THE CHURCH

Wesleyan Theological Perspectives

Series Editors
John E. Hartley
R. Larry Shelton

VOLUME IV

Contributors
Joseph E. Coleson
Milo L. Chapman
Alex R. G. Deasley
M. Robert Mulholland, Jr.
Paul M. Bassett
Melvin E. Dieter
Clarence Bence
Daniel N. Berg
David L. Cubie
Donald M. Joy
James Garlow
Everett E. Richey

THE CHURCH

An Inquiry into Ecclesiology
from a
Biblical Theological Perspective

Edited by
Melvin E. Dieter
Daniel N. Berg

Published by
Warner Press, Inc.
Anderson, Indiana

Scripture passages are taken from the Revised Standard
Version © 1972 by Thomas Nelson Inc. unless otherwise
indicated.

Contents

Part III: The Church and Ministry

Preface

The Church's understanding of itself and of its mission in the world has demanded continual theological explication throughout its history. In times of transition and change, however, it seems that the necessity for definition becomes more acute. The uncertainty of the times in which we are living and a certain halting uncertainty within the Church itself as to how it should respond to the times has brought about a rash of efforts to provide a "sure word" of direction for the people of God as they are about to enter their third millennium of witnesses in history.

The contributors to this volume have tried to help in that effort by bringing to the discussion the biblical, theological, historical, and practical understanding of the Church as it is set within their personal and professional commitments to a Wesleyan understanding of God and the world. No effort has been made to come to any common final definitions of a "Wesleyan" ecclesiology. It is difficult for scholars to agree upon whether John Wesley worked with a concept of the Church which was defined clearly enough for them to set its parameters. His pragmatism ruled by his strong commitment to the final authority of the Scriptures in all matters of faith and life served him well in meeting the challenges of fulfilling his evangelistic mission, but those who attempt to bring his theological foundations into logical summaries are not so well served. The readers of this volume, therefore, will have to approach the various discussions not only chapter by chapter, but chapter with chapter. It is hoped that they then can come to some comprehension of how Wesleyan presuppositions help one to see the place and mission of the Church in society.

The structure of the volume itself is a Wesleyan one. The Bible was Wesley's ultimate court of appeal, God's true and fully reliable Word to humankind; the discussions begin with a biblical theology as it comes to definition in the two Testaments. But Wesley was keenly aware that the Bible was not only God's book but a book for men and women as well; its precepts were not only God's living Word but God's Word to be lived. The second section threats the questions of the Church and its mission within the context of history and systematic theology, which reflects humankind's understanding of what God has done and said in his life in Christ and the people of God. It would be totally inappropriate to project a Wesleyan view of ecclesiology without a pragmatic extension of all of the preceding into application to the contemporary mission of the Church; the final section of the volume attempts to address this.

Melvin Dieter

I. The Church in Biblical Perspective

Joseph E. Coleson (Ph.D., Brandeis University), chairman, division of biblical studies and professor of Hebrew Scripture and ancient near eastern studies, Western Theological Seminary

Covenant Community
In the Old Testament

IT IS AXIOMATIC in Christianity that the Church is the true and proper successor to the covenant community of Israel.[1] Of course, this view was not axiomatic to the infant church; it regarded itself, and was regarded by both the Jewish religious authorities and the Roman civil authorities, as one of the several sects of Judaism.[2] The Council of Jerusalem, in ruling the Gentiles did not have to enter the edifice of Christianity through the door of Judaism, ensured an eventual and final schism between Christians and the several groups within Judaism who did not accept Jesus as the hoped-for Messiah. As the schism developed, the question naturally arose as to who were the rightful heirs of the ancient heritage and covenant.

The New Testament writers began by demonstrating and illustrating that believers became the rightful heirs through their acceptance of Jesus as Messiah and Lord. Paul argues the point very carefully in Romans 4 and Galatians 3. In Galatians 4 he uses a typological interpretation of the roles of Abraham's sons and asserts that believers, like Isaac, are "children of promise" (Gal. 4:28).

It did not take long, however, for this view to become so well established within the Christian community that it came to be assumed. Writing possibly as early as when Paul wrote to the Galatians, but to people who had been longer in the faith,[3] James could address his epistle to "the twelve tribes who are dispersed abroad" (James 1:1, NAS), knowing that the Christian believers who would hear the letter would understand and identify with his position. Even John in the Revelation (though he used the classically Jewish genre of apocalypse, drew on and developed many of the themes and imagery of the Hebrew prophets, and incorporated the restoration of the people of Israel within his eschatological vision) did not feel it necessary to argue that Christian believers had become the heirs of God. That point was already established; his purpose was to encourage believers by affirming the final triumph of the kingdom of God whose citizens they were. The Apostolic and later Fathers,[4] the medieval church,[5] the Reformers,[6] Wesley,[7] and most modern Christians have accepted the succession of the community of Christian believers to the covenant position and promises of God to Israel as set forth in the Hebrew Scriptures. This has been true whether they have interpreted this succession in an exclusivistic or non-exclusivistic manner with respect to Jews and Judaism.[8]

But having accepted this premise, what are we to understand that it means? Of what sort of community are we the heirs, and in what way are we its heirs? We will investigate here Israel's covenant community and leave direct discussion of the nature of the succession for a later time. We would stress, however, that a proper understanding of Israel's covenant community is essential to, and constitutes an important element in, a proper understanding of the Christian covenant community.

Our first task is to discover what term or terms, phrase or phrases, are used to designate the covenant community in the Hebrew Scriptures. We will then be in a position to investigate the nature of that community, and perhaps to draw some conclusions.

THE TERMS *QĀHĀL* AND *'EDAH*

In the discussion of whether a technical term designating the covenant community exists in Hebrew, two nouns are usually considered. They are *qāhāl*, usually translated, "assembly," and ' *ēdāh,* usually translated "congregation."[9] Our first consideration will be whether one or both of them are technical terms; then we will consider whether they are synonymous. That the basic meaning of *qāhāl* is "assembly" is not in dispute. While some would derive *qāhāl* from the same root as *qôl*, "voice," in order to establish an etymological connection between the assembly and the one who calls the assembly together, this identification is dubious at best.[10] The real debate has been over whether *qāhāl* is a technical term that can be understood as "the Old Testament church."

Probably the most extreme statement in favor of this interpretation is that of T. F. Torrance:

> *Qāhāl* denotes the Old Testament church actively engaged in God's purpose of revelation and salvation, that is, caught up in the mighty events whereby God intervenes redemptively in history, and involved in the forward thrust of the covenant toward final and universal fulfillment. *Qāhāl* is the community expecting eschatological redemption.[11]

The other end of the spectrum is stated most succinctly by Schmidt. In discussing the Greek terms used by the LXX to render *qāhāl* and *'ed*āh and the distribution of these two terms throughout the Hebrew Bible, he says, "This unevenness [of distribution] makes it clear that neither [Hebrew] word is intrinsically a technical term."[12]

The proper court of appeal is the actual usage of the term *qāhāl* in the Hebrew Scriptures. It is true that *qāhāl* may designate an assembly of the people in which the primary or even sole purpose was religious. Examples are Leviticus 4:21; Deuteronomy 9:10; Joel 2:16; and Nehemiah 5:13. However, *qāhāl* is also used of assemblies of less than all the people of Israel, of groups other than Israel, and of groups whose purpose is not only not religious, but positively evil. First Samuel 19:20 refers to an assembly of prophets; Psalm 89:5 refers to an assembly of holy ones who are either less than all of Israel, or who include individuals from outside Israel. In either case the assembly is not coextensive with Israel. Psalm 26:5 speaks of the assembly of evildoers; Genesis 35:11 and Jeremiah 50:9 speak of assemblies of nations; Proverbs 21:16 makes reference to the assembly of shades; Ezekiel 38:13, to the assembly of Gog; Ezekiel 27:27, to the assembly of Tyre; and Ezekiel 32:22, to the assembly of Assyria. At none of these places can *qāhāl* be understood as "the Old Testament church."

A similar situation obtains for *'ēdāh*. The meaning of "congregation" in the sense of a "company gathered together by appointment or acting concertedly"[13] is generally accepted. Coenen is representative of those who see in *'ēdāh* a technical term for Israel as the covenant community:

> In contrast to *qāhāl*, *'ēdāh* never refers to any people other than Israel and clearly needs no other special qualification: only four times is the name of Yahweh added. . . . If one compares the use of the two Hebrew words, it becomes clear, from the passages in which both occur in the same context, that *'ēdāh* is the unambiguous and permanent term for the covenant community as a whole. . . . This conclusion is reflected in the translations.[14]

Lewis takes the opposite position in his statement that "the noun itself does not imply the purpose of the gathering."[15]

For *'ēdāh* the range of possible applications is even broader than for *qāhāl*, inasmuch as we find it used of a swarm of bees (Judg. 14:8), and a herd of bulls (Ps. 68-39 [MT 31]). With reference to humans *'ēdāh* has the same range as *qāhāl*. It parallels "nations" and "the earth" in Jeremiah 6:18. Psalm 22:16(MT 17) and Job 15:34 speak of the congregation of evildoers, and Psalm 86:14, of the congregation of the godless. In Numbers 16 when the story of Korah's rebellion is related, and in Numbers 26 when the story is recalled, the people who stood with Korah are called the congregation or company (*'ēdāh*) of Korah, and in Numbers 14: 27, 35 the congregation (*'ēdāh*) of Israel is designated as evil. In Job 16:7, Job speaks of "my company (*'ēdāh*)," referring to the family and servants he had had before the calamities came upon him. Thus, by itself, the term *'ēdāh* is not a technical term for Israel, gathered or ungathered, any more than is *qāhāl*.

Are the two terms synonymous? It would seem that, in general usage as it appears in the Hebrew Scriptures, they are.[16] Some would understand *'ēdāh* to have a more restricted meaning in the context of the gathering of all Israel. They would take it to mean either all the men of war, or the heads of families, or a judicial/advisory council.[17] The passage most strongly supporting this view is Leviticus 4:13-21, which prescribes the purification (sin) offering to be sacrificed if "the whole congregation (*'ēdāh*) of Israel" commits an inadvertent sin that at first is hidden from the assembly (*qāhāl*), then made known to it. But even here the final statement of this prescription is, "It is a sin offering of the assembly [*qāhāl*]" (Lev. 4:21). In other places where it may refer to a smaller group than all of Israel, it is also possible that it does not; in any case, it is the context, and not the word *'ēdāh* itself that gives it particular definition beyond the general meaning of "congregation."

A few passages contain both terms; these seem to support the opinion that they are essentially synonymous. An example is Judges 20:1-2, which contains the noun *ʿēdāh* as the subject of a denominative verb from *qāhāl*; this same group of people is then referred to as "the assembly [*qāhāl*] of the people of God."

Sometimes translations can give insight into the semantic range of words in the language being translated. In the case of the LXX translations of the terms *qāhāl* and *ʿēdāh*, the LXX supports the idea that these terms are synonymous.[18]

For the sake of completeness, four other terms must be mentioned. The first is *miqrā;* unmodified, it means "convocation," and is synonymous with *qāhāl* and *ʿēdāh*. It often is modified by being placed in construct with the noun *holiness* and then refers to "a convocation of holiness" or "a holy convocation." This term merits only passing attention by reason of the fact that it occurs only twenty-five times in the Hebrew Scriptures, twelve times in the Book of Leviticus.[19]

A second term is *ʿatsarāh* or *ʿatseret;* it also means "assembly." However, it is used only eleven times, and six of its occurrences have reference specifically to the last day of one of the feasts.[20]

Two other terms are at the opposite end of the spectrum of frequency. Both the terms "Israel" and "people" (*ʿam*) have been proposed as terms that meant for God's people in the Hebrew Scriptures what we may mean by "church" or "God's people" today.[21] "Israel" occurs more than twenty-four hundred times in the Hebrew Scriptures.[22] If we were to add synonyms like "Jacob" and "Judah" (used sometimes after 722 B.C. as Israel was sometimes used before 722 B.C.), and occasions of synécdoche (such as "Ephraim" at many places in Hosea) and other literary devices, the number of references to the nation of Israel would be substantially larger. The term '*am* occurs more than eighteen hundred times.[23] Many times it does refer to the people or nation of Israel, but it can also refer to other people(s). Even when Israel is in view, it is obvious that a great many occurrences of both these terms will have reference to the people as an ethnic, political, or military, rather than a religious, entity.

In sum, then, we may say that there are a number of individual terms that *may*, in a given context, refer to the covenant community in such a way that we may see in that covenant community the forerunner and a likeness of our own. However, there is no single term that, by itself and always (or even usually), has reference to that community in that light.

TERMS DESIGNATING THE COVENANT COMMUNITY

While none of the terms just discussed expresses intrinsically the concept of the covenant community, several of them are components of expressions that do. As Schmidt points out, everything depends on whether Yahweh or Israel is added to *qāhāl* or *'ēdāh* or *'am*, to give the expression the sense of "the people (or assembly or congregation) of Yahweh (or Israel)." This addition may be explicit or implicit, but it is necessary if the term is to give this sense.[24] Even "Israel," while its addition to another word can form the type of expression under discussion, can do so only because in this usage it is already implicitly understood as designating the people of God.

The word *qāhāl* occurs in the expressions "the assembly of Yahweh" (*qᵉhal*[25] *Yahweh*) and "the assembly of Israel" (*qᵉhal Yisra'el*). *Qāhāl* also frequently stands alone, but if it is to be understood as the covenant community, the context readily indicates that "the assembly of

Yahweh" or "the assembly of Israel" is intended. Craigie discusses the assembly of Yahweh:

> The assembly (qāhāl) of the Lord refers to the covenant people of God, particularly when they are gathered in his presence. . . . Here the word has general reference to Israel as a worshipping community. Thus to enter the assembly of the Lord would indicate a person who became a true Israelite and who therefore shared in the worship of the Lord. The expression is somewhat narrower in its intent than Israel, taken as a whole, for there would be resident aliens and others who, though a part of the community, were nevertheless not full members of it.[26]

The identification of 'ēdāh as "the congregation of the sons of Israel" is the most frequent when the identification is explicit. "The congregation of Yahweh" occurs only four times. But more often 'ēdāh stands by itself, and the context indicates that the sense "the congregation of God" is implicit within the term 'ēdāh, if that is how it is to be understood.[27]

The phrase 'am Yahweh, "the people of Yahweh," occurs only a handful of times in the Hebrew Scriptures. It is used twice in the Song of Deborah, Judges 5:11, 13. In Numbers 16:41(MT 17:6) the people use it in a complaint against Moses and Aaron to add gravity to their charge. Of course, many times when 'am is used without explicit qualification, it has reference to Israel or a portion of Israel as God's people.

However, the most significant use of 'am is with a personal pronoun referring to God. This is done very often in the third person, with a human speaker referring to "His people," and in the second person, with a human speaker referring to "thy people." Even more importantly, it occurs many times in the first person singular, with God as the speaker referring to "my people." The number of such references approaches two hundred. Thus, God himself, as well as his spokesmen, recognizes and acknowledges that there is a people with whom he has entered into a special relationship. Of course, the *nature* of that relationship is not described by God's use of the term "my people." But the *fact* of the relationship is established as no single word can establish it, and more convincingly perhaps than any other phrase can do.

We have considered at some length the words and phrases which are most often cited as the general designations by which the Hebrew Scriptures refer to the covenant community. We have done so because of the imprecision with which most of these terms often have been handled. It remains the soundest course to allow the biblical author to invest the text with the meaning he wishes it to have. To lift out a term which may, even in many contexts, denote the covenant community, and treat it as though that were its meaning in all its contexts is to handle the Word of God carelessly.

There are two further reasons for care in investigating whether and how a given pericope designates and characterizes the covenant community. One is the necessity always of guarding against the tendency to read into the ancient text modern notions of how the covenant community was constituted and what characterized it. This can happen even after we have determined legitimately that the text indeed refers to the covenant community. The other reason for care is that the biblical authors possessed as well other means of designating and discussing, addressing and/or characterizing the covenant community. The covenant community can be under consideration even though none of the terms discussed is present in the text. Other terms are available, terms that are more particularly descriptive and thus less apt as general designations. Metaphorical language also is used frequently of the covenant community, both as appellation and as characterization.

Composition of the Covenant Community

To this point we have discussed the designation of the covenant community. We consider now briefly some aspects of eligibility for inclusion within the community.

We begin by noting that the covenant community traced its own inception ultimately to God's covenant with the individual, their ancestor, Abraham. Abraham's response of faith made him eligible for inclusion within what was, at that point, a human "community" of one. At least three elements are discernible in this inaugural covenant that became factors in determining eligibility for inclusion within the larger covenant community established at Sinai. The first of these is God's sovereign initiative in establishing the covenant and the covenant community. This is obvious in the establishment of the covenant with Abraham. Though sometimes less obvious in consideration of the succeeding covenant community, it is equally true of it; that community was established at God's initiative, and individuals were included in it only because of God's grace individually extended.

The second element would seem at first glance to be contradictory of God's initiative. It is that membership within the covenant community was primarily through belonging to the line of Abraham's offspring. Most of these who ever belonged to the covenant community were physical descendents of Abraham. This element is explicit within the canonical record of the covenant community much more pervasively than is the first; it is likely that it was self-consciously embraced by a much greater proportion of the community than was the first.

What keeps the primarily ethnic character of the covenant community from contradicting the primacy of God's initiative in its establishment is the third element, the necessity of the response of faith for inclusion within the community. It was possible to be born into the community and reject membership through a number of specified actions or conditions.[28] It was also possible to be born outside the covenant community and become a member of it by deliberate choice. The provisions for this are explicit, and many examples are recounted of individuals and even groups who did choose to join the covenant community from outside ethnic Israel.[29] The number of these episodes, and the prominence that some of them are according in the history of the covenant community, suggests that stress on this element was deliberate and more or less constant. The covenant community was never intended to be a closed community.

Not only was a response of faith necessary for individuals to come into the community from outside, but it was the faith response of the community that made possible the institution of the covenant initially. The form of the Sinaitic covenant is that of the suzerain-vassal treaty of the second millennium B.C.; these treaties followed a regular pattern, which included a public (oral) ratification ceremony in which vassals swore obedience to the suzerain, and called down upon themselves the curses described in the treaties if they rebelled.[30] In the case of the Sinaitic covenant, Yahweh was the suzerain and Israel the vassal. Israel's responsibilities were both collective and individual; naturally, the collective aspect is brought to the fore in the narratives relating Moses' (as Yahweh's agent) presentations and Israel's acceptances of the covenant, both at Sinai (Exodus) and again in the plains of Moab (Deuteronomy). The response of faith of the community is prominent in the narratives which describe recommitment of the covenant in later periods as well. The occasions of Joshua's farewell (Josh. 24), Hezekiah's reinstatement of Yahweh worship (2 Chron. 29-30), Josiah's discovery and reaffirmation of the covenant (2 Kings 23:1-3), and Ezra's actions in rectifying a breach of the covenant (Ezra 10) are examples.

The Covenant Community Defined
By Instruction (*Torah*)

Of course, the most direct manner of defining the covenant community was through the instruction given the community at its inception at Sinai.[31] The most important precept was that they were to be a holy community. Since holiness is always relational, a separation *from* someone (or something) *to* someone (or something) else, this meant that the covenant community was an entity separated to Yahweh above anything and everything else. The very term *covenant community* at least implies this, for a covenant with one party precludes entering covenants of equal standing with other parties.[32]

The most direct expression of this expectation that the community be holy to Yahweh is in the command "Be [*ye*] holy, for I am holy" (Lev. 11:44). This admonition itself occurs with slight variations at several other places, such as Leviticus 19:2, 20:7, 26, and of course it is implicit in many other passages. Holiness—separation—to Yahweh is thus *a* characteristic of the covenant community.

Great significance attaches to the reason Yahweh gives for demanding holiness of his people. They are to be holy *because* he is holy. Their holiness is to be of his holiness, as its source and in its kind. The idea of dedication to special use was very common in the ancient Near East. Since it was usually done in a religious context, it most often meant removal from common (profane) use and restriction to sacred use. However, since the gods to whom persons (and objects) were consecrated as holy were no more (in fact were often less!) upright in their conduct than were their worshipers, ethical and moral ideals did not enter into the practice of holiness for most ancient peoples.

With Yahweh it was completely different. His holiness consisted in his attributes of love, righteousness, faithfulness, graciousness, and mercy. He was holy—separate—because he possessed infinitely these qualities, while his creation with which he had endowed them as a reflection of his image had forfeited them in Adam's fall. For the covenant community of Israel, then, to be called to holiness to Yahweh was for them to be called to reflect again his ethical and moral qualities. They were to be like the God who called them into covenant with him (for good), as the nations around them were like the gods whom they worshiped (too often for evil). It is this reflection of God's character in the context of keeping covenant with him that is the origin of the ethical and moral dimensions of the covenant community's conduct.

In setting forth how this is to be worked out in day-to-day practice, the instruction (*tôrāh*) goes into great detail on a great many subjects. As the organizational principles are not always immediately clear to our minds, it is difficult for us initially to extract principles of action or attitude that may be said to characterize the covenant community. However, such principles do underlie the corpus of edicts; in fact, they are explicitly stated from time to time, and a few may be mentioned briefly.

The covenant community is to be a worshiping community. While this may be implicit in the fact that they were holy to Yahweh, it becomes explicit in a number of ways throughout the instruction (*tôrāh*). The Second Commandment, by enjoining the fashioning and/or worship of other gods, becomes at the same time a directive to worship Yahweh. While many of the sacrifices were for the purpose of dealing with sin, Leviticus 7:16 mentions two—an offering for a vow and a freewill offering—that are entirely associated with worship.[33] The tithe, the Sabbath rest, and the offering of firstfruits are also fundamentally acts of worship.

The covenant community is to be a just community. Oppression of the unfortunate and the powerless is forbid-

den. The rights of the widow, the orphan, the resident
alien, the slave, the debtor, even of the inadvertent
homicide, are safeguarded. The punishment of crime is
concerned as much with restitution to the victim as with
vengeance upon the criminal.

The covenant community is to be a caring community.
This is expressed negatively by the prohibition of injustice
and oppression, but also by admonitions to guard against
the accidental infliction of injury upon a neighbor's person
or property, such as those found in Exodus 21 and 22. It is
expressed positively in as direct a manner as is possible in
Leviticus 19-18, "Thou shalt love thy neighbor as thyself." Specific positive expressions of caring are the laws
providing for gleaning (Lev. 23:22), the inclusion of the
entire household—even to the animals—in the Sabbath
rest (Exod. 20:10; Deut. 5:14), the prohibition against lending at interest to the poor, or keeping overnight the cloak
taken in pledge (Exod. 22:25-27); obviously, many other
examples could be adduced.

The covenant community is to be a faithful community.
False witness is forbidden and is punishable by death, if
death would be the result for another of the false witness
(Exod. 20-16; Deut. 19:16-21). Adultery is punishable
by death (Lev. 20:10), for it is the ultimate unfaithfulness
between persons and symbolizes most closely unfaithfulness to God. A vow made or an oath taken must be
fulfilled (Num. 30:2).

THE COVENANT COMMUNITY DEFINED
BY PROPHETIC ADMONITION

It is evident from even a cursory reading of the record
preserved in the Hebrew Scriptures that the covenant
community often strayed far from the ideals set forth in
God's instruction. In a continuing effort to bring them
back to himself, God sent a long line of prophets, deliver-

ing essentially the one central message of repentance as the only means of avoiding disaster. Though the message was essentially one, the means used in delivering it were many and varied.

Even before the entry into the land, Moses delivered a long and impassioned admonition to remember Yahweh's faithfulness and to remain faithful to him; this admonition is preserved in Deuteronomy 4-12 as a general summary of the treaty (covenant) stipulations. (It was intended to be read aloud to the people periodically as a positive reinforcement toward faithfulness.

When the community proved faithless, one means used by God's prophets to persuade them to repent was to describe in some detail the transgressions of the covenant that had been committed and rehearse the punishment that could be expected as a result. These warnings were often prefaced by a plea to the community to hear (and by inference to obey); they are often stark and harsh in their recital of covenant transgressions, and even more so in their threats of punishment. Yet the reality of the visitations of terror upon Israel and Judah made the threats seem mild by comparison. A few of the many examples of this type of admonition are the ''Woes'' of Isaiah 5; the ''Woes,'' ''Hear this,'' and ''Listen'' of Isaiah 28-29; the ''Hear the word of the Lord'' of Jeremiah 2; and the ''Hear this'' of Amos 8. Sarcasm can even be a feature of these messages, as in Haggai 1:6, 9 and Malachi 1:8.

God used tender reasoning to try to woo back his people. Some examples that ought to have melted the stoniest hearts are Isaiah 55 (''Why do you spend money for no-bread?''); Jeremiah 3 (''Return, . . . I will not maintain [my wrath] forever.''); Jeremiah 8:18-22 (''Harvest has passed, summer has ended, and we have not been saved.''); and Hosea 11 (''How can I give you up, O Ephraim?''). There can be no question of God's love for his errant people.

A method of special interest is the adoption of the language of the courts of law in God's dealing with his people. Several prophets picture God as bringing a lawsuit (*rîb*) against the community because of their violation of the covenant. A good example is Jeremiah 2:9, "Therefore, I will again bring a lawsuit against you [utterance of Yahweh], and against your sons' sons I will bring a lawsuit." The rest of the chapter continues the language of the law, as God rejects the validity of Judah's countersuit (s. v. 29), then pronounces a verdict of guilty over their protestations of innocence (v. 35), and finally passes sentence (vv. 36-37). Hosea and Micah also used this language (Hos. 4:1; 12:2 [MT 3]; Mic. 6:2). In each of these cases the charges are carefully presented in some detail. This is not just a rhetorical device, but a real lawsuit (*rîb*), with God as plaintiff and judge, the prophet (acting as God's agent) as prosecutor, and the covenant community as defendant. As the lawcourt setting has always been one of extreme gravity and solemnity, where casualness and frivolity are completely out of place, this represents another approach in God's attempt to gain the people's attention and convince them of the need for repentance.

What does all this tell us about the character of the covenant community? The obvious point is that they were not faithful to the relationship with God into which they had entered. They were not faithful in carrying out the obligations of the covenant which they had assumed. Yet two other points need also to be made. One is that God never left himself without a remnant or without a witness. God himself is faithful; his faithfulness guarantees that in the midst of a covenant community that has largely become unfaithful, a faithful remnant and a faithful witness will remain. This is an exceedingly important point, for it locates trust and hope where they must be located, in God rather than in humanity.

The other point is that in spite of all the shortcomings of

the covenant community, God found them worth all the efforts that he invested in them. At any point he had the option to take the pot that had become spoiled as he fashioned it, and reshape it into another vessel of his choosing, or even discard it if he wished (Jer. 18:1-11). But in fact, God did not abandon or destroy his covenant community. That he continued to work with it, fashioning it until it took the shape he desired, is an indication that he put a value on his community that we can neither calculate nor understand. Its incalculable value by God's reckoning must be listed as another characteristic of the covenant community.

THE COVENANT COMMUNITY DEFINED
IN THE WRITINGS (*KETHUBIM*)

The Hebrew Bible is divided into three sections. The first is the *Tôrāh*), and includes the five books designated as the Pentateuch in the English arrangement. The Prophets (*Nebî'îm*) includes Joshua, Judges, 1 and 2 Samuel, 1 and 2 Kings, and all the "Major" and "Minor" Prophets except Daniel and Lamentations. All the rest of the books are included within the third section, called the Writings (*Kethûbîm*).

The covenant community is seen actually at worship in the Psalms. They show us that when the community is functioning as it should, it is characterized by worship. This was mandated in the instruction (*Tôrāh*); we see the mandate put into action in the Psalter. This worship includes corporate and private worship; it includes praise and complaint, thanksgiving and supplication, great joy and great thoughtfulness. The Psalms demonstrate that openness, not secrecy; candor, not deceitfulness; and sincerity, not hypocrisy are to characterize the covenant community. The full range of joy and sorrow, hope and despair, trust and honest doubts, is expressed, and the worshiper is accepted because his heart is inclined toward Yahweh.

In Job and Qoheleth the covenant community is characterized as committed to intellectual integrity, even when that involves wrestling with hard theological and philosophical questions. The pursuit of wisdom and understanding is not limited, but rather expanded, by genuine piety.

Ruth and the Song of Songs acknowledge and celebrate the presence and providence of God in the everyday affairs of life. What is more commonplace than agricultural pursuits? Yet in the providence of God a sequence of the most mundane events is given cosmic and eternal significance. What is more ordinary and predictable than that some young man will begin to love some young woman, and she will begin to love him? Yet the Song of Songs celebrates with fierce joy this common miracle, and in so doing confirms and affirms a number of features that characterize individual members of the covenant community. One is that they are dust, and physical participants in a physical world. That is not a lot to be pitied, borne, cursed, or denied. It is a gift to be celebrated, and it cannot be celebrated better than when a man and a woman celebrate it properly together.

The covenant community is depicted in the Book of Proverbs as it considers the ramifications for the marketplace of its covenant with Yahweh. Actually, several marketplaces are in view, among them the marketplace of goods and services, the marketplace of ideas and intellectual pursuits, the marketplace of value systems, and the several marketplaces of interpersonal transactions. For all of these, the conclusion is the same: the covenant relationship with Yahweh is not a liability, but an asset.

The Writings (*Kethûbîm*) are a more diverse collection than the other two sections of the Hebrew Scriptures. There is much else that could be included within the discussion, but the total effect of the Writings is to affirm that the characteristics of the covenant community envisioned in the instruction (tôrāh) given at its inception and labored for by the prophets would bring blessing upon the community as promised. The Writings did point out that this blessing would not always be material prosperity, as many, then as well as now, expected. But to live in faithfulness to the covenant was wise as well as right.

The Writings also allow us to correct one misapprehension that consideration of the prophets alone could produce. Active as they often were at times of crisis, and concerned singlemindedly with calling the community to repentance from their transgressions, the prophets normally could not describe what was right with the community. The Writings are another witness, then, that at least a remnant of the faithful was always preserved. By way of example, one collection of proverbs, ascribed to Solomon and now included within the Book of Proverbs, was made in the reign of Hezekiah, almost certainly under his sponsorship (Prov. 25:1). Hezekiah reigned two hundred years after Solomon; how were those proverbs preserved during that time, if not by faithful adherents to the covenant?[34] Again, though there were times when the worship of Yahweh in the Temple ceased, or became so contaminated by syncretism with pagan deities as to be blasphemous, yet there remained those who utilized certain of the psalms in private worship. Thus, the Writings provide an important witness to the continuity of the covenant community.

SUMMARY

We began by stating that the covenant community depicted in the Hebrew Scriptures has been of interest throughout the history of the Church, because the Church has considered itself, to a greater or lesser extent, (one of) the heir(s) to that community.[35] We proceeded to investigate the designations of the covenant community in the Hebrew Scriptures, and concluded that no single word functions as a technical term, designating always and exactly the covenant community, especially if viewed as "the Old Testament church." There are, however, a number of words and phrases that *may* designate that group of people who had entered into a covenant relationship with Yahweh. Whether any of them does at a given place in the text depends upon the context.

Inclusion within the covenant community depended upon the sovereign initiative of God, and the faith response of the community itself, whether viewed collectively or individually. While most members were physical descendents of Abraham, most outsiders were eligible, if they wished to join themselves to the community.

The character of the covenant community was determined by the character of the God with whom the covenant was made. Yahweh was a God of faithfulness, love, righteousness, and mercy. Holiness unto Yahweh therefore meant that the covenant community partook of those attributes as well. When the community proved faithless, as they often did, a remarkable factor came into play. Yahweh demonstrated, through his continued patience and refusal to destroy them, that the covenant community was of inestimable value to him. Finally, the witness of the Writings demonstrates that the covenant and the covenant community were not just for the sanctuary; they were intended to be operative in every aspect of life.

If the Church today indeed wishes to consider itself a rightful heir to this covenant community, we aspire to a worthy station. But we, as they, will attain it only by God's gracious enabling.

Notes

1. One cannot use the qualifier "orthodox" with "Christianity" in this context, because it is precisely in their descriptions of how they are the true and proper (and only) inheritors of Israel's covenant relationship with God that many heretical movements have strayed from orthodoxy.
2. Cf. Acts 4; 5:17-18; 6:12; 15; 18:12-16; Claudius's expulsion of the Jews from Rome about A.D. 49 is further evidence. For a discussion of this as it relates to Christianity, see F. F. Bruce, *New Testament History* (Garden City, N. Y.: Doubleday and Company, Inc., 1969), pp. 291-304.
3. Donald Guthrie, *New Testament Introduction* (Downers Grove, Ill.: Inter-Varsity Press, 1973), pp. 761-64. For the general New Testament development of this theme, see F. F. Bruce, *New Testament Development of Old Testament Themes* (Grand Rapids: Wm. B. Eerdmans Publishing Company, 1968), pp. 51-67, and E. P. Sanders, *Paul, the Law, and the Jewish People* (Philadelphia: Fortress Press, 1983), pp. 173-76.
4. Many references could be cited; one will suffice: *Didache* IX:2.
5. For example, Augustine's *City of God* exhibits this understanding.
6. Cf. Luther's statements, conveniently in Ewald M. Plass, compiler, *What Luther Says: An Anthology*, vol. 1 (St. Louis: Concordia Publishing House, 1959), p. 247.
7. Cf. the introduction to his sermon "The Ministerial Office," in *The Works of John Wesley*, vol. VII (Grand Rapids: Zondervan Publishing House), pp. 273-75. See also William M. Arnett, "A Study in John Wesley's *Explanatory Notes upon the Old Testament*," *WTJ* 8 (Spring, 1973), pp. 29-30, and John N. Oswalt, "Wesley's Use of the Old Testament in His Doctrinal Teachings," *WTJ* 12 (Spring 1977), p. 47.
8. Three positions have been taken with regard to the place of national Israel in God's program. One is that national Israel has no more place, another that national Israel has been set aside temporarily but will be restored as the end approaches, the third that national Israel has continued to

occupy a place and that Christians have been added as a "second community." Whichever of these three positions is taken, the accession of the Christian community to the status of heirs of ancient Israel is not questioned.

9. As an example, cf. Robert L. Thomas, general editor, *New American Standard Exhaustive Concordance of the Bible* (Nashville: Holman, 1981), pp. 1570b, 1590a.
10. James Barr, *The Semantics of Biblical Language* (Oxford: Oxford University Press, 1961), pp. 119-27.
11. T. F. Torrance, "The Israel of God," *Interpretation* 10 (July 1956), p. 306.
12. K. L. Schmidt, *"Ekklesia,"* in Gerhard Kittel, *Theological Dictionary of the New Testament*, vol. 3 (Grand Rapids: Wm. B. Eerdmans Publishing Company, 1965), p. 529.
13. Francis Brown, S. R. Driver, and C. A. Briggs, *Hebrew and English Lexicon of the Old Testament* (Oxford: Oxford University Press, 1972), p. 417a.
14. L. Coenen, "Church, Synagogue," in Colin Brown, ed., *The New International Dictionary of New Testament Theology*, vol. 1 (Grand Rapids: Zondervan Publishing House, 1975), pp. 294-95.
15. Jack P. Lewis, *"'Eda,"* in R. Laird Harris, Gleason L. Archer, Jr., and Bruce K. Waltke, *Theological Wordbook of the Old Testament*, vol. 1 (Chicago: Moody Press, 1980), p. 388.
16. Cf. Lewis, p. 388, and M. H. Pope, "Congregation, Assembly," in G. A. Buttrick, ed., *The Interpreter's Dictionary of the Bible*, vol. 1 (New York: Abingdon Press, 1962), p. 670.
17. See G. J. Wenham, *The Book of Leviticus* (Grand Rapids: Wm. B. Eerdmans Publishing Co., 1979), p. 98, with references.
18. Cf. Barr, pp. 124, 128.
19. George M. Landes, *A Student's Vocabulary of Biblical Hebrew* (New York: Charles Scribner's Sons, 1981), p. 4.
20. Solomon Mandelkern, *Veteris Testamenti Concordantiae* (Tel Aviv: Schocken Publishing House Ltd., 1971), p. 910.
21. Barr, p. 124; see also George W. Anderson, "Israel: Amphictyony," in Harry Thomas Frank and William L. Reed,

Translating and Understanding the Old Testament (New York: Abingdon Press, 1970), pp. 150-51.

22. Thomas, p. 1534c.
23. Thomas, p. 1574c.
24. Schmidt, p. 529.
25. The change in spelling from *qahal* to *qehal* does not mean that we are dealing with a different word. It is due to a phonological phenomenon of the Hebrew language, called the "construct state."
26. P. C. Craigie, *The Book of Deuteronomy* (Grand Rapids: Wm. B. Eerdmans Publishing Co., 1976), p. 296. Cf. also Calum M. Carmichael, *The Laws of Deuteronomy* (Ithaca, N. Y.: Cornell University Press, 1974), pp. 172-73.
27. Coenen, p. 294, thus mistakes the significance of *'edah*'s standing alone when he states, "*'Edah* . . . clearly needs no other special qualification."
28. Deuteronomy 23:1-8(MT 2-9). Cf. Craigie, pp. 295-98; Of course, any capital crime also involved rejection of, and being cut off from, the covenant community.
29. Exodus 12:38, 48; Deuteronomy 23:7-8(MT 8-9); Joshua 6:25; Ruth 4:13-22; 1 Chronicles 2:55.
30. For discussion see, with references, K. A. Kitchen, *Ancient Orient and Old Testament* (Downers Grove, Ill.: Inter-Varsity Press, 1966), pp. 90-102, and Meredith G. Kline, *The Structure of Biblical Authority* (Grand Rapids: Wm. B. Eerdmans Publishing Co., 1972).
31. "Instruction" is a better translation of *torah* than is "law," when reference is to the entire body of material received by Moses at Sinai, and recapitulated (in Deuteronomy) in the Plains of Moab, or to the entire Pentateuch.
32. Of course, the reference here is to covenants that establish allegiance, not to normal business agreements.
33. Cf. Wenham, pp. 76-81.
34. Cf. Derek Kidner, *The Proverbs* (Downers Grove, Ill.: Inter-Varsity Press, 1964), p. 24.
35. In this regard should be mentioned also the discussion in the important work of Hans Kung, *The Church* (New York: Sheed and Ward, 1967), pp. 107-125.

Milo L. Chapman (Th.D., Pacific School of Religion), president emeritus, Warner Pacific College

The Church in the Gospels

TO SAY that Jesus of Nazareth is Christ and Lord is to say that his coming to this earth is the pivotal point of all history. It is perfectly in order to divide the calendar in reference to him, B.C. and A.D., for he has initiated a new era in the history of the world. Not only is Jesus the founder of the Christian religion, but accepting the New Testament view of his significance means that all of history becomes the history of God's redemptive activity. His coming marks the coming and subsequent growing of the kingdom of God. The Christian religion affirms that he is that one decisive fact upon which the salvation of persons is completely dependent. The Gospels, of course, are our primary source of information about his life and teachings and work. The question we ask then is, Do the Gospels tell the story of the founding of the Church?

Many answer this question quickly by applying some preconceived criteria. For example, some divide biblical history into three segments: the period of Israel, the period of Jesus' ministry, and the period of the Church. The Church in this case is an outgrowth of Jesus' ministry and, therefore, is not to be found during his lifetime. Others say that the Church is a fellowship of the redeemed and since redemption—atonement—cannot take place until the sacrifice for sin is made, the Church cannot have come into existence until after the sacrificial atoning death of Jesus.

Yet others look for signs of specific organization and structure to mark the beginnings of the Church. But we look in vain for a formalized plan whereby a society of Jesus' followers can be maintained as an entity of itself. Jesus apparently had no such plan in mind, and if an organized structure is what we have in mind, then the Gospels have nothing to say to us about the origins of the Church.

It becomes apparent that the definition one has in mind for the Church will largely determine the outcome of the search for the Church in the Gospels. It is our intention to show that the Church is a fellowship that is dependent upon a relationship with Jesus based upon acclaiming him as Christ and Lord. This will be done by showing that the Church is the outcome of God's search throughout history for a people who will respond to him in faith and obedience. But first, let us look at the meaning of the word translated "church" in the Gospels.

The English word *church* is derived from a Greek word, *kuriakon*, which means "of or pertaining to the Lord." Ultimately it passed into our language in association with the idea of ownership recognized in the dedication of a building for public worship. Since the early church had no such facility for their meetings, this usage came into being much later than The New Testament period. Indeed this word is not associated in Scripture with *church*.

The term that does find New Testament usage in this connection is *ecclesia*. Paul is the first to use it. The basic meaning that it carries is that of a group of citizens gathered together for some public purpose. They are "called out" or called together to form an assembly. In Greek literature the term has only a secular meaning. It is used in this secular sense in Acts 19:32, 39, 40. Elsewhere it speaks of those who are gathered together because they belong to God. They are the *ecclesia* of God even though at times this relationship is only implied instead of being explicitly stated. This is the term, for reasons which are not known aside from the literal meaning, which the translators most often chose for the Hebrew rod *qahal*—the assembly of Israel (Josh. 21:8; 1 Chron. 29:1; and so on)—when the Old Testament was translated into Greek. Almost always the qualifying phrase "of the Lord" is used in connection with *ecclesia*. It is comonly assumed that the New Testament use of *ecclesia* afforded them an easy distinction between themselves and the Jewish synagogue. Thus the early Christians, referring to themselves as the "*ecclesia* of God," were identifying themselves as the reconstituted, messianic, people of God.[1]

Inasmuch as *ecclesia* is used a great deal in the Pauline literature and beginning in Acts 5:11 in Luke's writings it continues to appear often, it is somewhat strange that the term appears only three times in the Gospels, and then only in the first Gospel—Matthew 16:18 and twice in 18:16. This fact has caused many scholars to doubt the authenticity of these sayings. If these sayings are put on Jesus' lips by the evangelist, then Lohfink's observation that we cannot speak of the "church" until the word is used has significance for our study.[2] However, on textual grounds there are no objections to either 16:18 or 18:17. There are no known Greek manuscripts or ancient versions that do not contain these passages.[3] Nor is the fact that these words from Jesus are recorded only by Matthew and not supported by the other Gospels sufficient reason to deny their authenticity. Other savings of Jesus are to be found only in Matthew, yet no doubt is cast upon their originality.[4]

A part of the hesitancy to accept these words as coming from Jesus is, perhaps, due to the resistance encountered in Protestant circles to the use made through the centuries of these words to support the claim by the Roman Catholic church that Peter was the first Bishop of Rome and that Jesus gave to him and all succeeding popes authoritative jurisdiction over the administration of grace. But theological bias is not a sound basis for judging the validity of a passage such as this. As Nygren observed, "Our conceptions ought to be corrected by the New Testament and not contrariwise."[5]

The real question that must be raised is, Did Jesus found the Church? The answer to this question must certainly be in the affirmative. On a textual basis we must assume that the Church was closely, even inextricably, linked with the gospel from the outset of Jesus' ministry. But the reasons for making this claim go beyond the use of the term. That which we hope to show is that the conception is present even when the term *church* may not be used.

By saying that Jesus, indeed, did found the Church is not to say that he established, or that there grew in his lifetimes, an organized institution. Neither occurred. As Brunner says so well, "Jesus wills to have a people . . . but certainly not an institution."[6] Rather, what is claimed is that he brought together a people who found their meaning and their fellowship in relationship to him as they, in faith, claimed him as Lord and Savior.

Jesus' ministry is not the first time that we meet with the necessity of identifying the people of God. In fact, it may be said that the story of the Bible, both Old and New Testaments, is the story of God's search for a people who will respond to him in faith and obedience. Thus, there is no specific date that marks the founding of the Church. It began in those who were responsive to Jesus' call to repentance because of the imminence of the kingdom of heaven. The story of the establishment of this community of the faithful began with the old covenant and extends to the calling together of the true Israel of God.[7] When Matthew says, "From that time Jesus began to preach saying, 'Repent, for the Kingdom of Heaven is at hand,' He was at one and the same time calling men to enter the Kingdom and to join the brotherhood of the reconciled."[8] He who heeds Jesus' words and becomes his disciple will be so thoroughly identified with Jesus and his work that he will participate in his life, sharing its deprivations and sorrows as well as its glorification in the age to come (Matt. 10:24-33; Mark 8:38; Luke 12:3-9).

It is in this sharing of the disciples with Jesus in the achieving of his purposes that we have the strongest illustration of Jesus' intention to establish his Church. Subsequently this personal relationship based upon having been with Jesus is one of the tests by which the early church judged the qualifications of a man when they sought to find a replacement for Judas Iscariot. The Scripture says, "So one of the men who have accompanied us during all the time that the Lord Jesus went in and out among us, beginning from the baptism of John until the day when he was taken from us—one of these men must become with us a witness to his resurrection" (Acts 1:21, 22). This election criterion illustrates the strong group identity that the disciples had based upon their common relationship with Jesus, and it shows that there was this sense of group identity not only immediately after Jesus' death and resurrection but also that there must have been such awareness from the very beginning. Not only so, but we notice that the fellowship of relationship with Jesus went beyond the select group of twelve. It included also the many others who were his disciples. These had heard and heeded his invitation to enter the kingdom of God. Those who followed him and remained with him participated in what God gave to him. "You are those who have continued with me in my trials; and I assign to you, as my Father, assigned to me, a Kingdom, that you may eat and drink at my table in my kingdom" (Luke 22:28-30). From the masses of Jewish people Jesus called forth a company of those who were willing to follow him. They stood in sharp contrast to those like the Pharisees who are described as unwilling to enter and hindering those who would (Luke 11:52). Jesus' followers were also markedly different from those unrepentant, stiff-necked people who refused to be obedient to the call (Acts 7:51). Those who heeded "represented the true people of God (i.e., the *ecclesia*).[9] These are those to whom it is the "Father's good pleasure to give . . . the kingdom" (Luke 12:32). But we may well ask what Jesus meant by "kingdom."

It has already been noted that Jesus' public ministry was marked by his preaching that persons must repent because the kingdom of God is at hand. Repentance should be viewed more from the Hebrew perspective than the Greek. Whereas the Greek word *metanoeō refers to a change of mind, the Hebrew word shub* means "to turn back"— specifically "to return to God." Jesus' parable of the prodigal son (Luke 15:11ff.) is the classic illustration of this meaning. Thus at the very outset Jesus' invitation to the Kingdom is a matter of the wayward, disobedient sinner returning to the household of God. The way into the Kingdom is by way of the path back to God. Such would not be the case if the kingdom that Jesus envisioned and came announcing had been of a political and geographical nature. That kind of kingdom would belong to the strong and mighty and influential, but Jesus said that his kingdom was not of this world; if it were his servants would have fought (John 18:36). Rather, the kingdom of God belongs to the childlike (Mark 10:15) and to those who do the will of the Father (Matt. 7:21). The Old Testament looks forward to the time when God will send his anointed to complete the

destiny of Israel. It is clear that the Jewish people in the
first century were looking for a Messiah who would bring
them independence from Roman suppression. The Messiah they expected would establish a Davidic kingdom that
would reverse their lot. No longer would they be the oppressed and dispersed people of the world. Rather the nations would come to them and hold them in honor as some
of their prophets seemed to say. (See Isaiah 45:1-17.) In
this hope the Jewish people were destined to be disap-
pointed. Jesus had no intention of involving himself in an
effort to reestablish the physical throne of David. Others
had tried this and failed.[10] Probably Jesus' temptations at
the beginning of his ministry should be seen in this light.
He considered himself to be the Messiah but refused to
pervert the power inherent in that role for personal convenience, to win the Kingdom by inappropriate means, or
to stoop to the spectacular in order to gain support from
the masses. A popularly conceived Messiah would have
done all these things without any qualms. Jesus, however,
refused to compromise his messianic role by making terms
with the power of evil. He understood that to do so would
be to negate the very purpose for which he was sent—the
bringing in of the rule of God. But before we go further in
defining the nature of the Kingdom, it is to this messianic
consciousness that we must turn.[11]

Jesus is presented in the Gospels as coming to complete
what God had begun centuries earlier. Frequently it is said
that such and such a thing happened as a fulfillment of
what God had planned or promised (Matt. 4:14, 5:17; Mark
14:49; Luke 1:20; and so on). Mark relates the story of
Jesus' baptism at the hands of John as a confirmation to
Jesus of a special relationship between himself and God:
"Thou art my beloved Son; with thee I am well pleased"
(Mark 1:11). That this must have also been the signal or
call to his special task is agreed upon by all of the Gospels,
since it is directly after this experience when he was

endowed with the Spirit and began "preaching the gospel of God, and saying, 'The time is fulfilled, and the kingdom of God is at hand; repent, and believe the gospel'" (Mark 1:14, 15; cf. Matt. 4:17). Luke describes the same sequence, but he tells of Jesus' beginning his public ministry by going into the synagogue at Nazareth where he read from the Book of Isaiah to those assembled:

> The Spirit of the Lord is upon me,
> because he has anointed me to preach good news to the poor.
> He has sent me to proclaim release to the captives
>   and recovering of sight to the blind,
> to set at liberty those who are oppressed,
> to proclaim the acceptable year of the Lord (Isa. 61:1, 2).

Then he calmly announced, "Today this scripture has been fulfilled in your hearing" (Luke 4:21). It is hard to imagine an announcement that would be more clear than this of his messiahship. Further, Jesus affirmed that prophets and righteous men of old looked forward with longing to see what was occurring in his ministry (Matt. 13:17). In him the great prophetic expectations come to fruition. In answer to the Pharisees' request for a sign from him that would test his authenticity, he said that all of the proof that was necessary was already there because a King greater than Solomon was present (Matt. 12:42); Jesus was greater than the Temple (Matt. 12:6); in him was to be found the rightful heir to David's throne (Mark 12:35-37; 15:2), the Son of Man (Dan. 7:13ff; Mark 13:26), and the Suffering Servant (Isa. 53; Mark 10:45).[12] The evidence becomes conclusive that Jesus truly intended to claim for himself the messianic role.

Furthermore, it is clear that the Gospels represent Jesus' doing those things that might well be expected of the Messiah, but that would be beyond the ability of an ordinary individual to perform. He healed the sick (Mark 1:41; Matt. 9:2; Luke 5:20), and announced himself as being Lord of the Sabbath (Mark 2:28; Matt. 12:8; Luke

6:5). In addition, he had power over demons. Far from proving, as his enemies charged, that he was in league with Satan in performing this exorcism, Jesus pointed out that just the opposite was evident: "If Satan casts out Satan, he is divided against himself; how then will his kingdom stand? . . . But if it is by the Spirit of God that I cast out demons, then the Kingdom of God has come upon you" (Matt. 12:26ff.). When, therefore, in response to Jesus' inquiry into the disciples' opinion of his identity, Peter said, "You are the Christ the Son of the living God," Jesus readily acknowledged that this was true and affirmed that Peter's knowledge of this fact came as a result of divine revelation (Matt. 16:16, 17).

In light of the preceding discussion it appears that the conclusion must be drawn that Jesus did indeed see himself as the predicted and looked-for Messiah whose task it was to bring about the rule of God. We can now return to a consideration of that rule—the Kingdom—which was his consuming passion.

The most instructive teaching the Gospels contain in this regard comes from the parables of Jesus. In these descriptive and colorful narratives he tells what the Kingdom is like. For the purposes of this study these parables may be considered under two general headings as we attempt to get a clear picture of Jesus' teaching.[13] The first group deals with the coming of the Kingdom and the second deals with the gracious manner in which God receives those who come into the Kingdom.

We have already noted that the era of which Jesus speaks is one that had been anticipated for many years (Luke 20:23) and it is now beginning. The fact is that those who are alert enough and spiritually sensitive enough can see it already in their midst. The signs of its arrival are given in the words of Isaiah (29:18, 19; 35:5, 6; 61:1) to John the Baptist as he lay in prison. For many years God had been planting the seed and now the harvest was ready

(Luke 10:2). The new age had begun. Under these circumstances one does not put new wine in old skins, nor
does he sew new unshrunk cloth on the old garment (Mark
2:21, 22). Watch the woman as she puts leaven in her
bread. See how a small—even hidden—amount of yeast
can permeate the whole. Understand by this that the small
beginnings of the rule of God do not limit its ultimate
growth (Luke 13:20ff.). Or again, the Kingdom resembles
a man scattering seed and mysteriously it grows and brings
forth a harvest (Mark 4:26-29). Sometimes in the sowing of
seed, bad seeds get mixed up with the good, just as in
fishing both good and trash fish are caught in the net. So in
the kingdom of God the time to separate the good from the
bad will come and God will be the one who judges the
individual's worthiness (Matt. 13:24-30; 13:47-50). The
Kingdom grows as men and women are delivered from the
bondage of Satan (Mark 3:23-27) and the life once dominated by the enemy must be kept clean and properly controlled (Luke 11:24-26). Thus the rule of God that Jesus
proclaimed is the time when the power of evil will be broken. The Messiah is victorious over Satan. Those who
wish to benefit from this victory are, as it were, invited to
a wedding feast, there to enjoy and rejoice in the presence
of the bridegroom (Mark 2:19ff.).

In the parables God is pictured as a gracious heavenly
Father. He is a beneficent employer who pays wages in
kindness as he wishes rather than on the basis of strict
justice (Matt. 20:1-15). He is also like a father whose two
sons both are requested to work in the vineyard. One refuses but later obeys. The other promises but does not
produce. The lesson is plain. Repentant sinners receive
God's grace rather than those who profess righteousness
but who do not live up to their claim (Matt. 21:28-31).
Again, the Kingdom resembles a great feast to which many
are invited. Those whom one would expect to attend made
excuses and refused to attend. Whereupon the gracious

host tells his servants to fill up the banquet hall with any who can be found who will heed the invitation (Luke 14:16-24). No parable describes God's mercy to the repentant sinner better than the parable of the Pharisee and the tax collector. In this story we are made to understand that justification comes as a result of the admission of guilt and the seeking for forgiveness rather than pleading one's case on the basis of good works done (Luke 18:10-14). But the joy of God over restored relationships appears in the parables told about what was lost: the sheep, the coin, the son. In each case the parable ends on a note of rejoicing over the restoration of what was lost (Luke 15:4-7, 8-10, 11-32). The story of the prodigal has become the classic illustration of the restoration of the wayward individual back into the family relationship. We shall look more closely at the relationship and fellowship that result from such a reclamation, for this is that for which the Messiah came—to seek and save that which is lost, and the Kingdom is made up of those who are sought and found.

As we have already noticed, Jesus viewed himself as the Messiah whose task it was to gather together the true people of God. This he did from the beginning by preaching that the rule of God had begun and all who would could be a part of that Kingdom. But he also brought together a more intimate group who would learn from him and who would form a nucleus of a society that would carry out his work. He called the twelve disciples. After some time he "called to him the twelve, and began to send them out two by two, and gave them authority over the unclean spirits. . . . So they went out and preached that men should repent. And they cast out many demons, and anointed with oil many that were sick and healed them" (Mark 6:7, 12, 13; compare Matthew 10:1). Luke specifies that they were to preach the kingdom of God (Luke 9:1). The authority and the mission that he gave to his disciples were the same as his own. Luke tells of Jesus' sending out another group of seventy with the same commission and similar results. Upon their return they joyfully reported the results of their mission. In commenting upon this, Jesus recognized that he, indeed, had given his emissaries power over evil, but this was secondary. The real cause for rejoicing lay in the fact that they had joined the ranks of the people of God. The fellowship thus established was even closer because it resulted from their knowing both the Father and the Son, for the Son had revealed this to them (Luke 10:22). Jesus lovingly called them his little flock (Luke 12:32).

The most significant event in the life of Jesus and his disciples that points to a community of fellowship occurred at the Last Supper, which was held in connection with the celebration of the Passover. This passover was to be different from any they had experienced before, which was evidenced by the rising pressure of resentment by the scribes and priests as they sought to find some justifiable reason that would permit them to arrest Jesus and put him to death. It was also marked by the unusual way in which the place of celebration would be found—just follow a *man* with a water pitcher. Furthermore, Jesus emphasized his keen desire to eat this passover with them before his suffering (Luke 22:15). It would appear that Jesus thought of this meal as the culmination of all that he had done, short of his crucifixion. Up to this point he had repeatedly called to Israel as a whole to follow his teachings, only to meet with repeated rejection. Now he turned to his friends and never again did he make a direct appeal to Israel. ''You are those who have continued with me in my trials; and I assign to you, as my Father assigned to me, a kingdom that you may eat and drink at my table in my kingdom, and sit on thrones judging the twelves tribes of Israel'' (Luke 22:28-30). Thus was a fellowship established that would not be forgotten. ''In that community later generations have recognized the prototype and essential embodiment of the idea of the *Ecclesia*."[14]

The statements that Jesus made as he instituted this rite are particularly important to this study. When he identified the bread as his body and gave it to his disciples to eat, he was emphasizing as fully as possible their identity with him. Could it be that these words contributed to Paul's understanding that the Church is the body of Christ? Such is not unreasonable to assume in light of Nygren's statement:

> It is the unanimous view of the New Testament that the Church is the body of Christ. Even though the name itself is not encountered uniformly throughout the New Testament, nevertheless the substance of the idea is everywhere present. Here we can refer again to Matt. 16:18. The Church is given an immediate connection with Christ, and of the Church it is said that 'The powers of death shall not prevail against it'. The Church belongs to the new age and has participation in its imperishable life.[17]

Matthew and Mark agree that when Jesus took the cup and blessed it he said, "This is my blood of the covenant" (Matt. 26:28; Mark 14:24). Paul reports him saying, "This cup is the new covenant in my blood" (1 Cor. 11:25). In either case the resemblance of this statement to the new covenant promise of Jeremiah (31:31ff.) cannot be coincidental. Jeremiah's promise—the days are coming—had to do with the performance of God's will, the rule of God. In that new day obedience would be possible because God's will would be written upon the heart—internal instead of external, and the new covenant would provide for the forgiveness of sin. As he gave the cup to the disciples, Jesus said that the new covenant was then present. His action anticipated his death a short time later. The sacrifice that Jesus was making would provide for the reconciliation of the sinner to God. It is important to remember that *cove-*

nant in the Old Testament is the word used to describe God's effort to make Israel his people.

> For the prophet, a covenant was not a contract or a bargain but an approach by God to His people, an offer of His Grace, a statement of His will, and accompanied by manifestations of His power to redeem them.[16]

Even so Jesus uses the conception of covenant as the highest expression of his redeeming activity and sacrifice in bringing together the new Israel, the *Ecclesia*, and in giving his disciples a share in the redemption of persons. Thus the "institution of the Lord's Supper is . . . an act in the establishment of the Church."[17]

That meal and that evening were climactic in the life of Jesus and his disciples. Jesus had warned them that one of them would betray him. He had on a number of occasions spoken of his own death. He warned them again that this was about to happen. There followed the experience during the night on the Mount of Olives and eventually of the betrayal. Then followed the trial and finally the Crucifixion. Jesus did not go up to Jerusalem just to die, but to live out the demands of his self-acclaimed identity as the son of man who was suffering as the servant of the Lord.

Early in his ministry Jesus referred to himself as the son of man (Matt. 8:20) and after Peter's confession (Matt. 16:16) it was his favorite appellation for himself. Manson places this title in its proper perspective:

> The Son of man in the Gospels is the final term in a series of conceptions, all of which are found in the Old Testament. These are the Remnant (Isa.), the Servant of Jehovah (II Isa.), the "I" of the Psalms, The Son of Man (Dan.). . . . The Son of Man is, like the Servant of Jehovah, an ideal figure that stands for the manifestation of the Kingdom of God on earth in a people wholly devoted to their heavenly King.[18]

Mark affirms, "The Son of Man came not to be served but to serve, and to give his life as a ransom for many"

(10:45). The phrase "ransom for many" is reminiscent of Isaiah 53:1-16. Jesus, the son of man, is the suffering servant.

As with the conception of the Son of Man, a great deal has been written about the role and the identity of the servant of the Lord. For the Church, all of the mystery as to the Servant's identity was removed with the life and death of Jesus. As has been frequently recognized, Isaiah 52:13-53:12 could be transposed into the passion narratives of any of the Gospels and no one would feel that it was out of place. Furthermore, it appears that this description of the Servant helped to form in Jesus' mind what was to happen to him. Jesus understood his mission as the Messiah against the background of this statement.[19] Jesus saw himself as the son of man—suffering servant of the Lord who was destined to die for the sinful. His death was not a martyrdom. Rather his life was given freely on behalf of those in need of redemption. Thus Isaiah makes clear the meaning of his death: "He was wounded for our transgressions, he was bruised for our iniquities; upon him was the chastisement that made us whole, and with his stripes we are healed" (52:5).

Thus Jesus' life was a continuum of God's search for a people. The story of this search began in the earliest stages of the religious life of Israel through all of those whom God sent to bring his people an awareness of his will. It continued through the life, teachings, death, and resurrection of our Lord. It continues in the life of the Church whenever and wherever men and women are brought into fellowship with him through an obedient response to Jesus' invitation to follow him. If this be true, then becoming a genuine disciple of Jesus and entering into the kingdom of God amounted to the same thing. As Manson has said, "It . . . appears that an essential part of the messianic office as Jesus conceived it was not to bring the Kingdom of God to men but to bring men to the Kingdom of God."[20]

Becoming a disciple—entering the Kingdom—is costly. Those who are unwilling to deny themselves and take up a cross (Luke 9:23), or who look back on their decision (Luke 9:62) are not fit for the Kingdom. Nothing must come before the Kingdom (Matt. 6:33), not even father or mother, son or daughter (Matt. 10:37). One cannot be a follower of Jesus and postpone the discipleship until the convenience of caring for personal matters is satisfied (Luke 9:57-62). Persons should not enter into such a self-giving discipleship without being certain that that is of the utmost importance to them. They must "count the cost" (Luke 14:25-35). In the story of Dives and Lazarus it is suggested that being poor—even poverty stricken—may be of greater ultimate security than riches (Luke 16:25). Zacchaeus, as he joyfully met the Master's requirements, pledged to give a half of his wealth to the poor (Luke 19:8). But more than paying a price for discipleship is required. A life that will match the ideals of the Kingdom is also required.

Jesus' teaching which is comonly called the Sermon on the Mount as recorded in Matthew 5-7 lays out a strict code of attitude and conduct that serves as the moral ideal of the Kingdom of God.

The Beatitudes promise God's special favor toward those who will live under his rule. The kingdom of heaven belongs to those who recognize their own spiritual poverty (5:3). Those who mourn and those who yearn after righteousness will find comfort and satisfaction. The pure in heart and the peacemakers will enjoy God's presence and will be called his sons. Those who are meek rather than those who are mighty are the powerful, while those who show mercy are also the ones who will receive mercy. Persecution, far from being unusual in the Kingdom, is to be expected, but those who endure will live under the beneficence of God's rule.

In a series of statements on practical morality, Jesus

contrasted the rule of the Kingdom with the Mosaic standards. It is not enough, Jesus said, to abstain from actual deeds such as murder, lust, and giving false witness. The inward motives and desires that produce these actions must be avoided. Love for the neighbor and brother is commendable but must also extend to the enemy.

Pious action for show is not countenanced. Prayer should be simple and straightforward, and we can expect to be forgiven our own sins in direct proportion to our willingness to forgive those who wrong us. Righteousness must be in more than words. Meritorious action, even in the name of the Lord, is inadequate. In addition to these, our lives must demonstrate the integrity of discipleship.

It is often objected that the Sermon on the Mount represents an impossible ethic. And of course it is impossible for the sinner to live at that level. But that is the point. This new "community is expected to live on a loftier level of achievement than was possible hitherto . . . this life is to be lived out by the power of God, since such a life is His will."[21] As Barclay says, "We need Christ to enable us to obey Christ's command."[22]

We have attempted to show in this study of the Gospels that the messianic age dawned with the preaching of the Kingdom as being then present. We have not said that there was no future sense in which the Kingdom is yet to come. In the prayer that Jesus taught his disciples to pray, the future coming of the Kingdom is clearly implied. The Kingdom—God's rule—is an ongoing process throughout history; God is searching for an obedient, faithful people as he will continuously do to the very end of the age. Those persons who will heed the call of the Lord—and the invitation is extended to all—may enter that Kingdom. A special kind of life is required of them. All are expected to live out in their daily lives the will of the heavenly Father. To enter the Kingdom is to enter a domain in which God's will is done on earth.[23] To such is given the incomparable love and grace of God.

Thus when we understand the nature of this Kingdom we understand the meaning of Jesus when he said to Peter:

> Blessed are you, Simon Bar-Jona! For flesh and blood has not revealed this to you, but my Father who is in heaven. And I tell you, you are Peter, and on this rock I will build my church, and the powers of death shall not prevail against it. I will give you the keys of the kingdom of heaven, and whatever you bind on earth shall be bound in heaven, and whatever you loose on earth shall be loosed in heaven'' (Matt. 16-17-20).

What is it that will open the doors to the Kingdom? It is the confession that Jesus is the Christ, the Son of God: "If you confess with your lips that Jesus is Lord and believe in your heart that God raised him from the dead, you shall be saved" (Rom. 10:9; cf. Matt. 10:32). This Peter did under divine revelation, not by human intellectual discovery. And that is the subsequent role of Peter and all of those who follow after him. They are to witness to and confess Jesus so that others also may learn who he is and find their way into the Kingdom. Thus the Kingdom comes and thus the Kingdom is entered. Here the discovery is made—Jesus is the door to the Kingdom.

Once more we ask the question, Do the Gospels tell the story of the Church? To that question we must respond in the affirmative even in the virtual absence of specific use of the term or definitions of the Church. What we have seen is that the presence of the Kingdom was proclaimed and clear instructions as to its entry and the life lived under the rule of God have been given. When at a later time definitions were given and instructions came for being a member of the Church, what was immediately noticed was the similarity between the Church and the Kingdom.[24] We may wish to distinguish between the Church and the Kingdom[25] on a technical basis such as, the Church is God's instrument to bring persons to the Kingdom, but it will also be recognized that those who are in the Church are in the Kingdom and those in the Kingdom are the Church.

The Church—the citizens of the Kingdom—are to live the life of Christ and witness to his redeeming love. Christ and his church cannot be separated or defeated.

Notes

1. Alan Richardson, ed., "Church," in *A Theological Wordbook of* the Bible) London: SCM Press Ltd, 1957).
2. G. Lohfink, *Die Sammlung Israels: Eine Untersuchung zur lukanischen Ekklesiologie* (Munich, 1975) p. 56, as quoted in K.N. Giles, "The Church in the Gospel of Luke," *Scottish Journal of Theology,* vol. 34, no. 2 (1981).
3. K.L. Schmidt, "Ecclesia," G. Kittel, ed., *Theological Dictionary of the New Testament*, vol. III, G. Bromiley, trans. (Grand Rapids: Ferdmans, 1965), pp. 501-536.
4. Anders Nygren, *Christ and His Church* (Philadelphia: The Westminster Press, 1956), p. 16.
5. *Nygren.*
6. Emil Brunner, *The Christian Doctrine of the Church, Faith and the Consummation*, D. Cairns, trans. (Philadelphia: The Westminster Press, 1962), p. 22.
7. John Bright, *The Kingdom of God* (New York: Abingdon Press, 1953), p. 225.
8. Brunner, p. 199.
9. Schmidt, p. 520.
10. For example, Theudas, Acts 5:36.
11. A full discussion of the issues that may be raised over Jesus' Messianic consciousness is beyond the purview of this effort. It is sufficient to show that the Gospels represent him as recognizing this as his role, since his messiahship is the fact upon which the kingdom of God and the existence of the Church depend.
12. William Sanford La Sor, et. al., *Old Testament Survey* (Grand Rapids: William B. Eerdmans Publishing Co., 1982), p. 2.

13. Following Archibald M. Hunter, *Interpreting the Parables* (Philadelphia: The Westminster Press, 1960), pp. 42ff. Hunter identifies four groupings. The first two of his designations are relevant to this portion of our discussion.

14. C. Newton Flew, *Jesus and His Church* (London: The Epworth Press, 1951), p. 19. See also K.N. Giles, "The Church in the Gospel of Luke," *Scottish Journal of Theology*, vol. 34, (1981), pp. 121-46.

15. Nygren, p. 97.

16. Flew, p. 73.

17. Schmidt, p. 521.

18. T.W. Manson, *The Teaching of Jesus* (Cambridge: University Press, 1951), p. 227. The literature on the origins of the term *son of man* and Jesus' use of it is extensive. Manson has placed it in the appropriate context for our purposes.

19. Nygren, p. 58.

20. Manson, p. 206.

21. Flew, p. 53.

22. William Barclay, *The Gospel of Matthew* (Philadelphia: The Westminster Press, 1975), vol. 1, p. 175.

23. Flew, p. 25.

24. See Manson, p. 205, where he compares the requirements of Church and Kingdom in parallel columns in order to show their similarity.

25. E.g. Archibald M. Hunter, *Work and Words of Jesus* (Philadelphia: The Westminster Press, 1950), p. 76, and Flew, p. 24.

the life of Jesus at the expense of others. Their character
as faith-documents has been stressed. Comparative or al-
legedly comparative material in Greek literature has been
adduced in an attempt to demonstrate either their kinship
with or dissimilarity from the prevailing literary forms of
their time.[10] The net effect of this has been to stress the
theological character of the Gospels at the expense of the
historical. Talbert's summary statement is not unfair:
" 'The canonical gospels are not biographies. They are the
apostolic kerygma built up into a vivid narrative form.'
For over a generation this has been the virtually unchal-
lenged contention of critical scholarship."[11]

This points directly to the second reason why discussion
about the character of Acts has remained alive: namely the
organic connection between Acts and the Third Gospel.
The prologues to these works make this plain (Luke 1:1-4;
Acts 1:1). If then the Gospels are primarily theological
documents, does it not follow that the same will be true of
Acts; and that whereas, in his Gospel, Luke works up the
kerygma into a narrative about Jesus, in Acts he works it
up into a narrative about the Church? Even Cullmann is
prepared to say, "By its purpose as well as by its literary
form, this book is not different from the Gospels. It is still
a *euangelion*."[12]

There are reasons for regarding such a position as going
beyond the evidence. This is not to deny that the Gospels
and Acts are written from the perspective of faith and
therefore are written with the intention of commending the
faith. Nor is it to deny that, being addressed to individual
situations, they manifest emphases and interests that bear
upon these situations. But to describe them as theological
documents in the same sense as the New Testament epistles is to define their theological character too sharply. A
more plausible account is such as was suggested by C. F.
D. Moule some years ago in his essay "The Intention of
the Evangelists"[13] to the effect that the early Christians

"recognized that their faith stood or fell with the sober facts of a story, and that it was vital to maintain the unbroken tradition of these facts. Would they not," he asks, "from time to time, rehearse the narratives *as such*, first of one incident, then of another, doing their best to keep within the historical limits and not embroider the tale anachronistically, however well they knew its sequel and its inner meaning?"[14] To quote a phrase Professor Moule has used more recently in reaffirming the same position, "the Synoptic Gospels [are] ancillary to the apostolic gospel"[15]; that is to say, they tell the story upon which the gospel message rests. This still leaves the *kerygma* as the determining factor in what is preserved of the story: the gospels tell as much of the Savior as is necessary to convey the message of salvation. But the distinction between the story and the message is recognized.[16] A kindred understanding is implied in Professor Martin Hengel's statement that "when we inquire about the purposes of a New Testament author, we can never ignore the fact that such an author, who has a position within the Christian community and is at its service, does not seek primarily to display his theological individuality and originality, much less his rhetorical skill and historical learning. Keeping his own personality in the background, he works with existing traditions about the saving event which, while lying in the past, utterly governs the present of the community."[17]

If this is sound, it has important implications for the character of Acts. For unless Acts be regarded as a totally different *type* of book from the Third Gospel—which is improbable—[18] then Luke's primary concern here also will be to tell the story. No more than with Luke's Gospel does this imply mere chronicling. On the contrary the needs of the situation addressed and the underlining of points of particular interest have left their mark. And the needs of the situation and the points of particular interest are chiefly theological in character. Hence the increasing tendency by many—I. H. Marshall, W. van Unnik, M. Hengel, Alfons Weiser—to see Acts as a theological history.[19] But the theology arises out of the history and is not imposed on it, much less is the history a factitious creation fabricated to be the vehicle of the theological or religious message.

The Purpose of the Book of Acts. A second assumption of consequence for this study concerns the purpose of the Book of Acts. In some measure it follows from what has been said regarding the character of the book. But can it be defined more precisely? Numerous answers have been given. It has been suggested that Acts was written to confirm that the saving activity of God in Christ was continued after Christ's departure through the ministry of the apostles;[20] or to show how the gospel spread throughout the whole of the Roman world;[21] or to demonstrate that the Church was a law-abiding community and not a nest of political subversives;[22] or to refute Gnosticism;[23] or to show the Church that the delay in the return of Christ was not a disaster but rather an opportunity for global evangelism;[24] or to solve the problem of how rich people can truly be members of the Christian community.[25] The list could be extended and the permutations multiplied almost indefinitely. And in a way, that is the trouble; for with so many possibilities for which there is at least something to be said, how does one seek for a secure conclusion?

G. Schneider has suggested four questions that may be taken as guidelines in this regard.[26] (1) What is the expressed aim? (2) What details in the work clarify this? (3) What main themes are discussed? (4) Can purpose be illuminated by genre? For the expressed aim we are directed to the prologues. The exegetical alternatives here are legion.[27] With regard to the prologue to the gospel it must suffice to say that the intention indicated appears to be to give an account of the events on which the gospel message rests. Nothing in the terms of the prologue forbids this understanding. As van Unnik points out, Luke does not speak of *aletheia* ("the truth") but *asphaleia* ("the certainty"). "The 'truth' had already been expounded by his predecessors (v. 1-2), but he was concerned with the 'infallibility' of the facts."[28] The prologue to Acts may be taken consistently with this. For one thing Acts stands under the umbrella of the prologue to the gospel, especially if van Unnik is right in his contention that "former book" (Acts 1:1) means "first part of a connected work."[29] If, moreover, the prologue of Acts consists of 1:1-8, then the programmatic statement of verse 8 constitutes an implicit statement of purpose[30] and the "certainty of the things accomplished among us" will be confirmed by the record of the continuance after his death of "all that Jesus began to do and teach" (1:1) prior to his ascension.

The genre of the work—Schneider's fourth guideline— discussed previously under the heading of character, is consonant with this, but also points farther. For the most striking feature about Luke the author is that he is the only Gospel writer who felt it necessary to add a second volume to his first. What does this say? R. A. Maddox replies,

> [Luke's] innovation is to show that the gospel-story is incomplete without the church-story. Luke thus emphasizes, on the one hand, that the character of the Christian life in the church cannot be understood apart from its foundation in the incarnation, mission, death, resurrection, and ascension of Jesus. Conversely, the story cannot properly be appreciated without following it through to its outcome in the church. Hence the basic scope and shape of the work will show a major concern to explore and explain the nature of the church.[31]

Whether, in fulfillment of Schneider's second and third requirements, the details and main themes of Luke-Acts clarify and confirm this conclusion, is something that must be explored in the rest of this essay. At all events there exists a *prima facie* case for seeing ecclesiology as an overarching (even if not the only) interest of Acts. We must now indicate the method by which this theme will be examined.

The Method of the Inquiry

In order to do justice to Luke's account of the Church we must cast the net widely. The use of the term *church* (*ekklesia*) in Acts will serve as a guideline, as well as terms associated with it such as *believers, people, brethren*. Beyond this, however, it will be necessary to note ideas that are linked with the concept of the Church: vocabulary alone is too narrow a base to sustain this, for the Church may be in mind even in passages in which it is mentioned. On the basis of evidence of this kind we may attempt to construct the picture of the church or the ecclesiology of Acts and in conclusion, ask what this has to say of the church of today.

THE ECCLESIOLOGICAL VOCABULARY OF ACTS AND ITS IDEOLOGICAL RELATIONS

We may begin by reviewing a sample or cross-section of the terminology used in Acts to speak of the Church in its various aspects. On this foundation we shall analyze the ideas that come to expression through this terminology. This procedure will entail a degree of repetition, but any method would do the same, and this has the virtue of grounding the analysis in the terminology which is thereby able to exercise a control over the ideas in terms of which the Church is viewed.

Church (ekklesia)

We may begin with the term *church* (*ekklesia*). It occurs a total of twenty-three times, though three of these may be discounted at once: 19:32, 39 and 41 where the reference is to the civil assembly of Ephesus.

The striking feature about the examples referring to the Christian community is *the range of their use and meaning*. Sometimes it is used to refer to a single local assembly: the church in Jerusalem (11:22), in Antioch (13:1), in Ephesus (20:17). This is confirmed by the occasional use of the distributive: "they appointed elders in every church" (14:23); or the plural: "they passed through Syria and Cilicia strengthening the churches" (15:41), or "the churches were strengthened in the faith and increased in numbers daily" (16:5). Sometimes, however, the singular is used intensively. Thus at 9:31 it is noted that—with Paul's departure to Tarsus—"the church[32] throughout the whole of Judaea and Galilee and Samaria had peace." Clearly a number of local congregations is intended, and the use is collective. In 15:22, following the recording of the decision of the Jerusalem Council in the preceding verse, we read, "It pleased the apostles and elders with the whole church" to send men from Jerusalem to accompany Paul and Barnabas in taking the decree to Antioch; and the prologue to the narrative of the council (15:6ff.) makes it clear that this was a representative gathering of the churches.

Haenchen states flatly that "Luke elaborates no doctrine of the Church."[33] No doubt much depends on what is meant by the word *elaborates*.[34] But unless we are to accuse Luke of using words in an undiscriminating way, it would seem that the following ideas entered into his understanding. (1) The Church as a whole is constituted of the churches severally, though this does not mean that it takes a certain number of churches to constitute the Church. The Church existed when the Jerusalem congregation was the only one, as is implied in the first instance of the term in Acts: "fear fell on the whole church and on all who heard these things" (5:11). (2) The fullness of the Church is present in each constituent congregation. This is shown not only by the use of the same term to denote both, but also inasmuch as qualities, powers, and privileges are attributed to the local manifestation which apply to the collective whole. Thus, Paul enjoins the elders of the church of Ephesus to "care for the flock in which the Holy Spirit has appointed you as overseers, to shepherd the church of God which he purchased with his own blood" (20:28). That is, the church in Ephesus, though only a small part of the whole church, was procured at no less a price than the whole church.

If this is not an elaborate ecclesiology, it can hardly be described as insignificant.

Brethren (adelphoi)

A second term used by Luke is *brethren*: indeed, this is the term used first (at 1:15) and most in Acts. Apart from instances in which the context shows it to be referring to the Church by implication, there are examples in which it is used in association with *ecclesia*, each term explaining the other. Thus 9:30, "When the *brethren* knew . . . they sent (Saul) to Tarsus," is followed in 9:31 by the statement "Then the Church . . . had peace." There are twenty-nine examples in Acts, though fourteen of them mean "fellow-Jews" as in 2:37: "Men and brethren, what shall we do?" This tends to dull the flavor of the term. However, one particular example discloses its full force. It is the term by which Ananias, subduing all his understandable apprehension, greets the newly converted persecutor of the Church: "Brother Saul" (9:17; 22:13). R. P. C. Hanson states that "it is likely that this word was in fact the earliest Christian word for members of the Christian Church."[35] The term is expressive of the sense of new horizontal relationships to persons that came along with the sense of a new vertical relationship to God, and it expresses the idea of community and belonging.

Believe (pisteuein)—Word (logos)

We may take as our third example a pair of terms that stand together ideologically even if in Acts they are frequently used absolutely: the terms *believe* and *word*.

The former appears either as a verb or noun substitute no fewer than thirty-two times (though two examples refer, not to Christian faith, but to believing the Law (24:14) and the Prophets (26:27). The first example is a comprehensive description of the church: "all those who believed were together" (2:44). The analysis of uses is interesting. Thus: (a) a group of examples specifies *the object of belief* variously as "the word" (4:4) or "the Lord" (9:42, 14:23, 16:31); (b) another group of examples refers to *the believing subjects*: Samaritans (8:12), Jews (14:1), Gentiles (15:7), Pharisees (15:1), Corinthians (18:8); (c) a third group describes *the consequences of belief*: unity (4:32), forgiveness (10:43), justification (13:39), eternal life (13:48), salvation (16:31).

We may place alongside this, examples of the term *word*, which is frequently the expressed object of the term *believe*, though it has other relationships also. There are twelve instances altogether. Their general import is well represented by examples such as 2:41, 4:4, 10:44, 13:48 where the hearing of the Word in faith leads to baptism, the reception of the Holy Spirit and being added to the Christian community. Of special interest are 6:7, 12:24 and 19:20, which say, in only slightly varying terminology, that the Word of God increased and multiplied. These sayings are three of the six summary statements that C. H. Turner identified as concluding the six panels into which he believed the picture of Acts was cut.[36] It is therefore remarkable that in two of the three other summary statements (9:31 and 16:5)[37] it is the Church or the churches that are said to increase and multiply. What seems to be implied is that, since the Church is created by the proclamation and reception of the Word in faith, the term *word* can be used by extension for *church* so that to say "the

Word grew'' really means that ''the Church grew.'' One may observe incidentally that, if Turner's reading of the structural significance of these summary statements is sound, it goes a long way toward showing how central is the story of the Church to the purpose of Acts.

We may conclude our sampling of vocabulary at this point. The least that can be said is that a *prima facie* case exists for the judgment that ecclesiology is a significant concern of the author of Acts. Indeed, it is possible to go further and say that it shows some kind of reflection on the following aspects: (1) the nature of the Church; (2) the function of the Church; (3) the mission of the Church; (4) the ministry of the Church. It remains to be seen whether closer investigation sustains this. On the basis of the foregoing limited examination of the evidence we may include other terms and ideas that serve as tributaries to the ecclesiological river.

THE NATURE OF THE CHURCH

At least four ideas appear to be contained in Luke's understanding of the nature of the Church.

The Church—The Creation of God

Acts 20:28 is the only context in the book in which the word *church* is qualified by the phrase ''of God'' (taking *tou theou* to be the true reading).[38] The genitiv is posses sive rather than of origin. Indeed, it is this that gives definition to the use of *ekklesia* not only in Acts but throughout the New Testament. The term *ecclesia* in itself carries no necessary theological overtone (despite its use in the Septuagint to render the Hebrew *qahal* (''congregation'') and is used in a thoroughly secular way in Acts 19:32, 39 and 41 to refer to the civil assembly of Ephesus. It is its identification as the Church ''of God'' that ex-

presses its distinctive character; and—says K. L.
Schmidt—"even when ("of God") does not occur, we
should understand it since otherwise the full significance of
ekklesia cannot be appreciated. The congregation or
Church of God always stands in contrast and even in opposition to other forms of society."[39]

However, Acts 20:28 goes beyond indicating the ownership of the Church to indicating its origin. It is the
Church "which God has purchased with the blood of his
Own One."[40] That is to say, the Church is owned by God
because it is the product of his redemptive activity in the
death of his Son. It is true that this is the only example of
the application of this idea to the Church in Acts, but it is
not to be discounted for that reason. The corporate aspect
rests on the echo of Psalm 74:1-2 with its mention of the
redeemed flock of God; and the idea of the Shepherd who
places the safety of his flock above his own is sufficiently
common in the Old Testament (e.g. Ezek. 34) to rise naturally to expression here.[41]

But it is not chiefly in this way that the divine origin of
the Church is described in Acts; rather the Church is presented as the creation of the Holy Spirit. If one poses the
question "When did the Church come into existence?" the
answer of the Book of Acts is, "On the Day of Pentecost."[42] For the Church is the community of the New
Age; the distinctive gift of the New Age is the Holy Spirit
(Joel 2:28, Acts 2:17); the coming of the Spirit was the
divine response to the departure of Jesus (Acts 1:6); and
the Spirit was given on the Day of Pentecost (Acts 2:33).
The subsequent story of the Church in Acts is but a chain
of illustrations of this. As Jackson and Lake express it:

> The Church is the home of the Spirit; when Ananias and
> Saphhira deceive the Church they lie to the Spirit; Barnabas
> and Paul are appointed missionaries by the Spirit; the elders
> of Ephesus are said to have been made *episkopoi* by the Spirit
> . . . Christians were men who had been given the Spirit; the

Church was the supernaturally endowed society of those who had received the gift; only through it could this normally be obtained; and the case of Cornelius was so exceptional as to warrant his immediate reception in the Church.[43]

To this proposition that in origin the Church is the creation of God must be added a second which—in some measure—stands in tension with it.

The Church—The Ongoing People of God

F. Bovon observes that Acts is paradoxically the most universalist book in the New Testament and the book most favorable to Judaism.[44] It is this paradox that lies at the heart of the question, and has given rise to the debate, as to the relation of the Church to Israel. Did Luke regard the Church as a *new* Israel, forged out of both Jews and Gentiles, failure to accomplish which had led to the rejection of the old Israel? An impressive case for this view can be made by appealing to such features as the movement of the action in Acts away from Jerusalem to Rome; the formal turning from the Jews in Pisidian Antioch (13:44-8); and the progressive hardening of the Jews culminating in the concluding scene in the book in which Paul pronounces the rejection of the Jews on the leaders of Roman Judaism (28:25-28).[45] On the other hand the opposite case has also been advocated, notably by J. Jervell, that far from separating from Judaism, the Church is the Old Israel with the Gentiles added on. "Luke never saw the Church," says Jervell, "as the *new* or *true* Israel. When the Gospel was preached, the one people of God was split, Jews who refused the gospel being purged from Israel. The history of the people of God continues among Jews who accept Jesus who in turn take the gospel to Gentiles as foretold."[46] Of both of these positions it would seem to be true to say that they are right in what they affirm and wrong in what they deny. There is indeed an element of newness in the

Church, but not a newness that is exclusive of the past. On the other hand, there is a continuity with the past, but not a mere perpetuation without a difference.

This finely calculated view comes to expression in Luke's use of the term *laos*, for 84 of the 140 examples of which in the New Testament he is responsible, 48 of them in Acts.[47] While the customary sense in Luke-Acts is "crowd" or "people,"[48] and while it is also used in the technical sense of "Israel,"[49] yet there is also evidence of metamorphosis at work. This may begin as early as Luke 1:17 in which the purpose of the ministry of the Forerunner is stated to be "to make ready a people (*laos*) prepared for the Lord." The same idea, even if not the language, is present in Luke 3:8 where the possibility of creating offspring of Abraham out of stones is envisaged. It is such a notion that comes to expression in Acts 15:14: "Simeon has related how God first visited the Gentiles (*ethne*) to take out of them a people (*laos*) for his name," a statement which, in Strathmann's words, was

> for Jewish ears an astounding and even a revolutionary saying. . . . Thus far *laos* and *ethne* had been mutually exclusive terms. Now there rises up to God's name from the *ethne* a *laos* independent of all national preconditions. The circle of the word *laos* is given a new center. Only faith in the gospel decides. The title is not herewith taken from Israel. But another *laos* now takes its place along with Israel on a different basis. This means, of course, that within Israel only those who meet the decisive conditions belong to this *laos*.[50]

That this is the intended meaning seems to be confirmed by the quotation of Amos 9:11-12 which follows, according to which the restoration of the fallen house of David takes place in order that "the rest of men may seek the Lord, and all the Gentiles who are called by my name" (Acts 15:17). A further example of this idea is found at Acts 18:10 where Paul is encouraged in a vision to persist in his ministry in Corinth because God has "a sizable people" (*laos polus*) in that city.

This interpretation has been criticized on the grounds that Luke's usage in Acts 15:14 and 18:10 may be no more than linguistic imprecision.[51] However, the striking nature of the phrase plus the aptness of the Old Testament quotation in the former do not look like "happen-stance." In any case, it is in much more fundamental ways than this that Luke exhibits his belief that the Church, while standing in continuity with Israel, nonetheless represents a new departure. It was by recognition of Jesus as Messiah that his followers became the people of the Messiah—because Messiah and People are correlatives. This is the thrust and appeal of Peter's Pentecostal sermon in which "all the house of Israel" is enjoined to recognize that God has made the crucified Jesus both "Lord and Christ" (Acts 2:36). The Church is not simply the Old Israel; it is the Old Israel which has recognized that its Messiah has come in the crucified Jesus and which on this new foundation now advances to include all the nations of the earth among its number.

This leads readily to a third proposition in Luke's understanding of the Church:

The Church—Composed of Believers in Christ Jesus

The point need not be labored, since the terms *believe* and *Word* have already been reviewed and it was shown not only that "believers" was a common designation for the Church, but the object of their faith—"the Word," "the Lord"—and its results—forgiveness, justification, salvation—were indicated. The same conclusion follows from the immediately preceding section. It is acceptance of Jesus, that is, faith in him as Messiah, which alone brings inclusion in the people of the Messiah.

The Church—Both Local and Universal

Again, we may refer to the earlier treatment of the term
ecclesia,[52] which showed that, while the parts are constituents of the whole, the whole is in each of the parts.
The church in Corinth is part of the whole church. But the
whole of the Church, that is, all that constitutes the essence of the Church, is in the church in Corinth. As K. L.
Schmidt expresses it, "The congregation in different
places is simply called *ecclesia* with no question of precedence. . . . It must also be emphasised that the singular
and plural are used promiscuously. It is not that the
ecclesia divides up into *ecclesiai*. The one *ecclesia* is present in the places mentioned."[53]

We may put all this together by saying that for Luke *the
Church is that organ divinely created to serve as the instrument of God's universal saving purpose; fitted in consequence to discharge its task in all parts of the world;
and admission to which is secured on the basis of faith in
Jesus as God's Messiah.*

From the nature of the Church we may turn next to a
second theme disclosed by our preliminary examination of
terminology.

THE FUNCTION OF THE CHURCH

The word *function* is used here in the double sense of
what the Church does as well as how it does it. Task and
means are not finally separable. Three aspects must be
considered.

The Ministry of the Word

Our earlier examination of the term *word* included the
claim that, according to Luke, "the Church is created by
the proclamation and reception of the Word in faith."[54] If
this is a true reading of Luke's teaching, then the ministry

of the Word deserves primacy in any description of the function of the Church. Nor are there wanting those who read Luke in this way. "For Luke," writes C. K. Barrett, "the apostles are essentially witnesses; in particular they are witnesses of the resurrection (Luke 24:48; Acts 1:22; 4:33; 10:40f.). This role lays upon them the task of preaching, and Luke represents them as devoted to the ministry of the Word (6:2, 4). They are not, in his view, administrators."[55] But this is not the only view that is heard. The Anglican Bishop R. R. Williams, writing with Professor Barrett's statement in mind, insists that he sees in Acts, "a Church equally governed by, and devoted to, the Word of God, but also a Church in which the institutional arrangements—ministry, sacraments, calendar—have their part to play in the preservation and propagation of that Word."[56] To run the whole gamut we may add Ernst Käsemann's celebrated declaration: "The Lucan work as a whole is totally incomprehensible if it is not seen that only in the stream of apostolic tradition does one also belong to the one holy Church as the earthly realm of salvation;"[57] and also his equally celebrated deliverance: "To put it in a nutshell: the Word is no longer the sole criterion of the Church, but the Church is the legitimation of the Word and the apostolic origin of the Church's ministerial office provides the guarantee of a valid proclamation."[58]

Clearly the issue of the ministry of the Word spills over into that of the ministry as such, but since the latter will be given separate treatment later, we may concentrate at this point on the former. If the question could be settled by the counting of heads then the matter could be disposed of quickly, for the amount of space given in Acts to describing both the fact and content of early Christian proclamation tells its own story. The ultimate issue, however, is the finer one of the *relation* of the Church to the Word. Attention has already been drawn to the summarizing statements in Acts in which the terms are used interchangeably: to say that the Word grows is to say that the Church grows.[59] But although the terms are used interchangeably the meaning can hardly be that the Church causes the Word to grow; it must be the other way around. Church and Word are interdependent, but the dependence is not of the same order. The Word is dependent on the Church for proclamation; the Church is dependent on the Word for its creation. This is the point of the acute observation of R. Newton Flew that "at every point of the *kerygma* we see the idea of the Ecclesia declared or implied. . . . The *kerygma* contains the idea of the Ecclesia, but it also creates the Ecclesia."[60] If this is so, it is not surprising that the ministry of the Word should hold pride of place in Luke's understanding of the function of the Church.

The Ministry of the Sacraments

It will be convenient to treat separately the Lord's Supper and baptism.

1. *The Lord's Supper.* The prior issue to be determined here is not how often Acts speaks of the Lord's Supper but whether it speaks of it at all. In the five contexts in which it may be spoken of (2:42, 46; 20:7, 11; 27:35) the language used is that of the "breaking of bread" and in four of these (all except 20:7) there are features that raise the question as to whether the Lord's Supper is in mind rather than a fellowship meal (e.g. in 2:46) or even an ordinary meal described with Christian overtones (e.g. 27:35). The language of the "breaking of bread" is used descriptively in the Lucan account of the institution of the Lord's Supper[61]; and the probability is that in Acts 2:42 it is this that is in mind, distinguished from the *koinonia* or common meal. On the other hand the "breaking of bread" in the storm context (27:35) on all counts is unlikely to refer to the Lord's Supper, although the same language is used. It appears, therefore, as though the same language

could be used to describe distinct though not necessarily unrelated activities; that is to say the normal eating of food was an activity in which the presence of the Lord could be realized; and this was uniquely the case in the fellowship meal, particularly when it was enacted so as to recall the Last Supper.

If this is a valid interpretation of the data of Acts,[62] then two inferences may be drawn regarding the observance of the Lord's Supper. First, it was celebrated regularly. In Acts 2:42 it is listed among features that were characteristic of the life and worship of the primitive church. This is confirmed by the specific note in 20:7 where the first day of the week is described as the day on which they "met together to break bread." The second feature of their observance of the Lord's Supper was its relative informality. The way in which breaking-of-bread language could be transferred from one setting to another is suggestive of this, as is the impression made by a specific account such as that in 20:7-12 where the meal and breaking of bread are delayed, first by Paul's extended sermon, and then by its almost fatal consequences for Eutychus. C. K. Barrett's summing up is as judicious as it is terse: "(Luke's) allusions to the eucharist . . . are as slight and informal as they could be."[63]

2. *Baptism.* If the Lord's Supper is mentioned rarely, the same cannot be said of baptism, which is referred to in either verbal or substantival form approximately twenty times. Probably no subject in the study of Acts has given rise to more debate because it is so difficult to reduce the evidence to any kind of consistency. "Acts is full of obscurity and difficulty," says Barrett, "as anyone will readily detect who attempts to reconstruct, for example, a clear picture of how baptism was practised, and what was believed about it, in the earliest Church. . . . How were water-baptism and Spirit-baptism related to each other? Did the rite of immersion require the laying-on of hands

for its completion? Did the gift of the Spirit precede, accompany, or follow baptism? How was baptism related to
the forgiveness of sins, and to eschatology?"[64] It is not
necessary, even if it were possible, to deal with all of these
issues since our primary concern is with the ecclesiological
implications of Luke's understanding of baptism; and
even here a few summary observations must suffice.

a. It seems clear that the norm for admission to the
Christian community was the rite of baptism understood as
expressive of repentance which preceded it and the reception of the Holy Spirit which followed. Acts 2:38 states the
principle and it is confirmed in the instances of Samaria
(8:4-17), Saul (9:1-18; 22:3-16), and the disciples at
Ephesus (19:1-7). The problem lies in the exceptions,
though it may be that these are as much the clues to the
answer of the ecclesiological question as they are the problem. Thus, the gift of the Holy Spirit prior to baptism in
the case of Cornelius and his fellow-Gentiles (10:44-48),
however it is to be explained, certainly shows that in
Luke's mind the Holy Spirit was not tied to the baptismal
rite as being conditional upon it.

Again, if, as seems most likely,[65] the rebaptism of the
Ephesian disciples was insisted upon because they had not
received the Holy Spirit whereas Apollos was not rebap-
tized because he had already received the Spirit, we have
another indication that for Luke the substantive *meaning*
of baptism rather than the correct ordering of its components is of paramount importance.

Baptism is a single reality of which repentance, the rite
itself, and the reception of the Holy Spirit are constituents,
so much so that in some instances where only baptism is
mentioned (e.g. acts 2:41) we may reasonably infer that all
of the constituents were present.[66]

b. In keeping with Luke's concern for reality over form
in baptism is his picture of its administration. There are
eleven contexts in Acts in which the verb is used descrip-

tively of an act of Christian baptism. In one only is the verb in the active voice with the agent specified: "They both went down into the water, Philip and the eunuch, and he baptized him" (8:38). The remaining ten examples may be classified as follows: (1) one in which the verb *baptize* is used in the passive with no indication of the agent (2:41); (2) eight in which, although the agent might be readily inferred from the context, the passive is used nonetheless. This is the case in which one might infer the agent to be Philip (8:12, 13); Ananias (9:18; 22:16); Paul or Silas (16:15, 33; 18:8; 19:5); (3) one in which it is specifically intimated who did *not* baptize: Peter at the Gentile Pentecost (10:47-8). It is difficult to see in this pattern of usage anything other than an attempt to throw attention away from the agent to the act itself, suggesting that it is the act that matters. If the alternative and somewhat hazardous option be insisted on of seeking to infer the identity of the agents, then they would range from an apostle (though not one of the Twelve)—Paul; to one of the Seven—Philip; to a "disciple"—Ananias.

This provides a ready background for the evaluation of the two examples of the imposition of hands which are connected with baptism: Samaria (8:17) and Ephesus (19:6). These will be considered later[67] in connection with the mission of the Church to which it is maintained they properly refer.

Meanwhile we may turn to a third area of the Church's ministry described in Acts.

The Ministry to Material Need

It will be asked whether it is not incongruous to place the meeting of material need in the same column as the ministry of the Word and sacraments and therefore as a normative function of the Church. It might well be argued that the ministry to material need is given a deliberately inferior status in Acts 6 where the Twelve declare that it is not right for them to leave the Word of God and serve tables (6:2). It is undeniable that this is so. The ministry of the Word of God *is* given pride of place over "serving tables." However, it is possible to overdraw the contrast. For one thing, though the Twelve do not undertake the task themselves, they make provision for it to be done by others with the requisite wisdom and qualities of spirit (6:3). For another, both tasks are described as aspects of *diakonia*. The problem arises because the Hellenists' widows are overlooked in the daily *diakonia* of food (6:1). The Twelve will not abandon the Word to engage in the *diakonia* of food distribution (6:2), insisting on giving themselves to prayer and the *diakonia* of the Word (6:4). But the Seven are appointed, with the laying-on of the apostles' hands, to supply this need, or *diakonia* (6:3).

Diakonia or the related verb are used literally in Luke-Acts to denote either food-preparation (Luke 4:39; 10:40) or table-service (Luke 12:37; 17:8) or providing material support (Luke 8:3; Acts 11:29; 12:25). At the other extreme it is used to refer to the ministry of the apostolate (Acts 1:17, 25); or—in the case of Paul—his ministry to the Gentiles (Acts 20:24; 21:19); or—as in Acts 6:4—the ministry of the Word. It might seem, therefore, that *diakonia* is a perfectly general term that takes its meaning from its context. This, however, would be to ignore the use of the term by Jesus in whose hand the meaning of service and lordship were reversed. "It is clear," says Hermann Beyer, commenting on Luke 22:26-27, "that Jesus is not merely bringing about a radical change in the academic estimation of human existence and action; He is instituting in fact a new pattern of human relationships."[68] That this is the Lucan emphasis is made the more clear by verses 28-30. These stand in place of the ransom sayings in Mark 10:45 and Matthew 20:28. The remarkable thing is that a saying on the servantlike suffering of the Son of Man is replaced by a saying on the suffering of Jesus and the Twelve, followed by a declaration that they will be guests at his table: "You are those who have continued with me in my trials; and I assign to you, as my Father assigned to me, a Kingdom, that you may eat and drink at my table in my kingdom." What the entire sequence amounts to is that there is a *diakonia* shared by Jesus' followers because it is grounded in his own *diakonia*. That is to say, *diakonia* is a function of the community; and one in which moreover, every type of activity from table-service to preaching the Word finds its place. We are not far from the Pauline doctrine of the gifts of the Spirit.

Attempts have been made to extend the service-motif in Acts still further. R. J. Karris,[69] for example, has argued that in the community to which Luke-Acts was written, although there were poor, the rich were dominant—Simon Magus, the Ethiopian eunuch, Cornelius, Sergius Paulus. On this view Luke is responding to the question, Do possessions prevent us from being genuine Christians? His reply is to point to the dangers of wealth (Luke 14:10-12; 12:33-4; 16:1-31) and to urge the obligation of using wealth in a spirit of Christian generosity and responsibility (Acts 2:41-7; 4:31-5). This overpresses the evidence. No emphasis is laid on the wealth of the leading converts in Acts. On the other hand there is no doubt that the early church felt it a part of its ministry to provide for the needy, and it went to considerable lengths in order to do so.

THE MISSION OF THE CHURCH

There is a degree of artificiality and even distortion in treating *mission* apart from *function*. Mission might well be viewed as a function of the Church, if not its primary function; while function expresses the way or ways in which the Church executes its mission. Mission, however, is such a large theme in Acts that it merits independent treatment. Two aspects receive special emphasis.

The Nature of the Mission

This will necessarily be closely related to the nature of the Church. If therefore we have already correctly interpreted the nature of the Church as being to gather together, in continuity with the people of Israel, the people of the Messiah from among the nations, then the nature of the mission is clear. The programmatic statement of Acts 1:8 is sufficient indication of it.

There are some indications that the nature of the mission was not clearly or fully perceived at the start. The question about whether the kingdom was about to be restored to Israel (1:6) seems to reflect a concept of global mission cast in apocalyptic thought-forms[70]; and the closing words of Peter's Pentecostal sermon, "Save yourselves from this crooked generation" (2:40), have the same flavor. Neil comments:

> Peter's words reflect the conviction of the early Christians that they formed the faithful Remnant of Israel (cf. Joel 2.32). His invitation to the crowd is to join this messianic Remnant and accept Jesus as their Savior from the wrath to come (1 Thess. 1:10) which will fall upon the mass of faithless Israel.[71]

In an important measure the remainder of Acts recounts a wrestling with the definition of the term *Israel*, partly without but also partly within the Church. The first significant breach is made by Stephen and the Hellenists; for Stephen's speech in Acts 7 is a brilliant manifesto for the position that God's presence has never been confined to one locality—thereby undermining the sanctity of the Temple; and that God's message has always been resisted and rejected by the people of his choice—thereby undermining the security of the Jews. From here the ripples widen: to include the Samaritans (chap. 8), the Gentiles (chap. 10)—though not without a struggle recorded in chapters 11 and 15—and finally the Romans themselves, though not without Jewish resistance to the bitter end

(28:25-28). Evidently, the worldwide mission in the sense previously defined was an occasion not only of confusion but also of dissension and—in the case of some—of their rejection of the new faith.

Such a state of affairs raises the question as to how success was achieved; and we turn naturally to that issue.

The Accomplishment of the Mission

The story of the mission recounts how the Church went about its task or more accurately explains how God overcame the tardiness of the Church to understand or its reluctance to act or both. Here one encounters the variously phrased but frequently expressed idea that the Acts of the Apostles is fundamentally the Acts of the Holy Spirit.[72] This is true throughout the book, but nowhere is it more ture than in regard to the mission. Of Acts 13:1-3, I. H. Marshall writes, "The importance of the present narrative is that it describes the first piece of planned 'overseas mission' carried out by representatives of a particular church, rather than by solitary individuals, and begun by a deliberate decision, inspired by the Spirit, rather than somewhat more casually as a result of persecution."[73] We may summarize the matter thus.

1. First, the Holy Spirit is the initiator of the mission. This is made clear beyond misunderstanding in 1:8 where the description of the cause of the mission is prefaced by the promise of the Spirit's power to accomplish it, which in turn points back to the command not to leave Jerusalem until they had received the promise of the Father (1:4; cf. 2:33). While it is true that every new departure is carried out in the power of the Spirit even when it is occasioned by events such as the persecution following Stephen's death (8:1, 5) or the enquiry of the Gentile Cornelius (10:19), it remains the case that the first corporate initiative of the Church was that at Antioch, and that it took place in response to a directive of the Holy Spirit—

doubtless through one of the prophets[74]—to separate Barnabas and Saul for the mission to Asia Minor (13:1-3). The point is underscored in the description of their departure: "Being sent out by the Holy Spirit, they went" (13:4).

2. Second, the Holy Spirit is the director and guide of the mission. At critical moments of deciding in which direction the next step lay, guidance and direction were received from the Holy Spirit. A conspicuous instance is 16:6ff: "And they went through the region of Phrygia and Galatia, having been forbidden by the Holy Spirit to speak the word in Asia. And when they had come opposite Mysia, they attempted to go into Bithynia, but the Spirit of Jesus did not allow them." Again it is likely that a prophet was the medium of the directive. Indeed, it is not to be overlooked that Barnabas and Saul are themselves numbered among the prophets and teachers in the church in Antioch (13:1). At the same time, intelligent decision is not dismissed, and the second missionary journey is born out of the reasonable desire to see how the churches were faring which had been established during the first journey (15:36).

3. Third, the Holy Spirit was the seal of the mission. The terminology is not Lucan but seems to be faithful to his meaning. For it can hardly be accidental that at precisely those points at which the mission strikes out in a new direction, the Holy Spirit is given in an unusual way.[75] It is conceded that the interpretation of some of these instances is contested, and it can only be affirmed that to the writer the interpretation suggested is the most plausible. This would apply to the evangelization of the Samaritans in which the Holy Spirit is not given until the Jerusalem apostles pray for the Samaritan converts, laying their hands on them (Acts 8:14-17). That there was some defect in the baptism of the Samaritans, as suggested by J. D. G. Dunn, is improbable;[76] and while C. K. Barrett's contention that the narrative as a whole shows that the

Holy Spirit cannot be brought under human control is sound,[77] it takes insufficient account of the Samaritan background. Prayer with the laying on of hands in non-mission contexts (e.g. 6:1-6, 28-8) appears to be an expression of solidarity with and support for those upon whom hands are laid, and there is no clear evidence that its meaning is different in mission contexts;[78] and given the history of Jewish-Samaritan relations, nothing could have been more appropriate. A similar explanation would apply to the case of Paul, specially noteworthy being the description to Ananias of his mission to the Gentiles (9:15); and of Ananias' fraternal greeting: "Brother Saul" as he lays hands on him that he might recover his sight and be filled with the Holy Spirit—before baptism (9:17-18). The falling of the Spirit on Cornelius and his household without any human mediation—apostolic or otherwise—is taken by Peter to indicate direct, divine approval of the incorporation of the Gentiles (10:44-8; 11:17-18). The episode at Ephesus (19:1-7) involving those who knew only John's baptism and therefore implying the crossing of a salvation-historical frontier is probably to be interpreted in the same way. In short, the giving of the Spirit was the authentication that the mission was staying on course; and that this happened in unusual ways arose not from a love of the unpredictable so much as from a matching of the mode of impartation to the circumstances of each case in question.

THE MINISTRY OF THE CHURCH

We turn to a final aspect of the ecclesiology of Acts: the ministry. Reference has been made already to the suggestion that Acts is a repository of early Catholicism (Frühkatholizismus),[79] and Käsemann's statement has been cited to the effect that "the Lucan work as a whole is totally incomprehensible if it is not seen that only in the stream of apostolic tradition does one also belong to the only Holy Church as the earthly realm of salvation.''[80] Such a view inevitably carries implications for the form of the ministry. The question is whether the evidence sustains them.

The whole notion of early Catholicism, which in any case never achieved universal acceptance,[81] has come under renewed pressure. Early Catholicism, says Martin Hengel, is a "misleading cliché" and the features of church organization held to validate it are to be found in both Jesus and Paul and are part of the legacy of Judaism.[82] J. Dupont refers to attempts to do more justice to the evidence by speaking of the "ecclesiastical dualism" of Acts, distinguishing the institutional forms of ministry from the spiritual, and arguing that we are not to choose between the two since they are complementary.[83] The institutional apostolate of the Twelve and the spiritual apostolate of Paul are both divinely ordained; likewise the other forms of ministry. It is doubtful, however, whether the evidence supports such a distinction; for the features distinguished are frequently found in the same individual.

Three summarizing statements may be offered as epitomizing the picture of the ministry found in Acts.

1. The general impression is that ministerial order is rudimentary. Various roles are mentioned but while these are distinct they are not given sharp definition. Thus while the Twelve are called apostles (Acts 1:26; 8:1) the term is also applied to others such as Paul and Barnabas (14:4). Again, Paul and Barnabas, though labeled apostles as noted, are also listed among the prophets and teachers (13:1). The Seven, though appointed to care for the material needs of the Hellenist widows to enable the Twelve to devote themselves to the ministry of the Word (6:2), are soon launched into the ministry of the Word in the persons of Stephen (6:8-10) and Phillip (8:4-40). The label 'epis-

kopos' ('overseer') (20:28) is attributed to the 'elders' ('presbyters') of the church at Ephesus (20:17). This does not give the impression of precision in job description. Eduard Schweizer's characterization is apt that such a picture of continuity and discontinuity, order and freedom is suggestive of newness and a floating definition of the Church.[84]

2. Appointment is to function rather than office. This may be illustrated with reference to a variety of roles.

a. The prime example is the apostolate as embodied in the Twelve. Their position as described in Acts is, to say the least, curious. At the beginning of the book they occupy the center of the stage; by the end of chapter 15 they have disappeared. An intelligible reason lies behind each side of this phenomenon. Their prominence derives from their role as witnesses to the historical ministry of Jesus, his death and resurrection (1:21-2), and it is this aspect of witness that is repeatedly referred to in connection with them (2:22f.; 3:12f.; 4:8f.; 5:29f.; 10:34f.). At the same time this role is, by definition, self-limiting and it is no surprise that when, for example, James is murdered, there is no hint of an attempt to replace him (12:1ff.). This explains the other side of the phenomenon—their progressively diminishing role. However, it carries within itself an important implication: that there was no other ingredient in their role to preserve their visibility when the function of witness was exhausted. That this was so is confirmed by other data such as that their suggestions were not implemented automatically but required the approval of the community (1:15; 6:1-6); that Peter could be called to account by the whole church for his action in eating with the household of Cornelius (11:2, 15:3f.); and that at the Jerusalem Council the authority-figure was James, the Lord's brother (15:13). In short, their preeminence as witnesses did not convert into ecclesiastical authority for themselves, let alone for others whom they might appoint to carry out specific tasks.

b. A similar result in principle is obtained from the evidence of Acts regarding elders. These appear first in Acts as part of the leadership of Judaism (4:5, 8, 23; 6:12), where seniority was a component in any title to the exercise of authority.[85] Their earliest emergence in the Church in Acts is as functionaries of the churches in Judaea (11:29-30). This may be a clue to their origin and significance: Christian elders were patterned after Jewish; no explanation of their role was needed because it was familiar and fully understood. If one collates the evidence of Acts, the picture of the elder that emerges is of a group of church leaders to whom alms might be given for distribution to the congregation (11:30); who, in company with the apostles and the whole church might adjudicate on matters of faith and practice (15:2, 4, 6, 22-3; 16:4; 21:18f.); and who might exercise oversight and pastoral care over the church (20:28)—indeed this role of 'overseer' (*episkopos*) is one that has been given by the Holy Spirit. Since no church could survive without responsible leadership it is not surprising that Paul and Barnabas appointed elders in every church (14:23) after earnest deliberation and prayer. There is no suggestion of ordination, but there is evidence of solemn appointment of those with the maturity and good judgment that normally come with age.

c. A number of ministries are so described as to render definition in other than functional terms impossible. This applies to the Seven who exercise a *diakonia* but are never called "deacons" (*diakonoi*) (6:1-6); and who, moreover, are never *described* as "serving tables" but are rather presented as exercising the role of apologist in the case of Stephen (6:8—7:53) and evangelist in the case of Philip (8:4-40; cf. 21:8). Are we to infer that, having duly solved the problem of the *diakonia* to the Hellenists' widows, they promptly moved on to other tasks, that function having been accomplished?

The work of the prophets in the early church in general

and the Acts in particular has long been a tantalizing problem.[86] The central difficulty is that while the function is broad, apparently including exhortation (15:32), prediction (11:28; 20:23; 21:11), and instruction (13:1-3), the noun *prophet* appears to be used in a restricted way (11:27; 13:1; 15:32; 21:10); or to put the same point otherwise, while prophesying is implied to be a function of all Christians (2:17f.; 19:6; 21:9), yet there appears to have been a group regarded particularly as "the prophets." The suggestion has been made that the more general references are to those (who might include all Christians) who might prophesy occasionally, and the narrower references to those who might do so on a more regular basis.[87] Ellis writes:

> In part the ambiguous nature of the specified ministries in Acts is traceable to the differing terminology in Luke's sources, terminology that he is unconcerned to conform to a consistent pattern. But the lack of concern itself suggests that for Luke no less than for his traditions there is a certain ambiguity and fluidity in the designation of ministries. On the one hand, the Spirit is itself the gift and to be "full of the Spirit" implies the empowerment to manifest a variety of gifts (Acts 2:33; 6:3, 8ff.). On the other hand, certain persons may be so identified with a specific gift as to be recognized and set apart in the community on that basis.[88]

The important point for our present purpose is that those who exercised the prophetic gift regularly were not qualitatively different from those who prophesied in lesser measure.

3. Appointment was based on spiritual qualities and qualifications attested by the Spirit. To say that importance was attached to spiritual qualities is not to say that other abilities were overlooked. Thus the Seven who were appointed to care for the distribution of alms were not only to be "full of the Spirit" but "men of good repute" and "full of wisdom" (6:3). We may further note that they all had Greek names (6:5)—which may be significant since

Greek-speaking widows were complaining of being short-
changed (6:1); and we may note still further that the choice
of individuals was left to the congregation (6:3, 5): they
were not imposed from the top. The importance attached
to spiritual qualities, however, is unmistakable. Again, the
Spirit appoints Paul to his mission to the Gentiles in general (9:15), and to his missionary enterprises in particular
(13:2-4). At the same time, Paul uses his judgment to decide not to take Mark, and receives the support of the
Church for his mission with Silas instead (15:36-41).

What we seem to be seeing in all this is that, while the
Church could not dispense with organization, there was no
fixed pattern to which conformity was required. The
forms, in Newton Flew's phrase, are "entirely dependent
on the divine life which governs the Ecclesia."[89] Thus the
prophetic ministry spans the entire Church from the
humblest individual to those so gifted as to be accorded
"prophet" as a designation; and means of appointment
can range all the way from prophetic utterance to apostolic
appointment to congregational choice. William Neil writes:

> Thus the overall picture of the government of the church as a
> whole in its earliest stage is one of diversity, which we might
> even call pragmatic. Apart from the unique position of the
> twelve Apostles there is no common pattern, and certainly
> nothing that could be called "church order" in the modern
> sense. Leadership was essential in each congregation, but it
> seems to have been stereotyped neither in form nor by de-
> signation. The authority and continuity of the Church was
> safe-guarded, not by apostolic succession, but by adherence
> to the apostolic tradition concerning Jesus, by the legacy of
> the Old Testament and by the presence of the Spirit.[90]

CONCLUSION

In conclusion we may ask, What is the message of the

ecclesiology of Acts for the church of today? In what sense are we to try to "get back to the beginning"? If the foregoing interpretation is sound, then the answer is: in some senses not at all. For the forms in which the life of the primitive church coagulated were necessarily derived from its own situation and in response to its own needs.[91] Acts gives no hint of a polity to be adopted by all subsequent generations; or a ministerial order; or a sacramental format. What Acts does show us is a church alive, throbbing with a sense of mission, open to and dependent on the dynamic activity of the Holy Spirit and refusing to encase itself in forms that would inhibit that activity. Yet at the same time it is also passing itself constantly under the judgment of the teaching of Jesus as witnessed to by the Twelve. In this context of creative tension the primitive church found its way in its earliest days; perhaps that is the lesson it has to teach the Church today.

Notes

1. W. van Unnik, "Luke-Acts, a Storm Center in Contemporary Scholarship" in Leander F. Keck and J. Louis Martyn, eds., *Studies in Luke-Acts* (Nashville: Abingdon Press, 1966; reprinted Philadelphia, 1980), pp. 15-32.
2. Although the author does not say so in as many words, this is the implication of the review of this period by W. Ward Gasque, *A History of the Criticism of the Acts of the Apostles* (Grand Rapids: Eerdmans, 1975), Chapter 1, "Precritical Study of the Book of Acts."
3. For an account of Baur see Gasque, chap. 2, especially pp. 26-31; W. G. Kümmel, *The New Testament: The History of the Investigation of Its Problems* (ET London: SCM Press, 1973), Part IV, chap. 1, especially pp. 126-43; and (more briefly) Stephen C. Neill, *The Interpretation of the New Testament, 1861-1961* (Oxford: University Press, 1964), pp. 19-27. It is not implied in the text that Baur's only critics

were English. See Gasque, chap. 3; Kümmel, part IV, chap. 3. However, the decisive refutation of Baur came via Lightfoot's work on the Apostolic Fathers: an aspect overlooked by Kümmel, p. 174, but fully recognized by Neill, chap. 2, Gasque's treatment somewhat obscures the point by placing nineteenth-century British work on Acts in a separate chapter; however, he is fully aware of the scale of Lightfoot's contribution; pp. 113-23.

4. Of Ramsay's voluminous writings see especially *St. Paul the Traveller and Roman Citizen* (London: Hodder and Stoughton, 1897), and *The Bearing of Recent Discovery on the Trustworthiness of the New Testament* (London: Hodder and Stoughton, 1915). For evaluations of Ramsay's work see W. F. Howard, *The Romance of New Testament Scholarship* (London: Epworth Press, 1949), chap. 6; S. C. Neill, pp. 141-46; and W. Ward Gasque, *Sir William M. Ramsay: Archaeologist and New Testament Scholar* (Grand Rapids: Baker, 1966); and *History of the Criticism of Acts*, pp. 136-42.

5. Ramsay, *The Bearing of Recent Discovery*, pp. 37-42.

6. See his three works on the Lucan writings: *Luke the Physician* (ET, London: Williams and Norgate, 1907); *The Acts of the Apostles* (ET, London: Williams and Norgate, 1909); *Date of the Acts and of the Synoptic Gospels* (ET, London; Williams and Norgate, 1911). S. C. Neill, in *The Interpretation of the New Testament*, p. 57, notes Harnack's awareness of the greatness of Lightfoot's contribution.

7. E.g. W. L. Knox, *The Acts of the Apostles* (Cambridge, The University Press, 1948), and especially F. F. Bruce, *The Acts of the Apostles* (London, Tyndale Press, 1951); "The Acts of the Apostles Today" in *Bulletin of the John Rylands University Library of Manchester* (henceforth, *BJRLM*) 65, 1982, pp. 36-56.

8. E.g. Philipp Vielhauer, "On the 'Paulinism' of Acts" in Keck and Martyn, pp. 33-50.

9. E.g. Martin Dibelius, *Studies in the Acts of the Apostles* (ET London: SCM Press, 1956). For an account see Gasque, *History of the Criticism of Acts,* chap. 9.

10. For surveys see R. H. Gundry, "Recent Investigations into

the Literary Genre 'Gospel'" in R. H. Longenecker and M. C. Tenney, eds., *New Dimensions in New Testament Study* (Grand Rapids: Zondervan, 1974), pp. 97-114; C. H. Talbert, *What Is a Gospel? The Genre of the Canonical Gospels* (Philadelphia: Fortress Press, 1977); D. E. Aune, "The Problem of the Genre of the Gospels: A Critique of C. H. Talbert's *What Is a Gospel?*" in R. T. France and David Wenham, eds., *Gospel Perspectives: Studies of History and Tradition in the Four Gospels* (Sheffield: JSOT Press, 1981).

11. Talbert, p. 2.

12. Oscar Cullmann, *The New Testament: An Introduction for the General Reader* (ET, Philadelphia: Westminster Press, 1968), p. 53.

13. First published in A. J. B. Higgins, ed., *New Testament Essays: Studies in Memory of T. W. Manson* (Manchester: University Press, 1979), pp. 165-79; reprinted in C. F. D. Moule, *The Phenomenon of the New Testament* (London, 1967, reprinted 1981), pp. 100-14.

14. Moule, p. 109.

15. Moule, Preface to the New Impression, vii.

16. Moule, pp. 100, 102.

17. Martin Hengel, *Acts and the History of Earliest Christianity* (Philadelphia: Fortress Press, 1980), p. 56.

18. Van Unnik takes "former book" (Acts 1:1) to mean "first part of a connected work" and insists that Luke and Acts cannot be given different treatment. "Even when the totally different problems which the divergent material of the two books present are taken into account—in spite of exceptions—the gospel and the Acts will in the future have to be increasingly viewed from one angle so that the 'historical part' will be integrated where appraising the whole." "Remarks on the Purpose of Luke's Historical Writing (Luke 1:1-14)" in *Sparsa Collecta* I (Leiden: E.J. Brill, 1973), pp. 7ff. To the same effect M. Hengel, "Both (Luke and Acts) must be read as a unity," p. 37.

19. Cf. the suggestive title of I. H. Marshall's book *Luke: Historian and Theology* (Exeter: Paternoster, 1970). Van Unnik stresses the uniqueness of Acts as a *religious* (as opposed to political) history: "Luke's Second Book and the Rules of

Hellenistic Historiography" in J. Kremer, ed., *Les Actes des Apotres, Traditions, redaction, theologie* (Bibliotheca Ephemeridum Theologicarum Lovaniesium XLVIII, Leuven, 1979), p. 38. M. Hengel writes, "The genre of the work is that of a very special kind of 'historical monograph,' a special history which describes the missionary development of a young religious movement," p. 36. Weiser concludes a consideration of the formal characteristics of Acts thus: "Die Summe der einzelnen Gestattungselemente lässt erkennen, das die Apostelgeschichte unter formaten Gesichtspunkt zur Litteraturgattung der biblisch-frühjüdischen, hellenistisch-römischen *Geschichtsschreibung* gehört . . . Bie der Zuordnung der Apostelgeschichte zur Litteraturgattung der antiken Historigoraphie müssen freilich die *Unterschiede* beachtet werden, die sich aus dem religiösen Inhalt und aus der theologischen Zielsetzung ergeben"; *Die Apostelgeschichte*, Kapitel 1-12, *Ökumenischer Taschenbuch-Kommentar zum Neuen Testament*, 5/1/ Würzburg, Echter Verlag, 1981, p. 31.

20. W. van Unnik, "The 'Book of Acts' the Confirmation of the Gospel" in *Sparsa Collecta I* (Leiden, 1973), pp. 340-73.

21. E. Haenchen, *The Acts of the Apostles: A Commentary* (Oxford: Blackwell, 1971, translated from the fourteenth German edition, 1965), p. 144.

22. H. J. Cadbury, *The Making of Luke-Acts* (London: Macmillan, 1927), esp. pp. 308-16.

23. C. H. Talbert, *Luke and the Gnostics* (Nashville: Abingdon, 1966), p. 15.

24. H. Conzelmann, *The Theology of St. Luke* (ET, London: Faber, 1960).

25. Robert J. Karris, "Poor and Rich: The Lukan Sitz im Leben" in Charles H. Talbert, ed., *Perspectives on Luke-Acts* (Danville: Va.: Association of Baptist Professors of Religion, 1978), pp. 112-25.

26. Gerhard Schneider, "Der Zweck des lukanischen Doppelwerks" in *Biblische Zeitschrift*, NF 21, 197, pp. 45-66.

27. For a critical analysis of the chief options see Schuyler Brown, "The Role of the Prologues in Determining the Purpose of Luke-Acts" in C. H. Talbert, ed., *Perspectives on Luke-Acts*, pp. 99-111.

28. W. van Unnik, "Remarks on the Purpose of Luke's Historical Writing (Luke i 1-4)," in *Sparsa Collecta I*, p. 13.
29. van Unnik, p. 8.
30. See Schuyler Brown, p. 108.
31. Robert Maddox, The Purpose of Luke-Acts (*Forschungen zur Religion und Literatur des Alten and Neuen Testaments*, Goettingen-Vandenhoeck amd Ruprecht, 1982), p. 10.
32. Cf. B. M. Metzger, "The range and age of the witnesses which read the singular number are superior to those that read the plural," *A Textual Commentary on the Greek New Testament* (New York: United Bible Societies, 1971), p. 367.
33. Haenchen, p. 93.
34. The German is: "Lukas entwickelt keine lehre von der Kirche," *Die Apostelgeschichte* (*Kritisch-exegetischer Kommentar uber das Neuen Testament*, Goettingen, 1968), p. 83.
35. R. P. C. Hanson, *The Acts* (*The New Clarendon Bible*, Oxford: The Clarendon Press, 1967), p. 46.
36. C. H. Turner, "Chronology of the New Testament" in James Hastings, ed., *A Dictionary of the Bible* (Edinburgh: T. and T. Clark, 1898), vol. 1, p. 421.
37. The sixth summary statement is at 28:30-31 and constitutes the conclusion of the book.
38. The ms. evidence for the reading "of God" is as weighty as that for "of the Lord," and not only is the latter very rare; it also obviates theological difficulties in the latter part of the verse if it is read, thereby providing strong motives for scribal alteration.
39. K. L. Schmidt: "*ekklesia*" in G. Kittel, ed., *Theological Dictionary of the New Testament* (ET, G. W. Bromiley, Grand Rapids: Eerdmans, 1963), vol. 1, p. 505.
40. The point under discussion is unaffected by the choice of textual-exegetical alternatives as to whether one prefers "his own blood" (favored by the ms. evidence) reading the antecedent as 'Lord'; or "the blood of His Own One" which is both grammatically possible and partially paralleled in the Pauline writings (Rom. 8:31; Col. 1:13).

41. C. K. Barrett has argued covincingly that a *theologia crucis* in the sense of a "continuous life of discipleship" is very much present in Acts. Though Luke's emphasis is pastoral and practical, it is not un-Pauline even in its language. "Luke, who is telling a story, is content to show the result, without either the presuppositions or the connecting working. This is the main (though not indeed the only) difference between Luke and Paul" ("Theologia Crucis—In Acts?" in C. Anderson and G. Klein, eds., *Theolgia Crucis—Signum Crucis*, Festschrift für Erich Dinkler [Tübingen: Mohr-Siebeck, 1979], pp. 73-84, esp. pp. 76, 77ff.).

42. F. J. Foakes Jackson and Kirsopp Lake, eds., *The Beginnings of Christianity*, Part I, *The Acts of the Apostles* (Grand Rapids: Baker, 1979 reprint), vol. 1, pp. 328ff. For the view that the Church was regarded by Luke as already existing during Jesus' ministry see K. N. Giles, "The Church in the Gospel of Luke," *Scottish Journal of Theology*, 34 (1981), pp. 121-46.

43. Jackson and Lake, pp. 324ff.

44. Francois Bovon, *Luc le Theologien*, Vingt-Cinq ans de Re cherches (1950-75) (Neuchatel-Paris: Delachaux et Niestlé, 1978), p. 342.

45. For an elaboration of this view see J. C. O'Neill, *The Theology of Acts in its Historical Setting* (London: SPCK, second revised edition, 1970).

46. J. Jervell, *Luke and the People of God* (Minneapolis: Augsburg, 1972), p. 15.

47. The statistics are from Strathmann, "*Laos* in the New Testament," in Kittel, *TDNT*, IV (Grand Rapids: Eerdmans, 1967), p. 50.

48. Strathmann, p. 51.

49. Strathmann, p. 52ff.

50. Strathmann, p. 54.

51. Stephen G. Wilson, *The Gentiles and the Gentile Mission in Luke-Acts* (Cambridge: University Press, 1973), p. 225.

52. See above.

53. K. L. Schmidt, "*ecclesia*" (TDNT), vol. 1, p. 505. Cf. L. Coenen, "In Acts, as in Paul, *ecclesia* denotes first Christians living and and meeting in a particular place. But ulti-

mately it is one. The particular places always imply the totality. The singular and plural are always qualitatively identical." "Church" in C. Brown, ed., *New International Dictionary of New Testament Theology* (Exeter: Paternoster,
1975), vol. 1, p. 303.

54. See above.
55. C. K. Barrett, *Luke the Historian in Recent Study* (London:
The Epworth Press, 1961), p. 71.
56. R. R. Williams, "Church History in Acts" in D. E.
Nineham, ed., *Historicity and Chronology in the New Testament* (London: SPCK, 1965), p. 145.
57. Ernst Käsemann, *New Testament Questions of Today*
Philadelphia: Fortress Press, 1969), p. 247.
58. Käsemann, p. 22.
59. See above.
60. R. Newton Flew, *Jesus and His Church* (London: The Epworth Press, 1938), p. 169.
61. Luke 22:19a. The point is unaffected by the textual problem.
See B. M. Metzger, *Textual Commentary*, pp. 173-77 for a
discussion of the textual options.
62. For a full treatment of the problem see I. H. Marshall, *Last
Supper and Lord's Supper* (London: Paternoster, 1980), pp.
123-33. A recent treatment that finds only fellowship meals
in Acts is Kevin Giles, "Is Luke an Exponent of 'Early
Protestantism'? Church Order in the Lucan Writings," Part
I, *Evangelical Quarterly*, LIV, 4 (1982), pp. 193-
205. He writes: "The gathering together of the disciples for
a common meal is nothing more than a fellowship meal in
which their oneness with each other and their ever-present
Lord is affirmed," p. 205.
63. C. K. Barrett, *Luke the Historian*, p. 75.
64. C. K. Barrett, *Luke the Historian*, p. 23.
65. So I. H. Marshall, *The Acts of the Apostles, Tyndale New
Testament Commentaries* (Grand Rapids: Eerdmans, 1980),
pp. 303-4.
66. S. New, "The Name, Baptism and the Laying on of Hands"
in Jackson and Lake, *The Beginnings of Christianity*, vol. 5,
p. 134.
67. See below.
68. Hermann W. Beyer, "*diakoneo*," *TDNT*, vol. 2, p. 84.

69. R. J. Karris, "Poor and Rich: the Lukan Sitz im Leben" in
    C. H. Talbert, ed., *Perspectives on Luke-Acts*, pp. 112-25.
70. W. Neil thinks it impossible that the Eleven could have been
    so obtuse as to entertain such a notion after the long period
    of instruction on the subject referred to in verse 3; and ac-
    cordingly he suggests that a wider audience is in mind (*Acts*,
    pp. 65ff). C. S. C. Williams however, sees here an illustra-
    tion of the hardness of the disciples' hearts, removed only
    by the outpouring of the Spirit, *The Acts of the Apostles,
    Black's New Testament Commentaries* (London: A. and C.
    Clark, second edition, 1964), pp. 55ff.
71. Neil, p. 79.
72. E.g. A. A. T. Ehrhardt, "The whole purpose of the Book of
    Acts . . . is no less than to be the Gospel of the Holy Spirit"
    (*The Framework of the New Testament Stories* [Manches-
    ter: University Press, 1968], p. 75).
73. I. H. Marshall, *The Acts of the Apostles* (1980), p. 214.
74. So I. Howard Marshall, *The Acts of the Apostles*, p. 216.
75. See S. S. Smalley, "Spirit, Kingdom and Prayer in Luke-
    Acts," *Novum Testamentum* 15, 1973, pp. 59-71. "In both
    Luke and Acts, *Spirit, kingdom* and *prayer* are all closely
    related at important moments in the progress of salvation
    history," p. 64. He cites Acts 1; 4:24-31; 8:4-25. "If it is true
    that the critical moments in the progress of the *Heilsges-
    chichte* are associated with petitionary prayer, as a response
    to the petition, it is also true that prayer is the means by
    which the dynamic power of the Spirit of God is realized and
    apprehended for purposes of salvation in history," p. 62.
    Not all of the examples he cites are equally convincing as
    turning-points in salvation history (e.g. 4:24-31); while his
    inference that the virtual disappearance of the triadic struc-
    ture after chapter 13 is explained by the fact that once Paul's
    mission to the Gentiles is under way the Kingdom can be
    seen to have arrived and therefore prayer for its coming is
    no longer needed overlooks the possibility that other
    salvation-historical turning-points are spoken of although
    not all elements of the triad are named (e.g. Acts 19:1-6).
    The deciding factor in determining a turning-point is not the
    presence of the triadic structure but the contribution of the

episode in question to the expansion of the gospel. If an event answers to this description, it constitutes such a point even if one of the triadic elements be lacking. The critical fact in all examples is the giving of the Spirit, and it appears that in most if not all of these this takes place in an unusual way.

76. J. D. G. Dunn, *Baptism in the Holy Spirit* (London: SCM Press, 1970), pp. 55-68.

77. C. K. Barrett, "Light on the Holy Spirit from Simon Magus (Acts 8,4-25)" in J. Kremer, ed., *Les Actes des Apotres* (1979), pp. 282-95.

78. For a contrary point of view which finds a variation in the significance of the laying on of hands in different contexts, see J. Coppens, "L'imposition des mains dans les Actes des Apotres" in Kremer, pp. 405-38.

79. See above.

80. *New Testament Questions of Today*, p. 247.

81. Cf. H. Conzelmann: "There is no trace in Luke of the idea which would form a necessary part of such a programme of reform, i.e. an assertion that the Church has declined from its original high ideal. Further, in his account of Paul's missionary activities he never sets up the primitive community as a model" (*The Theology of St. Luke* [ET London, 1969], p. 209. See also pp. 211ff). A similar perspective underlies E. Schweizer, *Church Order in the New Testament* (ET, London: SCM Press, 1961), pp. 63-76.

82. *Acts and the History of Earliest Christianity*, p. 122. For an earlier critique of early Catholicism see I. H. Marshall, "Early Catholicism in the New Testament" in R. N. Longenecker and M. C. Tenney, eds, *New Dimensions in New Testament Study* (Grand Rapids: Zondervan, 1974), pp. 217-31. He argues (among other things) that many of the features placed under the umbrella of early Catholicism were in fact there all the time and are better labeled "Early Protestantism" (p. 229).

83. J. Dupont, *Etudes sur les Actes des Apotres* (Paris, 1967), pp. 103-5.

84. Schweizer, pp. 72-75.

85. The quotation of Joel 2:28 (LXX) at Acts 2:17 where

"elder" (*presbyteros*) is contrasted with "young man" (*neaniskos*) reflects the mentality that was to prevail in Judaism, viz. that "older" means "wiser."

86. For a discussion see E. E. Ellis, "The Role of the Christian Prophet in Acts," in W. Ward Gasque and Ralph P. Martin, *Apostolic History and the Gospel* (Exeter: Paternoster, 1970), pp. 55-67.
87. See Ellis, pp. 62ff., for references.
88. Ellis, pp. 62ff.
89. *Jesus and His Church*, p. 203.
90. *The Acts of the Apostles*, p. 52.
91. See A. J. M. Wedderburn, "A New Testament Church To-day?" in *Scottish Journal of Theology* 31, 6 (1978), 517-32.

M. Robert Mulholland, Jr. (Th.D., Harvard Divinity School), associate professor of New Testament interpretation, Asbury Theological Seminary

The Church in the Epistles

METHODOLOGICAL CONSIDERATIONS

A SUPERFICIAL STUDY of the terms for the Church in the Epistles forces us to realize that we are up against a phenomena that eludes all attempts at rational, logical, cognitive organization into clear, concise categories. Simply to list the various terms utilized for the Church is mind-boggling: city, body, bride, temple, stones, building, house, vineyard, kingdom, nation, family, flock, God's people, army, sons of light, salt, leaven, firstborn, priests, servants, and many others. Minear is absolutely correct when he asserts:

> No list can exhaust the vivid imaginative power of the NT writers or do justice to the fluidity, vitality, and subtlety of their conceptions.

> None of the separate titles or pictures can be taken as comprehending the total range of thought. None of them can be

reduced to objective, qualifying definitions. These words and pictures are channels of thought rather than receptacles of ideas with fixed meanings. This is due, not alone to the character of the thinking, but also to the qualitative, relational character of the reality being described.[1]

This situation suggests that before we can understand the Church in the Epistles, we need a breakthrough in our perception of the term *church*. Through almost two thousand years the various terms for *church* have been invested with a diversity of limited, parochial, "this-worldly" perspectives. We are the recipients and the promulgators of an ingrained, cultural/religious perspective of *church* that has been highly influenced by the sociological, psychological, political and economic dynamics of human existence.

Along with this more or less unconscious and ingrained perspective that attaches to the term *church*, we also convey by the term the individual dimensions that emerge from our own unique Christian experience. We have a strong tendency to perceive the Church in our own image, to define it in terms of our own Christian experience. Then, having defined the Church in our own image we impose it upon others: either defining the Church narrowly as the community of those whose Christian experience is identical to ours, or defining it pluralistically as the community of those who have had any kind of experience that they themselves identify as "Christian." At either extreme, *church* is heavily overlaid with very subjective and individualized perspectives.

Whenever we encounter the term *church*, it immediately triggers a response from within a complex perceptual horizon. This perceptual horizon is formed by the ingrained dynamics of perspective passed on to us by our culture and by the individual dimensions of perspective arising out of our own Christian experience. This perceptual horizon is the context within which our understanding of *church* takes place.

The same reality of perceptual horizon existed for the writers of the New Testament. The terms and images that they selected to convey meaning to their readers operated within a particular perceptual horizon. This horizon was shaped by the perspectives received by the first-century world from the past coupled with the individual perspectives arising out of their Christian experience.

These two horizons give rise to what modern scholars call the hermeneutical problem: How is meaning transferred from one horizon of perception into another? The solution in modern biblical scholarship is labeled *Horizontverschmelzung*—a "merging of horizons."[2] Through detailed critical study of the New Testament world we can overcome the gap of perceptual understanding between the two horizons. Through analogical study of human existence we can discover those points of commonality (*Einverständnis*—"unity of comprehension")[3] that become the foundations within each perceptual horizon for building the bridges across which meaning can be transferred.

While this process has certain value in the enhancement of our understanding of the New Testament, it fails to break the hermeneutical circle. The hermeneutical circle results from the fact that when modern interpreters look for points of commonality with the New Testament world they make their observations through the prism of their own horizon and tend to read themselves into the text. But a questionable presumption lies behind the whole hermeneutical endeavor: the presumption that understanding is communicated primarily, if not wholly, at the cognitive level of human existence; if only we could merge the cognitive horizons of the New Testament writers and the modern interpreter, then meaning could be communicated. This presumption has so prevailed in critical biblical scholarship that the various philosophical epistemologies of modern naturalistic humanism have become the norms of biblical interpretation.[4] In reaction to this trend, conservative scholars have tended to stress the affective level of human existence. If only we have what we think is the same experience the New Testament writers had, then we can automatically understand what they are communicating. Wesleyan scholarship has in its tradition a dynamic that can bridge the gap between the cognitive and affective polarities just sketched. This is found in Wesley's life-long purpose to "conjoin the two so long disjoined, knowledge and vital piety."[5] Wesley clearly saw that the cognitive and affective dimensions of human existence must be conjoined in mutual interdependence if Christians were not going to fall into the extremes of sterile intellectualism on the one hand or mindless enthusiasm on the other.

How does this relate to biblical studies? The biblical writers utilized verbal images from within their perceptual horizon to express the reality of their experience with God. Their images are cognitive portraits of an affective involvement with the living God, the "knowledge" of a "vital piety." Their images necessarily contain the conditioning of their perceptual horizon, but there is a new and radically different level of communication to their readers who have also entered into this experience with God. Aelred Squire succinctly describes this aspect of the communication of meaning:

> It is the man who lives a certain kind of life who is in a position to understand the doctrine. There are some kinds of knowledge to which experience is the only key.[6]

Paul seems to express the same realization when he concludes an extended discussion on the contrast between the communication of the gospel and philosophical knowledge (1 Cor. 1:18-2:16) with the statement:

> That which we communicate [we communicate] not in taught words of human wisdom but in taught spiritualities of the Spirit, expounding spiritual things (1 Cor. 2:13).[7]

Then he further elaborates:

> The unspiritual person does not receive the things of the Spirit of God for they are foolishness to such a one who is not able to understand because such things are spiritually discerned. But the spiritual person discerns all things (1 Cor. 2:14-15).

What is suggested by this is that although the verbal images of the New Testament are necessarily conditioned by the perceptual horizons of the first-century world (requiring our diligent study of that world to recapture, as much as possible, the inner dimensions of their horizon), the New Testament writers employ them as the only linguistic means available to communicate to their Christian audience the deeper dynamics of their common experience of life in a new order of being in Christ. In brief, what we have in the New Testament is literary inconography—word pictures that serve as windows into a reality that is radically different from the world view in which the words usually functioned.

Alan Jones writes, "The journey (inward to God) involves the exploration of images, mythologies, ideas, pictures in the hope that one or two may become an icon, a window into reality."[8] This could be expressed another way: What are icons for those whose lives are intimately involved in that reality are but images, myths, ideas, pictures for those who stand outside that reality. Here lies the conundrum of biblical studies. No matter how perfectly biblical scholars reproduce the perceptual horizon of the New Testament world as the context for understanding the terms and images utilized by the New Testament writers, no matter how objectively and accurately they reproduce the dynamics of human existence in that era, or how adequate their cognitive grasp of the life and experience of the Christian community—unless they also participate in the experiential reality of life in the new order of being in Christ, their ultimate understanding of the New Testament writings will be one of seeing images, myths, ideas, and pictures that they will then analyze or demythologize in the light of their own experience of human existence.

The idea of iconography, while alien to Western perception and comprehension, is an essential one for our deepest understanding of the Church in the Epistles. The Epistle writers were participants in a radically new order of being in Jesus Christ. Of necessity they were constrained to utilize the language of the old order of being, the language of the first-century world, to convey the breadth and length and height and depth of their experience to one another. But in so doing language became iconographic, verbal windows into reality. This idea is not so far fetched when we consider the iconographic nature of the Roman-Hellenistic world of New Testament times.[9] The art, architecture, coinage, and sculpture of the Roman-Hellenistic world served to portray the ''spiritual realms'' that were thought to form the context for human existence and society. Literature was simply the written expression of the perceptual framework in which visual iconography played such an important part. For instance, the literary device of personification was one means utilized to bring the dynamics of an iconographic culture into literary expression. This practice is seen in Paul's personification of sin (Rom. 6:16), death (1 Cor. 15:55), and Law (Gal. 3:24). Literary iconography is seen even more clearly and vividly in the pictoral imagery of Revelation. It is within this broad perceptual framework that the Church in the Epistles must be viewed.

The focus, then, is precisely upon the truly iconographic nature of the images of the Church in the Epistles: ''Participation in the life of the church was considered necessary for comprehending the implications of the pictures.''[10] In other words, for those who lived within the reality of the new order of being established by God through Jesus and actualized by the presence and work of the Holy Spirit, the multiple and diverse images of the Church became icons through which they perceived and experienced ever new and deeper dimensions of the infinite reality of life as God's covenant people.

For our purposes in this chapter, we will examine three of the most focal icons of the Church in the Epistles: Temple, City and Body.[11] First, however, we must examine the central and essential dynamic that energizes all the icons of the Church: the focal reality of Christian existence that is "incarnated" in each image of the people of God—the Love Command.

THE DYNAMIC OF LOVE

While it doesn't always stand out sharply, the Great Commandment of Jesus to love God, self, and neighbor (Mark 12:28-34) pervades the Epistles. It expresses the essential dynamic of a radical new order of being that shapes Christian life in the midst of the old order of being. Eric Osborn has stated it well:

> The love command has an eschatological rather than a humanitarian basis. The kingdom of God, by its presence, implies the royal command of love and forgiveness. Love indeed is the new age itself, powerfully present and creative in history.[12]

The primary reason why the new age, the kingdom of God, the inbreaking eschatological new order is characterized by love is because its inception is an act of God's love. Repeatedly[13] the writers of the Epistles bear witness to the fact that God's sacrificial, redeeming love in the cross of Jesus opens for alienated humanity the way of return to God; it is the restoration of a relationship wherein we can love God with all our heart, soul, mind, and strength, the establishing of a community wherein this love for God results in transformed human relationships of loving neighbors as self.

The presumption of the first part of the command, to love God, surfaces in a variety of ways in the Epistles. The Christian community is identified as "those who love God" (Rom. 8:28; 1 Cor. 2:9; Eph. 6:24; 1 Pet. 1:8). This is more than simply a theological affirmation or creedal statement. Paul affirms that this love for God actually controls the living of Christians so that they live no longer for themselves but for the one, who, for their sakes, died and rose again (2 Cor. 5:14). Love of God is the central reality of Christian experience. This is why Paul prays for the Thessalonians, "May the Lord direct your hearts to the love of God" (2 Thess. 3:5), and why his great prayer for the Ephesians to be filled with all the fullness of God is based upon their being rooted and grounded in love (Eph. 3:14-19). This is why Jude exhorts his readers to keep themselves in the love of God (Jude 21). The love of God is that primary reorientation of life at its center that actualizes that life in the new order of being in Christ. John stated this reality succinctly: "If anyone loves the world, love for the Father is not in him" (1 John 2:15), clearly indicating that love is the primary dynamic of all human existence and that the context of that existence is determined by the object of its love. From this brief survey it can be seen that although the first part of the Love Command does not manifest itself blatantly in the Epistles, it is the presumed foundation of Christian experience. It is the deep, central and continuous reorientation of being toward God that results in the transfer of life from a context of existence wherein God is not loved to a context of existence wherein love for God is the ruling principle of all being and doing.

While the first part of the Love Command is more presumed and understated in the Epistles, the last part is strongly and repeatedly affirmed. Love for God is manifested in loving actions and relationships in the world:

This is the love of God, that we keep his commandments (1

John 5:2-3). And this is his commandment, that we should
believe in the name of his Son Jesus Christ and love one another, just as he has commanded us (1 John 3:23). Whoever
keeps his word, in him truly love for God is perfected (1 John
2:5). If anyone says, "I love God," and hates his brother, he
is a liar; for he who does not love his brother whom he has
seen, cannot love God whom he has not seen. And this command we have from him, that he who loves God should love
his brother also (1 John 4:20-21).

Life in the new age that God has inaugurated through
Jesus is not only loving God as noted in the first part of the
Love Command; it is also the manifestation of that love in
loving obedience to God in the affairs and relationships of
daily life.

This dimension of the new age pervades the writings of
Paul. He exhorts the Romans, "Let love be genuine . . .
love one another with brotherly affection" (Rom. 12:9-10),
and then reminds them, "He who loves his neighbor has
fulfilled the law," since all the commandments "are
summed up in this sentence, 'You shall love your neighbor
as yourself'" (Rom. 13:8-9). He urges the Corinthians to
make love their aim (1 Cor. 14:1, as conclusion to chapter
13), and to let all they do be done in love (1 Cor. 16:14).
He tells the Galatians that "neither circumcision nor un-
circumcision is of any avail, but faith working through
love" (Gal. 5:6), which, in an exact parallel in 6:15, is described as a "new creation." Therefore they are exhorted
"through love be servants of one another. For the whole
Law is fulfilled in one word, 'You shall love your neighbor
as yourself'" (Gal. 5:13-14). After praying that the Ephesians, "being rooted and grounded in love . . . [may] know
the love of Christ" (3:17, 19), Paul calls them to "walk in
love, as Christ loved us" (5:2). Paul strives for the Colossians "that their hearts may be encouraged as they are knit
together in love" (2:2), and then exhorts them, above all
the other qualities of Christian character, to "put on love,

which binds everything together in perfect harmony"
(3:12-14). He prays that the Lord may make the Thessalonians "increase and abound in love to one another and to
all . . . so that he may establish [their] hearts unblamable
in holiness" (1 Thess. 3:12-13). Even though God has
taught them to love one another, and they are doing it,
Paul exhorts them to "do so more and more" (4:9-10). In
his instructions Paul reminds Timothy that the goal of their
exhortations is love issuing from pure hearts (1 Tim. 1:5).

This emphasis continues in the other Epistles. The
writer of Hebrews urges his readers to "consider how to
stir up one another to love and good works" (10:24).
James points to the "Royal Law . . . 'You shall love your
neighbor as yourself,'" as the ruling principle of the
Christian community in dealing with partiality and meeting
the needs of others (chap. 2). Peter urges his readers that,
"having purified [their] souls by . . . obedience to the truth
for a sincere love of the brethren," they are to love one
another earnestly from the heart since they have been born
anew (1 Pet. 1:22-23). As partakers of God's new order of
being, Peter twice more urges them to love the brethren
(2:17, 3:8), and finally exhorts them "above all hold unfail-
ing your love for one another" (4:8).

Another dimension of the command to love others
emerges from John's report:

A new command I give you, that you love one another; even
as I have loved you, that you also love one another. *By this
all will know that you are my disciples*, if you have love for
one another (John 13:34-35, emphasis added).

Love is the hallmark of the Christian's life in the new
order of being. Paul frequently employs the witness of love
as evidence of the reality of the Christian experience of
those to whom he is writing: "I have heard of . . . your
love toward all the saints" (Eph. 1:15); "We have heard of

. . . the love which you have for all the saints" (Col. 1:4); "Timothy has . . . brought us the good news of your faith and love" (1 Thess. 3:6); "I hear of your love" (Philem. 5). Love expressed in action continued through the second century as the central characteristic of Christian life.[14] Even into the third century Tertullian coined the famous remark, "See how these Christians love one another!" (*Apol*, 39).

Perhaps the most profound aspect of the Love Command is the injunction to love even enemies. Paul urges the Romans to "bless those who persecute you" (Rom. 12:14), and "if your enemy is hungry, feed him; if he is thirsty, give him drink" (12:20). He sets an example before the Corinthians, "When reviled, we bless; . . . when slandered, we try to conciliate" (1 Cor. 4:12-13). Peter urges his readers, "Do not return evil for evil or reviling for reviling; but on the contrary, bless" (1 Pet. 3:9). In the second century, Justin Martyr viewed this love of enemies as an eschatological miracle (*Dial*. 85:7). It is the most complete evidence of the inbreaking of the new age of God into the midst of fallen human history. It most fully reveals human life lived with a radically different dynamic of being and doing. If *enemy* is defined as anyone who, in their relationship with you, is not what God would have them be, then love of enemy is the call to be with them, *in that relationship*, all that God would have you be. Such response requires a fullness of love for God wherein we totally consecrate ourselves to be God's servants in the lives of others, no matter what the nature of their relationship with us might be. Such response calls for a life lived in a new order of being wherein the love of God is poured into our hearts through the Holy Spirit (Rom. 5:5).

This brings us to the "hidden" aspect of the Love Command: love for self. Jesus said, "You shall love your neighbor *as yourself*" (Mark 12:31, emphasis added). At first glance, the Epistles seem to say nothing on this di-

mension of the Love Command. This apparent silence becomes a loud affirmation, however, once we ask what
"self" we are to love. Obviously it is not the old self, "the
old man with his deeds" (Col. 3:9). We are enjoined to
"put off" this old self (Eph. 4:22), to "put to death" its
principles (Col. 3:5ff.), for "our old self was crucified with
him" (Rom. 6:6). In its place there is a new being, a new
person, a new creation that is being made in the image and
likeness of God (Col. 3:10).[15] It seems reasonable, therefore, to presume that it is this new self of God's making
that we are called to love. Thus, an integral part of loving
God is loving what he is doing in our lives. When this reality becomes operative, then our relationships with others
take on two new dimensions. First, others become agents
through whom God can and does do his work of recreating
us in his own image, *even the enemies*![16] Second, our relationships with others become the arena in which we live
out the new being that God is creating in us, a being whose
essential dynamic is love as is its creator's. This radical
transformation of human existence must not be viewed as
simply some sort of "individual" salvation. The individual
aspects of this radical new being are the particularized
form of a whole new order of being which has broken into
human history in Jesus Christ.

In the Epistles, the Church is the community of this new
order of being. It is the community whose essential
dynamic is love: *love for God* in an inner posture of consecrated response of the whole being to God; *love for self*
in an inner posture of willing receptivity to God's shaping
of a new being created in his own image; *love for others* in
an inner posture of relationship wherein both love for God
and love for self are actualized in the daily experience of
being available to God for others and available to others
for God.

This community whose essential principle is love is also
a community whose essential characteristic is holiness.

Several hints of this appear in the passages we have noted,[17] and others could be added: "He chose us in [Christ] before the foundation of the world, that we should be *holy* and blameless before him in *love*" (Eph. 1:4); or the setting of 1 Thessalonians 4:1-8:

3:12-13: "May the Lord make you increase and abound in love to one another and to all men . . . so that he may establish your hearts unblamable in holiness.

4:1-8: "For this is the will of God, your sanctification (v. 3). "For God has not called us for uncleanness, but in holiness" (v. 7).

4:9-10: "Concerning love of the brethren . . . you yourselves have been taught by God to love one another and indeed you do love all the brethren."

Perhaps the most focal statement regarding the holiness of this community of the new order of being is in 1 John, that one Epistle that most clearly and strongly sets forth love for God and others as the essential reality of Christian experience. In 1 John 3:1-3, John draws love into the character of holiness: God's love in the cross (1 John 4:10) has made us his children (characterized as those who love God and obey him by keeping his commandment to love others), and will make us like himself ("we shall be like him," v. 2). On the basis of this reality, John states, "Everyone who thus hopes in him [hope acted out in love for God and others as well as hope awaiting God's acting out of his re-creation of us in his likeness], sanctifies himself as he is sanctified."

Since holiness is also wholeness, the joining of humanity's being to the image of God in love, the Church is also a community whose essential quality is wholeness. Kenneth Leech equates this with the "catholicity" of the Church, noting that *catholic* "comes from the Greek *kath'holou* which denotes inner wholeness and fullness. The church is a symbol of the recreated world."[18]

Thus, if "love indeed is the new age itself," as Osborn suggested at the beginning of this section, then the Church in the Epistles is the community of that new age, the society of God's new order of being, or, to use Leech's phrase, the "symbol of the recreated world." This recreated world, of which the Church is the manifestation in the fallen world, has love as its essential dynamic, holiness as its essential characteristic, and wholeness as its essential quality.[19]

We now turn to three of the focal icons of the Church in the Epistles, three windows into the reality of God's new order of being that provide more detailed and specific parameters of how this community of love, holiness, and wholeness can be understood and experienced.

THE TEMPLE

The experiential reality of Christian life is multi-dimesional, poly-dynamic, and many faceted. The Epistles employ a wide diversity of icons to express the fullness of this reality. This is best seen in the amazing fluidity of the icons through which the various dimensions of the new order of being in Christ are portrayed. For instance, in Revelation 21-22, the Christian community is first the Bride of the Lamb, then becomes the New Jerusalem which, in turn, is also the Temple with God and the Lamb in the midst. Or consider Ephesians 2:19-22, where the Christian community is first citizens, then members of a household, then a building, then a holy temple—a dwelling place of God. Or, finally, consider the icons of Jesus himself who, on the one hand is a Temple (Rev. 21:22), but also High Priest (Heb. 3:1 *passim*), altar (Heb. 13:10), and sacrifice (many places[20]). While the examination of each icon is valuable, we must realize that no single icon provides the whole picture of the reality of the new order of being in Christ, for the whole is a living reality that is greater than all its icons. The icons are simply the cognitive lenses of human experience through which we see darkly the profound reality of that new order of being that continually intrudes into history as the Church.

The icon of the Church as Temple is directly related to the first part of the Love Command: love for God. An alternate biblical expression for love of God is *worship*. Just as we have seen that all human existence is determined by the object of its love,[21] it can also be said that all human existence is determined by the object of its worship. This is most clearly portrayed in Revelation, in which every living being worships: those of the heavenly host and the followers of the Lamb worship him who sits upon the throne and the Lamb; the rest worship the Beast in his varied manifestations.[22] Even the great call to repentance in Revelation 14:6-7,[23] is a call to "worship him who made heaven and earth." This is coupled with the warning of judgment upon those who "worship the beast and its image" (14:9). The profound dimensions of the nature of worship are seen in the mark of the Beast and the seal of God.[24] The mark of the Beast is upon the forehead, the seat of perception, and upon the right hand, the symbol of action or life-style.[25] Thus the worship of the Beast denotes life lived within a particular order of being which conditions both perception and action. The same is true of those who worship God. The seal of God is upon their forehead and, although the right hand is not noted in this case, action or life-style is clearly indicated in the repeated description of Christians as those "who keep the commandments of God and bear testimony to Jesus."[26] It is seen, therefore, that the two alternate orders of being for human existence are characterized by worship, and that the nature of human worship manifests itself in the quality of human existence. The church is the community of that order of being whose worship is true.

The identification of the worshiping Christian community as a Temple has many facets. In Revelation 11:1-2,
the Christian community is portrayed as worshiping in the
Temple of God, which is surrounded by and whose courts
are trampled by "the nations," one of the terms for those
who worship the Beast.[27] Interestingly, the command to
measure this Temple in 11:1 is unfulfilled until 21:15ff.,
when the New Jerusalem (which is also a Temple since
God and the Lamb fill it and they are its Temple [21:11,
23—*glory* is the very essence of God himself, 21:22—
Temple]) is measured. It is found to be a thirteen-
hundred-mile cube (21:16). In biblical imagery, the only cube
in which God dwells is the Holy of Holies in the Temple.[28]
Intriguingly, if a thirteen-hundred-mile overlay is placed
upon a map of the Roman Empire with its center at
Patmos (the place of John's vision, 1:9), the resulting
square encompasses Rome on the west, Jerusalem on the
east, and the northern and southern boundaries of Roman
domination. John seems to envision the community of
those who worship God as a "Holy of Holies" set down in
the midst of the community of those who worship the
Beast. Or, in other words, the Church is the dwelling place
of God in the midst of the world.

The icon of the Church as Temple being the dwelling
place of God in the midst of the old order of being is also
found outside of Revelation. We previously noted the
merging of icons in Ephesians 2:19-22,[29] in which the final
picture is the Church as a "holy temple in the Lord" into
which the Ephesian Christians have been incorporated
"for a dwelling place of God in the Spirit." In the light of
this icon, Paul subsequently prays for them that they
"may be filled with all the fullness of God" (3:19). In the
same vein Paul also reminds the Corinthians, in the midst
of the factionalism that threatens their existence as a
Christian community (1 Cor. 1:10—4:21), "Do you not
know that you are God's temple and that God's Spirit

dwells in you? If anyone destroys God's temple, God will destroy him. For God's temple is holy, and that temple you are" (1 Cor. 3:16-17). The intrusion of aspects of the old order of being that threaten the Corinthians causes Paul to remind them of what they are in Christ: God's holy temple in which his Spirit dwells! Paul had previously[30] reminded them of this reality by emphasizing that the new order of being in Christ cannot continue to operate under the principles of the old order, and then affirmed,

> For we are the temple of the living God; as God said, "I will live in them and move among them, and I will be their God, and they shall be my people. Therefore come out from them, and be separate from them," says the Lord, "and touch nothing unclean; then I will welcome you . . . and you shall be my sons and daughters," says the Lord Almighty (2 Cor. 6:16-18).

As the Temple of God, Paul then exhorts them, "Let us cleanse ourselves from every defilement of body and spirit, and make holiness perfect in the fear of God" (7:1). For Paul, therefore, the Church as Temple is a community of the new order of being in whose midst God himself dwells through the Holy Spirit. When members of the old order of being respond to God's love and grace in Christ, they are incorporated into this profound reality (Eph. 2:19-22) and must undertake the disciplines of love/ worship that will enable God to truly dwell in their midst (2 Cor. 6:16—7:1).

Another dimension of the Church as Temple is found in Hebrews. Here the Christian community is seen as participating in the heavenly Temple (8:1-7) of which the earthly temple in Jerusalem was but a shadow. The old covenant with its cultus of sacrifice was incapable of cleansing the "conscience" of the participants (9:9), thus requiring constant repetition of the cultic sacrifices for the guilt of transgression (10:1-4). The old cultus could deal with the consequences of the sin nature in human exist-

ence (9:13; 10:11) but it could not deal with the sin nature
itself (what Hebrews calls *conscience*[31]), thus never enabling persons to come into the presence of God (9:7-8).
But now, in Christ, a sacrifice has been made that cleanses
the sin nature (9:14, 26) and sanctifies (10:10, 14) so that
the believer can draw near to God (7:19), even enter into
the Holy of Holies (10:19ff.; 6:19) and approach with bold-
ness the throne of grace (4:16).[32] This is Hebrews' rather
detailed cultic iconography for viewing the Christian
community as those who have been sanctified, who have
entered into the Holy of Holies, and who live in the very
presence of God. This is a variant of what we have already
seen in Revelation and Paul. But there is another facet of
Hebrews's icon of the Church as Temple: the Church as
the "firstborn" (12:23). This puzzling use of *firstborn* may
be a continuation of the whole Temple imagery of Hebrews. In the old covenant, the Levites became the sanctified ministers of the Aaronic priest in place of the
firstborn males of Israel (Num. 3:6-9, 8:14-19). Now
Christians become the sanctified (10:10) servants of Jesus,
the great High Priest (4:14) who has replaced the Aaronic
priesthood (7:11). Just as the Levites were sprinkled and
washed, had atonement made for them by Aaron, and
entered into the tent of meeting (Num. 8:7, 21-22), so
Christians are sprinkled and washed, have been atoned for
by Jesus, and enter the sanctuary (Heb. 10:19-22).[33] Thus,
under the new High Priest, Jesus, the Christian community
exists to live and serve him in the Temple of God. For the
writer of Hebrews, the outcome of the Temple icon is the
exhortation to "offer to God acceptable worship, with
reverence and awe" (12:28).

The inner reality of the Temple icon is worship in the
very presence of God. It is life lived out of a deep inner
dynamic of loving adoration and submission to the presence and purpose of God at the center of our beings. This

is not so much "Christ in us" (where it is so easy to find ourselves subtly controlling the relationship) as "us in Christ" (where he is truly in control and everything is given over to his sanctifying power and purpose).

As we begin to grasp, even superficially, some of the deep dimensions of the icon of the Church as Temple, we can begin to comprehend more adequately why the early Christian community was such a disruptive influence in the fabric of the society in which it lived. The inner orientation of its being in worship/love of God and its experience of the living presence of God in its midst empowered it to live in the world a life whose radiance and power set at nought the imprisoning dynamics of the surrounding culture and the dehumanizing consequences of its false worship. The Church as Temple is the inbreaking into history of an order of being whose worship is true and whose community of love provides a matrix of nurture for wholeness that militates against the fragmenting brokenness and bondage of the world order of being's false worship. As a community of nurture for wholeness, the Church as Temple becomes the Church as City.

THE CITY

The icon of the Church as City is directly related to the more hidden dimension of the Love Command: Love for self, where, as noted previously,[34] this is a loving yieldness and response to the wholeness of being that God purposes for us in his own image. In the New Testament world, *city* represented the total complex of human existence. It was the entire matrix of political, economic, educational, social, cultural, and religious dynamics that served as the context of meaningful human life. It was a "free subjection of the citizens to the laws which protect the common welfare . . . each . . . furthering the whole to the best of [their] ability. . . . In this common life [human existence] genuinely comes to [it]self, to the unfolding of [its] nature."[35] In brief, *city* was the order of being that gave life meaning, purpose, and value. So strong was the role of *city* in giving meaning, purpose, and value to human existence that Socrates chose death as a citizen of Athens as preferable to life banished from the nurture of its citizenship.[36] This model of *city* as the matrix for the conduct of life is seen biblically in Hebrews 11, which states that the great examples of faith lived their lives "looking forward to the City which has foundations, whose builder and maker is God" (11:10). Although they did not receive it, "they saw it and greeted it from afar" (11:13), living their lives as "strangers and exiles"[37] in the midst of the world *city* because "they desired a better country" (11:13, 16). For these, God "has prepared for them a City" (11:16).

The biblical image of *city* as the order that gives meaning, purpose, and value to human life is much more pervasive than just Hebrews. It stretches from the beginning to the end of the scriptural revelation. In Genesis 4:16-17, Cain "went away from the presence of the Lord . . . and he built a city." Having left the intended context of human existence, life in relationship with God, Cain sought to create an alternative context for his existence. The deeper dimensions of this situation are more fully portrayed in Genesis 11:4:

a. "Let *us* build a city for *ourselves*." Here a human-centered, human-created structure and context for life is portrayed.

b. "And a tower with its top in the heavens. . . ." This human-generated order of being even attempts to exercise its rule over and to supplant the true realm of human existence.

c. "And let *us* make a name for *ourselves*. Since *name* has to do with the very nature of what is named,[38] we see here the human-centered effort to determine the nature of its own being.

d. "Lest we be scattered." Inherent in this concern is the awareness of the fragmentation of human existence when separated from a realm of being that gives it meaning, value, and purpose. Cain and Babel represent a deep, central posture of human autonomy that seeks to develop and maintain its own order of being, its own context of existence. This lies close to the heart of what Paul describes as the "flesh" life (Rom. 8:5, 7-8), and what John speaks of as the "world" (1 John 2:15-16).

This City of rebellion makes its final biblical appearance as Fallen Babylon in Revelation (14:8, 16:19, 17:1—19:10). In Fallen Babylon we see the epitome of the rebellious order of being and how it rests upon the foundation of the Beast (17:3), who is the agent of the Dragon (12:3, 13:1-2), who can be seen as the ruler of the realm of Death and Hades. But at the very beginning of Revelation, Jesus' initial self-description is as the one who has the keys of Death and Hades (1:18)! The judgment of God in the death of Jesus has undone the very foundation of Fallen Babylon, the rebellious order of being that fragments and destroys human existence.

At the same time, the keys that Jesus possesses also open the door into the heavenly City, New Jerusalem. This is the new order of being in which human existence finds wholeness, true meaning, purpose, and value.[39] This true order of human existence as *City* is most fully portrayed in Revelation 21-22, with remarkable correlations to the rebellious city of Genesis 11:

a. "He showed me the Holy City Jerusalem coming down out of heaven from God" (21:10). Here we see that the true context of human meaning, purpose, and value is given by God who provides the structure and dynamics for fulfilled human life.

b. "Down out of heaven. . . ." Instead of humanity attempting to lift itself to heaven as in Genesis, God comes to provide for humanity his new order of being.

c. "His name shall be on their foreheads" (22:4). The very nature of God himself shall be the nature of those who inhabit New Jerusalem. They shall be in his image; the nature of God is what determines the nature of their being.

d. Instead of scattering, the flow is *into* this City (21:24, 26, 27). Here is the antithesis of that order of being that fragments and scatters and destroys human existence. Here is that true order of being that heals (cf. 22:2b) and nurtures (cf. 22:2a) the integrity of human existence in the image of God.

John's vision further implies that this City is the present context of the Christian community in the world. As we have seen,[40] the City is envisioned as a thirteen-hundred-mile cube (21:16). If the cube is laid over a map of the eastern Mediterranean with its center on Patmos, that area would encompass the entire Christian community in the world at the time of John's writing.[41] John seems to be saying that the New Jerusalem interpenetrates the historical realm in which Fallen Babylon seems to rule.[42] This cubic city is the dwelling place of God (21:3, 11, 22; 22:3).[43] Here we see a merging of the Temple and City icons, clearly delineated in Revelation 3:12, where victorious Christians become pillars *in the temple of God* and receive the name of *New Jerusalem* (which is also the name of God and the Lamb!), which is coming down[44] out of heaven. Thus John indicates that the Christian community in history is the earthly portion of the population of the City of God; they are the City in which the wholeness of human existence in the image of God is to be fulfilled.

If anyone questions the validity of this aspect of John's magnificent iconographic tapestry, confirmation of the icon of Church as City is found in the rest of the Epistles. Hebrews, as Revelation, merges its strong Temple iconography with the icon of the City, especially the City as the present context of the Christian community. As we have already noted in the introduction of this section, the great examples of faith in Hebrews 11 lived their earthly lives "in the shadow" of the City whose builder and maker is God (11:10). But they did not, in this life, participate in that City (11:13, 39) because only in the time of the writer of Hebrews has the actuality of participating in it become possible (11:40). Now the Christian community has come to "the City of the living God, the Heavenly Jerusalem" (12:23). Paul also affirms the icon of Church as City when he reminds the Galatians that the "Jerusalem above is free, and she is our mother" (4:26). Another Pauline reminder in more technical *city* terminology is found in Philippians, a letter to a church whose earthly context of existence was a Roman colony with all its deep sensitivity to the privileges of Roman citizenship. Paul reminds the Philippians that their "citizenship is in heaven" (3:20), and earlier in the letter exhorts them to "live as worthy citizens of the gospel of Christ (1:27).[45] Thus, in a powerful city context, Paul reminds the Philippians that they constitute another City and that City is the context of their living. He also reminds the Ephesians that whereas they were once alienated from the *citizenship* of Israel (2:12), they are now fellow *citizens* with the saints (2:19).[46] Just as Paul's central injunction to the Ephesians is that they might be increasingly conformed to the image of Christ (4:13, 15, 24), so his exhortation to the Philippians to live as worthy citizens of the gospel is immediately followed by the profound appeal that their lives be formed by the dynamics of Jesus' life (2:1-11); that as citizens of the gospel their beings be conformed to the image of Christ.

The Church as City, therefore, is an icon that portrays the Christian community as a new order of being in Christ, provided by the grace of God, in which God's purposes for the transformation of human existence into his own image are fulfilled. As such, the Church is a radical alternative to the world's structure of existence. In the midst of an order of being that imprisons, fragments, scatters, and destroys the intended wholeness and integrity of human life through its false meanings, purposes, and values, the Church manifests an order of being that frees, integrates, unifies, and reshapes human life in the wholeness of the image of God. But this life of increasing integration and wholeness in God's new order of being is not simply the Church's special "possession." It is also the Church's responsibility to bring this realm of wholeness to the brokenness of the world. This is seen in the icon of the Church as Body.

THE BODY

The icon of the Church as Body is directly related to the final injunction of the Love Command: Love others. Human existence is lived out in relationships. We may have true worship of God as the center of our lives; we may have God's new order of being as the context of our living; but our lives take place in the physical, creaturely, historical daily flow of the fallen created order. Our lives are lived out within the same complex of relationships in which God incarnated himself in Jesus. The icon of the Church as Body is a window into the profound reality of the Church's involvement in the deeper dimensions of the Incarnation.

In Luke's account of the Transfiguration (9:28-36) we see the extension of the Incarnation into the past. Moses and Elijah are present with Jesus and discuss "his departure, which he was to accomplish at Jerusalem" (v. 31). Here, in some sense, the Law (Moses) and the Prophets (Elijah) are integrally involved in the culmination of the Incarnation, bringing the past history of God's interaction with humanity to a consummation. The same image is portrayed even more graphically in Revelation 11, in which the culmination of the testimony of the two witnesses,

clearly depicted as Moses and Elijah,[47] is death at the
hands of the Beast (11:7). Their death is intimately associated with the crucifixion of Jesus (11:8), and with his
resurrection and ascension (11:11-12). The crucifixion of
Jesus as the culmination of the Incarnation extending back
through the past is more explicitly stated in Revelation
13:8, in which Jesus is described as the Lamb slain "from
the foundation of the world." Luke utilizes the same
phrase to speak of "the blood of all the prophets, shed
from the foundation of the world," which is to be culmi-
nated in Jesus' day (Luke 11:50).

The Incarnation extends not only into the past but also
into the future. This is the profound meaning of Paul's
puzzling pronouncement in Colossians 1:24: "I rejoice in
my suffering for your sake, and in my flesh I complete
what is lacking in Christ's afflictions for the sake of his
body, that is the church." Is Paul implying that Christ's
death was not sufficient and that additional human effort is
necessary to inaugurate God's new order of being? Not at
all. Paul is realizing that the death of Jesus reaches out
into the future to deal with the brokenness and alienation
of the old order of being and, as an ambassador of Christ
having a ministry of reconciliation (2 Cor. 5:18-20), Paul
finds himself an extension of the Incarnation into ongoing
human history. It is as such that he can make the statement "It is no longer I who live, but Christ who lives in
me" (Gal. 2:20) and repeatedly voice the outrageous
exhortations "Be imitators of me" (1 Cor. 4:16); "Be imitators of me, as I am of Christ" (1 Cor. 11:1); "Join in
imitating me" (Phil. 3:17); "Be imitators of God"
(Eph.5:1). The clearest indication of Paul's understanding
of the Church as the extension of the Incarnation into
human history, however, is in his icon of the Church as
the body of Christ (1 Cor. 12:27; Eph. 1:23; 4:12; Col.
1:18, 24; Rom. 12:5).[48]

The role of the Church as the body of Christ is most

focally described by Paul in conjunction with the Eucharist
(1 Cor. 11:17-34). The larger context of Paul's statement is
the factionalism that rends the Corinthian church and pre-
vents them from being the body of Christ. This is seen in
Paul's statement "When you assemble as a church . . . it
is not the Lord's supper that you eat" (vv. 18, 20). As we
shall see, if it is not the Lord's Supper they eat, then they
are not the body of Christ. There are three aspects of the
Eucharist that Paul stresses and that reveal to us the focal
dimensions of the Church as the body of Christ. *First,* the
Eucharist is a remembrance. But it is a remembrance in
the biblical sense of the term. The Passover of the Jews
was such a "remembrance," in which the participants,
through the rituals, understood themselves to be incorporated into that original Passover in Egypt and thus, in the
present time, called out by God to be his covenant people
in the world. The Church, in the Eucharist, "remembers"
Jesus' death and in that "remembrance" is incorporated
into that death and all its consequences. The Eucharist is
for the Church the experience of the continuation through
its history of the death with Christ it experienced at baptism (Rom. 6:3-4). *Second,* Paul focuses the Eucharist
upon the Body. A woodenly literal translation of 11:24 is,
"This, of me, is the body—the for (concerning) you
[body]"[49] The ambiguity of the expression can be seen in
the later textual variants that add "broken," "crushed" or
"given" after "for you" in an attempt to clarify the relationship between "body" and "for you." But in the light
of Paul's focal vision of the Church as the body of Christ,
it seems Paul meant it to be understood that Christ's body
is also the Church's (i.e. they are his body). He had just
reminded the Corinthians, "The bread which we break, is
it not a participation in the body of Christ? Because there
is one bread, we who are many are one body, for we all
partake of the one bread" (1 Cor. 10:16-17), and almost
immediately after the eucharistic words in 11:24, Paul

makes discernment of the Body essential for genuine participation in the Eucharist (11:29). Clearly for Paul, the call to "remembrance" is also a call for the Church to realize that it is the body of Christ. *Third,* the Eucharist is an extension of the death of Jesus into ongoing history until his return: "You [continuously] proclaim the Lord's death until he comes" (11:26). The term Paul uses for *proclaim* might also be translated "show," "display," "manifest."[50] It is not the usual term Paul uses for the proclamation of the gospel.[51] Paul is saying that when the Church, in its central act as the worshiping community of God's new order of being, truly "remembers," truly "discerns the Body," it is then the body of Christ that manifests the extension of the Incarnation into the history of its own time.

Immediately following the discussion of the Eucharist in 1 Corinthians 11, Paul turns to the gifts of the Spirit. Interestingly, in the two other places in which Paul speaks of the gifts of the Spirit, the Church as the body of Christ is also prominent (cf. Rom. 12:4-8; Eph. 4:11-12). In 1 Corinthians 12:12-27, we find Paul's premier illustration of the Church as the body of Christ set in a framework of gifts of the Spirit (12:4-11, 28-31). These gifts are the empowerment of God through the Holy Spirit that enable the Church to function in the world as Jesus functioned. Rather than disruptive and disturbing elements of "super spirituality," which many in our day as in Paul's take them to be, the gifts of the Spirit are the empowerment of the Church of God which enables it to be the body of Christ in the world. The gifts enable the Church to continue the ministry of Christ in the world,[52] to be the extension of the Incarnation through ongoing human history until Christ returns.

The gifts, however, are secondary to the fruits of the Spirit, especially love. In all three instances in which Paul deals with the gifts of the Spirit in the body of Christ, he also brings the focus to love. Romans 12:4-8 is immediately followed by the injunction "Let love be genuine" (v. 9). Ephesians 4:11-12 is followed by the affirmation "Speaking the truth in love, we are to grow up in every way into him who is the head, into Christ, from whom the whole body . . . when each part is working properly, makes bodily growth and upbuilds itself in love" (vv. 15-16). And the premier illustration of the Church as the body of Christ empowered with the gifts of the Spirit (1 Cor. 12:4-31) flows directly into the premier portrayal of love as the focal principle of all the gifts (1 Cor. 13). The fruit of the Spirit is the consequence of that work of the Spirit in the life of the Church that conforms it to the image of Christ in the nature of its being and the quality of its character. Thus the Church as the body of Christ incarnates, through the transforming and empowering presence of the Holy Spirit, both the being of Christ and the action of Christ in ongoing human history.

This perception is not unique to Paul. John also caught this profound vision of the Church when he wrote, "As he is so are we in this world" (1 John 4:17b). This follows John's affirmation of the gift of the Holy Spirit (4:13) and the perfection of love (4:17a). John received this emphasis from Jesus, for in his Gospel, John reports that Jesus, after praying that his followers might be sanctified (17:17), says, "As thou didst sent me into the world, so I have sent them into the world" (17:18).[53] Following the subsequent crucifixion, in his resurrection appearance to the disciples, John again reports Jesus' saying, "As the Father has sent me, even so I send you" (20:21); then Jesus breathes the Holy Spirit upon them (v. 22).

It is noteworthy that Paul and John are the two Epistle writers who also stress the dynamic of the Church's being "in Christ." In Paul's perception the Christian community has entered into the very being of Jesus himself and, through that incorporation, has become the "Body" in which and through which, by the person of the Holy

Spirit, he continues his redemptive ministry to a fallen world. John also claims, "We are in him who is true, in his Son Jesus Christ" (1 John 5:20), and, "He who says he abides in him ought to walk in the same way in which he walked" (2:6). The abiding in Christ results in an "incarnational" life in the world.

The Church as Body, therefore, is an icon that portrays the Christian community as the extension of the Incarnation into ongoing human history. In the Church the redemptive, regenerative, sanctifying grace of God continues to minister to a lost and broken world in sacrificial love. As such, the Church is a radical alternative to the world's incarnation of the rebellion of Satan. In the midst of a world that incarnates a life of practically unmitigated self-centeredness and humanistic enmity toward anything that might claim rule over human destiny, the Church is the incarnation of One who so loved the world that he gave his only Son, and is thus the vehicle in which he continues to give his only Son for the world. The Church as Body is the community that takes up the cross daily and follows him. It is the community that exists not to be served but to serve and to give its life as a "ransom" for many. This community becomes obedient unto death, even the death of the cross, and though despised and rejected by the world, is the means through which the manifold wisdom of God is made known even to the principalities and powers in the heavenly places. When Jesus appears, this community will be like him.

CONCLUSION

The writers of the Epistles utilize images from their own cultural horizon of perception to portray the Church. These images, infused with the reality of the writers' experience of a new order of being in Christ, become icons that reveal the Church as the community of God's new order of being. This, in turn, represents a radical disturbance in the world's status quo. The Church is the Temple whose focal dynamic of true worship/love of God militates against the world's idolatry in any form. The Church is the City whose inner structures of true human existence/love of self militate against the world's restrictive and destructive structures of human existence. The Church is the body of Christ whose ongoing incarnation of divine life/love of others sacrificially militates against the world's living death.

These three icons are inseparably interconnected and, with their manifold variants, constitute the multifaceted unity of God's new order of being in Christ. The true worship of the Temple must flow into the structure of our being (City) and the nature of our doing (Body) lest it become idolatry. The structure of our being (City) must maintain true worship (Temple) and result in a valid expression in life (Body) lest it become Fallen Babylon. Our life in the world (Body) must have true worship (Temple) and proper structure of being (City) lest it become the incarnation of death.

Finally, these three icons represent the Church as the fulfillment of the Lord's Prayer:

Notes

1. P. S. Minear, "Church, Idea of," *Interpreters' Dictionary of the Bible,* G. A. Buttrick, ed. (Nashville: Abingdon, 1962), I:616a.
2. For an excellent treatment of this aspect of biblical studies see Anthony C. Thiselton, *The Two Horizons: New Testament Hermeneutics and Philosophical Description* (Grand Rapids: Wm. B. Eerdmans, 1980).
3. Cf. Thiselton, "The New Hermeneutic," in *New Testament Interpretation,* I. Howard Marshall, ed. (Grand Rapids: Wm. B. Eerdmans, 1977).
4. For example, the work of Bultmann, who utilized the existential philosophical perspective of Heidegger as the ruling perspective for N.T. interpretation.
5. John Wesley, *A Collection of Hymns for the Use of the People Called Methodists* (London: John Mason, undated), Hymn 473, stanza 5. The most recent publication is by Oxford University Press, 1983, Frank Baker, ed., p. 644.
6. Aelred Squire, *Asking the Fathers: The Art of Meditation and Prayer* (New York: Morehouse-Barlow and Paulist Press, 1976), p. 3.
7. The antecedent for *ha* laloumen ("that which we communicate") is *ta* hupo tou theou charisthenta hēmin ("the things 'graced' to us by God") in verse 12, and the *ha . . .* hēmin de apekalupsen ho theos dia tou pneumatos ("the things God revealed to us through the Spirit") in verses 9-10, that is, an experiential reality. In vv. 6-7, that which is communicated (laloumen!) is wisdom, but not a wisdom of this age. It is the wisdom of a new order of being that must be communicated in dynamics different from the wisdom of this age. This is clearly seen in the parallelism of verse 13:

ha kai laoumen that which we communicate)	ouk en (not in)	didaktois (taught	anthrōpinēs of human	sophias logois wisdom words)
pneumatika (spiritual things	all'en (but in) sugkrinontes expounding*)	didaktois (taught	pneumatos of Spirit	pneumatikois spiritualities)

120 M. Robert Mulholland, Jr.

*Cf. Friedrich Büchsel, "*sugkrinō*," G. Kittel, ed. *Theological Dictionary of the New Testament,* G. W. Bromiley, trans. (Grand Rapids: Eerdmans, 1965), III, pp. 953ff.

8. Alan W. Jones, *Journey into Christ* (New York: Seabury Press, 1977), p. 13.

9. Cf. Richard Oster, "Numismatic Windows into the Social World of Early Christianity: A Methodological Inquiry," *Journal of Biblical Literature* 101 (1982), pp. 195-223, for an excellent portrayal of the iconographic aspects of the culture of the first century A.D.

10. Minear, I. 616b.

11. Each of these icons is a gem with many facets: the Temple icon displays facets of kingdom of priests, Jesus as High Priest, holy people, holy priesthood, building, and so on; the City icon displays the facets of kingdom, nation, household, family, house, vineyard, flock, God's people, and so on; the Body icon displays the facets of member, bride, servant, head, and so on. These icons are extremely flexible and can interrelate with one another as will be seen below (*infra.* 103).

12. Eric Osborn, "The Love Command in Second-Century Christian Writing," *The Second Century* 1 (1981), 225. Cf. also V. Furnish, *The Love Command in the New Testament* (London: 1972).

13. Cf. Paul: Rom. 5:8, 8:37 (cf. vv. 31-32); 2 Cor. 5:14-15; Gal. 2:20; Eph. 2:4-7; 5:2, 25; 2 Thess. 2:16; *et. al.* (Heb. 9:13-14); Peter: 1 Pet. 2:24-25, 3:18 with 1:3 and 2:3. John: 1 John 3:16; 4:10, 19; Rev. 1:5; *et. al.*

14. Osborn, p. 225.

15. Cf. new creation: 2 Cor. 5:17; Gal. 6:15. New birth: 1 Cor. 3:1; 1 Pet. 1:3; 2:2. New life: Rom. 6:4; Eph. 4:24. Image of God: Rom. 8:29; 2 Cor. 3:18; 1 John 3:2; Col. 3:4; 2 Pet. 1:4.

16. Paul's repeated injunctions to give thanks in all circumstances, to rejoice always, are only possible when the basic posture of our being is one of grateful receptivity to the great work God is doing in our lives through all circumstances (i.e. when we love the self he is creating in us in all the situations of our lives).

17. First Thessalonians 3:12-13—"May the Lord make you increase and abound in love to one another and to all men . . .

so that he may establish your *hearts unblamable in holiness.*" First Timothy 1:5—"The aim of our exhortations is love that issues from a *pure heart.*" 1 John 4:12—"If we love one another, God abides in us and love of him is *perfected* in us." Colossians 3:14—"Put on love which is the bond of *perfection.*" Hebrews 10:22-24—" . . . with out *hearts sprinkled clean* . . . let us consider how to stir up one another to love . . ." First Peter 1:22—"Having *purified* your souls . . . love one another earnestly from the heart."

18. Kenneth Leech, *True Prayer* (New York: Harper and Row, 1980), p. 95.
19. From this brief survey of the centrality of the Love Command as the warp and woof of the new order of being in Christ, we can appreciate the biblical soundness of Wesley's insistence upon perfection in love as the hallmark of holiness and the essential dynamic of the Christian community.
20. Cf. Heb. 9:26; 10:12; 7:27; Eph. 5:2; Gal. 1:4; 1 Pet. 1:19; 1 John 1:7; Rev. 1:5.
21. *Supra.* p. 95.
22. Heavenly hosts: 4:10; 5:14; 7:11; 11:16; 19:4. Christian community: 11:1. Fallen humanity: 9:20; 13:4, 8, 12, 15; 14:9; 11; 16:2; 19:20.
23. The call is to "those who dwell upon the earth and every nation and tribe and tongue and people"—a standard phrase in Revelation for the inhabitants of the fallen order who worship the Beast (cf. 3:10; 6:10; 8:13; 11:10; 12:12; *13:8, 12, 14*; 17:2, 8; and 5:9; 7:9; 10:11; 11:9; 13:7; 17:5).
24. Mark of the Beast: 13:16ff.; 14:9, 11; 15:2; 16:2; 19:20; 20:4. Seal of God: 7:3, 4; 9:4 (14:1, 22:4, 3:12).
25. Jacques Ellul, *Apocalypse,* G. W. Schreiner, trans. (New York: Seabury, 1977), p. 96. Cf. also, Walter Grundmann, *"deksios,"* G. Kittel, ed., *Theological Dictionary of the New Testament,* G. W. Bromiley, trans. (Grand Rapids: Eerdmans, 1964), II, pp. 37f. In the Old Testament, the rebellious perceptual framework of life is symbolized as a "hard" forehead (Isa. 48:4; Ezek. 3:7), a "harlot's forehead" (Jer. 3:3), or, in one instance, a "leprous forehead" (2 Chron. 26:19f.); and repeatedly the hand is representative of action [Eduard Lohse, *"cheir,"* G. Kittel,

ed. *Theological Dictionary of the New Testament,* G. W. Bromiley, trans. (Grand Rapids: Eerdmans, 1974), IX, pp. 424ff.]

26. Rev. 1:2, 9; 6:9; 12:17; 14:12; 19:10; 20:4.
27. *Supra,* note 23.
28. 1 Kings 6:20, n. b. that it is entirely overlaid with gold, and in Revelation 21:18, the cubic City "was pure gold." In Ezekiel 41:4, the Holy of Holies is twenty by twenty cubits (as Solomon's) but no height is given; the same is true of Josephus' description of Herod's temple (*War* V, 215-19).
29. *Supra,* 103.
30. Second Corinthians 6:14-7:1, which, in its content, seems to be the letter mentioned in 1 Corinthians 5:9-13.
31. This can be seen in 10:22: Christians can "draw near" to God (note this technical use of proserchomai [to come to] in Hebrews—4:16; 7:25; 10:1; 11:6; 12:18, 22) with a true heart because their hearts are "sprinkled clean from an evil conscience." The cultus cannot "perfect the conscience of the worshiper" (9:9), but the blood of Christ can (9:14).
32. On the "Throne of Grace" as the Mercy Seat in the Holy of Holies cf. F. F. Bruce, *The Epistle to the Hebrews* (Grand Rapids: Eerdmans, 1964), 86ff.
33. Cf. M. Robert Mulholland, Jr. "Firstborn," *Beacon Dictionary of Theology* (Kansas City: Beacon Hill Press, 1983), pp. 218-19.
34. *Supra,* pp. 199ff.
35. Hermann Strathmann, *"polis,"* G. Kittel, ed. *Theological Dictionary of the New Testament,* G. W. Bromiley, trans. (Grand Rapids: Eerdmans, 1968), VI, p. 520.
36. Plato, *Apology* and *Crito.*
37. Note the frequent use of this type of *city* iconography in the Epistles: Eph. 2:12, 19; 4:18; Col. 1:21; 1 Pet. 1:1, 17; 2:11.
38. Cf. Hans Bietenhard, *"onoma,"* G. Kittel, ed. *Theological Dictionary of the New Testament,* G. W. Bromiley, trans. (Grand Rapids: Eerdmans, 1967), V, pp. 242-83.
39. In the letters to the seven churches (Rev. 2-3), various elements of the vision of Jesus in chapter 1 are used to introduce him in each letter. The keys are used for this purpose in the letter to Philadelphia (3:7), where the conquerors re-

ceive the name of the New Jerusalem (3:12). In Revelation 21-22, this New Jerusalem is the context of fulfilled human existence.

40. *Supra,* pp. 107ff.

41. This assumes that John wrote in the late 60s A.D. But this would still be basically true of the later date for Revelations in the 90s.

42. It is a mistake to think that Fallen Babylon is a cipher for Rome. The opposite is the case: for John, Rome was the historical manifestation of Fallen Babylon in his day.

43. *Supra,* p. 104.

44. In both 3:12 and 21:2 and 10, the term *katabainousa(v)* ("coming down") is a present participle that, as Caird notes, is "an iterative present, denoting a permanent attribute of the New Jerusalem." (G. B. Caird, *The Revelation of St. John the Divine* [New York: Harper and Row, 1966], p. 55, cf. pp. 263, 271).

45. The Greek term *politeuesthe* meant to conduct one's life as a citizen of the *polis* ("city").

46 Greek *politeias* (v.12) and *sumpolitai* (v. 19); both technical citizenship terms in the first-century world.

47. Fire consumes their foes (Moses—Num. 16:25-35; Elijah—2 Kings 10:12); power to shut the sky (Elijah—1 Kings 17); smite the earth with plagues (Moses—Exod. 7-11).

48. Minear, p. 571; also, "Christ, Body of" *loc. cit.* pp. 614f. Eduard Schweizer, *"sōma",* G. Kittel, ed. *Theological Dictionary of the New Testament,* G. W. Bromiley, trans. (Grand Rapids: Eerdmans, 1971), VII, pp. 1067-1080.

49. *touto mou estin to   sōma to huper humōn* [*sōma understood*]
    this of me is the body the for   you   [body]

50. Paul uses *kataggelō,* which appears elsewhere in Paul only at Romans 1:8; 1 Corinthians 2:1; 9:14; Philippians 1:17-18, Colossians 1:28. While most uses by Paul can simply mean to "proclaim" (=*kērussō* Phil. 1:15-17), 1 Cor. 2:1 may be instructive for a more significant use by Paul. Here Paul reminds the Corinthians that he did not come to them *kataggelōn* the mystery of God in superior rationality or wisdom (v. 1), but in a demonstration (*apodeiksei*—a showing forth, a manifestation) of Spirit and power (v. 4) so that

their faith might not be in human wisdom but in the power of
God (v. 5). Obviously something more than simple "proclamation" is involved here. There is some acting out of the
mystery, some manifestation of its reality. The context of
Colossians 1:28, suggests the same use of *katagellō*. In 1:27,
the mystery is defined as "Christ in you." If in verse 28, the
relative pronoun (hon) takes "mystery" as its antecedent,
then Paul "manifests" (*kataggellomen*) the mystery of
"Christ in you" in order to bring others to the completeness
of this reality.

51. Paul's usual terms are *gnōridzō*—"to make known" (18 of
    24 New Testament uses); *euaggelidzomai*—"to announce
    good news" (twenty-two of fifty-five New Testament uses,
    plus seven in Acts; [*euaggelion*—the news which is an-
    nounced is used by Paul sixty-one of the seventy-seven New
    Testament uses]); *kērussō*—"to proclaim" (nineteen of
    sixty-one New Testament uses).
52. Cf. John 14:12—"greater works than these" in the context
    of the presence of the Spirit.
53. The Greek *kathōs* ("just as") is a strengthened form of *hōs*
    ("as") and means "in the same way as." It appears eight
    times in John 17 (vv. 2,11,14,16,18,21,22,23), almost all in
    formulations that bring the believers into the same relation-
    ship with God as Jesus and the same role in the world.

II. The Church in Historical and Theological Perspective

Paul M. Bassett (Ph.D., Duke University), director of M. Div. program and professor of history of Christianity, Nazarene Theological Seminary

A Survey of Western Ecclesiology to about 1700

Part I: Major Concepts in Ecclesiology from the Second to the Fifteenth Centuries

THE IDEA OF CHURCH IN EARLY CHRISTIANITY

Elsewhere in this volume, Alex Deasley deals with the idea of "Church" in the New Testament.[1] This essay picks up the development of this idea in the succeeding generations, when the vocabulary for expressing it had narrowed and become more mundane but when the form of the Church was becoming much clearer. The culling of the vocabulary used to describe and define the nature and role of the Church did not simplify the necessary process of giving it precise organizational and theological content.

Always, the Church spoke to at least three audiences, each of them working at a different level of discourse. These were the Christian audience, the nonbelieving audience of Jews and pagans, and the schismatics and heretics. The Church described and explained itself to each of these, and to their diverse subgroups, in *ad hoc* bits and pieces.

Yet, this occasional manner did not arise from pragmatic roots. On the contrary, most of the Christian writers whose works have reached us seem to have assumed that they were articulating selected portions of a complete and generally well-known understanding of the nature and role of the Church.[2]

In fact, their perception contradicted reality. The early church had nothing like a rational, reflective theology of its nature and role until late in the fourth century. And yet, while those earlier writers assumed a rational theological basis that simply did not exist, they were caught up in a unity that was quite real and formative.

Everywhere, Christians organized themselves to worship as joyful penitents. Gathered since the first Christian Pentecost from among earth's many tribes and tongues, and usually from among its faceless poor or enslaved, they knew themselves to be the "no people" now made "God's own nation" by the redeeming work of Jesus of Nazareth. Their Master had spoken of the kingdom of heaven and its inner life. Of this kingdom, they understood themselves to be citizens—citizens here and now with the full realization of the Kingdom and of the meaning of that citizenship lying in a glorious future. Here was reason to rejoice and here was a hope to proclaim.[3]

But the good news of the Kingdom was tempered by the earthiness of its temporal expression, the Church. The Church, founded by the One who had spoken much more of the Kingdom than of the Church, was to be taken with utmost seriousness but not with ultimate seriousness. What was obvious to all was the moral distance between earthly Christendom and the fully realized kingdom. And yet, it was not an unbridged distance. Christ had spanned the gap, as it were, and in his continuing presence forgave the sinfulness that created it. And, the Spirit had come to it, too, as the fully divine agent who applies the benefits of that forgiveness and guides the people of God on to full identification with the very King himself.[4]

So, the church was organized as a society, a *civitas*, of joyful penitents bent on rendering worship and service—and seeing the two as one process. The precise social structure of this *civitas* was of little concern to the early generations of Christians. They aimed to organize so as to proclaim, to celebrate, and to maintain their true citizenship and its hope. And they aimed to draw the whole world in with them. Form was important only as it served function. So, in organizing, they cast a wide net, borrowing from far and wide—and sometimes from unlikely sources. The appropriation of administrative forms, or even ritual, from Jewish or pagan sources—on the surface of things appearing to be sheerly pragmatic—was but another way of saying, "The earth is the Lord's and the fulness thereof."[5]

At the center of its worship, the Church celebrated baptism and the Lord's Supper. And it did so with rituals that it borrowed and transformed.

The baptismal rite "for repentance and the forgiveness of sins" was borrowed largely from the tradition represented by John the Baptizer. But the Christians transformed it by a simple addition—they did it in the name of Jesus, later in the name of the Trinity, with the laying on of hands. John's baptism washed away the filthiness of the old era and prepared one to enter the new messianic age; Christian baptism washed away the filthiness of the old era and actually ushered the believer into the new. The rite of the Lord's Supper drew upon both Jewish and pagan sources; but again, Christianity transformed the borrowed elements. Christ, represented in the bread and wine, was the once-for-all Passover Lamb. The pagan meal celebrating the mythological dying and rising of a god became a celebration of a real physical death and a real physical resurrection of the God-man, Jesus of Nazareth, at a determined time and place in human history. And the eating and drinking of the bread and wine, far from symbolizing participation in a cosmic idea, declare participation in the very life—past, present, and future—of that same Jesus.[6]

Organizational patterns, too, were freely borrowed by the early church. Much of the earliest-used terminology seems to have come from the Jewish *diaspora* and from paganism. This is especially evident in Paul's letters as he speaks of apostles, prophets, and teachers.[7]

The Jewish apostle was an official emissary from one congregation to another, sent to make a special appeal or to carry a very special message. The Temple in Jerusalem often sent such persons to groups of Jews in distant places. The Jewish teacher interpreted Scripture.

Paul's apostles were also specially commissioned and sent with an urgent appeal, but primarily to unbelievers. They itinerated. Paul's teachers were also, as in Judaism, biblical interpreters to believers. And they itinerated, but were not as mobile as the apostles.

The role of prophet in both Judaism and earliest Christianity had undergone transformation. It now bore more of a Hellenistic than an Old Testament stamp. In certain sects of pagan religion, it was the responsibility of the prophet to deliver his or her special word from the god(s) and lead adherents in prescribed rituals. Paul's prophet is an itinerant with an especially urgent word from the Lord who also leads the congregation in worship by praying and preaching as well as by fore-telling and forth-telling.[9]

Apostles, prophets, and teachers were the extraordinary leaders of the Church. The phalanx of officials conducting its daily affairs held such titles as helper, president, elder or bishop, and deacon.[10] The extraordinary leaders were understood to have been chosen by direct divine appointment somehow; the day-to-day officials were elected by their respective congregations. Of course, the vote, however taken, intended to express the mind of God, but these leaders were not seen as being especially charismatic. They were the servants of a given local fellowship.[11]

Apostles, prophets, and teachers, on the other hand, were essentially charismatic and were sent by the Spirit to minister to the wider church.

The local officials' roles and titles seem to be Christian innovations, by and large.[12] At least they have no clear analogies in either the religious or secular structures of the Empire. And even in the Church itself, where the titles were in common use long before the end of the first Christian century, the functions denoted by the titles were not clearly delineated or universally the same until well into the second century.

The *Didache,* a Syrian church order from about A.D. 100, describes the situation as the charismatic offices of apostle, prophet, and teacher began to yield authority to the local offices of bishop and deacon. Very strict regulations now governed itineracy. Apostles were to stay in one place no more than two days and were not to ask for money;[13] prophets and teachers were recognized as more or less itinerant, too, but were not forbidden to settle in one locality.[14] And bishops and deacons, though locally chosen, were now said to "perform . . . the ministry of the prophets and teachers."[15]

By about A.D. 120, Ignatius, bishop of Antioch, produced a series of letters in which he reflects on the day-to-day governance of local (and perhaps regional) Christian communities—a series that later would become a standard source of guidance in matters of ecclesiastical organization. Ignatius rarely mentions the offices of apostle, prophet, and teacher as they had come to function; he prefers to restrict these titles to their biblical denotations—*apostle* meaning Paul or one of the Twelve, *prophet* meaning an Old Testament writer, and *teacher* meaning simply an instructor.[16] This preference and the care and intensity with which he writes of the roles of the local officers—bishops, presbyters, and deacons—raise the suspicion that it is precisely the ministries of the charismatic itinerants with which he is concerned. They are not to disrupt the discipline and ministries exercised by the "located" local officers.

Ignatius makes it clear that the bishop is the presiding officer in a local congregation, and in calling himself bishop of Syria probably indicates his own presidency over all of the congregations in a given area. Ignatius is in no way careless about doctrine, but he does insist that it is unity with the bishop, and not simply adherence to some tenet, that makes one a Christian. This holds true because, on one hand, the bishop represents the Church, and on the other, he represents God the Father. True doctrine arises only out of sound spiritual relationships.[17]

Assisting the bishop are the presbyters and the deacons. The presbyters are deputized to administer the sacraments, to preach, and to catechize. The deacons carry forward the mundane business of the institution and administer its philanthropic enterprises.[18]

While the offices of bishop and presbyter, and perhaps deacon, seem to be Christian inventions, for the most part, Ignatius does not view them as mere pragmatic responses to the Church's needs. He believes that the ecclesiastical hierarchy reflects or parallels that of the heavenly kingdom. So the bishop presides in the place of God or as a type of the heavenly Father; the presbyters serve as types of the Apostles, not in terms of the Apostles' earthly ministry but in terms of their heavenly role as judges of "the twelve tribes of Israel"[19]; the deacons carry out the continuing earthly ministries of Jesus himself.[20]

Without bishops, presbyters, and deacons, Ignatius believes, there is no Church. This is probably a simple extension of his analogy: the Church is inconceivable without bishops, presbyters, and deacons because the heavenly kingdom is inconceivable without the Father, the Son, and the Apostles.[21]

Whether forms were borrowed or not, it was evident by

Ignatius's time that the Christian society, the Church, was essentially an anti-type of Graeco-Roman society.[22] While the Empire deliberately impressed, or sought to impress, itself and others, the Church developed as an invisible commonwealth—a "hidden and publicity-fleeing tribe," as one Christian writer was to put it late in the second century.[23] But it was a commonwealth, a *civitas*, nonetheless. No less than the Empire, it called for strict allegiance to its head. But rather than advocating such allegiance primarily as a means for holding society together, a practice increasingly common in the Empire—even to the point of permitting cynicism about the person of the emperor so long as the external symbols of allegiance were maintained—the Church insisted that Christ's *is* the Kingdom. Christ was no mere symbol of the commonwealth but its source, reason for being, and end.[24] The law of the Christian commonwealth, far from being coercive and established for the protection and maintenance of the *civitas*, was seen to arise as a voluntary expression of gratitude for the privilege of citizenship; but it was, nonetheless, a gift of divine grace.[25]

Ignatius's insistence on the authority of the bishop, then, expresses little, if any, love of power or place. But it does reflect both strictly Christian and Roman influences. The understanding of the Church as the servant of the Kingdom, and its reflection as well, demands that there be a head. That the administrative head should represent the whole people to the divine power and represent the divine power among the people is a Roman idea.[26] Ignatius stops short of apotheosizing the bishop, of course. But he does give him high place in calling him a type of the Father.[27]

Ignatius also paves the way for administrative authority and priestly authority to be placed in the same hands in the Christian commonwealth—a union more reflective of Roman society than of either Judaism or of earlier Christianity.[28]

Slowly, the entire church moved toward the Ignatian system and then beyond it to monarchical administration, though it would be nearly a thousand years before one bishop would claim administrative and spiritual jurisdiction over the whole universal church, including jurisdiction over all other bishops. By the end of Ignatius's century, claims would be made for a unique spiritual precedence for the bishop of Rome.[29] But in his own geographical area, a bishop came more and more to rule the Church as a monarch would rule the society at large. He controlled both the administration and the spiritual life of his diocese.[30] But, as in Roman society, the controller exercised his role as the principal representative of the controlled.

Here we must consider a philosophical point: the similarity in perceptions held by the Roman empire of its emperor and by the Church of its bishops. Both Rome and the Church were convinced that they were the special concern and favorite of divine power and wisdom, though, of course, they were at odds over who or what that divine power and wisdom were. Both Rome and the Church also believed that they had special insight into the will and way of the divine power and wisdom, an insight that they believed explained their astounding successes. This was their *genius*. Both also believed that this *genius*, possessed by the people as a whole, had entailed the privilege of self-direction in accountability to the divine power and wisdom. This was their *imperium*. And both believed that the whole people could bestow this *imperium* on an individual or group of individuals, who then became the expression, even carried the *genius*, of the whole people. The Empire called its *imperium*-bearer, "emperor"; the Christians called theirs "bishop."[31]

Again, Christianity had both borrowed and transformed. The Christian *genius* was the acceptance by faith of a grace-given revelation of the will of God in Christ.[32] And the Christian *imperium*, far from autonomy or independence from the divine power and will granted or developed because of some supposed inherent harmony with that power and will was understood to be an ethical and moral responsibility.[33] Christians could not save themselves, nor could the Church save them, but they and the Church were responsible for maintaining and deepening the channels for the influx of divine grace—the believer *through* the Church.[34] Further, the Church had, by its episcopal elections, bestowed this responsibility in a special way on the bishop.

But, ideally, the bishop's model for exercising this responsibility and character was Christ—Christ as the lordly servant.[35] The bishop, in this moral sense, was the Church and the Church was in the bishop.

By the end of the second century, this whole process had allowed two undesirable things to happen. Bishops were too often tempted to overlook their representative character and their servant role and to become autocratic. And Christianity tended to become externalized—a matter of institutional relationship instead of a matter of hearty commitment of life. Tertullian, a North African, lays down the most penetrating criticism of the situation: the Church had allowed custom too much authority and had created an inappropriate separation of clergy and laity.[36]

For good or ill, Tertullian's complaint was little heeded, largely because what seemed then to be the best remedy also seemed to be worse than the problem. It seemed to be an inopportune time to trust new revelations and certainly an inopportune time to curtail clerical authority.

Two major doctrinal-administrative problems confronted the church of Tertullian's day, and they forced responses on two very different fronts. On the one hand were the

Gnostics, and on the other were the Montanists. The types
of Gnostic were legion, but they agreed in disparaging the
historical character of Christian faith. And they all saw
cosmological or metaphysical insight, wrapped in esoteric
language and symbol, as "knowledge" and such "knowledge" as the way to salvation. The declaration that Christ
was an authentic human being, born of woman, who really
suffered and died and who was actually raised in the flesh,
seemed to them crude and blasphemous. They preached
and taught that he was an idea or a force or a spirit who
rescues our souls from our bodies and from the material
world, basing their message on a philosophical exegesis of
Scripture.[37] The Montanists, on the other hand, differed
not a whit from Christians in general in their understanding
of salvation. But they believed that the Holy Spirit still
had revelations to give to the Church through latter-day
prophets and they believed that the church at large, because it had slipped morally, was in desperate need of
these revelations. They saw the hierarchy as increasingly
self-interested and therefore as a source of the moral decline and an obstacle to the freedom of the Spirit.[38]

The Church's response to the Gnostics could only
exacerbate Montanist criticisms that the hierarchy was already too powerful, while its response to the Montanists
seemed to the Gnostics only to prove the unwillingness of
the Church to take either the Scriptures or the Spirit seriously.[39]

Caught in this pincers, the Church struggled to speak to
its three audiences without contradicting itself. We cannot
here review its doctrinal response; we look only at its perception of what it meant to be the Church and at how that
perception affected structure.

Internally, it had to meet its own admitted spiritual
weakness by more careful catechesis and discipline while
at the same time continuing to receive increasing numbers
of persons who had little or no acquaintance with the cul-

tural "givens" upon which Christian morality drew in preaching its own ethic. Suspicion was strong in some circles that it was precisely this influx that was creating the spiritual decline.[40]

Already in the early decades of the second century, the idea that the Church must be a society of the spiritually perfect was seriously questioned.[41] (Ironically, the letters that came to be included in the New Testament reveal anything but a spiritually perfect church; but by the end of the first century, there seems to have been a general conviction that it had been and that such is the norm for the Church in every age.) The *Shepherd of Hermas,* the work of a prophet in the Roman church, urges a more lenient attitude toward a believer who had sinned. The Epistle to the Hebrews (6:4ff.; 10:26ff.) seemed to most to allow for no repentance—and therefore no hope—for sin committed after baptism. Apostasy seems to be the sin in view. Hermas is not clear but seems to allow for one repentance to an apostate provided the apostasy was not premeditated or a consequence of habitual spiritual carelessness and provided the offender underwent some self-imposed penance.[42] Adultery and murder seem to have been irremediable under any circumstances until the first quarter of the third century.

While Hermas apparently thought in terms of self-imposed penance, Clement of Alexandria at the close of the second century, explicitly advocated public repentance.[43] And by mid-third century, a regimen was in general use that included confession (early on, public; later, to a bishop or designated confessor), acts of repentance, prayers for the transgressor by clergy and congregation, and rituals of reconciliation and restoration.[44]

As this process was developing and taking fixed form, however, a conservative reaction set in, especially in the Roman church. There, the presbyter Hippolytus (d.236) defined the church as "the saintly society of those living righteous lives."[45] He thus contended that penitential schemes and rituals had no place among believers except as they might recall their prebaptismal state.[46] So severe was the tension that Hippolytus's supporters, believing the laxity of much of the Roman church to be incurable, elected him bishop and went into schism. The regularly elected bishop of Rome, Callixtus (d.223), argued that the Church is like Noah's Ark with its clean and unclean animals and the field growing wheat and tares together. It is mixed company.[47]

Hippolytus, attempting to be faithful to his perception of apostolic tradition, wrote a church order meant to guide and sustain his "saintly society." He emphasized the authority of the clergy, especially that of the bishop, and elevated them theologically in his concern to strengthen their disciplinary role. Congregations elected bishops, but bishops were ordained by other bishops; and priests and deacons were ordained by bishops only.[48] Further, the episcopacy took on the character of the Aaronic priesthood established in ancient Israel. The bishop now mediated between God and the believers, offering up sacrifice for them and regulating their participation in the divine purpose.[49] The laity now had to depend upon the clerical hierarchy not simply for the ordering of the Church and the stewardship of its means of grace but for salvation itself.[50]

Ironically, a profound contradiction affected the future of Hippolytus's notions. Hippolytus had developed his rules in order to maintain the spiritual purity of the Church, but in their Levitical character they assumed that the Church was not pure and could not be pure this side of the return of Christ. The whole idea of Levitical priesthood falls meaningless if Israel, or the Church, be pure, for it is a system of propitiation for sin. So it was that Hippolytus's *Apostolic Tradition*, conceptually elaborated by Cyprian and Augustine of Hippo, became a veritable manual for the development of the admittedly mixed character of the medieval church while the purpose for which he wrote it was decisively rejected.

Some twenty years after Hippolytus's death the first empire-wide, official government persecution of Christianity added yet other dimensions to the idea of Church, building upon Hippolytus's ideas. In fact, the nature of the persecution itself shaped those dimensions.

At the base of the great persecution of A.D. 250 was the recognition of the antithetical nature of the Church to that of the Empire by the highest circles of the Imperial government.[51] The Church appeared to them to be an alien state within the State, and therefore a threat.

Emperor Decius, therefore, planned to destroy the alien state by exterminating its organizational leaders and by sowing discord among its citizenship. He died just as his scheme really came to reality and his successors did not pursue his plans with rigor. So, many whose positions made them marked men were spared; but the discord took root and grew, especially after the persecution stopped.

Trouble brewed with greatest intensity in Rome and North Africa. The specific issue was whether those who had apostatized in the persecution should be allowed restoration to the Christian fellowship as communicants. In the diocese of Carthage, North Africa, both sides were taken—that there should be no readmission under any circumstances and that all should be readmitted who wished to be. And there was a middle-of-the-road party, too, advocating a case-by-case approach. Bishop Cyprian, a moderate who would himself die as a martyr in A.D. 258, called a council of bishops to resolve the issue but in the meantime (c. A.D. 251-254) readmitted only those who were penitent and about to die; he insisted that others who wished readmission undergo severe penance. The council decided that each case must be considered separately but that no one be readmitted without sincere penance.

Returning clergy could never again exercise clerical office.[52]

In Rome, Bishop Cornelius (A.D. 251-253) took much the same stance as Cyprian and the council.[53] But like Cyprian he ran into stout opposition from the rigorists, under their leader, Novatian. In fact, the rigorists in both Rome and Carthage elected counter-bishops; and Carthage had a laxist rival to Cyprian as well as a rigorist one.

The rigorists, soon to be called Novatianists, believed that congregations readmitting lapsed persons to communion, penance or no, lost their identity as the Church of Christ. The lapsed were, after all, apostates for whom there was now no hope. Receiving them into the Church destroyed its purity.[54] Novatianists then took their position one step further: a new church must be constituted, a pure church maintaining both the doctrine and the discipline of the apostles.[55]

Both the Novatianists and their rivals (the Catholics) adhered to the same doctrines and to the same organizational form. The schism demonstrated all too conclusively that doctrinal agreement was an insufficient basis for unity. Nor was simple episcopal succession sufficient, for both sides agreed that some sort of succession was necessary, though each defined it differently. The Novatianists defined it in terms of purity or holiness (i.e., freedom from apostasy). A bishop held his see legitimately only if he were free from apostasy, if his predecessor had been free as well, and if he had been consecrated by bishops likewise pure.[56] While the Novatianists sounded a bit like Hippolytus when they talked of the Church, calling it the "Congregation of the Sanctified," their first concern was the sanctity of the bishops and lower clergy.[57] So, in fact, they implied that the Church is the congregation of the sanctified bishops. They participated fully in the developments that separated clergy and laity and destroyed the confidence that the latter were of the essence

of the Church. Definitions or descriptions of the true
church anchored in the Church's holiness, a holiness determined primarily by the clergy's freedom from apostasy.[58] The laity were adjective to the essence of the
Church.

Cyprian and his ideological kin took a different point of
departure and developed a different ecclesiology, though
they, too, made the laity adjunctive. Cyprian bases his
definitions and descriptions of the true church in its unity
instead of its holiness. For him, sanctity depends upon
unity—a diametric contradiction of Novatian priorities.
Unity, says Cyprian, is a matter of the fidelity of the lower
clergy and laity to the local bishop, and, more nearly essential, of the fidelity of the bishops to each other.[59]

Cyprian's logic is clearly demonstrated in his demand
that any who come to the Catholic church from heresy or
schism must be baptized in the Catholic church even if the
form of their baptism at the hands of the dissidents was
correct. There is but one baptism and that is because there
is but one church to whom it is entrusted.[60] The one baptism does not make the Church one; rather, the one church
is the only source of the one, true baptism.

The Church came to reject Cyprian's sacramental exclusiveness but, somewhat inconsistently, granted his
theological point: unity is the fundamental mark of the true
church. Further, it accepted his notion that there is no
church without episcopacy: "The bishop is in the Church;
the Church in the bishop. And anyone not with the bishop
is not in the Church."[61]

But what to do if one's clergy are unworthy? Cyprian
says, "Separate!" And he sharply rebukes clerical slip-
shoddiness in ethics and morality.[62] But he seems to account rejection of a bishop to be only a remote possibility
given the presence of the Holy Spirit in the process of
episcopal election and that Spirit's concern, as it were, to
maintain unity.[63] Then, too, any bishop stands accounta-

ble to all other bishops, just as he represents the entire Church to his territory. So, his decisions are reformable only by a consensus among his episcopal colleagues.[64] Beyond them, there is no higher "court."

As for the presence of ethically and morally questionable persons in the Church, made almost inevitable when unity supercedes sanctity as the fundamental mark of the Church, Cyprian accepts as valid Callixtus's belief that the Church is a mixed society—wheat and tares, an ark of clean and unclean creatures. But he takes the ark-symbol in a novel direction. Only those in the ark will be saved; outside the church there is no salvation.[65] Conceptually, Cyprian would scarcely think in terms of three hundred denominations, or even of two, which might be authentically "the Church." He had the institutional church of his day in mind because it was the only one meeting his definition of unity.

Not everyone was thinking as concretely as Cyprian, however. In the Mediterranean city of Alexandria, Egypt, several very well-educated, sophisticated Christians were working on the New Testament's paradoxical way of speaking of the Church. They strove to understand the Church as Body and Bride of Christ on the one hand and the haunt of obviously imperfect persons on the other without overemphasis upon either side. To do this, they drew upon the platonic philosophical tradition.

The platonic tradition taught that our world of things and people is but a collection of reflections or shadows of ultimate reality. Every earthly thing imitates or participates in ultimate reality, more or less. Ultimate reality itself is a realm of eternal forms, perfect and unchanging. Earthly things are more or less real, depending upon the extent to which they imitate or participate in the forms.

By the beginning of the third Christian century, this tradition had revived and had taken on a decidedly religious and theological cast. Neo-Platonism, as the revival later came to be called, simplified the older realm of the forms to consist of only one form—Being or Reality Itself. Being Itself has no parts and is changeless. All else that has any ultimate reality at all has it as an emanation or a spark or an overflow of Being Itself. The human being participates in ultimate reality or in Being Itself—not as one is a human body, for that body changes and even comes into existence and passes from it—but as a soul. The human soul is a spark of Being Itself, caged in a body. And the body, not being real in itself is evil—or at least it is a source of evil, for it tempts the soul to regard it as ultimately real.

In Alexandria, Clement (d. about A.D. 215) and Origen (d. A.D. 255) saw in this philosophical system a way to explain how the Church could be both perfect and obviously imperfect. Their principle problem in this matter was to affirm, as Christians must, that this world, including the human body and the institution called the Church, is real in itself and is not evil simply because it is physical or material. They confessed with all Christians that God actually created the world and human beings, and the Church. These are not accidental consequences of some divine attribute or activity.[66]

Clement and Origen fuse the platonic tradition and Christian faith by talking of two churches. One is the earthly, the other the heavenly. This is a platonic perspective. The earthly reflects the heavenly. But a platonist would insist that the two are by nature mutually exclusive, while Clement and Origen teach that they intertwine along the course of human history.[67] The heavenly church is surely holier than the earthly, but this is only the empirical fact; it is not a metaphysical or a soteriological necessity.[68]

Origen calls the heavenly church "the assembly of the sanctified or perfect"; and the earthly church is but "the assembly of believers." Nonetheless some of the latter are already present in the former, which means that the former is present in the latter. The two are not parallel; the earthly makes manifest the heavenly. It is much more than mere shadow. It makes the heavenly church visible.[69]

Notice that the definitions of Clement and Origen refer to the whole people of God as the Church. Their thinking had little of the clergy-centered tendency developed in western Europe and in the province of North Africa. In fact, Origen emphasizes the priesthood of all believers, though not so much the priesthood's intercessory aspect as its role in worship and its need for ethical and moral rectitude.[70] This universal priesthood holds force in both the heavenly church and the earthly.[71] This emphasis arises from Origen's attention to the social character of the heavenly realm.

Origen almost always counterbalances his written thoughts on the ordained ministry with thoughts on the universal priesthood. The ordained clergy, especially the bishops, do appoint others to clerical office, and bishops are the ordaining authorities. But no nominee is to be ordained without ratification of his appointment by the appropriate congregation.[72] Further, Origen underlines the servanthood of the ordained ministry rather than its administrative authority.[73] On this point, he stands in some contrast to his contemporaries in the province of North Africa and in the western European provinces of the Empire.

In the three centuries following the first Christian Pentecost, the Church had gradually transformed itself from being a society of joyous penitents celebrating forgiveness and liberty to being a highly structured, clerically directed corps of persons confessing the same dogmae.

This is not to say that the clergy had no managerial responsibilities to begin with; nor is it to say that there were no dogmatic commitments from Christianity's earliest day; nor, yet, is it to say that after three hundred years the Church had lost its joyfulness and spontaneity and gained only a dictatorial directorate bent only on control.

Several factors inhibited stagnation. The older, freer language remained, and a healthy regard for tradition kept it alive in practice. Persecution, or the threat of it, inhibited most forms of administration from digging in: a congregation or "diocese" had to be prepared to press on even with the loss of the ordained "stewards of the mysteries." The influx of "new people" into the Empire and into the Church, and the crossing of the Empire's boundaries to evangelize, encouraged at least some concern with organizational novelty, though it did encourage even stricter, conservative dogmatic articulation. Then, most importantly of all, the worship of the Church with its vivid sense of the divine presence still reminded Christians that the earthly institution's validity utterly depended upon its servant-response to the gospel of the heavenly kingdom and its Lord.

THE IDEA OF CHURCH CRYSTALIZES

In the late-fourth and early-fifth centuries, the several ecclesiological strains already mentioned were brought together in the powerful, synthesizing mind of Augustine (d. A.D. 430), bishop of Hippo, North Africa. It is primarily to Augustine that western Christianity traces the durable elements of its understanding of the nature and role of the Church.[74].

But Augustine's views did not arise from reflection on abstractions. He had been forced to think ecclesiologically by a fifty-year struggle in Carthage, the capital city of his own province, North Africa. A schismatic Christian "Church" had been organized there in A.D. 312 or 313 under the leadership of a rigoristic dissident priest named Donatus, with funds supplied by a wealthy Spanish matron named Lucilla, then living in the African coastal city of Ceuta. The schism was given the name Donatism because

Donatus was its effective leader from the beginning to his death in A.D. 355. (Surprisingly, he was not its first bishop, but its second, taking his seat in A.D. 316.)

Donatism was doctrinally orthodox and presented no ecclesiological arguments not long since heard. But unlike its predecessors, it established itself well as a serious, continuing rival to Catholic Christianity. In fact, only the Muslim advance in the second half of the seventh century saw to its demise.[75]

Theologically, Donatism recalled the Hippolytan notion that holiness, not unity, is the fundamental mark of the true church. And, reflecting the hieratic understanding of "Church" that was typical of all Christianity by that time, it was the holiness of the clergy that really mattered. The Church was understood to be holy only as the clergy were holy.[76]

The mark of holiness that counted for the most at that time was steadfastness in the face of persecution. Some bishops, considering petitions for reconciliation on a case-by-case basis, were allowing priests who had succumbed to the pressure of the great persecution under Diocletian to be reinstated to service at the altar after completing appropriate penance. The rigorists were offended. Many of them felt that even readmission to the table as communicants was a blasphemous leniency—especially for priests, who should have shown exemplary faith and courage. Readmission to priestly functions was, to the rigorists, an unthinkable sacrilege.[77]

The Donatists carried the sense of outrage further by declaring that any official duty carried forward by a readmitted priest was illegitimate and an act of blasphemy.[78] This cast a cloud over many a baptism, many an offering of last rites, many a reception of the Eucharistic elements by innocent believers, and, since some of these priests even became bishops, it called significant numbers of ordinations of presbyters and other bishops into question. And, from the Donatists' perspective, passing generations only deepened the corruption. Church order was shaken and the ecclesiastical waters stirred for generations.

Such was the immediate context in which Augustine developed his understanding of the nature and role of the Church. He did it hoping to encourage, even to induce, reunion of the contending parties, and for that reason he seldom accused them of being totally in error. Of course, what truth they did know and experience was "what they had retained of the essence of the Church." If they lost it, they would die quickly.[79] He was himself elected the Catholic bishop of a city in which the conflict was sharp—in A.D. 395, almost a century after the original break.

Unlike his Catholic predecessors in the West, Augustine accepted as valid the rigorists' belief that the fundamental mark of the true church is holiness.[80] But while accepting their postulate, he develops novel content for it. The holiness of the Church does not depend upon the holiness of the clergy. The Church is holy, he says, because its redeeming Lord and Head is holy. Christ, not the clergy, is the essence of the Church. He is the reason for its rites and their center; he is the subject of the Church's preaching; and he is, through the Spirit, the true life of the Church. So the rites, preaching, and life of the Church do not depend upon its goodness and purity, upon the purity and goodness of its clergy.[81]

Augustine has no intention here of allowing or excusing ethical carelessness, but he does not see ethics to be central to the definition of *church* or essential to describing its nature and role. Rather, the basic ecclesiological point, from which all else follows, is the Church's identification with Christ himself. Christology, not ethics, controls Augustine's ecclesiological reflection.[82]

Because the Church is the body of Christ the Redeemer and has Christ as the essence and source of its life, salvation inheres in it.[83] Like Tertullian and Cyprian before him, Augustine believed that in order for one to have God as saving Father, one must have the Church as Mother.[84] The Church as Mother nourishes in faith and disciplines with the authority of the Father himself. The Church as bride of Christ brings forth many "children."[85]

Vivifying the Church is the Holy Spirit, "Lord and Giver of Life." What the soul is to the human body, the Spirit is to the Church.[86] And what the Spirit is to the life of the Trinity, so it is in the life of the Church.[87] To both, it is the bond of love. So, the Church is the creation of God's love, through the Spirit, and is itself, through the presence of that Spirit a community of lovers of God and of lovers of one another. It is the fellowship of the Spirit.[88]

As the Church is the fellowship of the Spirit, who is the bond of love, the Church is one. Those who do not love God or his church therefore stand outside of it; they are strangers to the Holy Spirit. Such were the Donatists. And yet, the Donatists were schismatic, not fully heretical. They did possess sacraments, valid in form and material, which could have been infused by the life-giving Spirit— but only in the true fellowship of the Spirit, the Catholic Church.[89]

Augustine pressed both elements of this point, for he saw baptism and eucharist as the unique channels of holiness and expressions of Christian unity.[90] The Donatists were so near and yet so far away from salvation. They possessed the sacraments but their peculiar definition of holiness, as a mark of the Church, cut them off from salvation itself.[91] The legitimacy of these quintessential symbols and channels of both holiness and unity does not depend upon the sanctity of their celebrants. It lies in the divine presence that inhabits them.[92]

So it is that for Augustine, the Church is holy because Christ is holy and because, through the sacraments, it is united with him. The Holy Spirit maintains this union and vivifies the Word and the sacraments so that they induce and produce holiness in the believers.

Here in this last point, Augustine may at first glance appear to grant some validity to the Donatist's argument that the Church is holy only as its clergy is holy. But he turns the notion to say that the holiness of the Church is demonstrated not so much by the holiness of its members (i.e., the clergy) as by the fact that only within the Church may anyone attain perfect holiness.[93] No other institution or socio-religious body possess that character.

Historically, the visible church is a "mixed body"—so Augustine. There are "tares" or "vessels unto dishonor" in the Church insofar as they are "adjoined to the communion of the saints." But they are not the Church itself, and the Church keeps itself from being corrupted by them as it refuses to approve evil and controls the administering of the means of sanctifying grace (i.e., the sacraments).[94]

But in fact, Augustine confesses, the empirical church does become corrupt and that fact has to be taken into account.[95] And yet, paradoxically, the Church is confessed to be holy. The former fact belongs to the realm of experience, the latter to the realm of faith.[96] And to Augustine, it is the realm of faith that is the nearer of the two realms to absolute reality and truth.[97] The empirical church must be understood as being real, but it is more distant from the source of reality than is the Church confessed in faith to be holy. The empirical church encloses the true church but is not itself that true church.[98] Here, then, Augustine appeals to that fundamental element in faith, the belief in divine election. The true church is "the fixed number of saints predestined before the foundation of the world." But even that true church is holy only as it is in Christ; it is not holy because of the sanctity of its members. So the holiness of either church has the same source and character, and the same must be said of the unity of either one.

The Donatists err in believing that the holiness of the Church depends upon the holiness of its clergy, especially its bishops, and they err also in believing that the unity of the Church depends upon that holiness. They would make the Church a human institution only, though they intend the opposite effect.[99]

Because they have created a human institution, they have created a limited one. Morally, it is confined to those who meet their judgment with respect to sanctity, and geographically it is circumscribed by its own unwillingness or inability, for whatever reasons, to move beyond North Africa. And, it is limited in time, having begun, by the Donatists' own confession, as late as the time of Constantine.[100]

By contrast, says Augustine, the Catholic church, against all humanly calculated odds and against all of the obstacles posed by the world, the flesh, and the devil, extends across time in a conscious unity of faith. And this corresponds to prophecies made concerning the Church centuries earlier.[101] This corresponds, too, with the announced intention of God to spread his glories and the benefits of his redemption in Christ across the world. Christ is the universal savior; his body is a universal body.[102] Donatism's confinement to North Africa testifies to the falsity of its claim to be the one true church. Further, the Catholic church is that holy society that stands in the succession of the apostles, prophets, and patriarchs.[103]

This succession, from the patriarchs to the apostles and their successors, has been forsaken by the Donatists in their breaking of communion with the Catholics. So, though it is true, says Augustine, that the Donatists did retain the Scriptures, which contain the message born by the succession up through the apostles, in refusing the fellowship and authority of the apostolic church, the Donatists were refusing the only agency entrusted with the legitimate, authoritative interpretation of the Scriptures. This places all of their teaching in doubt.[104] And in refusing that fellowship and authority, the Donatists were also cutting themselves off from the guidance of the Spirit, who protects the Church from error, for the Spirit was sent to the apostolic church and has made it his unique instrument for the proclamation and maintenance of truth.[105]

Any truly Catholic congregation, says Augustine, can trace its episcopal succession back to the twelve apostles. The succession does not guarantee that a given congregation enjoys apostolic faith and life, but it does guarantee that it may, indeed. The Catholic church at large does enjoy that faith and life. Outside of that succession, there is no possibility of enjoying true apostolic faith and life. Such is the status of the Donatists.[106]

So it is that Augustine develops the notion of the "marks of the Church": holiness, unity, catholicity, and apostolicity. His fundamental concern was to build a bridge across which the Donatists could come to reenter the Catholic church. He had no interest in continuing schism. To call him "an ardent exponent of absolute and unbending ecclesiastical authority" is to be both unfair and incorrect.[107]

However, it is quite correct to say that Augustine's ecclesiology is inconsistent—even paradoxical. And it is precisely this paradoxical character that has made him the authority for opposing sides in many an argument over the nature and role of the Church.

His doctrine of election is the source of several fundamental ecclesiological inconsistencies. For instance, he refers to the empirical church as the kingdom of heaven or kingdom of God while insisting that it is a mixed society of elect and nonelect, of wheat and tares.[108] This paradox is further complicated by his confidence that some of the elect are not within the Church at all.[109] Another instance: Augustine attempts to distinguish between the invisible

(and thus true) church and the visible and then drains the
distinction of any but abstract meaning by insisting that
the true church is built up by sacraments, which are surely
celebrations of the visible church.[110] And while the sacraments may be divine gifts and necessary vehicles of grace,
they may come to the believer through an evil person.[111]

Augustine does reflect the earliest church to a higher degree than had been done for two hundred years on one
significant point. He consistently defines the church in
terms that do not distinguish between clergy and laity. On
the other hand, in discussing apostolicity as a mark of the
church, with its corollary, apostolic succession, he points
to Peter as "a type of the whole Church."[112] His reasoning here was later to lend itself to the hieratic or hierocra-
tic view.

Augustine did not write with posterity in mind. He
wrote in response to problems at hand. But he reasoned so
well and so profoundly, and the problems to which he responded happened to be so persistent, that later ages con-
sulted his works as standard resources across wide ranges
of theological concern, including ecclesiology. Commentaries on those works and collections of excerpts from
them, arranged topically, circulated for twelve hundred
years or more.

But neither the commented Augustine nor the excerpted
Augustine was the real Augustine; and even the real Augustine, cited from this work or that, is often a lopsided
Augustine. He thought subtly and wrote occasionally,
which means that he spoke from several angles to any
given problem, holding the several in tension, or even
harmonizing them, in his own mind. And, he did
occasionally contradict himself, sometimes knowingly.
Nowhere was this more true than in his ecclesiology.

But a later generation would take advice from one or
another angle of Augustine's perception, seldom from the
whole of it, leaving a still later generation to appeal to yet

another angle. For instance, in the period from about 1378 (the beginning of the Great Schism) to at least 1563 (the close of the Council of Trent), ecclesiological debate often found one Augustinian view in heated conflict with another Augustinian view. Nonetheless, Augustine, or Augustinianism, dominated Western ecclesiology until the end of the sixteenth century and then continued more potent than any other thinker or system of thought, though the dominance was gone.

In the van of Augustine's disciples throughout the Middle Ages one finds the papacy. In fact, it is quite correct to say that he "develop(ed) the system of Cyprian and (laid) the foundations of papal supremacy,"[113] provided one recognizes two other data as well: that Augustine also developed doctrines of grace and biblical authority that seriously undermined that supremacy and that "papal supremacy" never came to be "papal absolutism" on Augustinian grounds.

The story of the rise of the see of Rome, and its bishop, to preeminence in the West defies simple explanation. The worst of all simplifications is to credit it to the ambitions of the papacy itself; only slightly less reprehensible (and inaccurate) is assigning it to either the Holy Spirit or the Enemy.

The papacy itself was relatively slow to make claims to primacy, but as early as the end of the first Christian century the Roman congregation was presumed to possess some sort of precedence among Christian churches. One hundred years later, nonpapal writers were granting to the bishop of Rome a certain primacy.[114] By Augustine's time, papal primacy was almost everywhere presumed but hardly defined. Only in Augustine's lifetime did the papacy itself launch any self-conscious efforts to propound its own case. Popes such as Damasus (336-384), Innocent I (402-417), Leo I (440-461), and Gelasius (472-496)—the latter two serving after Augustine's lifetime—sought to extend papal authority throughout the Church by appealing to precedent, tradition, and biblical reference.[115] But, except for Leo, their appeals were generally narrowed to applying the principle of petrine primacy to specific areas involving rejection of their administrative claims. Leo I does appeal to the theological responsibility of the successor to Peter in his famous *Tome,* but even he usually limits his concern for primacy to administrative claims.

And yet, behind the development of even the claims for administrative precedence lay Roman presuppositions about the nature of a *civitas,* a society or commonwealth, and its governance.[116] As we have seen, the famed practicality of the Roman was not sheer pragmatism. Practicality had to meet criteria established by metaphysical and axiological consideration. And so it was in the Church, except that the criteria were theological and spiritual; administrative authority might be the thing demanded, but it is demanded on the basis of responsibility that must be borne for the whole church by Peter's successor. This is seen very clearly in the first of the few letters we yet possess written by Pope Siricius (384-399):

> Given the nature of our office, we are not free to play dumb or to keep silent. Our zeal for the Christian faith ought to surpass that of anyone else. We carry the burdens of all of the heavy-laden. Or rather, the blessed Apostle Peter carries them through us. And in everything—such is our confidence—he protects and defends those who are heirs of his rulership.[117]

So, while the papacy can rightly be accused of laying the claims to supremacy with some motives less than noble, its fundamental purpose was to gain sufficient authority to carry out what it, and many others, saw to be its assigned responsibility—the pastoral care of the whole church.[118] This profoundly ethical view of administrative leadership parallels that of the best civic administrators among the Romans from the time of Cicero to that of Marcus Aurelius.

But in the Church, ethical perspective was held to be but part of the necessary basis. Almost always, the Church came soon or late to call for theological rationale. In the matter of papal authority, that rationale had been developed outside of the papacy itself, for the most part.[119] Now the papacy itself began to see its need for it. And in the person and pontificate of Gregory I (590-604), the bonding of the ethical and theological perspectives proceeded apace.

Gregory had not sought the papacy. He had seen it closely and knew its rigors—and its spiritual dangers. Largely by default, the pope had come to be the political and executive leader of the Roman *civitas*. And Gregory knew that this position could either beguile or coerce one into betrayal of his spiritual role.[120]

Yet, it did not occur to Gregory to see himself, once he was pope, as the wearer of two hats—an ecclesiastical and a civil one. He believed, as did his era generally, that Roman society, now almost completely Christian by baptism, was itself the Church, even the City of God. He lacked either the silliness or the optimism to believe that the *civitas Dei* had yet come to perfect manifestation, but he did believe that it was essentially present. Coupled with this was his commitment as the successor to Peter to care for the flock—a flock that was now virtually conterminous with the *civitas* itself. Care for the flock had become care for the society.[121]

So it was that Gregory warred and then negotiated with the Lombards to bring relief to Rome; so it was that he rearranged the economic administration of the city and became its personnel director. So it was that he preached every day, often in physical misery that caused him to be carried into the pulpit and propped up through the entire homily. So it was that he sent missionaries to England. Here was territory once both Roman and Christian, now but feebly either; territories that therefore fell within the responsibilities of the chief Roman and Christian pastor. So it was that unbidden, except by conscience and an inarticulate expectation on the part of western Europe, he entered into a great deal of correspondence with clergy everywhere directing them in the discharge of their responsibilities. And so it was, too, that he wrote books: Bible commentaries, homilies, a manual for bishops, and a collection of illustrations for pious living.

But most notable about this prelate—notable in his own day as in those since—was the fact that his immense productivity and personal prestige came to mind always in company with two other characteristics: his emphasis on the interior and contemplative life and his confident humility.[122] A millennium later, Gregory remained the ideal for any bishop but especially for a pope. Prelate after prelate was constrained to recognize the force of Gregory's character and his example, even if it meant abusing them by public counterfeit.

Gregory's concern for the interior life, expressed precisely while carrying forward enormous enterprises and attending to myriad details with patent skill, sanctified activity as well as meditation. And his evident sincerity in calling himself and acting like "the servant of the servants of God," transformed, at least for a while, the whole idea of ecclesiastical leadership.[123]

Gregory's mind was not original. His ecclesiology, where it surfaces, clearly depends upon Augustine's. Nonetheless, in his circumstances, Gregory does redirect Augustine's view.

Perhaps his most significant contribution, however, lies in his inattention to Augustine's distinction between visible and invisible church, especially as he worked with the by-then venerable notion that church meant clergy, clergy meant sacraments, and sacraments meant salvation.

Augustine had said that the earthly church is the earthly manifestation of the *civitas Dei,* but he said this precisely by way of his distinction between the two churches. He could not believe that the earthly church is a smaller, concentric society within the invisible church. Rather, he saw the invisible church, the *civitas Dei,* as the more select of the two. Election is what places one in that *civitas.* Baptism, the means of entry into the earthly, visible church, may or may not symbolize election.[124] The earthly or visible church is composed of both those elect to salvation and those elect to damnation. It is a *corpus mixtum.*

Gregory did not have to battle schismatics. His world presented no effective anti-Church. The last sociopolitically significant body of heretics or schismatics in the West, the Arian Visigoths, had been converted to Catholic Christianity in A.D. 589. It was no longer necessary to dwell upon such questions as the marks of the true church, its authority, or even the doctrine of election.

It was now assumed that all within the Church were elect to salvation. Gregory did not have to contemplate the difference between the *civitas Dei* and the *civitas terrenae.* The Church had converted his world. The *civitas terrenae* had disappeared as a socio-political entity. All was now *civitas Dei.*[125]

This transformed the idea of the Church as a *corpus mixtum.* Augustine had used the term to refer to the earthly church as a society of both evil and good persons—of those elected to damnation and those elected to salvation. Some of the baptized and some at the Lord's Table are nonetheless reprobate. Even at Font and Table, evil and good are present. But Gregory took *corpus mixtum* to mean that in the true church there are those more and less worthy.[126] He could concede it as only theoretically possible that a given baptism would not be efficacious.[127] For Augustine, baptism was the symbol of election, but it was not an absolutely certain symbol. For Gregory baptism was more than the symbol of election; it was the means of election.

But what of those among the baptized whose lives fall manifestly short of usual Christian practice, to say nothing of missing the mark of the ideal? Here, Gregory protected the efficacy of the sacraments by appealing to the disciplinary authority of the Church. And he did this by giving official sanction to three long-standing notions common among the grass-roots believers: the notion of meritorious good works, the notion that penance is essentially sacramental, and the notion of purgatory as a place where believers who died unfit for heaven could be made fit. These were means of repentance and correction for the believer.[128]

He also gave official sanction to the idea of the Mass as primarily an instrument of penance rather than primarily a celebration of Christ's once-for-all sacrifice and a celebration of Christian *koinonia*.[129] As an instrument of penance it is a uniquely clerical instrument. The laity are not so much members of the Church as its subjects.

Here were giant steps in the direction of an essentially penitential view of the nature and role of the Church. And here, too, were further steps in the direction of absolutely Church-centered, Church-dependent salvation. It was to Gregory, and to Augustine as his thoughts were translated by Gregory, that the medieval church owed its understanding of itself, especially its view of ecclesiastical leadership and its confidence in itself as the dispenser and guardian of Christian faith itself.

THE IDEA OF CHURCH EXPANDS

For a variety of reasons, modern scholars and lay persons have generally been betrayed into perceiving the medieval church in western Europe as a monolith with a pyramidal organization, autocratically directed by the Bishop of Rome. Its thought, too, including its ecclesiology, gets short schrift because nearly everyone is believed to have been thinking the same things from the same premises. Where there was debate, so many moderns believe, it was generally either obscure or piddling or both.

The facts belie this perspective. Medieval ecclesiastical practice and ecclesiology fairly roil with tensions and contradictory claims and ideas. Simply to cite extremes before examining the matter in closer detail, Boniface VIII (1294-1303) claimed absolute papal authority over the entire society while Marsilius of Padua (1270-1343), his younger contemporary, argued that the Church must submit to civil authority.[130] On the strictly theological side of medieval ecclesiology, the extremes were no less distant: Pope John VIII (872-882), or someone close to him, wrote that the Church, precisely defined, is the clergy; John Wycliffe (c. 1302-1384) defined the Church precisely as "the universe of the predestined faithful."[131] Marsilius, a lay person, and Wycliffe, a cleric, were condemned as heretics, to be sure, but this was clearly because their views were sufficiently attractive to become problematic to ecclesiastical administrators. In fact, both lived long lives, generally protected by civil authority though Wycliffe did suffer toward the end of his career.

To cite one more example of extreme views before returning to closer investigation: Gregory VII (1073-1085) said that a pope judges all others, including the emperor, whom he may depose, but can be judged by none;[132] the Council of Constance (1414-1418), an ecclesiastical convocation, held that a general council, like itself, could judge and even depose a pope.[133]

These citations should disabuse us of any notion that the Middle Ages endured a monolithic ecclesiology or uniform ecclesiastical administrative behavior. However, it is true to say that even in the face of the cited contradictions, and other tensions and contradictions not cited, the medieval papacy did develop a rather consistent view of the nature and role of the Church and of its role therein. That point of view never actualized itself fully, but it did influence profoundly the entire range of medieval socio-political development, ecclesiastical and civil. And that point of view was also the point of reference for all medieval ecclesiology, even for that which was most virulently anti-papal.

This being the case, attention should be given now to the details of the papal point of view as it developed after the watershed pontificate of Gregory I.

The Church in western Europe in the seventh and eighth centuries was a web of offices and jurisdictions whose relationships to one another were complex and often ill-defined. But for all of the legal confusion, one assumption governed the scene: the belief that there was and should be interrelation. And as the establishment of stable government slowly replaced the turmoils of Germanic migration, thoughtful ecclesiastics increasingly demanded that theoretical unity be replaced by unity in fact.

This had become an especially significant theme in the face of the corruption that had infected the Church in the West in the seventh and eighth centuries, and in some of the ninth. In these centuries, especially before the rise of the Carolingians, local church and local lord were thrown together for the sheer survival of either. The lord needed the order, especially the economic order, that the church could provide or at least inculcate; the church needed civil protection, physically and legally. Bargains were struck, usually in feudal style, which is to say that they took the form of contractural arrangements based on fairly clear understandings regarding the relative ranks of the contracting parties. In the majority of cases, the superior party to the contracts was understood to be the civil or temporal authority. A lord might eke out a living without the order and measure of prosperity that the Church could afford, but the Church—a parish, a monastery, an episcopal residence or benefice—could not withstand the troubles that would accrue should it attempt an unprotected, or even merely separate existence.

All of these, and some other factors as well, had created a church that could be bought—and often was. In those centuries, it sometimes seemed to be little more than the best managed among several economic sectors of many a local jurisdiction. Under Charlemagne, the Church had become an instrument of the temporal power in maintaining an orderly, moral society.

Of course, everyone knew that the Church saw to everyone's eternal salvation—in exchange for minimal attendance upon its rites, minimal fidelity to its precepts, and minimal contributions in goods, labor, or (rarely) money to its treasury. And, as crude as even ecclesiastical justice could be in those days, the Church often offered some shelter from oppression by rapacious local aristocracy. This was especially true before the reforms imposed by Charlemagne and again became true as the Church withstood the socio-political collapse of the Frankish "Empire."

Everyone believed that in faraway Rome sat the vicar of Christ, successor to St. Peter, master of the entire soteriological—and socio-economic—system. This belief, really not much more than theory in the mid-seventh century, was to become fact, increasingly, as the centuries passed—though not without protest regarding the form that that mastery could take.

The theory was there all along. But it took four hundred years before the long-standing claims of the papacy and the long-standing grievances of bishops and abbots against lay control (and corruption) of the Church intersected, giving the papacy practical reasons for advertising its claims. But first the papacy had to free itself from local politics.

The story is long and complex, but finally, and thanks to the German Holy Roman emperors, it can be said, it did free itself. Leo IX (1049-1054) made the papacy visible and brought it new respect by traveling incessantly across Europe, holding court with an even-handed justice;

Nicholas II (1059-1061) changed the rules for electing popes, placing the matter primarily in clerical hands; and he curtailed the rights of secular rulers over ecclesiastical matters as well.[134] Then came the greatest of all reforming popes, Gregory VII (1073-1085), a Benedictine monk who was not even a priest at the time he was elected pope. He turned his reforming zeal in two directions: the raising of the moral and educational level of the clergy and the freeing of the Church from civil control.

To carry his program forward, Gregory simply put the long-held, and long-granted, papal claims to priority and primacy in the simplest practical terms. For example: everyone granted the superiority or priority of the spiritual over the secular; Gregory translated that into the superiority or priority of the pope over any civil ruler, even over the emperor. In fact, he could even release people from allegiance to unjust rulers. Everyone granted that the Holy Spirit would keep the Church from erring and everyone granted that the Church of Rome was under the special solicitude of the Spirit; Gregory translated that into the infallibility of the Roman church, though he said nothing of the infallibility of its bishop. Everyone granted the primacy of Peter among the Apostles and granted that the Bishop of Rome was Peter's successor; Gregory translated that into absolute administrative control of the Church by the papacy.[135]

By Gregory's time, however difficult (and finally impossible) it would prove to be to put these practical "translations" into daily operation, there had accumulated a vast body of legal decisions supporting them. No like body of law existed supporting, or even defining, either temporal authority or the authority of ecclesiastics in lesser posts.[136] Further, from this period and for another century, there blossomed a veritable industry bent on cataloging and interpreting that vast body of ecclesiastical decisions, even harmonizing those that seemed contradictory or inconsistent. And for the most part that industry and the papacy supported each other.[137] To most medieval thinkers, the contrast between the Roman orderliness of the papacy and its legal tradition and the haphazard, consuetudinary development of the various temporal governments with their legal and administrative traditionless-ness seemed only to testify to the validity of papal claims to primacy over even the secular realm.

What is more, it occurred to no one to think of the spiritual and secular as essentially separate. They were two sides of one coin, the Christian commonwealth of western Europe. True, the English had their king, the French theirs, and so forth, but the idea of nation wasn't born yet. These kings saw themselves as rulers over parts of a larger whole—the *corpus Christianum*. And the pope, according to papal theory, being directly responsible for the whole, was a unique sort of universal prince. The Church was the superior institution because of its catholicity.[138]

But all of this came clattering down in the fourteenth century. At the beginning of that century, Boniface VIII (1294-1303) made the tactical error of advocating the practical application of the most exalted claims for the papacy to issues raised by a rising nationalism. His bull, *Unam Sanctam* (1302), sounded all of the grand papal chords at precisely that moment in which much of western Europe, especially France, had decided to march to another sort of music. Boniface reviewed the ancient dogmas; the Church is the only way to salvation and it is one and the same Church everywhere (implying that it then supercedes "nation" as a focus of loyalty); the head of the Church is Christ, whose vicar is Peter, whose successor is the pope; the command of Christ to Peter was "feed my sheep" (John 21:16), and, says Boniface, that means *all* of the sheep—the whole church; further, Peter's two swords represent the temporal and the spiritual power—Peter holds both of them (Luke 22:38); and when Jesus says, "Sheath your sword" and Peter does so (John 18:11), it shows that the Church, in Peter, on command from Christ, has power over both of them.

Then, too, Boniface continues, Paul (Rom. 13:1-2) says that all things are ordained by God—ordained meaing "set in order." And since we know that the universe is hierarchically arranged and higher gives lower its meaning and order, and since we know that the spiritual is higher than the temporal, we must admit that the spiritual judges the temporal and governs it. Should the temporal resist spiritual governing, it resists the very will of God and the very order of the universe. For salvation's sake, all must submit to the spiritual authority, whose earthly apex is Peter and his successors, the bishops of Rome.[139]

The temporal powers were not slow to respond and by 1309, the French had managed to make the papacy once again dependent upon the temporal power, though in its outward appearance it was richer and more powerful than ever.

But now we must go back to the period of Gregory VII and show how the papal ecclesiology was challenged even within the ecclesiastical hierarchy.

No medieval thinker doubted the spiritual primacy of the bishop of Rome over the Church. The debates raged over what the term *spiritual* included and over the papacy's claim that spiritual primacy implies temporal primacy. The most explicit early rejection of the ideas represented in the *Dictatus Papae* of Gregory VII came from York, England, in about A.D. 1100. This document, the *Norman Anonymous,* said that papal primacy was a human invention that arose from the simple socio-political fact that Rome had been the capital of the world. The real Mother-Church is Jerusalem. The claim that belief in the primacy of the Bishop of Rome is necessary for salvation is untenable. All bishops are vicars of Christ and in spiritual matters none of them is to be judged by anyone else. On the other hand, bishops and clergy are not in any way the whole church. The Church is "the Christian populus," "the congregation of faithful Christians living together within God's house, united in faith, hope, and love." The only head of the Church is Christ. Furthermore, temporal kings are instituted by God and are his vicars. Their rule derives from him, especially as it is seen in the divine kingship of Christ, the Son. Priesthood is not an institution grounded in the divine character of Christ, but in his earthly humiliation. He is priest precisely because he became human. And as human priest, he was subject to kings and temporal authority. So should it be with priests, including bishops. Insofar as clerics have any temporal authority, they hold it as a trust from temporal rulers.[140]

The *Norman Anonymous* is the only theologically articulated direct response to papal claims from the temporal side. But there were other responses, practical and theoretical. In fact, controversy over the precise nature of ecclesiastical authority and its relationship to temporal authority raged for a half century, from the pontificate of Gregory VII to the Concordat of Worms in 1122, and then merely bubbled through the pontificate of Innocent III (1198-1216); it regained its old fury through much of the thirteenth century, raging again in the reign of Boniface VIII. Then it generally only simmered, with occasional moments of boil, from 1309 to 1903. It now lies largely dormant.

Of the contemporaries of the *Norman Anonymous,* the most thoughtful and effective inside critic of papal claims was the saintly Bernard of Clairvaux (1090-1153). He granted that the papacy had what had come to be called the *plenitudo potestatis,* the fullness of power.[141] But, he argued, the Church is the Church of God, and that means that it is the church of love itself.[142] When it concerns itself with honor and dignity, it is all too likely to take its power and its authority too seriously. They become bonds, chains, and the Church is unfree.[143] The Church's true honor and dignity lie in its status as Spouse of Christ, in the love which it has from him and gives to him. The exercise of this love is what should occupy the papacy. It should rise preeminent in love.[144] This would mean it would exercise a judicious curtailment of its own admitted power and authority. The pope should not think it necessary to do all that he could, by right, do.[145] He should take pains to show that he is the successor of Peter, not Constantine.

Underlying this view of the papacy is Bernard's concern that institution and individual live in mutual love and spiritual commitment. Both the believer and the Church are the spouse of Christ.[146] Ecclesiastical claims to honor, dignity, primacy, or whatever else must not interfere with the pure mystical union of the believer and of the whole Church with Christ, the Bridegroom.[147] On the other hand, this union is not the product of contemplation alone. It is a union born of both "Mary and Martha." And it will be maintained by both contemplative and active love.[148] For this, Bernard himself was to become the most compelling model.

Bernard did not see that the presuppositions of his concern with spirituality actually undermined the institutional church as it was in his day. And his own ceaseless activity on behalf of that institution kept others from seeing it as well. For him, the authority and power of the Church are instrumental; for Gregory VII and subsequent popes, they were essential. For Bernard, the clergy are servants of the mystical union between Christ and his Church, the pope being the chief servant; for most persons in his time, the clergy were the Church itself, the pope being the summation of the clergy and therefore of the Church.

Only in the sixteenth century would Bernard's

presuppositions take practical hold or even gain articulation. But from time to time, debate over the nature of authority in the Church did bring one or the other of them into play.

Among the less bizarre, but still schismatic forms of criticism of papal claims were those motivating the Albigensians and Waldensians. Both groups have commonly been claimed as forerunners of Protestantism, but it is a claim untenable in the case of the Albigensians.[149] The Albigensians, probably simply ascetics critical of ecclesiastical worldliness in origin, had become dualists by the end of the twelfth century. There are two churches, they said. Rome and its subjects, created by Satan; and their own community, founded by Christ. Within the good church, their own, there were two sorts of adherents: the perfect and the believers. Perfection was primarily a matter of denying oneself of anything physical, insofar as it were possible, for matter was regarded as evil.[150] The Waldensians' principle concern was for a renewal of the idea of the Church as a communion of saints. They reinstituted the notion of visible and invisible church in the form that Augustine had developed it: an invisible church of the elect known only to God, and a visible church that participates in the invisible more or less. They differed from Augustine in assuming that the visible church is more likely not to be within the invisible than to be. And they rejected as well the venerable notion that the Church defines the Scriptures, preaching, and the sacraments and exercises them as properties owned, as it were, by the Church. Rather, said they, the Church is defined by the Bible, preaching, and the sacraments.[151]

By the mid-thirteenth century, persons in several quarters of the Church were openly contesting the practical applications of papal supremacy that were being suggested in one case and another.

Generally speaking, the great scholars of the thirteenth

century accepted the main lines of Augustinian ecclesiology; the Church is the nuptial body of Christ, and while it must be admitted that there is a Church whose boundaries extend beyond that of the visible earthly institution, and while it must also be admitted that not all within the visible earthly institution are true believers, generally speaking, the visible church is the true church and is the kingdom of God; the Church is a mixed body (here, there was some revival of Augustine's understanding of "mixed" as Christian and non-Christian, but the general view was that of Gregory I that "mixed" means "good" and "bad" Christians); and the Church is the "congregation of the faithful."[152]

The thirteenth-century scholars also clung fairly closely to Augustine's concept of the marks of the Church—holiness, catholicity, apostolicity, and unity—though they did tend to sharpen the definition of each mark along lines taught them by Aristotelian logic. Holiness now referred not only to the holiness of Christ, whose Body the Church is, but also to the actual sanctification of believers. The Church was sacramentally the source of the sanctifying process.[153] Catholicity, primarily a geographical concept for Augustine, was now seen to include heaven and purgatory and to include as well all time, from Abel to the Second Coming.[154] Apostolicity, understood by Augustine primarily in terms of some sort of evangelical succession that may or may not include bishops, was anchored in Peter and the See of Rome, which had stood doctrinally steadfast while all other apostolic congregations had suffered lapses.[155] And the concept of unity was sharpened, usually along the lines of defining it in terms of unity of faith (meaning dogma), hope, and charity.[156]

On the question of the nature of the Church, especially as it had to do with the supremacy of the papacy, thirteenth-century scholars divided, though they all held some assumptions in common. They all believed that the spiritual and temporal realms were two parts of a single society. They all believed that the one society was a Christian commonwealth holding precedence over either ecclesiastical entities such as dioceses or political entities such as kingdoms. They all believed that the Church was the soul of that commonwealth. And they all believed that the Bishop of Rome directed the whole church. But these assumptions were variously explicated and beyond them lay a jungle of conflicting opinion, often devoutly defended.[157]

Continuing intense concern for reform of the Church, papal insistence on directing any such reform, growing national consciousness, new awareness of long histories of legal precedent, and a growing interest in representative government in Church and nation spurred the growth of that jungle. As the papacy worked to develop a new corporate image and personality as absolute lord of all Christendom, temporal authorities spurred legal experts to enlarge the base of their own power—often at the expense of the Church.

Each side claimed absolute fidelity to the tradition of societal unity and blamed the other for any and all societal imperfection; each called for thorough-going reform under its own direction.

The papacy had, to this point, been inconsistent in action but not in aim. And the reason for its inconsistency was its attempt to define the Church in two mutually incompatible ways. In its struggles with the temporal powers, and even in struggling with some of the more powerful bishops, it had claimed authority over the whole of Christian society by defining the Church as the encompassing social entity and then arguing that Peter and his successors had responsibility to rule the Church. This entailed the use of definitions referring to the Church as the faithful people or the congregation of the faithful or some such. But in its attempt to regain control of all ecclesiastical appointments, it had argued that temporal authorities had no right to invest anyone with church office precisely because they are temporal authorities, not spiritual. That is to say, they are not the Church. So, an ambiguity in defining *church* that pervaded canon law and tradition was turned to a contradiction that could not be tolerated in a society that was asking Aristotle to teach it to reason and classify.

The published pretensions of Boniface VIII probably did as much as any single thing could to animate open discussion of the nature of the Church vis-a-vis the nature of the papacy. The first rejoinder came from John of Paris—a calm, reasoned tract titled *On Regal and Papal Power*.[158]

John believes that the ultimate authority of the Church belongs to the Christian people as a whole, for they constitute the body of Christ.[159] Further, Christ, not Peter or the pope, is the head of the Church.[160] The pope, somehow elected by the whole Christian populace, is the principle servant of the Church, not its sovereign.[161] The pope dispenses the authority of the Church, directing the penitential and sacramental life, and he dispenses the resources of the Church in maintaining right faith and good practice. But in no way is he the owner of the Church's authority and resources. They are not his possession; they belong to the Church defined as the entire Christian people.[162] And the people, through councils, have the right and the responsibility to keep the pope accountable. Should he prove either doctrinally or administratively inept, a council may go so far as to depose him.[163] The pope does have God-given powers, but they are granted through the Christian people and are instrumental, not ends in themselves.[164]

John wrote in 1302-03. Six years later, the papacy moved to Avignon, technically not French but dominated by France. From here, the papacy spoke more calmly than it had in the person of Boniface, but it did not intend to mute his claims. Its problems were now different, however; and the way in which it made its claims while playing political games only frustrated those who would advocate absolute papal supremacy from an idealistic base and angered those who wanted a papacy spiritually uncompromised no matter what its authority.

One of the angriest responses came from Dante, who wrote his *De Monarchia (On Rulership)* between 1309 and 1317, apparently. His point was that God had given certain kinds of power to the papacy and other kinds to the temporal authority—had given them directly—and that the two authorities should work in harmony for the happiness and peace of society. The temporal ruler was to use his power to make temporal life good, peaceful, and happy. The spiritual power was to be used to bring people to eternal life. Of course, eternal life is more important than temporal and it has certain ramifications for the temporal that are the pope's responsibility; but even at that, there is no call for anything like the interference that the papacy habitually exercises in the name of primacy and it certainly gives no room for papal self-centeredness.[165] Cooperation between the temporal and spiritual powers can bring peace and happiness in this life and the next.[166]

Marsilius of Padua and John of Jandun, the former serving as rector of the University of Paris, further stung the papacy and afforded strong support for the superior authority of the temporal power in their book *Defender of Peace,* written in 1324. There can be but one authority in an orderly society, they said. And that is the people or a prince chosen by them. This "legislator," whether a group or an individual, has jurisdiction over all individuals or groups within its boundaries, and over their possessions as well. This jurisdiction applies to both clergy and laity, and it includes the conferring or taking away of certain ecclesiastical offices such as episcopacy.

In the Church itself, supreme authority belongs, again,

to the whole people of God, represented in a general council. Such a council may be convened only by the temporal ruler, who also chooses its membership: bishops, priests, and laity. It has responsibility for every aspect of the internal life of the Church: biblical interpretation, doctrinal interpretation, ritual, establishment of new sees and archdioceses, canonization, discipline, and sanctions of teachings and activities contrary to divine law.[167]

As to the primacy of the papacy, Marsilius denies it. He writes, "All bishops derived their authority in equal measure immediately from Christ, and it cannot be proved from the divine law that one bishop should be over or under another in temporal or in spiritual matters."[168]

Here was a call for radical rearrangement of the structures of power in Europe. And yet, it was but a rearrangement. It remained for William of Occam and John Wycliffe to call for the most revolutionary reform of all, tying together both structure and theology.

William, an English Franciscan working under the patronage of the Bavarian would-be Holy Roman emperor, Ludwig, addressed the problem of the nature of the Church and its reform in several of his works, most notably in his *On the Power of Emperors and Pontifs,* written in 1346-47. With genuine Franciscan revulsion, he scored the venality of the papacy precisely at a moment in which the curia, desperately needing funds, had established a complex system of taxation to extract them. As William saw it, the pope was walking ever farther away from the gospel, which, William believed, called all believers, but especially ecclesiastical leadership, to evangelical poverty.

As William saw it, the papacy was using its claims to temporal authority only to gain more temporal authority, thereby making Christianity a religion of bondage to certain human beings and human systems when the law of the gospel is a law of liberty and of the love of people through love of Christ.[169]

William denies that the papacy has either temporal or spiritual authority in the way in which it claims to have it. Citing such passages as Luke 22:25, he insists that Christ gave no such plenitude of power to Peter as the papacy claimed in the temporal arena. Further, plentitude of spiritual power is to be denied the papacy, for that would be power to burden the Church—as has already been demonstrated. It would result in the imposition of a burden greater than that of the old law, an imposition against which Peter himself spoke (Acts 15:10).[170]

William defines the Church as "the whole congregation of the faithful living this mortal life at a given time." It is "a community of palpable persons."[171]

Here, William's nominalism comes into play, of course. And it sets at naught any pleas to primacy that depend primarily upon historical succession or upon abstractions such as "the power of the keys." Instead, it places a premium upon actual practice, current practice, which should be a matter of demonstrating the "law of the Gospel." The current papacy gives the lie to all of its own claims to spiritual primacy because it fails to practice evangelical poverty.[172]

"Church" is not limited to those practicing evangelical poverty, for there are the ignorant and the immature among the baptized and faithful. And William seems to stop far short of suggesting that the papacy is outside the true church. He only rejects its claims to primacy, and he rejects them because they have nothing positive to do with the gospel.

William believed that the Church has the right to elect a representative body, a council, that would have authority to correct,or even to depose a pope; or it may elect a pope if the cardinals cannot do so. Ordinarily, a council would be convoked by the pope and convened by him, but in these tasks he would serve as executive officer, not as master. Further, such a council must be truly representative—clergy, laity, rulers, subjects, men and women.

William made his case for universal representation in
the council from Scripture. And he went on to argue that
one of the characteristics of the Church best preserved by
universal representation is infallibility. The truth could
conceivably perish from among even the highest clergy—a
fear based upon his reading of the situation. It could perish
from among Christian males. But neither of these groups
constitutes the whole church; each is a part of the Church.
None is the whole of it and none is essentially superior or
inferior to the others in spiritual capacity or insight. So
conceivably, truth, which cannot perish entirely from the
Church, could survive elsewhere than in the clergy or the
male constituency—perhaps among the women and children.[173] Only the spiritual rights and privileges directly
associated with the ordering and celebration of the mysteries are reserved to the clergy.

William of Occam died about 1349, still seeking reconciliation with the Church, which had excommunicated him in
1328. About a quarter-century after his death, a mature
Oxford scholar named John Wycliffe, a man with very
highly placed friends, delivered a series of lectures at the
university under the title "On Divine Lordship." His
thesis was somewhat radical but not really daring: any
proper human authority is a gift of divine grace and is thus
neither permanent nor unlimited. His conclusion was that
spiritual lords ought to recognize that their lordship is
really only stewardship of a divine gift.[174]

Wycliffe followed this series with one titled "On Civil
Lordship," carrying on some of the themes and proposi-
tions earlier adumbrated. To his previous observation that
all lordship is based upon grace, he now added his belief
that any power, whether civil or ecclesiastical, depends for
its legitimacy upon the state of grace of its holder. A
pauper in grace has more moral right to lordship than does
an immoral pope or king, he says. Yet, the unrighteous are

not to be overthrown for that reason. They do hold their offices "naturally."

An unrighteous or unworthy civil ruler, especially, must not be overthrown simply because of that unrighteousness. On the other hand, an unworthy or unrighteous cleric should be deposed. And where the Church is too corrupt to do it, civil authority should act. In fact, said Wycliffe, God has had to give the secular arm precisely that sort of lordship over the Church "in these times."[175]

Wycliffe now picked up on a theme of William of Occam: the heart of the Gospel is evangelical poverty. Clergy should not own anything, and their lordship should be expressed in servanthood, not in the dominion that they now exercise.[176] Wycliffe had clearly "gone radical."

In 1377, Gregory XI issued orders for Wycliffe's arrest and promulgated five bulls against him. But Wycliffe's friends kept him free.

In 1378, Wycliffe produced three major works: *On Pastoral Duty, On the Truth of Sacred Scripture,* and *On the Church.* In the first named, he reminded the clergy that it was their responsibility to cleanse the Church of moral stain. The means would be the practice of evangelical poverty, and where the stain remained because of the presence of an unworthy cleric, the people were to withdraw.[177] In *On the Truth of Sacred Scripture,* Wycliffe declared the Bible to be absolutely authoritative in matters of faith and practice and the sufficient guide in all matters, secular or ecclesiastical. Tradition, conciliar declaration, papal decree, and all other classes of doctrinal exposition must be tested against the Bible, for it is the supreme instrument of divine revelation.[178]

On the Church is the work most important to this essay. Here, Wycliffe defined the Church as "the universe of the predestined faithful."[179] This true church is invisible and all who are in it will be saved—something that cannot be said of all in the visible church. Not even possession of the highest ecclesiastical post in the visible church guarantees membership in the invisible. There are no *ex officio* memberships in the church of the predestined faithful.[180] The most that a pope, as pope, can claim is headship of the Roman portion of the visible church.[181]

There is no infallible way, said Wycliffe, to determine whether one is or is not a member of the true, invisible church. But a pious life, obedient to the will of God, is at least presumptive evidence of election to salvation. And an impious life, flouting the known will of God, is presumptive evidence of election to reprobation.[182] Both sorts of people are members of the visible church.[183]

In 1379, Wycliffe took up the question of papal authority in *On the Power of the Pope*. Primacy is a matter of character, not of office, he said. And character depends upon the gracious work of the Holy Spirit. Peter was given primacy because he loved Christ deeply and possessed especially suitable personal qualities. Election to the papacy does not confer these, nor does possession of Peter's chair make one a true successor to Peter. True Petrine succession depends upon one's possession of Peter's devotion to Christ, his faith, and his love.[184]

But more important than imitating Peter is the imitation of Christ. The pope who fails to follow Christ in simplicity and in evangelical poverty is Antichrist.[185]

Wycliffe only barely escaped excommunication. His idiom was clearly inflammatory and his legacy was sectarianism and, eventually, this caused schism. But he was to be vindicated, too. What he had said about the corruption of the Church and its causes came to public view even before he died (1384): there were two claimants to Peter's see, both of them experts in the lordly use of power and neither of them interested in the least in evangelical poverty except perhaps to quash it where it stood to rebuke them. Amid such corruption, the idea of the true church as the universe of the predestined faithful afforded no small comfort. But it could not stand as the sole response.

The Idea of Church Tested

Seldom has Christianity suffered as it did in the tortures of the Great Schism (1378-1449).[186] The unthinkable took on flesh and blood as the Church, the very model and preacher of unity among people across time and space, and the bond of unity between God and humankind, time and eternity, fell into disunity and parochialism. The papacy, focus of Christian unity in the West, actually promoted division. For nearly forty years (1378-1417) there were, simultaneously, two and even three popes; each with a retinue of lawyers, bureaucrats, sycophants, and self-seekers; each of them appointing bishops and other officials; each of them seeking to collect taxes and other funds to further their ends; each of them encouraging massive building programs; each of them directing a system of ecclesiastical discipline; and each of them developing systems of diplomats and other agents suitable to their plans and intrigues in games of high-stakes power politics with the great nobles of Europe.

From 1417 to 1424, there was again but one pope, but in the latter year schism appeared again and did not end until 1429. Then, from 1439 to 1449, Europe suffered the last gasp of the Great Schism: again there were two popes, two papal courts, and all the rest of it. But this time, thanks to some judicious changes of mind, and perhaps heart, by some leading advocates of the conciliar point of view, the council of Basle, assembled at Lausanne, submitted to Pope Nicholas V and an era ended.

The whole story of the Great Schism is too complex to review here, and some of it is beside the point of this essay. But significant ecclesiological notions having long-lasting effects were advanced in that period. The story of Western ecclesiology cannot even be summarized without them. So we must give them due attention.

It must be remembered that the Great Schism took place

in an age that had a profound passion for unity. Paradoxically, in fact, the Great Schism expresses that passion, albeit perversely. It should also be remembered that the conciliar side—that is, those parties believing that ultimate authority in the church rests with councils—had no monopoly on righteousness. The conciliarists were no less obstructing of truth and justice on occasion than the papalists. Protestants especially tend not to see this.

It was the question of reform that created the Great Schism and it was the question of reform that kept it in existence. It was obvious to many observers of the Avignonese papacy that until the Bishop of Rome resumed ruling the church from Rome there could be little or no reform. In Avignon, matters of finance and political alliance, and intrigue, had so preoccupied the papacy that its essentially spiritual character and responsibilities were neglected. And, as was the pope, so were his minions. Fourteenth-century bishops were like nothing so much as earthly princes. Their retinues were like nothing so much as temporal courts. The complaints of such persons as William of Occam and John Wycliffe were not made with references to obscure, unusual cases of petty corruptions. One did not have to travel far, if at all, to see first-hand precisely what they were complaining against.

Many believed that reform could only come, or at least best come, from the top down and that the first practical step to be taken would be removal of the Bishop of Rome to Rome. There, it was believed, he would be free of the temptation and the necessity of compromise with the temporal power.

Pope Gregory XI (1370-78) did go back to Rome, importuned directly by Catherine of Siena and indirectly by all but the French nobility. He went back and promptly died, necessitating the election of a new pope. The new pope was styled Urban VI (1378-89). He was Roman—and he also proved to be tactless, cruel, and viciously anti-French in an unconscionably short time. This precipitated the election by the pro-French cardinals of yet another Frenchman, who took the ironic title Clement VII and reigned in Avignon, claiming to be the true successor to Gregory XI.

So now there were Urban and Clement, each claiming to be true pope, and each spending much of his time seeking to undermine the claims and work of the other. Generally, Urban could count on the allegiance of England, Scaninavia, most of Germany, and north and central Italy. Clement had the loyalty of Scotland, Ireland, the Low Countries, France, and the various domains of the Iberian peninsula.

To the popes, and to their proponents, the obvious solution to the disunity was union on the given pope's terms. Meanwhile, intrigue, diplomatic maneuver, and, if necessary, war would serve to keep the claims of either one credible. To both papacies, reform meant only the end of schism and the reinstitution of full papal control. Others, especially many in the rising universities who were acquainted with the interconnections of law, theology, and social theory, advocated the calling of a general council to end schism and to institute reform of the entire ecclesiastical system. These people were seldom in agreement as to what was needed by way of reform, let alone agreeing on how to achieve it. But they did agree that schism was at least unacceptable and that the first step toward reform and reunion would be a general council.

So the University of Paris, by unanimous decision of its four faculties in May 1381, issued the first serious call for a general council to resolve the Great Schism. Later that year, Henry of Langenstein (1325-97), appealing to earlier church practice and noting the resolution of the university, suggested that while a council should convene, it should do so only after anyone "conscious of being a party" to the schism or its causes had, through penance, reconciled himself to God. Henry said that this process should be accompanied by the prayers and fastings of the whole church for divine mercy. Only after these things were accomplished, said Henry, should the temporal rulers—he specifies no one in particular—convene a council. But they should do it quickly.[187]

Henry seems to have assumed the general appropriateness of distinguishing between the universal church, defined as the congregation of the faithful, and the Church defined hierarchically (especially the Roman church constituted by the pope and the cardinals). He is in general agreement with John of Paris, William of Occam, and Marsilius of Padua that the universal church, represented in council, holds the plenitude of ecclesiastical power, indivisibly and inalienably. A council may bind the pope himself by its resolutions, may sit in judgment upon him, and may even depose him and give him over to the secular arm for punishment.[188]

The idea that the universal church holds the plenitude of spiritual power gained no new substance beyond this point in the conciliar epoch. But it did come to be refined and even applied briefly. Its principle advocates were Peter d'Ailly (1350-1420), chancellor of the University of Paris, bishop of Cambrai and cardinal; Jean Gerson (Jean Charlier de Gerson) (1363-1429), successor to d'Ailly as chancellor at Paris; and, later, Nicholas of Cusa (1401-1464), who later supported the papal cause and was bishop of Brixen and cardinal.

These, and a large circle of supporters, generally held that the pope did indeed have the right, and the responsibility, to exercise the plenitude of spiritual power but only as an executive officer, for the power itself is not his. It belongs to the general council, which may itself exercise it if it so chooses. The pope may exercise it only mediately.[189]

Further, the pope is answerable to the general council for his stewardship of that power. In fact, the council may overrule him, correct his abuses, judge him, depose him, and even inflict corporal punishment upon him.[190] Gerson's reasoning is instructive here: any element of Christ's mandate of power to the Church (e.g., the Petrine mandates in Matthew 16:17-19 and John 21, or the more general one in Matthew 28:18-20) must be seen in three ways. Considered abstractly and in its elemental simplicity, any element of the mandated spiritual power belongs to the Church, of which the pope is only a part. Considered in terms of the subject (person or office) in which the power may reside, it must be understood that it is resident there for a given time only. And, should the need arise, the terms under which the power is resident can be altered or the power taken away. This holds true even in the case of the office of the pope. Considered in terms of its exercise and use, the mandated spiritual power is alloted among various offices and organs of the Church according to the institution's constitution. That is to say, there is a practical division of that power. The pope, acting as the council's executive office, certainly does hold authority to distribute and to direct that division of power, so that in that sense he actually does hold it in plentitude—along with the council. In this way, the pope does hold the highest degree of ecclesiastical power, but it is his only so long as he recognizes that in assigning it he is assigning it from the council and assigning it with its due measure of fullness to the lower offices.[191]

Gerson and d'Ailly both recognized the tactical problem involved in advocating the superior authority of a general council. Even if it were to meet as frequently as the Council of Constance ordered (every ten years, normally), it would still run the risk of being outmaneuvered by those holding the reins day in and day out. Then, too, it would ordinarily be heavily burdened with procedural matters even before it got to the mountain of issues that had accumulated over the decade. So they advocated that the College of Cardinals be made a sort of executive review and policy committee, meeting regularly in the interim.

Philosophically, this would be the kind of government thought best by their teacher, Aristotle—a "mixed constitution" involving all three basic political styles, monarchy (papacy), aristocracy (the cardinals), and democracy (the council representing the whole church).[192]

What may surprise us nowadays is Gerson's insistence that there had to be a monarchical papacy. He believed that God had given the Church its monarchical constitution and that not even a general council had a right to undo it.[193] This, he said, is the difference between the constitution of the Church and the constitutions of temporal societies: the latter may indeed be monarchical, but their monarchies are not in themselves divinely mandated.[194]

The other side, the pro-papal proponents, had much to say during the Great Schism and its conciliar aftermath, too, though it was generally not represented in force at the councils themselves.

As we have already seen, the idea that the papacy holds absolute spiritual supremacy in the Church was first forwarded in a cogent and fairly complete form by Gregory VII. But Innocent III (1198-1216) was the first to use the phrase *plenitudo ecclesiasticae potestatis* to indicate that God had vested the fullness of ecclesiastical power in the pope and that from that fullness all other ecclesiastical power flows and is maintained.[195] The much more secular-minded Innocent IV (1243-54) seconded him and gave the claim a powerful push into the reaches of temporal jurisdiction as well.[196] On the theological side, Thomas Aquinas had advocated papal plenitude of power as it applied to the pope's office as teacher of the Church and as it applied to him as the person to call councils and set their agendas. Thomas also threw some confusion into the matter. To these two clear cases of advocacy, he adds a third, and troublesome one: he quite clearly does not support papal claims to supreme temporal authority but does appear to be making some sort of exception where "secular power is joined to spiritual power." Read literally, the passage appears to say only that the pope holds both temporal and spiritual primacy where he is the actual temporal lord, as in the Papal States. But read as a statement of systematic theology, with a certain propositional order understood, it advocates absolute papal supremacy.[197] The three instances added together tended to lead later scholars to align Thomas with the papal party.

Much clearer in its advocacy of papal *plentitudo potestatis* is the line from Aegidius Romanus (1247-1315)[198] through Petrus Paludanus (fl. 1329),[199] Augustinus Triumphus de Ancona (1243-1328),[200] and Alvarius Pelagius (fl. 1330s),[201] to Juan Torquemada (d. 1468)[202] and Petrus a Monte (d. 1457).[203] Its point is quite clearly made by Alvarius: the authority of the papacy is exceptionless, all-embracing, the basis of all power, sovereign, boundless, and immediate. Its only limitations, says Augustinus Triumphus, mitigating the hyperbole of Alvarius, are those imposed by divine law, natural law, the articles of faith, and the "new law of the sacraments." The pope's authority is never absolute, but it is pervasive.[204]

It is very useful here to take a closer look at Juan Torquemada, for unlike most supporters of papal supremacy, including even his contemporary, Petrus a Monte, Torquemada's point of view takes in the very real papal corruption that had helped to create the issues that pressed the Church so hard in the fifteenth century. He is especially alert to the more extravagant claims made for either the conciliarist or the papal side and the history of the struggle between the parties.

Torquemada grounds his ecclesiology in Augustine: salvation has to do with faith in Christ, not faith in the

Church; nonetheless, the Church is Christ's, and outside of it there is no salvation.[205] Not all who are baptized and within the Church are saved. Only those are saved who are united to Christ by the indwelling presence of the Holy Spirit. Yet, baptism and fidelity to the Church and her teaching are strong evidences, even if not conclusive, that the Spirit does dwell within. The community of those within whom the Spirit dwells, the true church, is one, holy, catholic, and apostolic, as Augustine had suggested, said Torquemada. But Torquemada seems to accept the modifications of those marks made by Gregory I, with the added conviction that they are not simply descriptive but are evaluative as well; i.e. they distinguish true church from false.[206]

To this point, most of the conciliarists agreed with Torquemada. But he parts company with them—at least with those in Gerson's train—with his notion of the origin of the hierarchical structure of the Church. Like Gerson, he argues that God has given the Church a monarchical constitution, but he goes on to tie this divinely given constitution to the specific orders of the clergy—deacon, priest, and bishop—and to accept the distinction in character between clergy and laity.[207]

Torquemada then says that the pope is head of the Church and the bond of its unity not because a council has given him authority but because of divine appointment.[208] The pope is the vicar of Christ with authority directly from Christ because he is the true successor to Peter, prince of the apostles by Christ's own appointment.[209] And, these things being so, all ecclesiastical jurisdiction derives from the *plenitudo potestatis* of the pope.[210]

Nonetheless, Torquemada repudiates the notion of papal absolutism. Faith in Christ, not adherence to the bishop of Rome, remains the substance of the Christian faith. The rock upon which the Church is founded is faith in Christ, not the person of Peter.[211] Should a pope forsake Christ, he would be heretical; and in forsaking Christ, he would no longer be a member of the true church, let alone its visible head. Yet, a council does not depose even such a pope. It simply anounces that God does not adjudge him pope any longer and it makes God's judgment effective in the Church.[212]

Torquemada believes that other than when it exercises this awful function, a council is largely an advisory committee to the papacy and is quite unnecessary to the *esse* of the Church. In fact, says Torquemada, the pope can even dispense with its advisory role as long as he has about him persons learned in divine law and in the administration of the Church.[213]

Torquemada died in 1468, by which time the papacy had regained its grip upon the Church. This was all the more true by the time his book was published in 1489. The book, titled *Summa contra ecclesie et primatus apostoli Petri adversarios*, became a manual for upholders of papal supremacy for the next four hundred years and more. Its chief strength lay in the fact that its advocacy of papal supremacy did not totally demolish the conciliarists' critiques of the Church or seek completely to silence their insistence that the Church retain the convening of councils for the ongoing process of reformation. It did help the papacy to regain control of the councils themselves.

From this side of the events, it appears to offer very hollow concessions. But, in fact, Torquemada had gone farther toward conciliation than any previous apologists for the papal position had done. Truth to tell, by the time of his death, the papacy had so far regained control, and the conciliarist party had fallen into such inprincipled ways that concessions from the papal side could be void of political motives.

In fact, so seriously decayed had the conciliarist program become that one of its most effective advocates took up the papal cause. This was Nicholas of Cusa, mystic, activist, scholar, reformer, bishop and cardinal, who was perhaps the keenest intellect in western Christianity in the fifteenth century.

Nicholas attended the Council of Basle in 1432, arguing on the conciliarist side. His *De concordantia Catholica* was written for the council itself, partly as a plea for a proconciliarist candidate for the archepiscopate of Trier. So effective was his work at the council that he soon became a leader of the anti-papal party and actually served on the deputation that accused Pope Eugenius IV of contumacy.

The council decided against his candidate for the see at Trier, largely with connivance from some temporizing conciliarists. The cynicism and opportunism that marked those conciliarists as they struck their bargains and trimmed their principles in other cases as well as his own turned Nicholas away. He had been a conciliarist because he thought it to be the best way to bring about unity and reform. Now he saw that the chances for unity and reform were better were he to align with the papalists. So, from 1438 to 1448, he was active in the papal diplomatic corps, and in later years, as a reward for gaining German support for Pope Eugenius, he served as a prince of the Church.

There is little need to question Nicholas's motives in changing sides. His overriding concerns were reform and unity. Party identification was incidental to them. Even in the *De concordantia Catholica*, Nicholas made it clear that he believed the papacy to be a divinely ordered office, essential to the unity of the Church. And while the *De concordantia Catholica* is a product of his conciliarist days, he continued to put the main lines of its theory into practice well past 1438.

Basic to Nicholas's thought is the conviction that sovereignty in the Church belongs to the people and that far from being a pragmatic principle, this is a rule of both divine and natural law. In fact, the people have ultimate sovereignty in the civil state as well for the same reasons.

This means that in the Church, as well as in the State, all lordship or superiority depends upon the consent and voluntary submission of the whole body politic to that lordship.[214]

Of course, all ecclesiastical power comes from God, ultimately;[215] but it is only the grace or gift, the form, as it were, that is immediately given. The content of power, which is coercive force, is granted by its subjects, voluntarily.[216] In the case of the papacy, such power or primacy as it has comes as a result of divine-human cooperation. So, with respect to the source or nature of its power, the papacy is not essentially different from secular power.[217] The use and *telos* of power constitute another issue.

The usual form that this divine-human enterprise takes is election, a well-ordered society being established by a pyramidal scheme of representation more or less popularly chosen. Even a council does not gain its authority from its leaders but from "the common consent of all."[218] And this, in some sense, places the council over the pope.[219] The pope is elected, by the cardinals, in the name of the entire church. And while God himself does authorize and confirm papal elections, the pope has only that authority that the whole church chooses to give him. His sole power is that of "administration and jurisdiction," conveyed to him by election and voluntary submission.[220] He is not a law unto himself but is bound by existing law.[221]

Because of his power of administration and jurisdiction, the pope is greater than any individual; but he is the servant of the people as a whole.[222] And, as servant, he can be judged and deposed.[223]

But there must be a papacy, a monarchical papacy. That is the divine plan for the Church.[224]

Nicholas, like Gerson, also believed that Aristotle was correct in advocating a mixed government as the best form for any society. So he sought to interpose the cardinals as an executive board between the democracy of the universal church and the papal monarchy.[225]

Oddly enough, neither Nicholas nor any other of the conciliarists envisioned any clear, active role in the affairs of the Church for the laity. The most that they allowed was a sort of secondary place to temporal rulers— secondary and vaguely defined. Only when one goes back to Marsilius and William of Occam does one find agitation for genuine lay participation beyond the usual "pay and pray" and elect.

The fifteenth century closed with the papacy firmly fixed as supreme in the Church, though now perhaps less willing to claim that supremacy as an absolute and immediately God-given right. The Church itself had done much talking about itself as the universe or congregation of the faithful, and about representative government, but beyond some rudimentary electoral powers the laity were no more participants in the institutional life of the fifteenth-century church than they had been in the twelfth or fourteenth. Practically, the Church was the hierarchy administering the sacraments—an ancient notion revived. And, in some quarters, in ways carefully qualified, there were those ready to say that the pope is the Church.[226]

Many, feeling the need for reform, believed that the situation was now almost hopeless. The papacy needed reform, but it had written the rules so that it could avoid reform.

Notes

1. Cf. *supra*, pp. 47-88.
2. E.g., Clement of Rome, *First Epistle to the Corinthians* 42-44. (This work is most often called 1 Clement.) Eusebius, *Ecclesiastical History* III.38.
3. E.g., *Odes of Solomon* 11; Clement of Alexandria, *Paedagogos* III.12; Tertullian, *Apologia* 39.
4. E.g., Clement of Alexandria, I.6; Origen, *In Jeremiam homil.* XX.1-3; *In Cant. Cantic. homil.* II.8.

5. On the variety of organizational patterns in the Church and attitudes toward it, cf. Adolph von Harnack, *The Constitution and Law of the Church in the First Two Centuries* (London: Norgate and Williams, 1910).

6. For solid studies of baptism in the early church, cf. André Benoit, *Le baptême chrétien au deuxième siècle* (Paris: Presses Universitaires de France, 1953) and G. W. H. Lampe, *The Seal of the Spirit: A Study in the Doctrine of Baptism and Confirmation in the New Testament and the Fathers* (second edition) (London: SPCK, 1967). On the Lord's Supper, cf. Werner Elert, *Abendmahl und Kirchengemeinschaft in der Alten Kirche, Hauptsächlich des Ostens* (Berlin: Lutherisches Verlagshaus, 1954) and Hans Lietzmann, *Mass and the Lord's Supper: A Study in the History of the Liturgy,* Dorothea H. G. Reeve, trans. (Leiden: E. J. Brill, 1953).

7. Cf. 1 Cor. 12:28-29; Eph. 4:11; *Didache* XI.7; XII.3; XIII.1-2. For thorough discussion, cf. Adolph Harnack, *The Mission and Expansion of Christianity in the First Three Centuries,* James Moffatt, trans. and ed. (Gloucester, Mass.: Peter Smith, 1972), pp. 319-34.

8. Regarding Jewish apostles, cf. Josephus, *Antiquities* XVII. 11.i; Justin Martyr, *Dialogue with Trypho the Jew* XVII; CVIII; CXVII; Eusebius, *In Isaiam comm.* XVIII. 1-2; Epiphanius, *Adversus haeresis (Panarion)* XXX.4.

9. Cf. Acts 11:27-30; 13:1-3; 21:10; Josephus, *Antiquities* XIII.11.2. Also cf. Acts 21:38 and Josephus, *Antiquities* XX.5.1.

10. E.g., Phil. 1:1. Cf. Harnack, 319-68. Also see Harnack's *The Constitution and Law of the Church in the First Two Centuries*.

11. On the historical development of the office of bishop, see Jean Colson, *L'évêque dans les communautés primitives* (Paris: Cerf, 1951). First Clement 40-44 indicates the local character of bishops (presbyters) and deacons.

12. These roles and titles appear to have no Jewish or pagan counterparts. It is quite likely that they are simply the result of the imitation of some primitive Christian congregation's practice. Antioch presents a possibility.

13. *Didache* XI.4-6.
14. Cf. *Didache* XI.7-12; XIII. 1-2.
15. *Didache* XV.1.
16. Such was his preference, but he was not altogether consistent, e.g., *Epistle to the Philadelphians* v.2.
17. E.g., *Epistle* VIII.1-IX.2.
18. *Epistle to the Magnesians* VI. 1-2; *Epistle to the Trallians* II.1-3; *Epistle to the Smyrnaeans* VIII.1. Also see, for the deacon's responsibilities, e.g., Justin Martyr, *First Apology* LXVII; Hippolytus, *Apostolic Tradition* I.9.
19. Matt. 19:28.
20. Ignatius of Antioch, *Epistle to the Magnesians* VI.1; *Epistle to the Trallians* III. 1.
21. Cf. Ignatius of Antioch; *Epistle to the Magnesians* III-VII.
22. Cf. Rom. 14:17; Matt. 5:3-7,27; Shepherd of Hermas, *Visions* I.1.6; *Similitudes* I. 1-5. On the theological foundations of the early Roman Empire, see Charles Norris Cochrane, *Christianity and Classical Culture: A Study of Thought and Action from Augustus to Augustine,* Galaxy Book edition (New York: Oxford, 1957), pp. 74-176. On the theological bases of the Christian commonwealth, cf. Adolph Harnack, *Mission and Expansion . . . ,* pp. 147-98.
23. Minucius Felix, *Octavianius* 8.4.
24. Early Christianity expressed both kinship and complete opposition between the kingdom of God and the kingdom of earth. Cp. Justin Martyr, *Apology* I. xii with Tertullian, *Apology* 21. For the christocentric focus, cf. Aristides, *Apology* ii and Justin Martyr, *Dialogue with Trypho the Jew* 123.
25. E.g., Justin Martyr, *Apology* 18.3; 23.1; 30.1; 93.1-3 and Tertullian, *Apology* 4, 33-34.
26. Cf. M. P. Charlesworth, "The Virtues of a Roman Emperor: Propaganda and the Creation of Belief," *Proceedings of the British Academy* XXIII (1937), pp. 105-133.
27. E.g., Ignatius of Antioch, *Epistle to the Trallians* III.1.
28. Cf. Ignatius of Antioch, *Epistle to the Magnesians* VI and *Epistle to the Smyrnaeans* VIII. Such was the purpose of designating the Emperor Pontifex Maximus, a practice begun in 12 B.C. Then also it became officially necessary

for the Roman citizen to render homage to the *genius* of the emperor, that is, to pay cult to Roman civic virtue as personified in the emperor. Cf. W. F. Otto, "Genius" in *Real-Encyclopädie für Altertumswissenschaft* VII.1 (1910), col. 1155-1170. Tertullian often speaks of the bishop as *summus sacerdos* (high priest), but he sneers at the idea of the Bishop of Rome as Pontifex Maximus or even as bishop of bishops—i.e., as both highest religious and highest administrative authority in the Church, Cf. *De pudicitia* I.13.

29. E.g., Irenaeus, *Adversus Haereses* 3.iii.2-3.
30. E.g., Ignatius of Antioch, *Epistle to the Philadelphians* VII.1-2.
31. On "genius," cf. *supra,* n.28; on "imperium," cf. Cochrane, pp. 99-113. For an example of Christian thinking that attributes something like *genius* to the bishop, cf. Hippolytus, *Refutatio omnium haeresium* praef. and IX.1.12; also Tertullian, Apology 21. For an example of the transfer of the Roman idea of *imperium* to the bishop, see Hippolytus, *Traditionis apostolicae* I.ii-iv.
32. Cp. Otto, "Genius" (*supra*, n. 28) and Harnack, pp. 219-39.
33. E.g., Clement of Alexandria, *Protrepticus* X. 108; Origen, *Contra Celsum* V.40.
34. E.g., Irenaeus, *Adversus haereses* III.4.1; III.24.1; Clement of Alexandria, *Paedagogos* III.12.
35. E.g., Ignatius of Antioch, *Ep. to the Magnesians* III.2; Irenaeus, IV.26.5.
36. Tertullian, *De exhortatione castitatis* 7.3. Also see, Eusebius, *Ecclesiastikē historia* VI.19 for an account of Origen's struggle with Bishop Demetrius over the right of the laity to give formal presentations in Church when the bishop was present.
37. Cf. Robert M. Grant, *Gnosticism and Early Christianity,* rev. ed. (New York: Harper and Row, 1966); Hans Jonas, *The Gnostic Religion: The Message of the Alien God and the Beginnings of Christianity,* second edition, revised (Boston: Beacon Press, 1963).
38. Pierre de Labriolle, *La crise montaniste. Les sources du Montanisme: Textes grec, latin, syriaques* (Paris:Cerf, 1913).

39. Cf. Eusebius, IV-V. Very few passages from the literature
of the period work with Montanism and Gnosticism simultaneously for obvious reasons. But it is generally understood that a principal strategy in opposing the Gnostics was
the strengthening of the hierarchy while Montanism was
combated by strengthening the idea of tradition as a source
of spiritual truth. These strategies gained the Church a
more nearly uniform structure, a more nearly uniform biblical canon, and a concern for discipline and liturgical
order but the cost in freedom of expression was high.
40. E.g., Tertullian, *Scorpiace* 1, speaks of "folks who are
Christians only when the wind is right"; also see *De
pudicitia* 1. Origen, too, in his commentaries sharply rebukes the moral level of all too many Christians; e.g., *In
Matt. comm.* I.2. Also see Origen, *Contra Celsum* III.9.
41. Cf. *Didache* VI.2; Origen, *In Luc. homil.* XVII, the comment on 1 Corinthians 1:2.
42. Shepherd of Hermas, *Mandates* IV. 3.6.
43. Clement of Alexandria, *Stromateis* II.xiii.56.1-59.1 and
IV.xxiv.154.3.
44. Cf. Tertullian, *De paenitentia* 7, 10. Also see the responses
to the penitential order of Callixtus, bishop of Rome (217-
222); Hippolytus, *Elenchos* ix.12 and Tertullian, *De
pudicitia passim*. The shift from public confession to private confession to a bishop or other confessor may be seen
to have occurred by the time of Origen. E.g., *In II
Psalm.homil.* xxvii. 2, 6; Cyprian, *De lapsis* 28.
45. Hippolytus, *In Daniel. comm.* I.17. Cp. Tertullian, 18.
46. Hippolytus, *Elenchos* ix.12.20-26.
47. Hippolytus, Elenchos esp. ix.12.22-23.
48. *1 Clement* 32.2; *Didache* XIII.3; Hippolytus, *Traditionis
apostolicae* I.ii.1-2; I.viii.i; I.ix.1-8.
49. Cf. Hippolytus, *Elenchos* praef.; *Trad. apost.* IV and X;
Origen, *Peri euchis (De oratione)* 28.9; Cyprian, ep. 67.1.
This view seems to have developed very rapidly once the
notion of levitical priesthood was generally held.
50. Cf. Hippolytus *Trad. apost.* XXVI-XXVII.
51. The precise wording of Decius' edict(s) is now unknown.
Cf. Cochrane, pp. 151-76 for an analysis of the

intellectual-spiritual crisis of the Empire in the third century. For an analysis of its consequences on the Church, see W. H. C. Frend, *Martyrdom and Persecution in the Early Church: A Study of a Conflict from the Maccabees to Donatus* (Garden City, N.Y.: Doubleday, 1967), pp. 285-323.

52. Cf. Cyprian, epp. 17-20; 30.3-5.
53. Cf. Cyprian, ep. 67; *De unitate ecclesiae* IV and V. Also see Cyprian, epp. 49 and 50. These are letters of Cornelius to Cyprian. Eusebius, *Eccl. hist.* VI.43, presents an extract of a letter from Cornelius to Fabius, bishop of Antioch.
54. Cf. Eusebius, *Eccl. hist.* VI.43.1; Cyprian, ep. 55.27.
55. Cf. Cyprian, epp. 55.24; 68.1; also Eusebius, *Eccl. hist.* VI.46.3; VII.5.
56. Eusebius, *Eccl. hist.* VI.43, where Eusebius quotes a letter from Cornelius to Cyprian (Cyprian, ep. 49).
57. Cf. Cyprian, ep. 50.3.
58 Cf. E. Amman, "Novatien," *Dictionnaire de Théologie catholique,* vol. 11, pp. 816-49 and A. d'Ales, *Novatien* (Paris, 1924), for basic studies of Novatian's theology, including his ecclesiology.
59. Cf. Cyprian, epp. 48.8; 67.5.
60. Cyprian, ep. 70.1. In Cyprian we see the fruition of the development of the notion that unity is the fundamental mark of the true church. Earlier, holiness has been seen as the fundamental mark: e.g., *Ep. of Barnabas* XIV.6; Shepherd of Hermas, *Visiones* I.3,4,6; Tertullian, *Adversus Marcionem* IV.13.
61. Cyprian, epp. 26.1 and 68.8.
62. E.g., Cyprian, ep. 67.3.
63. E.g., Cyprian, epp. 54.5; 67.5; 68.1; *De unitate ecclesiae* IV-VI.
64. Cf. *Concilium Carthag. sub Cypriano VII,* proem; Cyprian, ep. 43.5; *De unitate ecclesiae* V.
65. Cyprian, *De unit. eccl.* VI.
66. Our interest here is, of course, in the Church as a "creature" or creation. Cf. Clement of Alexandria, *Stromateis* VI.xiii.107.2 (also IV.viii.66); *Paedagogos* I.4.10. Origen repeatedly emphasizes its historical character, e.g., *Peri*

archon (De principiis) IV.1.3-5; *In Ezech. homil.* I.11; *In Exod. homil.* IX.3; *In XXXVI Psalm. homil.* 2.1.

67. E.g., Clement of Alexandria, *Stromateis* IV.viii; Origen, *In Cant. cantic. comm.* II.8.

68. Origen II.7.

69. CP. Origin I.1 and *In Exod. homil.* IX.3; *In Levit. homil.* VII.2; *In Cant. cantic. comm.* II.8.

70. Clement had worked with the same idea in a more abstract way; cf. *Stromateis* VI.xiii.106.1,2. See Origen, *In Levit. homil.* IX.1,9.

71. Origen, *In Levit. homil.* IV.4-6.

72. E.g., *In Levit. homil.* VI.3.

73. E.g., *Contra Celsum,* III.51; *In Num. homil.* XX.4.

74. In this essay, the Eastern Church after Nicea (325) is largely, though not entirely ignored simply because Eastern ecclesiology had little influence in the developments that finally bear on the ecclesiology of the American holiness movement. Whether it should have is quite another question.

75. Cf. W. H. C. Frend, *The Donatist Church: A Movement of Protest in Roman North Africa* (Oxford: Oxford University Press, 1952). Frend works primarily with the sociological issues, not the theological. But this work is still very pertinent to the present essay.

76. Cf. Optatus of Mileve, *Contra Parmenianum Donatistam* ii.20; vii.2; Augustine, *Contra litteras Petiliani* I.2,3.

77. Cf. Augustine, *Breviculus collationis cum Donatistis* iii.19-21.

78. Cyprian had already asserted this in the light of the Decian persecution. Cf. Cyprian, epp. 65.4 and 67.3.

79. Augustine, *De baptismo contra Donatistas* I.12.14.

80. This is both presupposed and declared in Augustine: presupposed in the very distinction between visible and invisible church, declared in numerous descriptions of the spiritual character of the members of the true church themselves. Augustine does seem to argue elsewhere that unity is the fundamental mark, but here one would take issue with a large number of interpreters. Unity is the fundamental mark of the *visible* church; holiness the fundamental mark of the *invisible* and *true* church. But even this dis-

tinction is not consistently applied. Authentic unity is itself known only among the saints "predestined before the foundation of the world." Cf. *De unitate ecclesiae* 7; *De civitate Dei* XXI.25; *De peccatorum meritis et remissione et de baptismo parvulorum* I.59;

81. E.g., *In I Ioann. homil.* VI.10; X.3; Sermon 341.9.

82. E.g., *De unitate ecclesiae* 7; *Enarratio 1 in Psalm.* 30.4; Serm. 272, *passim;* 354.1; *Contra Cresconium grammaticum* I.34.

83. Cf. *De bapt.* IV.17; ep. 173.6; *Tractatus in I ep. Iohann.* 10.3

84. Cf. *De bapt. I.10-17; IV.17; Contra litt. Petil.* III.10.

85. E.g., *De bapt.* I.10-17; Sermon 191.2-3; 192.2; *De bapt.* IV.24.

86. Sermon 267.4.

87. Cf. *De Trinitate* XV.29,38.

88. E.g., Sermon 267 *passim;* 268 *passim.*

89. Cf. Sermon 268.2; ep. 61.2; *In Iohann. tract.* 26.11. Augustine introduces the subtle and exceptionally problematic distinction between the validity of a sacrament and its efficacy in *De bapt.* VI.1.1. This has pertinence here.

90. Cf. *De civ. Dei* XXII.17; *In Iohann. tract.* 12.5; Sermon 88.5.

91. Cf. *De bapt.* II.8 and V.27; *Contra litt. Petil.* II.22.

92. Augustine believes that the sacraments of the Donatists are legitimate precisely because the Spirit is in them. But only the true church can bestow the Spirit that is in them. So they are valid but not efficacious.

93. E.g., Sermon 4.11.

94. *Contra litt. Petil.* III.4.

95. Augustine is even willing to believe that the majority of those within the visible church are reprobate, cf. *Enchiridion* 97. Also see *Contra litt. Petil.* III.4; *De bapt.* V.

96. Cf. *Enchiridion* 65.

97. Augustine never really settled the matter of how to distinguish between the two churches, but it is clear that it is more significant to believe in the holy church than to be able to point to the empirical. Cf. *De bapt.* V.38-39; *De correptione et gratia* 39-42.

98. Augustine seems inconsistent here, for he does indeed refer to the empirical church as the kingdom of God (e.g., ep. 36.17). But he is probably thinking theologically, not historically in such passages. That is to say, when one would observe and think upon the kingdom of God, one looks to the empirical church—and through it. Nonetheless, from the standpoint of philosophical theology, the idea that the true church is the number of the elect, which is known only to God, destroys the very possibility of ultimate significance to the empirical church. Cf. ep. 141.5; *Contra Cresconium gramm.* I.34; *Contra litt. Petil.* II.172.

99. Cf. Optatus, i.4; ii.20; iv.5; vii.2; Augustine, ep. 93.7; *Contra litt. Petil.* II.83.

100. Cf. Augustine, II.38.9; III.2.3; epp. 93.23; 185.5; sermon 46.32-33. Also cf. Optatus, ii.1.5; iii.2.3.

101. Cf. *Expos. in Psalm.* 56.7.

102. Cf. ep. 76.

103. Cf. *Expos. in Psalm.* 56.1; epp. 43.21; 44.3; 53.3.

104. Ep. 61.2; sermon 268.2; *Contra litt. Petil.* II.172.

105. *Contra litt. Petil.*

106. Cf. epp. 43.21; 44.3; 49.2-3.

107. E.g., Earl D. Radmachr, *What the Church Is All About: A Biblical and Historical Study* (Chicago: Moody Press, 1978), p. 44. (This work was originally titled *The Nature of the Church.*)

108. Cf. *De civ. Dei* XX.9.1; sermon 213.7.

109. cf. *De correptione et gratia* 9.22; *De dono perseverantiae* 2.2.

110. Cf. *De civ. Dei* XXII.17; *In Iohann. tract.* 12.5; sermon 88.5.

111. This is one way to state the thesis of Augustine's first full anti-Donatist tract, *De bapt.* Cf. also *Contra litt. Petil.* II.5.11.

112. Ep. 53.1.

113. Radmacher, pp. 50-51.

114. Cf. Irenaeus, *Adv. haer,* III.3.2-3. The precise meaning of this passage is highly debatable, but it is clear that Irenaeus does claim for the Roman church at least a place as the model of apostolic fidelity. Given the temperament dis-

cussed earlier, this role would be seen as summed up in the bishop of that church.

115. E.g., Damasus' letter in Theodoret, *Historia ecclesiastica* II.17; Innocent I, ep. 25.1-2; Leo I, serm.4.2-4.

116. Cf. Augustine, *De civ. Dei* I.15; XIX. 21-24; ep. 138. These show Augustine's analysis, interpretation, and transformation of the notion.

117. Ep. 1.1.

118. It is in this period, for instance, that the popes begin to refer to their care for the whole church in the very way in which they address others in their letters: e.g., Leo's frequent "our fatherly solicitude" and Damasus's use of "my sons" instead of the heretofore usual "my brethren" in his letter to the eastern bishops. (Cf. Theodoret, V.10.)

119. Cf. Cyprian, epp. 48.3; 59.14; and see its limitation in epp. 71.3 and 74 *passim;* Optatus, *De schismate Donatistorum* 2.2; 7.3; Augustine, epp. 43.7; 175.2-3; 176.1; 177.19. Also see the response of Innocent I to epp. 175-177 among the collection of Augustine's letters, i.e., epp. 181-84.

120. Cf. Gregory I, *Moralia in Iob,* epist. dedic. i; *Liber regulae pastoralis* I.1.

121. E.g., Gregory I, *Moralia in Iob;* VI.56.

122. On the former, see *Homil. in Ezech.* ii.2.2-4; *Mor. in Iob* IV.45; V.57-58; VI.37, 57-61. On the latter, see Book IV of the *Dialogi de vita et miraculis patrum Italicorum passim.*

123. E.g., *Lib. reg. past.* VI.44. Gregory's successors continually cite him as model, even when they have no intention of imitating him. For instance, his influence is still felt at the Council of Constantinople (680), and in 795, Pope Hadrian cites Gregory in resisting Charlemagne's position concerning the veneration of images. Cf. Migne, *Patrologia Latina,* XCVIII, col. 1291.

124. Cf. Augustine, *De bapt.* IV. 25.32; *Enarratio in Psalm.* 77.2.

125. Gregory was quite aware of non-Christian areas of his world and has harsh words for the Roman state in Constantinople. But he assumes that the fundamental religious commitment of Rome and its environs is Christian sufficiently so to say, "the present Church is called the kingdom of Heaven." Cf. *Homil. in evangel.* ii.38.2; *Mor. in Iob.* XXXIII.18.34.

126. Cf. *Homil. in evangel.*ii.38.7-8; *Homil. in Ezech.* ii. 4.16-17.
127. Cf. *Mor. in Iob* XXII.20.
128. Cf. *Dialogi* iv.25,39; Augustine, *Enchiridion* 107-109.
129. Cf. Gregory, *Homil. in evangel.* ii.37.7; *Dialogi* iv.58-59.
130. Boniface VIII, *Unam Sanctam* 13 and Marsilius of Padua, *Defensor pacis,* dictio II.6-7, 15-17.
131. Cp. John VIII, ep. 5 and John Wycliffe, *Trialogus* iv.22.
132. Gregory VII, *Dictatus papae.*
133. Council of Constance, *Sacrosancta* (cf. Mansi XXVII, 590-591).
134. Cf. both the papal and forged versions of Nicholas's decree of 1059. (In *Monumenta Germaniae Historica: Constitutiones et Acta* [Hanover and Berlin: Weidmann, 1893] I.537-46.
135. E.g., Gregory VII, *Dictatus papae;* ep. ad Otto, bp. of Constance (Dec., 1074). For the latter, see the English translation by E. Emerton, *The Correspondence of Pope Gregory VII* (New York: Columbia University, 1932), pp. 52-53.
136. An excellent place to begin study of this development is R. W. and A. J. Carlyle, *A History of Medieval Political Theory in the West,* 6 vols. (London: Blackwood, 1903), vol. IV.
137. This process is best represented in Gratian's *Decretum* (c. 1148), originally titled *Concordantium discordantium canonum.* It has two major sections: *Distinctiones* and *Causae.* The latter are divided into *Quaestiones.* This work is in vol. 1 of the *Corpus iuris canonici,* E. L. Richter, E. Friedberg, eds. (Leipzig: B. Tauchnitz, 1922).
138. The literature here is immense: cf., for instance, Bernard of Clairvaux, ep. 244 (to King Conrad, 1146); Thomas Aquinas, *Summa theologiae* II.I. q. 81, art. I; Augustus Triumphus, *Tractatus brevis de duplici potestate prelatorum et laicorum;* and more especially, Augustus's *Summa de potestate ecclesiastica* II. qq. 45-46.
139. Boniface VIII, *Unam Sanctam* (Nov. 1302).
140. *Tractatus Eboracenses* (also known as the *Norman Anonymous* or the *Anonymous of York*). It may be seen in

Monumenta Germaniae Historica: Libelli de Lite III (Hanover and Berlin: Weidmann, 1897), pp. 662-68.

141. E.g., Bernard of Clairvaux, *De consideratione* (1153) III.4.13-14. This five-part work is addressed to Pope Eugenius III.

142. Bernard of Clairvaux, *Sermo in Cantica canticorum* 83.3-4.

143. Bernard of Clairvaux, *Sermo in Cantica canticorum*.

144. Bernard of Clairvaux, *De consid.* I.iv.5; IV.ii.4-5;III.ii.6-12; III.iv.14.

145. Bernard of Clairvaux, *De consid.* I.vi.7; II.vi.9-11; III.iv.14; IV.iii.6.

146. Bernard of Clairvaux, *Sermo in Cantica canticorum* 29.7.

147. E.g., Bernard of Clairvaux, *Sermo in Cantica canticorum* 26.6-10; 84.3.

148. Bernard of Clairvaux, *Sermo in Cantica canticorum* 26.8.

149. Cf. Bernard Gui, *Practica officii inquisitiones heretice pravitatis* 5; L. Clédat, *Rituel Cathare* (Paris, 1887), pp. 470a-482b.

150. Gui, 5.1 (1); Raynier Sacconi, *Summa de Catharis* (A. Dondaine, ed., *Un Traité neo-Manichéen du XIIIᵉ siècle: Le Liber de duobus principiis* [Roma: Instituto Storico Domenicano di S. Sabina, 1939]).

151. Cf. A. Dondaine, "Aux origines du Valdéisme: une profesion de foi de Valdès," *Archivum Fratrum Praedicatorum* XVI (Roma: Instituto Storico Domenicano di S. Sabina, 1946), pp. 231-32.

152. E.g., Thomas Aquinas, *Summa theologiae* III. q. 8. art. 4; *Ep. ad Eph. comm.* cap. 1, lectio 8.

153. E.g., Thomas Aquinas, *S.T.* Ia. IIae. q. 90, art. 4; q. 107. arts. 1-4; q. 108. arts. 1-4; q. 109.

154. E.g., Thomas Aquinas, *S.T.* III. q. 8. art. 3.

155. *Summa contra gentiles* IV.76.1-4.

156. *Summa contra gentiles* IV.76 *passim; S.T.* I. q. 108. art. 2; *Lect. III ad I Cor.* 12.

157. Cf. Otto Gierke, *Political Theories of the Middle Age,* Frederic William Maitland, trans. (Boston: Beacon, 1958), pp. 9-21, 101-129 (nn. 3-64).

158. John of Paris, *Tractatus de potestate regiae et papali* (1302).

159. John of Paris, caps. 6, 10, 19, 20, 23.
160. John of Paris, caps. 18-19.
161. Cf. John of Paris, caps. 3, 6, 7, 10.
162. Cf. John of Paris, caps. 13-15.
163. Cf. John of Paris, caps. 6, 14, 21, 25.
164. Cf. John of Paris, caps 11 and 16.
165. Dante Alighieri, *De monarchia libri tres.* 3.16. He may have written as early as 1296; certainly no later than 1317.
166. Alighieri.
167. Marsilius of Padua (Marsilius Patavinus), *Defensor pacis* dictio II, cap. 20. sec. 1-4.
168. Cf. Marsilius of Padua, dictio III. cap 2. sec. 1-41. Quotation is sec. 17.
169. William of Occam (Ockham; Guilelmus Occam), *De imperatorum et pontificum potestate* 1.
170. William of Occam; and 10.
171. Cf. *Dialogus* I.1.4 and *Opera politica,* J. G. Sikes, et al. eds. (Manchester: University of Manchester, 1940), III.191.
172. Cf. *De imp. et pontif. potest.* XV.
173. Cf. *Dialogus* I.5.35.
174. John Wycliffe (Johannis Wycliffe), *De dominio divino* (1375) III.6.4.
175. Wycliffe, *De civili dominio* (1376) I. 3, 11, 28, 35.
176. Wycliffe, *De civ. dom.* I.37.
177. *De officio pastorali* I.1.8.
178. *De veritate sacrae Scripturae* 25, 47.
179. *De ecclesiae* 8
180. *De ecclesiae et membris eius* 1.
181. *De ecclesiae* 2.
182. *De ecclesiae* 1.
183. *De ecclesiae* 8.
184. *De potestate papae* John Loserth, ed. (London: Truebner, 1907), pp. 176-77.
185. *De potestate papae* pp. 178-79.
186. Cf. E. F. Jacob, *Essays in the Conciliar Epoch,* second edition (Manchester: University of Manchester, 1953); G. J. Jordan, *The Inner History of the Great Schism of the West* (London: Williams and Norgate, 1930); Walter

Ullmann, *Origins of the Great Schism* (London: Burns, Oates and Washbourne, 1948).
187. *Ep. concilii pacis* 4.
188. *Ep. concilii pacis* 12-15.
189. E.g., Peter d'Ailly (Petrus de Alliaco), *Propositiones utiles* 1-4. This and d'Ailly's other works are bound with those of Gerson. Cf. Jean Gerson, *Opera omnia* ed. Ellies du Pin; (Antwerp, 1706), vol. II, p. 112.
190. Cf. Jean Gerson, *Libellus de auferibilitate papae ab ecclesia, considerationes* X-XII.
191. *De potestate ecclesiae et origine iuris et legum, considerationes* VI-XI.
192. Cf. *Lib. de auf. pap. ab eccl. considerationes* XIII.
193. Cf. *Lib. de auf. pap. ab eccl. considerationes* VII-IX, XI.
194. Cf. *Lib. de auf. pap. ab eccl., considerationes* VIII, XX.
195. Gregory VII taught the idea without the phrase: cf. *Lib.* I. ep. 55 (1075). For Innocent III, see for example, *Lib.* I, ep. 127; *Lib.* VII. epp. 1 and 405; *Lib.* XI. epp. 82, 83, 130.
196. Cf. *Apparatus ad quinque libros decretalium* X. 1. 7; X. 2. 2; X. 2.27. The *App. ad lib. decret.* is Innocent's commentary on the *Corpus iuris canonici.* The first systematic theological statement of papal *plenitudo* was from Aegidius Romanus, *De ecclesiastica potestate* (1301).
197. *S.T.* II. II. q. 1. art. 10; *In quattor libros Sententiarum magistri Petri Lombardi commentarius* XLIV. iii. 4.
198. Cf. *supra,* n. 196. Aegidius was an educator and Augustinian monk who became the head of his order, then archbishop of Bourges.
199. Paludanus was Latin patriarch of Jerusalem. His principle work is *De causa immediata ecclesiasticae potestatis* (c. 1329).
200. *Summa de potestate ecclesiastica* (prob. post-1324) I. q.1. art. 8. 10-34; II. qq. 48-75. Augustus was an Augustinian monk and friend of Aegidius Romanus. He taught at Paris, as did Aegidius, became a court preacher at Padua, and then was political advisor and tutor to two generations of the French royal family.
201. *De planctu ecclesiae* (rev. ed., 1340) I. arts. 5-7; 11-12;

52-58. Alvarius (also Alverus) was a rigorist Franciscan, a doctor in canon law who taught at Bologna and Perugia, was confessor to Pope John XXII, and died as bishop of Silves (Portugal).

202. *Summa contra ecclesiae et primatus apostoli Petri adversarios* II. 54 and 65; *De pontificis maximi conciliique auctoritate* (printed as *De potestate papae et concilii generalis tractatus notabilis*). His works were only published posthumously. Also known as Johannes a Turrecremata, he was a Dominican, received a doctorate in canon law at Paris, was made Master of the Sacred Palace in 1431, and in 1439 was named cardinal in recognition of his contributions to the restoration of control of the Church to the papacy.

203. *De pot. Rom. pont. et gen. conc.* fol. 144-157.

204. E.g., *De pot.* I. q. 22. art. 1.

205. *Summa contra eccl.* I.21.

206. *Summa contra eccl.* I.22.

207. *Summa contra eccl.* I.6.

208. *Summa contra eccl.*

209. *Summa contra eccl.* II.22.

210. *Summa contra eccl.* II.254.

211. *Summa contra eccl.* II.93 and 102.

212. *Summa contra eccl.* IV.18.

213. *Summa contra. eccl.* III.16.

214. *De concordantia catholica* I.12-17. Torquemada, *De pont. max. conc. auct.* 38, seeks to overturn these principles. Cf. Nicholas's own attempts to modify them: *Opera omnia* (Basel, 1565), pp. 825-29.

215. *De concord. cath.* II.9.

216. *De concord. cath.* II.34.

217. *De concord. cath.* I.16; II. 13 and 34.

218. *De concord cath.* II.8 and 13.

219. *De concord. cath.* II. 17-34.

220. *De concord. cath.* II. 13, 14, 34.

221. *De concord cath.* II. 9. 10. 20.

222. *De concord. cath.* II.34.

223. *De concord. cath.* II.17-18.

224. *De concord. cath.* I.14.

225. *De concord. cath.* II.15.
226. E.g., Jacobus Almainus (d. 1515), *De auctoritate ecclesiae et conciliorum generalium versus Thomam de Vio Cajetanum* IV. art. 7. 29-31 (in Johannes Gerson, *Opera omnia* vol. II: 1098).

A Survey of Western Ecclesiology to about 1700

Part II: Ecclesiology in the Sixteenth to Eighteenth Centuries

R<small>ECONSTITUTING THE</small> I<small>DEA OF</small> C<small>HURCH</small>

THE PROTESTANT REFORMATION of the sixteenth century produced five distinct ecclesiologies: the Lutheran, the Reformed, the Anglican, the Anabaptist, and the Spiritualist—and each of these had its sub-forms, as it were. Each of them was in clear reaction to the medieval Catholic point of view, and each in some ways was in reaction to the other non-Catholic views as well.

Luther's intense revulsion against the works-righteousness scheme of much of medieval Roman Catholicism carries over into his ecclesiology, and is, in fact, basic to it. Simply put, Luther's point was that the Church must once again be established upon the gospel, finding its true unity in God's redemptive work rather than in human merit and human notions of organization.[1]

This perspective gave clarity and simplicity to Luther's ecclesiology: the Church is where the gospel is. And because Christ is the gospel, the Church is where Christ is. Christ is the living Word who is made manifest in the preached Word and in the sacraments. So the Church is that place in which the Word is truly preached and the sacraments are rightly celebrated. In contrast to the unceasing insistence of the papist that Christ had founded the Church, Luther insisted, "Christ has left nothing in the world except the gospel."[2]

But while this all seems simple enough, and seems to afford a test for determining whether any given body claiming to be the Church is that indeed, other elements of Luther's theology play upon it in such a way as to create paradoxes—perhaps even contradiction. He himself came to see that his understanding of the nature of the gospel, especially his doctrines of grace and the priesthood of all believers, undermined the very idea of Church as a body having authority of any sort over the individual. And then, when he did speak of Church in any super-individual way he often seemed to be talking of an ideal institution hardly related to what everyone else called the Church. He was accused, reasonably enough, of having only a platonic idea for a church.[3]

Luther did, in fact, believe that the true church, while authentically existing in space and time—a very non-platonic society—may be hidden, the saints being concealed.[4] It may be hidden, or it may exist quite openly. The Church's existence does not depend upon its visibility or invisibility, its empirical presence or absence. Physical location and material substance are not the Church itself; they do not really define the Church, though the Church cannot exist apart from them. To say that material substance and physical location—i.e., some thing in some place—constitute the Church or define it is to confuse living *in* the flesh with living *according to* the flesh. Christ lived *in*, but not *according to*, the flesh. In saying that the kingdom of God does not come with observation, that it cannot be identified by saying, "Here it is" or, "There it is" and pointing to something, Christ abolished reliance upon the flesh or the material world's constituting, identifying, or defining the Church. "The kingdom of God is within you," he said.

Rome errs critically, Luther says, in arguing as it does concerning apostolic succession and petrine supremacy, for in making the Roman church and her bishop absolutely necessary to the two notions, it ties Church to body and place. The Church is thus defined according to the flesh and is made worldly in the worst sense.[6]

Luther prefers to see the Church as analogous to the Incarnation. On the one hand, here is Christ visible, tangible, a person with empirical characteristics that make him both like and unlike other persons; but on the other hand there is Christ invisible, elusive, a mystery—living *in* the flesh but not according to the flesh. On this analogy, Luther avoids the force of the charge of platonism and retains the christocentric character of the Church.[7] Luther also avoids the pitfalls of the Augustinian doctrine of the visible and invisible churches.

There are not two churches. There is but one. But that one church does indeed have two aspects, the same two that characterize her Lord; both aspects are real. Of course, so long as she preaches the Word, she cannot be completely invisible; but so long as she is sought only within the limits of material substance and physical location she will not be fully known. The Church comes into view in preaching and in the celebration of the sacraments, for these both tell of Christ visible, tangible, identifiable. But they also proclaim his hidden side as well. So, "it is an exalted, profound, concealed thing, the Church."[8]

The Church is truly known only by faith, through baptism, the Lord's Supper, and the preaching of the Word. "Natural, real, authentic and essential Christian community exists in the Spirit—not in some external thing."[9]

Nonetheless, the believer needs some way to know when he or she has come to that reality. Luther recognizes this as a legitimate pastoral concern and in 1539 writes *On the Councils and the Church*, in which he lists and comments upon seven marks by means of which the Church may be recognized. these are: the Word of God, the rightly administered sacraments of baptism and the altar (Luther's term), the office of the keys (absolution) and the office of the ministry, public worship (which should include the recital of the Our Father, the Apostles' Creed, and the Ten Commandments), and the bearing of the cross.[10] Luther claims elsewhere that these are the legitimate marks because they were the marks of the ancient church. Nonetheless, these marks do not constitute the Church; they are only theologically unequal characteristics by means of which one may identify the Church.[11]

Luther is sure that the first of these marks, possession of the Word of God, is the most important of them all. He writes, "God's word cannot exist without God's people and, conversely, God's people cannot exist without God's word."[12]

But by God's Word, Luther does not mean the Bible alone. He means biblical preaching. He declares,

> We are speaking of the external word, preached orally . . . for this is what Christ left behind as an external sign by which his Church or his Christian people in the world should be recognized. . . . Whenever you hear or see this word preached,

believed, professed and lived do not doubt that the true holy catholic Church, a Christian holy people, must be there, even though their number is very small.[13]

Luther does seem to place the sacraments in a coordinate position with biblical preaching from time to time, but when his work is considered as a whole, there is no doubt that the one mark that most clearly identifies the Church is biblical preaching.[14] He writes, "The whole life and substance of the Church is the word of God. . . . Nor am I speaking of the written gospel, but rather the spoken word. . . . Only through the vocal and public declaration of the gospel can one know where the Church is and the mystery of the kingdom of heaven."[15]

It almost goes without saying that this notion completely negates the Roman Catholic understanding of the Church. In fact, Catholicism had long since decided that the preaching of the Word was not even essential to the worship of the Church. It had become a sort of bonus. The sacraments, administered by accredited clergy obedient to the pope, constituted and defined the church militant

Luther's view was too novel, too radical to survive him. For one thing, the Church of his day was too closely tied to the civil government and to its own past as a political instrument to allow his ideal to become reality. The doctrine of the priesthood of all believers, had it been consistently applied, would have made the Church a voluntary society, disciplining itself and spontaneously carrying on in mutual helpfulness. Its structures and its institutional character would have developed and continued on the basis of their usefulness to the spiritual growth of the believer and his or her concern to minister to others.

Luther's disappointment at this point was deep. The world was being allowed to shape the Church.[16] But, in fact, when the opportunity to develop his ecclesiology in almost pristine form did arise—in Hesse, in 1526—Luther backed away from it. He had seen in just the previous year the caricature of his views developed by Karlstadt and Müntzer. It had brought war and chaos. "Reality" chastened his vision. He had come to believe that there weren't enough Christians about who even wanted to help him fulfill it.[17] It would have to remain an ideal.

The second generation of the magisterial Reformation, led by Philip Melanchthon (1497-1560) and John Calvin (1509-1564), attempted to make the ideal the dynamic center of their ecclesiologies while at the same time recognizing what they supposed to be the realities of institutional existence in a fallen world. Generally speaking the difference between the first and succeeding generations of Lutheran and Reformed ecclesiologies is a difference between understanding the Church as an object of faith and understanding it as a institution.[18]

John Calvin's thought shows the movement from one way of thinking to the other. Calvin agreed with Luther that Christ is the center of the true church. This meant that the marks of the true church are the preaching of the gospel and the celebrating of the sacraments of baptism and the Lord's Supper. Churches holding these things "are without doubt entitled to be ranked with the Church."[19]

Early in his career, Calvin had held that there was a third mark of the Church as well—Christian behavior or discipline; and there are hints of a fourth—profession of faith.[20] But his later considerations place these among the matters of critical importance to the organizing and administering of the Church, as applications of the gospel, not among the essential marks of the Church.[21]

Perhaps under the influence of his own doctrine of election, which makes the Church the totality of all of the predestined,[22] he saw the problem of holding as a mark any characteristic or activity open to subjective or private judgment. At any rate, he tends to agree with Luther that Word and sacraments, being objective marks, are adequate criteria for determining the presence of the true church.[23]

At the same time, taking the Church strictly as the totality of the predestined, it is understood to be invisible and an object of faith. We are to believe in it, while we are to respect the visible church and to cultivate its communion.[24]

In fact, while the true church is indeed invisible, the presence of Word and sacrament in the visible church always infers the presence of the invisible,[25] and the person who disassociates himself or herself from the visible church where Word and sacrament are is denying Christ and the heavenly Father—a thing unthinkable among the elect.[26] It is precisely the work of the visible church to make itself the means of salvation for the elect, especially through the Word and the sacraments but also through discipline and instruction in doctrine. The visible church is a God-given instrument of sanctification.[27]

Here, Calvin ventures into territory not entered by Luther—the organization of the visible church as a theological and spiritual matter. Luther had credited the preaching of the Word with a mysterious power to order and galvanize the true church. Calvin believes that Christ has established "a ministry . . . as it were a vicarious work."[28] It is that ministry, employed by God for the governing of the church, that is the "chief nerve by which believers are held together in one body."[29] There are in this ministry "four orders, or kinds of offices, which our Savior has appointed for the government of his Church: namely, pastors; then teachers; then elders; and fourth, deacons."[30]

These offices, instituted by God, not by historical accident or perceived human need, have as their first responsibility the exercise of Christian discipline, discipline that extends as far as the very power to excommunicate.[31]

In this context, one can better see how separated Calvin had become from Luther in his ecclesiology. It can indeed be argued that it is as true of Calvin as it is of Luther that the marks of the true church are the Word, understood as biblical preaching, and the sacraments—the one absolutely essential mark of the Church being biblical preaching. But Luther's understanding of both Word and sacrament differs greatly from Calvin's.

Luther insists that law and gospel must not be confused. The Bible contains both because both are necessary to our salvation, but not in the same way. The Law is there to show us what sinners we are and to frustrate our attempts to save ourselves. It is to propel us out of trust in ourselves to trust in Christ alone. It should not be presented as if it could be kept. It should be declared in all of its strictness in order to beckon us to forsake that enterprise as the very essence of sinfulness and pride. The gospel is declared over against the Law. The Law should be presented in such a way as to show us our sin and guilt. The gospel should then be declared so that we know that in Christ our sin may be forgiven and our guilt taken away— that we are free from the Law.[32] This means that technically, not all of a sermon is the preaching of the Word. The preaching of the Word, in the strictest sense, is the proclamation of the gospel.[33] Law and gospel *must not be* confused, says Luther.

Calvin did not see such a chasm between law and gospel and saw little need for keeping the distinction as clear as Luther did. Calvin knew, understood, and positively appreciated Luther's distinction, but he believed Luther to have been too narrow.[34] The Law does indeed frustrate us to the point of trusting Christ but that is only one "use" of the Law. The Law does come from sovereign God, after all, and cannot be negative only. Citing such passages as Matthew 5:20ff, and Luke 16:17, Calvin insists that the Law is an external means that can help us attain the Christian goal—authentic sonship in Christ.[35] To be sure, in striving under grace to keep the Law, the believer will be made all the more aware of the need of Christ and his grace, but there is indeed keeping of the Law under that grace; there is positive growth in holiness.[36]

Preaching, then, for Calvin, includes both law and gospel, with the corresponding difference from Luther in what it means to say that biblical preaching is a mark of the Church. Biblical preaching, for Calvin, includes the preaching of the keeping of the Law, especially of the Decalogue, under grace. In fact, in this sense, the Law is really an aspect of the gospel—a notion not allowed by Luther. And the door is open to the preaching of good works primarily as a means of sanctification rather than solely as a response to justification.

This is not the place to dilate upon the specific differences between Luther and Calvin regarding the sacraments; but an obligation has been established to say something of them as marks of the Church in the light of the profoundly different ecclesiologies of the two men. Simply put, Luther believes that it is only through Word and sacrament that the Spirit comes to believers.[37] The sacraments are the "outward" vehicle; the Word, the "inward."[38] Of course, they depend upon faith and this faith "brings it to pass that the sacraments effect what they signify."[39] For Calvin, the sacraments have no vehicular function. Rather, they are means of reaffirming the mutual pledges of the covenant between the elect and God. A sacrament is an "external symbol by which the Lord seals to our consciences the promises of his benevolence toward us, and we, in turn, affirm our piety toward him."[40] They are testimonies to what has been done for the believer and they are the believer's pledge of faithfulness.

So, when Luther calls the sacraments a mark of the true church, he is reflecting his understanding of the Church as the dwelling-place of God—Father, Son, and Spirit—not "Church" as a thing in a place but Church as the unique conjunction of God and humanity in which God's saving work in Christ comes to confessing sinners for their ap-

propriation. When Calvin calls the sacraments a mark of
the true church, he is reflecting his understanding of the
Church as the congregation of the predestined, of those
elected to salvation, with whom a covenant has been
made.

For Luther, then, the sacraments are the means of en-
Spiriting the Church. They are the means by which Christ
is made truly present in and with his people. For Calvin,
the sacraments are the means of mutual reaffirmation by
God and his people that their promises and commitments
still hold and are active. They do make Christ to be truly
present when one's reaffirmations and his or her faith in
God's reaffirmation is sincere.

The language by means of which Luther and Calvin explained their ecclesiologies often sounds the same, or
nearly so, on the surface. And there are some comon beliefs, deeply held. But the two differed fundamentally on
almost every term in the ecclesiological lexicon and thus
created two very different traditions, though it would be
foolish to accuse either of being less than fully Protestant.

There were those, however, who were sure that Luther
and Calvin (and Zwingli) had not gone far enough in their
reforms; that, in fact, they had compromised with the
world, if not with Roman Catholicism, and were therefore
unworthy to be heard and heeded as teachers of Christ's
true church. One of the most vocal and troublesome
sources of such critique was the congeries of persons and
groups that came to be called the Anabaptists.[41]

The Anabaptists rejected the notion that the Church is a
mixed body. They found no warrant for the idea in Scripture. The "wheat and tares" passage so often used in
proof of the Church's mixed character on earth proved no
such thing, they said, for it clearly says "the field is the
world," not the Church. And as for Noah's Ark with its
clean and unclean animals—the Anabaptists could see no
analogy between church membership and the ceremonial

cleanness or uncleanness of the animals, though they did accept the analogy between the Ark and the Church.[42]

Everywhere they looked in Scripture, the Anabaptists saw a call for the Church to be pure—an insistence upon it, in fact. They recognized, of course, that from time to time persons of doubtful spiritual legitimacy would be found in the Church, but this was not to be taken as normal. Once known, it was not to be countenanced. Disciplinary action was to be taken at once, separating the sinner from the Church. But immediately, as well, action was to begin in the direction of the reestablishment of full fellowship.[43]

The Anabaptists insisted that moral purity lay at the heart of that holiness that nearly everyone accepted as a mark of the true church. Their way of interpreting the matter resounded a note long-forgotten in western Christianity. In the millennium and more during which Church and civil government had collaborated to create and maintain the Christian commonwealth, the Church had developed a penitential system that by its very existence implied that it was not necessary for the individual Christian to make holiness of life a fundamental concern. It threw the focus on minimal standards and on the details of Christian living at the expense of attitudes and ideals. Best, it said, to believe that one is sufficiently sanctified by belonging to Holy Mother Church, which has the authority to distribute and apply to superabundant merits of her incomparably holy Lord and the merits of her martyrs and other saints.

Roman Catholicism had not contravened the biblical insistence upon holiness as an absolute necessity for all who would finally see God and enjoy life in heaven. Rather, it had interposed institutional holiness in such a way that the common belief grew that its personal possession in this life was not an utter necessity and was, in fact, an improbability for all except a few monks. Personal holiness would be gained in purgatory as one suffered for what had been lacking in earthly holiness and good works.

The magisterial reform (Luther, Zwingli, Calvin and English), reacting to the vast schemes of works-righteousness created by the Roman Catholic system, had tended so to emphasize salvation by grace and apart from merit that almost any insistence upon moral effort was suspect. The door to works-righteousness was to be tightly shut, but so too, probably inadvertently, was the door to any strong doctrines of sanctification or even well-developed theological ethics.[44]

But the magisterial reformers did recognize the biblical demand for holiness understood as moral purity, and they recognized the need for giving it appropriate theological and spiritual place. They also recognized it as a mark of the true church. As to the holiness of the Church, they tended to follow Augustine and say that the Church is holy because her Lord is holy. What was said of the Church was then applied, *mutatis mutandis*, to the individual believer. Only in later generations did the magisterial systems elaborate systematic ethics or doctrines of sanctification. This earlier emphasis upon imputed righteousness, with all of that emphasis' careful theological articulation in polemics as well as apologetics, had made it difficult to make a legitimate place for a doctrine of imparted righteousness in a consistent theological system.

The Anabaptists soon came to see that the single-most effective element blocking commitment to moral purity in the ecclesiologies of the magisterial reform and Catholicism was their commitment to the venerable notion of the *corpus Christianum*, the Christian commonwealth. This insight did not usually mean that the Anabaptists despised or disregarded the civil state. But they severely criticized the Church since the era of Constantine, when Church and civil government had begun to see themselves as two sides of an indivisible coin. This, said the Anabaptists, had thoroughly corrupted the Church. It had engaged the Church in the worldly ways of secular politics, it had led the Church to rely upon the state for its maintenance instead of upon the Holy Spirit, and it had thoroughly confused the Church as to its proper task. The magisterial reformers, said they, had often enough begun well but in refusing to renounce the notion of the Christian commonwealth had stumbled into theological and ethical inconsistencies, ungodly compromises and bargains with the world, and hopeless temporizing.[45] The reformers were proving conclusively that the slightest compromise corrupts the entire enterprise of reform.[46] What is necessary, they said, is not reformation of the old but restoration or restitution of the original.[47] For this, the new Testament lays down the model, they believed.[48]

As they saw it, the New Testament church was an association of believers only, separated from the world, and guarding against infiltration by the world by means of strict discipline. They also understood that the New Testament church suffered profoundly for righteousness' sake. This, then, would be the model for restitution.

Basic to the requirement that the Church be an association of believers was the implication that it must be a voluntary society. This would be symbolized by the baptism of believers only. In the sixteenth century, this notion was radical, so old as to be novel, and seditious. Since Theodosius (d. 395), Christian baptism had made one a subject of the civil state; the Church was expected to inculcate loyal, subservient citizenship. Baptism was an act of civil obedience and allegiance. If it were now made voluntary, and there were vast numbers of unbaptized about, how could the Church hold any authority over or even within society, for its own sake or for the sake of the state and public order? To the magisterial reformers and to Catholic leadership, the idea of the Church as a voluntary society was sociologically unthinkable.[49] As they saw it, the Anabaptist idea would destroy the *corpus Christianum*.

The magisterial reformers and the Catholic leadership were quite correct as to the conclusion to which Anabaptism would have come, sociologically. But they were in error in their assumptions concerning the means by which the Anabaptists would attempt to bring it to pass. In error, but not without reason. The radical fury of Thomas Müntzer and the political maneuvering and then pious fraud that had produced the horrible debacle at Münster were taken as typical Anabaptist strategies. In fact, Müntzer was not an Anabaptist, strictly speaking, and the Münster Anabaptists were an aberration quickly repudiated by the majority of Anabaptists.[50]

More attractive to the majority of Anabaptists than the notion of sudden revolution were the notions implicit in the parables of the leaven and the mustard seed. As they saw it, to take up arms or to develop political strategies was to use the world's weapons and to run the risk, to say the least, of suffering the irony of contamination for the sake of purity.[51]

Nonetheless, the Anabaptists were radical. They believed that there are only two sorts of people in this world, and two kinds of association: God's and Satan's. And it is impossible that the two should mix, for the congregation of Satan will seek to corrupt and will persecute the congregation of God.[52] In practical terms, then, the danger of an Anabaptist destruction of normal society was negligible, for they were agreed that their ideal could be reached only in separation from the world and from the worldly church.[53]

As the Anabaptists read it, the New Testament pattern for the Church could not be followed where there is "sin in the camp," or where measures are but halfway, or where the world has influence in the Church. A church marked by any of these things is no church at all. The only true church is one consisting of believers only, totally committed to the gospel of the kingdom of heaven and, through the gospel, committed to each other.[54]

Generally speaking, the Anabaptists disavowed the notion of the invisible church and insisted on its very contradiction—that the true church should be, must be, visible.[55] So it was that they criticized the magisterial reform and Catholicism quite openly and in unvarnished prose, and, at the same time, made little effort to hide their "seditious" gatherings from the authorities. Leaven they would be, but not usually hidden leaven. Their separation from the world and from worldly churches did not usually lead them to isolation except where they were exiled or deported. Most frequently, it led them to persecution.

But suffering usually did not dishearten the Anabaptists. They saw it as an opportunity to imitate Christ. And they tended to see it as vicarious. They, like Christ, would suffer to save others.[56] Suffering, especially when it came from the hands of the religious authorities, or at their instigation, was also believed to be a certain sign that they were indeed the people of God at the end of time. So, if need be, they would suffer even death or exile and they would not hide. The true church must be visible precisely in its purity and suffering.[57]

Suffering and separation did indeed help to make the Anabaptists more visible. And they reasoned that if visible, all the more reason to be pure. So they emphasized the public character of discipline.[58] Within a voluntary association, this presented unique problems and opportunities. They hoped to show both the seriousness of God regarding sinfulness and sinning and his graciousness in forgiveness and restoration to fellowship in their exercise of moral and ethical rigor.[59]

The most serious form of discipline was the ban, exercised in various degrees. But care was to be taken to assure that it was truly disciplinary and not simple ejection, unless ejection was precisely what seemed to be called for—as in the case of presumptuous violation of biblical commandments without remorse.[60] Where there was ejection, it was understood to place the offender outside of salvation itself.[61]

Various sorts and degrees of discipline, all exercised as expressions of the Anabaptists' understanding of the power of the keys, rounded out the disciplinary system. All of them were supposed to aid the believer and the church to maintain moral rectitude, or holiness.

Several factors separate Anabaptist ecclesiology from that of the Donatists and the works-righteousness schemes of late medieval Catholicism. They had no interest in apostolic succession—at least not that of an episcopal sort—and would not see the purity of the Church depending on the clergy any more than on anyone else. Further, while holiness had originally meant moral rectitude in a rather broad sense, for the Donatists it had come to mean freedom from the taint of apostasy and not much else. The Anabaptist concern for holiness was anchored to the practice of the Sermon on the Mount. Anabaptist piety could look very much like late medieval works-righteousness, and there do seem to be some ties stronger than incidental between fifteenth-century Catholic lay movements and Anabaptism. But the Anabaptists ordinarily insisted that their piety was in response to the grace of God in salvation, not a system of works meant to gain their practitioner salvation. In this and in their insistence that the Bible be their ethical authority they were clearly evangelical.

Some cautionary notes should now be sounded about this review of Anabaptist ecclesiology. Anabaptism is really a generic designation and not the name of a well-defined group. So, exceptions can be found among them to almost every generalization made here. Further, Anabaptism was essentially a lay movement generally unconcerned with theologically refined exposition of its beliefs and practices. So, rational reflection on the phenomenon faces the dual prospect of giving reason where there was none and neglecting perfectly legitimate explanations simply because they were not preserved in writing.

With those notes, we can now move on to examine the ecclesiology of the English Reform, one branch of which, Puritanism, may be the most overarticulated, overrationalized system of them all.

The English reformation practically sprouted ecclesiologies—and with good reason. Each of the major continental reform movements had articulate adherents in England—some aliens, some immigrants, some native-born. And at times in the reign of Henry VIII and in that of Mary, English scholars and churchmen with Protestant leanings took refuge on the Continent. Even when they would have been safe in England, some made their way southeast to study.

The English merchant communities and the universities especially proved to be fertile ground for reforming notions—home-grown and imported.

As the break with Rome became clearer and more permanent, it became necessary for those favoring the reform and guiding it to explain that particular strategy for change. Theologically, they were forced to identify the true church within the visible church. It was clear that this was a conservative reform. It lacked the revolutionary fervor of its continental analogs. Much of the old was to remain, but how would it be determined what went and what remained?

The theological problem was paralleled by a pastoral one raised by an increasingly literate and history-conscious society: what did this royally imposed, though not altogether unwanted, reformation say of the salvation of their royally Roman Catholic forbears?

Thomas Cranmer (1487-1556), first Protestant archbishop of Canterbury, put the theological issue sharply.

> If we shall allow them for the true Church of God, that appear to be the visible and outward Church, consisting of the ordinary succession of bishops, then shall we make Christ, which is an innocent lamb without spot, and in whom is found no

guile, to be the head of ungodly and disobedient members.[62]

Richard Hooker (1555-1600), Master of the Temple at the Inns of Court, leaves his perception of the pastoral problem.

> Let me die, if ever it be proved, that simply an error doth exclude . . . utterly from hope of life. Surely, I must confess unto you, if it be an error to think that God may be merciful to save men even when they err, my greatest comfort is my error; were it not for the love I bear unto this error, I would neither wish to speak nor to live.[63]

Cranmer's specific target was the Roman Catholic claim that it was the one true church—a claim based, as we have seen, on certain interpretations of historical data. Hooker's specific target was the Puritan claim that since Roman Catholicism was clearly idolatrous, none who are or were its willing adherents could hope for eternal life.

Neither Cranmer nor any other of the moderate Anglicans wished so to define the true church as to keep Roman Catholicism out. Their principle concern was to assure the English that they were in. Neither Hooker nor any other moderate Anglican wished to gloss over what he believed was Roman Catholic error. They simply wanted to reform, not reject it.

The usual early English attempt to define the true church within the visible repaired to the classical Protestant understanding that the marks of the true church are at least the Word and the sacraments. Some English, as well as some on the Continent, had believed that there were one or two more marks.[64] But the English discovered what the continental reformers had—that these seemingly simple marks pose complex questions.

Perhaps as vexing as any was the Puritan exaggeration of the role of preaching in defining the true church.

Few, Anglican moderate or Puritan, would dispute the Protestant notion that "Word" in "Word and sacrament" meant "biblical preaching." In fact, they generally agreed with the Protestant rationale for it.[65]

The continental reformers believed that the Word is ultimately and essentially Christ himself.[66] But, of course, Christ manifests himself through several ancillary words, as it were.[67] From the standpoint of the public character and authority of the Church, the most important of these ancillary words is the external written word—the Scriptures. On the other hand, the Scriptures remain an unintelligible word until the Holy Spirit enlivens them, witnessing to their truth as it applies to the given reader or auditor.[68] This attested word, then, is the internal word and is no longer written in itself. In addition to the external written word and the internal word that comes through reading or hearing, there is the external oral word—the sermon. It is, of course, based upon the external written word. And, like the external written word, it is absolutely dependent upon the internal word for its effect.[69]

One need not fret over whether the Spirit will generate the inner word. Authentic proclamation of the external word will assuredly be accompanied by the inner word.[70] In fact, one of the most important characteristics of God is his speaking.[71] Then, too, the sermon was, after all, the original vehicle for the gospel.[72] So the external spoken word has a certain priority. As we have seen, most of the reformers accounted it to be the basic mark of the true church.

Enter here the Puritan caricature—the exaggeration of the role of the sermon. Some even referred to it as the usual means of grace, asserting that saving grace is granted only in conjunction with biblical preaching.[73] Some were even logically consistent enough to relegate private or public reading of the Bible, when unaccompanied by a sermon, to the rank of soteriologically inefficacious exercise.[74] The Bible must be preached to have effect, they said.[75] Perhaps the most untoward conclusion that developed from this position was the idea that the sermon is thus as important as Scripture itself—a point of view that very quickly tends to elevate the words of a preacher to the level of the oracles of God.[76]

The exaggeration of the role of preaching as the principle mark of the true church was accompanied in Puritan thought by a corresponding devaluation of the other mark: the sacraments. In part, this devaluation was a consequence of their having adopted something like the Reformed view of the sacraments. Not all Puritans were Reformed in theology, but by the 1590s the great majority of them were. As they saw it, the sacraments were, in the words of William Perkins, a Cambridge scholar, "a sign to represent, a seal to confirm, an instrument to convey Christ and all his benefits to them that do believe in him."[77] They were not certain means of grace, for that would fit poorly their doctrine of election. Of the sacraments' capacity to engrace, they had to be necessarily unsure. So they spoke in the language of "sign," "seal," and "symbol," and of a sure divine influence only among the elect. Here were covenant tokens of grace already received and affirmations that the gospel promises are fulfilled. They were celebrated primarily because they were commanded by Christ; this was the way in which God would have his people worship. In fact, the biblical passages read at sacramental celebrations were frequently called "Warrants." And with this view the Puritans believed they could avoid the twin evils of human invention in worship and "will-worship."[78]

The devaluation of the sacraments mentioned earlier comes at the point of their efficaciousness. Their benefits apply to the elect only. And the elect engage in them because they are thus commanded. This is in no way to say that they were not taken seriously or that they were drained of significance. It is to say that they tended to become necessary religious ordinances rather than welcome infusions of grace.

At the same time that Puritanism exaggerated the role of preaching as a mark of the true church, and devalued the sacraments, many of them added a third mark: discipline. Calvin had flirted with that idea, as we have seen. And more than a few of the earlier English reformers had held to it as well.[79] But generally, it had been abandoned by the magisterial reform—partly because of that reform's unwillingness or inability to separate from the civil government, partly on the theological ground that finally it becomes subjective and is, at any rate, too easily transformed into works-righteousness.

The Puritans retained discipline as a mark of the true church, largely on the basis of arguments developed by Martin Bucer early in the Reformation. Bucer's principle was "No ban, no Church."[80] Puritan literature is replete with references to discipline, not merely as an aspect of life in Christ but as one of the three marks of the true church. This, of course, followed logically on the conviction that love of a disciplined life is a "sign and note" of one's election to salvation.[81] The elect, of course, are the true church.

There were episcopalian Puritans, for it was not necessary that any in the Church of England believe that bishops were of the *esse* of the Church. In fact, one point continually made by the episcopalians in their struggles with the presbyterians and independents was that the New Testament presents no binding church order.[82] The church, they said, is constituted by the sincere preaching of the Word and the duly administered sacraments. No bishop is necessary to have these, nor is episcopacy necessary as a third, independent mark. The episcopacy was argued solely from historical and pragmatic grounds or expediency. Abuse of episcopacy, they insisted, is no reason in itself for destruction of episcopacy.[83]

Only with the second and third generation of Puritans did serious efforts arise to underwrite the presbyterian form of government from biblical bases.[84] But more effective in the long run than their positive *apologia* was their raising of doubts about the episcopal system. The presbyterian Puritans held the idea of a national church no less fervently than the establishment Anglicans and episcopalian Puritans—and at greater cost to theological consistency, for their doctrine of election could not admit of a Christian nation. Nonetheless, the obvious and carefully nourished relationship between the episcopalians and royal authority—especially as it was used to nurture sociopolitical conservatism—made an easy target for presbyterian Puritan propogandists. There was little doubt in their minds that the Church of England was yet too Roman Catholic and that a major programmatic reason for this flirtation with idolatry was the episcopal structure of the Church.

So convinced were many Puritans of the thoroughly idolotrous character of Roman Catholicism that they insisted with certainty that Roman Catholics had no hope of eternal salvation unless they repented of their false worship. This attitude stirred the waters greatly. Pastorally, it generated serious questions about the eternal welfare of ancestors who had lived and died (a good Anglican term!) loyal Roman Catholics. It also generated fears about one's own destiny: if one happened to live in a parish served by a staunch Puritan and one had considered certain pieties, such as signing with the cross at baptism, to be appropriate and even necessary to the rite, serious scruples could arise over their omission; if one lived in a parish served by a moderate or high Anglican and believed the signing with the cross to be a "popish superstition," another sort of scruple could arise. Crossing parish boundaries, except in very large towns and cities, simply could not be done.

It is this constellation of scruples that Richard Hooker set about to address in his first several years as Master of the Temple. Most notable in this enterprise was his sermon titled "A Learned Discourse of Justification, Works, and How the Foundation of Faith Is Overthrown." It was first preached 28 March, 1586, and then distributed in expanded form in several editions.[85]

Hooker will have nothing to do with the Roman Catholic claim that the visible Roman Catholic church is the one true church. On the other hand, he rejects the Puritan claim that the Roman Catholic church is a totally false church.

Historically, says Hooker, the Catholics do hold to a biblical, and hence a correct, view of the basic soteriological doctrine of true Christianity. They certainly err in their application of the doctrine of justification, but they are not in error concerning its content.[86] They have indeed overthrown the foundation of the Christian faith. But this is a consequence of their misapplication; it is not an intentional destruction. And surely those in unconscious error may be saved.[87] Of course, repentance is necessary for the forgiveness of even unconsciously committed sin, but this is, in part, precisely what the liturgy is for.[88]

Hooker is less hopeful for then-contemporary Roman Catholicism. The leadership at the Council of Trent deliberately set out to overthrow true faith. And for this, they must bear due responsibility.[89] But the principle still holds: those in unconscious error may be saved provided there is at least a general confession and repentance. And for this, the liturgy affords an avenue.[90]

Hooker's constructive response to the broader ecclesiological questions posed by presbyterian and (by now) independent Puritanism, and an oblique response to Roman Catholic ecclesiology as well, came in his book *Of the Laws of Ecclesiastical Piety*. The first four volumes appeared in 1593 and a fifth in 1597. Three more volumes appeared posthumously (1648-1662) under some cloud of inauthenticity, though it was known that at the time of his

death he had completed, but not revised the manuscript
for the three additional volumes planned. Generally, they
are accepted now as authentic but incomplete.[91]

Methodologically, this work is especially notable in that
Hooker discusses the Church without extended recourse
to the classical Protestant marks and with minimal concern
to distinguish, in usual Protestant fashion, between the visible and invisible churches.

Hooker nowhere gives the Scriptures less authority than
any continental reformer or Puritan, but he is careful to
define the kind of authority which they have.[92] They are
sufficient to salvation, even necessary thereto; but commitment to their sufficiency or necessity does not, says
Hooker, rule our reliance upon other sources of revelation
and authority.[93]

It is from this standpoint that Hooker moves in on Puritan theology and the Puritan ethos. As we have seen, the
Puritans tended to exaggerate the role of preaching and
came very close to making it the sole mark of the true
church. Hooker rejects that exaggeration emphatically and
simply bypasses the matter of the Word as a mark of the
Church insofar as "Word" be understood as "biblical
preaching."

In the first place, says Hooker, the moderate Anglicans
have no desire to devalue the sermon. In fact, says he,
"Wherefore how highly so ever it may please them (i.e.,
the Puritans) with words of truth to extol sermons, they
shall not herein offend us." But, "our desire is to uphold
the just estimation of that from which it seemeth unto us
they derogate more than becometh them."[94]

There had been strong Puritan reaction to the degree of
uncommented public reading of Scripture called for by the
Book of Common Prayer.[95] Hooker responds that historically, public reading of Scripture has been an instrument
used by the Holy Spirit to keep faith alive and vibrant.[96]

The Puritan objection had been tied to the argument that

the Anglicans were more concerned to read than to preach and that their preaching was, at any rate, often tepid.[97] Hooker countered that if the style and content of preaching were the issue, the Puritans were as much sinning as sinned against, but the real issue is the nature of the Word itself. It is not divided; it is one, be it read, taught, discussed in conference or conversation, or preached. The sermon does have an advantage, especially if people are taught to listen to sermons and to believe them to have a special benefit and if the preacher is artful. But this advantage is not necessarily a spiritual one, in essence.[98]

A basic tactical error of the Puritans, says Hooker, is their inclination to read or hear "sermon" whenever they read or hear the word "Word" or "Scripture." If they were consistent in their reasoning, says Hooker, they would then have to accept the sermon as having the force of Scripture itself—and that would include some Anglican homilies that some of them admit to be genuine sermons. If they were logically consistent, "then must we hold that Calvin's sermons are holie Scripture." How much better, says Hooker, to recognize that sermons are works of "human wit" and "often times accordingly taste too much of that over corrupt fountain from which they come." He continues, "Be they never so sound and perfect, his word they are not as the sermons of the prophets were; no, they are but ambiguously termed his word, because his word is commonly the subject whereof they treat, and must be the rule whereby they are framed."[99]

Hooker here has really leveled a serious charge at the direction in which the second and third generation of the reformation movement—especially those in the Reformed wing—were taking the doctrine of the Word. His appeal to its unitary character recalls the position of Luther, or more especially that of Calvin himself. But this understanding of the Word's unitary character was a subtlety lost on the Puritans.

In effect, then, Hooker revalues the place of the Word in Protestantism—revalues it upward. And this in the face of the Puritan use of Scripture and regard for preaching that would appear at first blush to place the Word on a very high pedestal indeed. He recognizes that "the necessary use of the Word of God" lies at the heart of the issue: the Puritans wanting to narrow "word of God" to Scripture and sermon and then subject all things to what is found in them; the moderate Anglicans wanting "word of God" to be understood to include Scripture, sermon, teaching, conversation on Scripture, and other ways in which and means through which the Holy Spirit communicates.[100]

Hooker would also revalue the place of the sacraments in Protestantism, especially as against the Puritan understanding of them. He revalues them upward in order to show the visible church as more significant to salvation than the Puritans would allow.

> The Church is to us that very mother of our new birth, in whose bowels we are all bred, at whose breast we receive nourishment. As many therefore as are apparently to our judgment born of God, they have the seed of their regeneration by the ministry of the Church which useth to that end and purpose not only the Word, but the Sacraments, both having generative force and virtue.[101]

The purpose of the Word—preaching, teaching, and so on—is to bring us to salvation. In this, it completes, and, insofar as intellect functions according to its fallenness, stands over against reason. The Word reveals the nature and plan of God as they affect our salvation. The purpose of the sacraments is also to bring us to salvation but in another dimension. They "serve to make us partakers of Christ."[102]

The Puritans had clearly come to another conclusion. They had come to "assign unto them (i.e., the sacraments) no end but only *to teach* the mind, by other senses, that which the Word doth teach by hearing.''[103] Now, Hooker could agree wholeheartedly with the highest that the Puritans say of them.

> For let respect be had to the duty which every communicant doth undertake, and we may well determine concerning the use of sacraments, that they serve as bonds of obedience to God, strict obligations to the mutual exercise of Christian charity, provocations to godliness, preservations from sin, memorials of the principle benefits of Christ; respect the time of their institution, and it thereby appeareth that God hath annexed them forever unto the New Testament, as other rites were before with the Old; regard the weakness which is in us, and they are warrants for the more security of our belief; compare the receivers of them with such as receive them not, and sacraments are marks of distinction to separate God's own from strangers: so that in all these respects, they are found to be most necessary.[104]

But this understanding of them is insufficient; they are means of grace.[105] So Hooker adds:

> But their [i.e. the sacraments'] chiefest force and virtue consisteth not herein so much as in that they are heavenly ceremonies, which God hath sanctified and ordained to be administered in his Church, first as marks whereby to know when God doth impart the vital or saving grace of Christ unto all that are capable thereof, and secondly as means conditional which God requireth in them unto whom he imparteth grace. For sith God in himself is invisible, and cannot by us be discerned working, therefore when it seemeth good in the eyes of his heavenly wisdom, that men for some special intent and purpose should take notice of his glorious presence, he giveth them some plain and sensible token whereby to know what they cannot see.[106]

Inasmuch as the sacraments are means of grace, they both bring the individual into the visible church and sustain his or her spiritual life there. Whether they also bring the individual into the invisible church and sustain spiritual life there is dependent upon the mysterious working of divine grace and the human will.[107] Again, they are means of participation in Christ or at least they may be.

The visible church, then, is elevated in Hooker's opinion beyond what the Puritans allowed. For Hooker, the Church was primarily the administrator of divine grace; for the Puritan, it was primarily the announcer of that grace.

Hooker's point of view tends to obscure the sharp difference that Protestants made between the visible and the invisible church, but not accidentally or out of some logical slippage.[108] The continental Protestants used the distinction to void the Roman claim that it was the true church, visible, and to cope with their own problems as territorial or magisterial churches with strong doctrines of election. Practically, the Church of England did not need the distinction until the last fifteen years or so of the sixteenth century, and its understanding of election was ampler and more optimistic than that of the continental Protestants. Until Robert Browne established the separatist congregation in Norwich in 1581, all was Church of England. The Thirty-nine Articles, published in permanent form in 1563, reflect a period in which there was little practical need to speak of any but the visible church and in which theoretical statement would have raised useless questions. This is the attitude Hooker reflects.

The invisible or mystical church is known to God alone. Salvation belongs to it; all who are members of it are saved.[109] But God has given the visible church the Word and the sacraments, and through them, salvation.[110] In this sense, the visible church is also mystical.[111] The sacraments, especially, express the relationship between visible and invisible. They are, in fact, the link between the two.[112] Granted, of course, the sacraments are not *ex opere operato* and when the participants lack proper fatih, their effect is negative. But what the effect of participation may be in any participant at any time is known to God alone.[113]

This means that while Word and sacrament are marks of the true church, they do not sufficiently define the visible church. And Hooker perceives that it is necessary, after all, to define that visible church in the struggle with the Puritans—not that his response satisfies them!

The visible church, says Hooker, is that society that professes "one Lord, one faith, one baptism."[114] Beyond this we cannot go, Hooker believed, in the assessment of the concordance of the visible church with the mystical or in finding the true in the visible. The mystical impinges upon the visible in Word and (especially) sacrament, making it betimes the "visible mystical body."[115] But just who belongs is known to God alone.[116] Hooker believes those to be excluded who lack "those virtues that belong unto moral righteousness and honesty of life" and, much more fundamentally, those who have no inward belief of heart, who despair and lack hope, and who are empty of Christian love and charity.[117]

Hooker recognizes that his definition of the visible church leaves room for many whom the Puritans could not accept as Christian—indeed, many of whom he would himself be suspicious.[118] But his purpose is not to argue that the visible church is the true church—a point that the Puritans seem not to have caught. His point is to show that the impurity of the visible church does not, can not, totally obscure the presence of the mystical church within it. The true reformation of the Church cannot come, Hooker holds, by separating in every way from Rome or even heretics as if they had no Christianity at all. The purpose of reformation is not to attempt to build a new ship but to change the course of that one church that has existed from creation itself.

Polity, then, must be built on the recognition of the character of the visible church—the society of those who *profess* one Lord, one faith, one baptism. The mystical or invisible church needs no polity.[119] For the visible church, the New Testament lays down no binding order. In fact, the Apostles could not have laid down such an order, for the visible church exists in a world that offers changing circumstances.[120]

No polity, then, including episcopacy, can be of the *esse* of the Church.[121] The Church is constituted by Word and sacrament (according to earlier Anglicanism) or the profession of one Lord, one faith, one baptism (Hooker). Episcopacy is simply a form of polity that has proven itself historically.[122] In fact, the Church of England does accept as valid other, nonepiscopal ministries. It does, however, draw the line with regard to England. There, it will not accept such ministries because it could divide the English church, and to divide the English church is to divide the English people. Revolt against episcopacy is political sedition. But it is not heresy, strictly speaking.

Moderate Anglicans responded to charges of inordinate submission to the civil ruler, made by both Puritans and Roman Catholics, by declaring that the sovereign's power over the Church is that of jurisdiction; it is not the power of ministry itself. So, for instance, the crown could nominate a cleric to be bishop but could not ordain him bishop.[123]

Further, the ordination of a bishop gives him power of jurisdiction over his diocese, and power to order the Church there—i.e., to ordain clerics, to be responsible for the sincere preaching of the Word and the due administration of the sacraments, and to administer the temporal affairs of his diocese—but in the power of ministry—i.e., the power of the keys, the right to administer the sacraments, and the right to the exercise of pastoral care in the congregations to which they are assigned—bishops and presbyters are equal because the power of the ministry does not admit of degrees.[124] The bishop's power of jurisdiction could indeed be transferred to others, such as a council, or to another person, should the Church so desire.

So, for moderate Anglicans, the episcopate is not indispensible. And it is certainly no mark of the true church, as the Roman Catholics allege.

Anglican ecclesiology, then, developed from a purely Protestant perspective to something genuinely unique in Hooker. Originally satisfied to identify the true church in the visible by its possession of at least the two marks of Word and sacrament, it was forced to defend itself as a visible manifestation of the true church by the Puritan overevaluation of preaching and by presbyterian Puritanism's biblicism with respect to polity. This had the unhappy consequence, much later, of a re-Catholicizing of Anglican ecclesiology, by which is meant a revival of the notion of bishops in apostolic succession as a mark of the true church. But such was not the view of Hooker and his intellectual progeny.

Puritan ecclesiology, on the other hand, developed to something unique as well, from a simple concern that certain practices and vestments be declared adiaphora in genuine Protestant fashion. It, too, was originally satisfied to identify the true church as the visible by its possession of Word and sacrament. But as "Word" generally meant "biblical preaching" (in a broad sense that included instruction and other elements) in Protestantism at large, it came to mean "sermons, paramountly" in Puritanism. And where earlier Protestantism, and continuing Protestantism at large, took the sacraments to be means of grace, the Puritans understood them to be testimonies to grace already given.

The entire Puritan enterprise was tied closely to a rather literal understanding of Scripture and in this it was ecclesiologically unique.[125] To the Puritan, *sola scriptura* meant "no other source may be used in establishing faith and practice"; to Protestantism at large, *sola scriptura* meant "in establishing faith and practice, Scripture is the sole arbiter." By the 1580s, Puritan ecclesiology consisted of locating and applying various biblical passages (or of pointing to Anglicanism's lack of them) in a wealth of attempts to build a wholly biblical church. This made division an inherent probability in Puritanism and it made it possible for Anglicanism to become indifferent to even the older and more nearly normative understanding of Word and sacrament as marks of the true church.

POINT-COUNTERPOINT IN EARLY MODERN ECCLESIOLOGY

In this section, very much more narrowly focused than its predecessors, two directions will be taken. On the one hand, effort will be made to trace the ecclesiological factors that came to impinge on the life and work of John Wesley. On the other hand, attempt will be made to outline very briefly the ecclesiological developments that shaped North American Christianity up to the eve of the birth of the holiness movement.

Most of the ecclesiological struggles of the seventeenth and eighteenth centuries rooted in the soil of sixteenth-century confessions and creeds. By and large, they involve refinements, glosses, and theological exegeses of and commentary on those earlier documents. This is especially true of developments on the Continent.

England, which is at the center of our interest, presents a somewhat different scene. There, the desires of both the Anglicans and the presbyterian and congregationalist Puritans that there be one national church led to some striking ecclesiological originality in both parties, though basic theological commitments stood about where they were at the end of Elizabeth's reign. The radicals' rejection of the idea and attempt to form a national church only added to the creative flow. In the closing third of the seventeenth century, the Society of the Friends of Truth promoted a truly unique ecclesiology to which attention must in due time be given.

We begin with Anglicanism—with Richard Field (1561-1616), friend of Richard Hooker and Dean of Gloucester from 1610 to his death. In 1606, while Prebendary of Windsor, Field published the first four books of *Of the Church;* in 1610, the fifth and final book appeared.[126] He wrote for much the same reason that Hooker had except that the now-reigning monarch, James I, believed himself to rule by divine right and in his disgust with the Puritans made it quite clear that his alignment would be with the Anglicans. And yet, the Puritans were not about to roll over and play dead. They rapidly gained support among the merchant class, and as the royal authority became more insistent and demanding, so did their propoganda and political maneuvering, especially in the cities of the realm. So the controversies that had inspired Hooker's work in the 1590s were hotter and more acrimonious when Field wrote.

Like Hooker, Field sought to answer the question of the locus of the true church within the visible church, especially as it was raised from the perspective of ecclesiastical discipline. Like Hooker, Field decided that it is impossible to identify it with certainty but that there are certain signs that point to it. He rejects the Puritan practice of speaking of the elect as being "of the Church" and thereby making the true church a secret society and the visible church of little or no positive spiritual significance except as it serves the elect.[127]

And yet, Field does not want to throw away the notion of visible/invisible churches. There is one church, he insists; it is visible at the point of its profession of one Lord, one faith, and one baptism, and visible as well in its possession of the sacraments and an ordained ministry; invisible as it is the company of the elect, but they are within the visible church. He arrives at this point by distinguishing between those who are in the Church and those who are of the Church.[129]

Unlike Hooker, Field ventures some marks of the Church: "the entire profession of those supernatural verities which God hath revealed in Christ his Son," "the use of such holy ceremonies and sacraments as he hath instituted," and "an union or connexion of men in this profession and use of these sacraments, under lawful pastors and guides, appointed, authorized and sanctified."[130] In short, Field's marks are doctrine, sacraments, and ministry.

Field was convinced that the three marks are best preserved by a triple order of ministry—deacons, priests, and bishops.[131] But he held that bishops and priests (presbyters) are really of one order and that where an entire episcopacy was somehow incapacitated, a presbyter could ordain as if he were bishop. That is to say, the bishop's power of order is no greater than a presbyter's; and it is also to say that bishops are not necessary to the Church. However, Field does insist that at least in England it would be folly to dispense with the episcopal system, for that would bring disorder.[132] Generally, apostolic succession through the bishops is affirmed, but it is succession in faith that must underlie ecclesiastical succession for the latter to be valid.[133]

Field was, of course, writing an *apologia* for the Church of England from the Anglican side, so his marks have specific points of reference. Doctrine means the Thirty-nine Articles; the sacraments are baptism and eucharist; the ministry is the episcopal order. And yet Field does not understand these points of reference to delimit or express the precise form that doctrine, sacraments, and ministry must take. Rather, he wants to show that there is but one church, of which the Church of England is a faithful part because it possesses the three necessary marks. Their special Anglican form is not the form that they must necessarily take everywhere but they are truly the necessary marks.

At the same time that Field was writing, and for several

decades thereafter, a number of Anglicans, feeling the force of the Puritan criticism that they were unscriptural and the Roman Catholic criticism that they were schismatic, took up serious study of the early church. They hoped thereby to establish a rationale for Anglican faith and order that would be properly accountable to both Scripture and tradition—Scripture being the foundation-stone, of course.[134] Especially effective in this enterprise were works by Lancelot Andrewes (1555-1626),[135] John Bramhall (1594-1663),[136] Joseph Hall (1574-1656),[137] John Hales (1584-1656),[138] Henry Hammond (1605-1660),[139] William Nicholson (1591-1672),[140] Herbert Thorndike (1598-1672),[141] Francis White (c. 1564-1638),[142] and his younger brother, John (1570-1615).[143]

In the day-to-day life of the Church of England, William Laud (1573-1645), Archbishop of Canterbury from 1633 until deprivation in 1640, paved the way for the application and enforcement of the scholars' work. Laud misjudged the strength and vitality of Puritan sentiment, and his high-handed methods only furnished that sentiment a clear target, costing him his life. But an adverse assessment of his character neither gives nor denies value to his ecclesiology. It must be judged by other canons.

What is clear in that ecclesiology is Laud's commitment to Scripture and to the *consensus quinquesaecularis*, the supposed general agreement among the leaders of the Church of the first five centuries on matters of faith and practice. Laud was convinced that his Church of England was part of the visible and true church, in clear continuity with the ancient church.[144] He said, in fact, "the Church of England in nearest of any Church now in being to the Primitive Church." And there were those in England and elsewhere who agreed with him.[145]

Laud agrees with the Puritans that "inward worship" is what is necessary in the true church, however much "external worship" be commanded and ordered. But he sharply disagrees with the Puritans' inclinations thus to reduce external worship—rites and ceremonies—to a minimum. Their logic is faulty and the consequence of following it is worse: some ceremonies may be unnecessary, he agrees, but that is no ground for saying that none are needed. Ceremonies help us to retain the real substance of religion. Besides, the Church of England practices in doctrine, ceremony, and government only what Scripture allows and what the early church practiced.[146]

But by appealing to the practice of the early church, Laud and his party did not intend to set that Church as a model for every detail. They made it abundantly clear that Scripture is the real authority.[147] The faith and practice of the early church are seen as exemplary interpretations and applications of Scripture in principle, but not necessarily in particulars. For the early church to be the model in particulars there would have to be a close parallel between the historical circumstances of that Church and any other.[148] The Church of England, so Laud and others believed, does imitate the early church in its theological and ethical perspective. It is not bound to apply that perspective in the same ways, however.

After all, the early church was not perfect. And that is why Scripture, which is the very work of God, "sufficient unto salvation," is the fundamental resource. Yet, Scripture and tradition are interdependent, in part because the question is not simply "What does Scripture mandate?" but, more broadly, "What does Scripture allow?" Laud writes,

> The Scripture where 'tis plain should guide the Church; and the Church where there's doubt or difficulty should expound the Scripture; yet so as neither the Scripture should be forced, nor the Church so bound up, as that upon just and farther evidence, she may not revise that which in any case hath slipt by her.[149]

That "just and farther evidence" could come from any

one of four sources but would always have to satisfy the integrity of the other three before it could be accounted authoritative. Those four sources, working in tandem, were to become increasingly useful in Anglican theological methodology over the next two centuries. They are (1) the traditional testimony and witness of the Church, (2) the tenor of Scripture itself as a whole, (3) the "inward testimony" of the Spirit, and (4) reason.[150]

This four-fold scheme did help the moderate Anglicans to avoid the theological and practical *cul de sac* into which the Puritans had driven with their understanding of *sola scriptura*. The Puritans had taken the principle to mean that Scripture should be the only source for faith and practice. This left them with the necessity for giving prooftexts for all things. The moderate Anglicans understood *sola scriptura* to mean that the Bible is the sole spiritual guide "sufficient unto salvation," the only infallible instrument used by the Holy Spirit to bring us to Christlikeness and eternal felicity. The Anglicans, therefore, did not believe that they were obliged to defend everything with biblical texts.

On the other hand, the moderate Anglican understanding did tend to make arguments from expedience and tradition too readily accepted, often giving them an appearance of theological respectability whether merited or not. And it did promote an ecclesiastical style very different from, even contradictory to, anything with which the Puritans could have anything to do.

The Anglican service now became a means of renewing faith in God; the Puritan service sought to aid the elect to perfect their understanding of God and self. The Anglican minister was a priest, an intercessor with God on behalf of the people, a mediator with Christ; the Puritan minister severely limited the priestly role in those days and emphasized his place as teacher and prophet. Anglican worship aimed at reconciliation between God and humanity;

Puritan worship aimed either at explaining the ways of
God to human beings or at counseling faithful acceptance
of divine inscrutibility.

Both paths were radical: the Anglican in its attempt to
be catholic without episcopacy as an essential, necessary
mark of the Church; the Puritan in its attempt to have a
Bible-warrant for all that it believed or did. But both paths
led to essential betrayals of the original radical bases: the
Anglican in its increasing concern to establish episcopacy
as normative finally came to argue apostolic succession as
if it had believed it all along; the Puritan in its theocratic
ambition becoming increasingly willing to compromise the
doctrine of election and the notion of the commonwealth
of the saints.

As early as 1606, John Overall (1560-1619), at the time
dean of St. Paul's, London, argued that the apostles "fully
communicated their apostolical authority" to those who
would be their successors and that it was their intention
"that the same order and form of ecclesiastical government should continue in the Church for ever."[151] But at
the time, even this much appeal to apostolic succession
was made by only a small minority, the majority view
being that of Hooker and Field.

By the time of Laud's reign in Canterbury, in addition to
keener advocacy of the apostolicity of episcopal government, strong arguments were being pressed for the
authority of the bishop as a divine gift or right.[152] By the
Restoration (1660), a significant number championed the
notion of apostolic succession as a necessary mark of the
true church.

One of the earliest and most effective cases for this later
position was actually written during the Civil War by
Jeremy Taylor (1613-1667), at the time chaplain to the Earl
of Carbery and after the Restoration, bishop of Down and
Conner. *Episcopacy Asserted* (1646) was Taylor's first
book and he knew that it would be troublesome.[153] Taylor

believed that episcopacy could be proven to be the one proper form of church government from Scripture, apostolic tradition, and "Catholic practice." Christ established this form of polity by committing to the apostles the power of the keys and the power to appoint successors. These successors were bishops. Christ also established the presbyteriate in the appointing of the seventy-two. So, "bishops are the ordinary successors of the apostles, and presbyters of the seventy-two." And, the evidence from the Fathers, so Taylor believes, shows that they believed this to be a divinely wrought arrangement ever to be followed in the Church.[154]

We shall examine the Puritan declension from its original reforming bases in the section on developments in ecclesiology in North America in the colonial and early national periods. For the moment, we remain in England.

The sharpest criticism of the pretensions of episcopal Anglicanism and both independent and presbyterian Puritanism was developed by George Fox (1624-1691), founder of The Society of the Friends of Truth, better known as the Quakers, and by his "Melanchthon," Robert Barclay (1648-1690).[155]

The basic ecclesiological proposition raised by Fox and Barclay is that there is but one true church, that it is the society of those called to be saints, and that its mark is its production of the fruits of righteousness and true holiness.[156] One may know the presence of this society by the signs of new life: evangelistic concern[157] and the expectation that its members will follow after holiness as defined by Scripture.[158] Where there is no real expectation of genuine moral transformation, there is no Church.[159] This is to say, of course, that the Church is to be defined in terms of its manifest life, its fruits, not in terms of such factors as apostolic succession, doctrine, ceremonies, or organizational pattern.[160]

Barclay knew that even the community of those called

to be saints needed organization.[161] But he insisted that
the headship or lordship of Christ over the Church be
immediate—priests and "ministers" tended to make it
mediate.[162] The absence of a ministerium or clerical orders
need not mean the absence of order, however.[163] This is
true for two basic reasons. First, the Holy Spirit is truly at
work, sensitizing the group to the diverse gifts among
them and drawing them to peace and harmony, not to
egoism and disorder.[164] They will be a group or a society
seeking God's will together, each having accountability to
all. Second, the business of the Church has been made
abundantly clear. It is to exercise compassion,[165] to adjudicate disputes among society members and to see to
their reconciliation, and to mete discipline.[166] It is to these
very ends that the Holy Spirit is at work among them in
his sanctifying work. And in such circumstances, disorder
is precluded.[167]

The Friends did not take organization of the Church to
be a concession to human sinfulness or simply an interim
arrangement. Rather it is an essential expression of
spirituality, friends of truth being impelled to fellowship
precisely because they know Christ and live in the
Spirit.[168] The Spirit himself gathers persons to wait upon
God, to worship, and to bear united testimony.[169]

"Inward prayer" is a constant necessity even apart from
the worship of the society,[170] but being human we find
corporate worship edifying in ways closed to private worship. Corporate worship, says Barclay, is "iron sharpening
iron"; it is a matter of joining candles so that there can be
"more of the glory of God."[171]

But while corporate worship is a natural part of being a
child of God, is required by our human nature, and is
mandated by Christ himself, we have been left no word as
to its order or method. The writers of the New Testament
say we are to pray, sing, and give attention to preaching, but
they left no word as to the order for any of it.[172] What is

needed, therefore, is worship that requires no extra-personal buttressing—especially none of that sort that may be exercised by a nonbeliever.[173] Barclay writes,

> Yet many and great are the advantages, which my soul, with many others, hath tasted of hereby, and which could be found of all such as would seriously apply themselves hereunto: for, when people are gathered thus together, not merely to hear men, nor depend upon them, but all are inwardly taught to stay their minds upon the Lord, and wait for his appearance in their hearts; thereby the froward working of the spirit of man is stayed and hindered from mixing itself with the worship of God; and the form of this worship is so naked and void of all outward and worldly splendor, that all occasion for man's wisdom to be exercised in that superstition and idolatry hath no lodging here; and so there being also an inward quietness and retiredness of mind, the witness of God ariseth in the heart, and the light of Christ shineth, whereby the soul cometh to see its own condition. And there being many joined together in this same work, there is an inward travail and wrestling; and also, as the measure of grace is abode in, an overcoming of the power and spirit of darkness; and thus we are often greatly strengthened and renewed in the spirits of our minds without a word.[174]

In this and in other passages, Barclay seems to agree with the Anglican, as contrasted with the Puritan, concerning the purpose of worship: it is to know the presence of God. On the other hand, Barclay believes that true worship demands a spirit of "holy dependence," something that the Puritan would understand better than the Anglican.

Silence is the principle, but not the sole expression and symbol of this "holy dependence."[176] Barclay anticipated praying and speaking in that same spirit. But silence serves as a "needful" element, "during which everyone may be gathered inward to the word and gift of grace, from which he that ministereth may receive strength to bring forth what he ministereth."[177] But seldom was silence unbroken in Barclay's day, for as in the early church, the Spirit moved someone—so Barclay—to "preach, pray, or praise."[178]

Perhaps the most controversial Quaker tenet was the refusal to celebrate baptism and the Lord's Supper in the longstanding forms. This seemed to Anglican, Puritan, and Catholic alike a complete repudiation of divine commandment and Christian tradition. For some, it seemed to leave the Quakers without any mark of identification as the true church.

Barclay argued that Christ brought a radically new order, one free of times and places and persons, one "performed in the Spirit and in truth."[179] If one truly knows Christ, no outward forms are necessary for true worship; if one does not truly know Christ, no outward forms will avail to bring that knowledge. Obviously, the New Testament does speak of baptism of several kinds, the truly efficacious now being Christ's. But Christ's is a baptism with the Spirit. This is the true, the real, baptism. It is an immersion in the love of Christ and a rising with him in newness of life. And, it is absolutely necessary if one is to be Christian.[180]

We need not follow through Barclay's argument here, but we should say that his is a consistent attempt to avoid giving any room at all to magic or to any form of the notion *ex opere operato* in Christian worship. He consistently reads the New Testament to be calling for a radical life in the Spirit free of external bonds or props, however innocent or anciently venerated. The Church is the body of Christ and needs such things no more than Christ did or does.

Barclay's argument regarding holy Communion is basically the same as that regarding baptism. He read the biblical references to feeding upon Christ as invitations or commands to a spiritual feast by the soul.[181] This places

Communion at the very center of Christian faith and worship, but it is not now that physical sacrament that Barclay believes drives the participant away from spiritual reality and agitates division among would-be believers. It is a direct, unmediated communion with Christ.[182] But Barclay would not take the traditional Supper away from those with deep scruples. He asked only that they not impose their views on others or judge adversely those who had "found themselves delivered" from the physical sacraments.[183]

Puritanism had gone far in removing the distinction between clergy and laity by recasting sacramental thought and removing baptism and the Lord's Supper from their eminence as means of grace. Their understanding of ministry, whether presbyterian or independent or separatist, had also served to destroy the Roman Catholic notion that ordination bestowed a special character upon its recipients. But the Puritans still celebrated baptism and the Supper, and they still ordained their clergy. And these practices were obviously sources of tension, even schism, for there was no firm agreement as to their meaning.

Barclay and the Quakers sought to bring a message of certainty in that situation. As to disputes concerning the meaning and practice of the sacraments, these could be banished by recognizing that the true sacraments are altogether spiritual. Wranglings over ministry, its authority and compass, could be ended by the realization that all may be immediately guided by the Spirit in mutual accountability and that the Spirit comes to direct the Church through the consensus of the whole, not through the cunning, however pious, of the few.

Here, then, was a radical critique of then-existing ecclesiologies, some of which were themselves radical. Here was also a self-consistent, positive perspective.

The Puritans retained the idea of the classical marks of the Church, exaggerating the role of the preached Word at the expense of other forms of "Word" and of the sacraments. And even where it was denied that discipline was a mark of the Church, practice stood in contradiction. Further, the Calvinistic majority among the Puritans was satisfied to say that finally the true church is known only to God anyway.

Anglicanism generally gave formal assent to Word and sacrament as the marks of the true church but invested its interest in the visible church as an expression of the true so that the functional marks were really "one Lord, one faith, one baptism." And by the time of the Restoration, many Anglicans were ready to insist on episcopacy as a necessary mark as well—at either the abstract theological or the functional level.

The Society of Friends of Truth took the mark of the true church to be the producing of the fruits of righteousness and true holiness.

It remains, now, to examine the ecclesiology (-gies) operant in North America in the seventeenth and eighteenth centuries.

In fact, the task is far less daunting than it may at first glance appear to be, for North American ecclesiologies were largely caricatures of Anglo-Saxon European ecclesiologies until well into the nineteenth century.

The caricatures were honestly come by, for religion in the North American colonies was predominantly dissenters' religion. This obtained especially in the English colonies but it was not unknown even in the French and Spanish settlements. In these latter, the form of Roman Catholicism was largely of the legalistic, simplistic, communal sort advocated by mendicant monasticism and the Jesuits. These monks were fiercely Roman Catholic and equally adamant in their implied critique of European culture-Catholicism.

Of the English mainland colonies, only Virginia had an Anglican establishment that was any way near successful.

In the Carolinas and in Georgia, the Church of England was established by law but in practice never held dominant place. In 1693, New York's Assembly made it the established church, but only 3 percent of the colony were Anglican; most of the rest were divided (about 55 to 41 percent, respectively) between Dutch Reformed and several types of British dissent. Too much history had passed in New York for an Anglican establishment to mean anything.

The remainder of the colonies either avoided establishment, or, in the case of Massachusetts Bay, had a dissenters' church as the established religion.

By the mid-eighteenth century, establishment had come to mean little in Virginia. The parish system operated fitfully, in part because the population was widely scattered; in the absence of a bishop, the aristocracy and those of the rural middle class tended to treat clergy as hired hands and got the quality that such treatment engenders; and in the western valleys, Presbyterian and Baptist preachers were gathering fervent and influential congregations. In Massachusetts, establishment Congregationalism had long since broken into doctrinally disparate camps and little had been done since the closing decade of the seventeenth century to keep the colony free of such groups as the Presbyterians, Baptists, Quakers, and even Anglicans.

But for all of the vitality and change, there were no new ecclesiological developments in the colonial period. The theories remained what they had been, with some groups, such as the Congregationalists in New England, simply tempering a distinctive tenet to meet certain socially generated demands. By the mid-eighteenth century, this process had produced an Anglicanism in Virginia that had overtones of "gathered church" perspective, and a Congregationalism in Massachusetts that was ready to confess that the Church is a *corpus mixtum*. But these accommodations, and others, were understood to be pragmatic, not theological. There would be no really novel ecclesiological development on the west side of the Atlantic until Barton Stone and the Campbells came along in the nineteenth century.

Generally, the religious climate favored the notion of the "gathered church" over that of the parish. Whether these gathered churches should then associate themselves congregationally or presbyterially, informally or constitutionally; whether leadership should be clerical or mixed, hierarchical or local; whether education or "gifts" should qualify for ministry; whether one group should accept as valid the baptisms and ordinations of another and whether participation in the Lord's Supper celebrated by another's group was licit or no—these questions tended to be answered on pragmatic or customary grounds by the time of the American Revolution. And since the Great Awakening, these "pragmatic and customary grounds" were deeply affected by considerations of religious sentiment and experience. Therein lay the wave of the future, ecclesiologically.

Notes

1. E.g., WA 17[ii]. 33 and 37; 50. 624. WA refers to *D. Martin Luthers Werke: Kritische Gesamtausgabe* (Weimar: H. Böhlau, 1883ff.). Citations in this section are even farther from being exhaustive than in the previous sections. They are presented as examples.
2. Cf. LW 31.31, 210, 230. LW refers to *Luther's Works*, American edition, Jaroslav Pelikan and Hlmut Lehman, eds. (St. Louis: Concordia; Philadelphia: Fortress, 1955ff).
3. WA 7.683.
4. WA 18.652.
5. WA 7.719-20.
6. WA 7.713; 39[i]. 191; 39th. 176-77.
7. Cf. WA 17[ii]. 262-63; 39[ii]. 161. Also see WA 1. 593; 2.603-606; 6.131; 12.486.
8. WA 51.507.

9. LW 39.69.

10. LW 41.148-60; 194-98.

11. Cf. LW 6.149.

12. LW 41.150.

13. LW 41.148-50.

14. E.g., WA 7.720.

15. WA 7.721.

16. LW 1.272.

17. WA 19.72-73.

18. Cf. Ernst Troeltsch, *The Social Teaching of the Christian Churches,* O. Wyon, trans. (New York: Macmillan, 1931), vol. 2, p. 518.

19. John Calvin, *Christianae religionis instituto* IV.i.9. This is the title given the first (1536) edition. References in this essay, unless otherwise noted, will be to the standard fifth edition of 1559, which was in Latin. It will be abbreviated, *Inst.* As in the case of Luther citations, Calvin citations are not exhaustive, only illustrative.

20. Cp. *Inst.* IV.i.9 in the first (1536) edition with the same section in the second (1539) and all subsequent editions.

21. Cf. François Wendel, *Calvin: Sources of évolution de sa pensée religieuse* (Paris: Presses Universitaires de France, 1950), pp. 297-99.

22. *Inst.*IV.i.2 and 7.

23. *Inst.* IV.i.7-9.

24. *Inst.* IV.i.7.

25. *Inst.* IV.i.9-10.

26. *Inst.* IV.i.10.

27. *Inst.* IV.i.1 and 5.

28. *Inst.* IV.iii.1.

29. *Inst.* IV.iii.2.

30. *Inst.* IV.iii.8; cf. IV.iii.4-9; IV.iv.1-5.

31. *Inst.* IV.xii.1-2.

32. E.g., WA 19.210, 226; 5.557. We but touch the surface of this complex matter here and then only from the direction of ecclesiology. Cf. Paul Althaus, *The Theology of Martin Luther,* Robert C. Schultz, trans. (Philadelphia: Fortress, 1966), pp. 253-56.

33. WA 39^i .442.

34. Cf. *Inst.* III.vii.6 and 8.
35. *Inst.* II.vii.12-13; III,xix.2.
36. *Inst.* III.viii.3 and 5.
37. WA 1.632; 2.112.
38. WA 2.112.
39. WA 2.715; 6.24.
40. *Inst.* IV.xiv.1.
41. This essay restricts itself to the Anabaptist movement within the so-called radical or left-wing Reformation because it is they—especially the Mennonites—who will later contribute more to holiness movement ecclesiology than any other groups or persons in the nonmagisterial religious revolution of the sixteenth century.
42. E.g., Balthasar Hubmaier, *Quellen zur Geschichte der Täufer.* IX Band *Balthasar Hubmaiers Schriften,* Gunnar Westin and Torsten Bergsten, eds. (Gütersloh: Gerd Mohn, 1962), pp. 434-57. Also see Henry Vedder, *Balthasar Hübmaier: Leader of the Anabaptists* (New York and London: G. P. Putnam's Sons, 1905), p. 135.
43. E.g., Menno Simons (Leonard Verduin, trans.), *Admonition on Church Discipline,* in *The Complete Works of Menno Simons* (Leonard Verduin, trans; John C. Wenger, ed. Scottdale, Pa.: Herald, 1956), pp. 410-15.
44. These did develop later and precisely from the groundwork done by Luther and Calvin, but they are quite undeveloped in Luther's thought and only somewhat more mature in Calvin's. Cf. Althaus, pp. 269-73, and Calvin, *Inst.* III.vi.3. Also see Paul M. Bassett and William M. Greathouse, *Exploring Christian Holiness,* vol. II: *Historical Foundations* (Kansas City: Beacon Hill, 1984), chapter 4.
45. Cf. Louis (Ludwig) Haetzer, *Eine kurze wohlgegründete Auslegung der zehn nachgehenden Episteln S. Pauli* (1524), *Mennonite Encyclopedia,* 4 vols. (Scottsdale, Pa.: Herald, 1955-59), vol. II, p. 622. Also see, e.g., Hubmaier, *Von Ketzern und ihren Verbrennern* (1521), p. 16. For source-based discussion see Leonard Verduin, *The Reformers and Their Stepchildren* (Grand Rapids: Eerdmans, 1964), pp. 95-131.
46. E.g., Hubmaier, *Von dem Schwert.* Vedder, pp. 275-310, translates the entire work. Cf. Verduin, pp. 21-62; 95-131.

47. For full discussion, cf. Franklin H. Littell, *The Anabaptist View of the Church* second edition (Starr King, 1958), esp. chapters 2 and 3. For an example among the primary sources, cf. Obbe Philips, *Bekenntnisse,* in *Bibliotheca Reformatoria Neerlandica* ('s-Gravenhage, 1903-1914), vol. VII, pp. 12ff. See the translation in *Spiritual and Anabaptist Writers,* George H. Williams and Angel M. Mergal, eds., vol. 25, *Library of Christian Classics* (Philadelphia: Westminster Press, 1957), pp. 112-35.

48. E.g., Peter Rideman (Riedemann), *Rechenschaft unserer Religion Lehr und Glaubens von den Brudern so man die Hutterischen nennt, ausgangen durch Peter Rideman* (154), II.ii. German edition; Fulda: Eberhard Arnold Verlag, Bruderhof-Neuhof, 1938. English translation by Kathleen E. Hasenberg, *Account of Our Religion, Doctrine and Faith, Given by Peter Rideman of the Brothers Whom Men Call Hutterians* (Place of pub. not given: Hodder and Stoughton w/ Plough Pub., 1950), cf. pp. 154-65.

49. Cf. W. Sohm, *Territorium und Reformation in der hessischen Geschichte, 1526-1555* (Marburg, 1915) for a thorough study of early serious wrestling with this issue in an area in which a clearly congregational, almost "gathered Church" ideology developed, though superficially the Church remained magisterial.

50. For the details, see George Huntston Williams, *The Radical Reformation* (Philadelphia: Westminster Press, 1962), pp. 362-403. Also see Rideman, II.vi (English translation, pp. 205-25).

51. E.g., Rideman, I.lxviii-lxxi (English translation, pp. 102-109).

52. *Schleitheim Confession of Faith* art. IV (John Wenger, trans. in *Mennonite Quarterly Review* XIX [1945], 249). Also see Robert Friednamm, "The Doctrine of the Two Worlds," in *The Recovery of the Anabaptist Vision,* Guy Hershberger, ed. (Scottdale, Pa.: Herald, 1957).

53. E.g., Rideman, I.lxiii-lxv (English translation, pp. 91-97).

54. Rideman, I.xxiii-xxvi (English translation, pp. 38-43).

55. Rideman. Some, such as Caspar Schwenckfeld, argued that they were themselves members of the invisible church. Cf.

Caspar Schwenckfeld, *Corpus Schwenckfeldianorum,* J.
Hartranft, R. Johnson, S. G. Schultz, eds. vols. 1-15[a]
(Leipzig, 1907-1939); vols. 15[b]-19 (Pennsburg, Pa.:Board of
Pub. Schwenckfelder Church, 1959-1961), vol. IV. pp.
830-31. The visibility of the Church is a presupposition
absolutely necessary to the whole disciplinary ideal of the
Anabaptists.

56. E.g., Jakob Hutter, *Apostolic Letter VIII* (1535). English
translation: Robert Friedmann, *Hutterite Studies* (Goshen,
Ind.: Mennonite Hist. Soc., 1961), pp. 203-13. Luther had
also believed that a faithful church will suffer.

57. Hutter. Also cf. Ethelbert Stauffer, "Anabaptist Theology
of Martyrdom," *Mennonite Quarterly Review* XIX (1945),
pp. 179ff.

58. Discipline, specifically the ban, became a basic tenet in
Anabaptist thinking by 1540. Already in 1527., the
Schleitheim Confession had made it one (the second) of its
seven articles. By 1541, Menno Simons published his *Admonition on Church Discipline* (cf. *Complete Works,* pp.
413ff.) Cf. F. C. Peters, "The 'Ban' in the Writings of
Menno Simons," *Mennonite Quarterly Review* XXIX
(1955), pp. 16-33.

59. In addition to the items cited in n.284, also see Rideman,
I.lxxxviii-lxxxix (English translation, pp. 131-33).

60. Cf. Menno Simons, *Instruction on Excommunication* (1558)
(cf. *Complete Works,* p. 287.)

61. E.g., *Schleitheim Confession,* arts. II and IV.

62. J. E. Cox, ed., *Miscellaneous Writings and Letters of
Thomas Cranmer* (Cambridge: Parker Society, 1846), 2.13.

63. John Keble, ed., *The Works of Mr. Richard Hooker,* 3
vols. (Oxford, 1836, rev. ed. R. W. Church, F. Paget; Oxford: Clarendon, 1888), 3.543.

64. E.g., Nicholas Ridley, *Works* H. Christmas, ed. (Cambridge: Parker Society, 1841), p. 123: "The works whereby
this Church is known unto me in this dark world and in the
midst of this crooked and froward generation are these—
the sincere preaching of God's word; the due administration of the sacraments; charity; and faithful observing of
ecclesiastical discipline according to the word of God."

65. E.g., John Jewel, *The Works of John Jewel, Bishop of Salisbury,* J. Ayre, ed., 4 vols. (Cambridge: Parker Society, 1845-1850), 4.1164. In this essay, "Anglican" will refer to those wanting to build a "biblical" Church, continuity or no.

66. E.g., Luther, WA 8.236.

67. Cf. WA 40[ii]. 548-50.

68. E.g., WA 10[i]. 130; 30[ii]. 687-88.

69. E.g., WA 2.112.

70. E.g., WA 2.112; *Smalcald Articles,* art. 321.

71. E.g., John Calvin, *Corpus Reformatorum: Johannis Calvini Opera quae supersunt omnia,* Baum, Cunitz, Reuss, eds., vols. XXIII-XLVI of the *Corpus Reformatorum,* Breitschneider and Bindseil, eds. (Halle, 1843-1860), XXIV.453.

72. E.g., WA 10[i]. 625-27; LW 35.123.

73. E.g., Henry Smith, "The Arte of Hearing in Two Sermons," in *The Sermons of Maister Henrie Smith gathered into one volume* (London, 1593), p. 646; Thomas Cartwright in John Whitgift, *Works* J. Ayre, ed., 3 vols. (Cambridge: Parker Society, 1851-1853), I. 26. Some of Cartwright's works appear here. Cartwright even argues, from the example of John the Baptist, that all baptisms must be accompanied by preaching. Cf. D. J. McGinn, *The Admonition Controversy* (New Brunswick: Rutgers, 1949), p. 101.

74. E.g., Cartwright, in John Whitgift, *Works* II.373-78.

75. Richard Hooker, *Of the Laws of Ecclesiastical Polity* in *The Works of Mr. Richard Hooker,* John Keble, ed., revision by R. W. Church and F. Paget, (Oxford: Clarendon, 1888) V.xxi-xxii. Hereinafter, *Of the Laws . . .* will be abbreviated EP. Also, Cartwright, in John Whitgift, *Works* II.374-92.

76. Cf. Hooker's critique of this issue, EP V.i.20.

77. William Perkins, *The Foundation of the Christian Religion gathered into six principles* (London, 1595), aif C4v.

78. Cf. Thomas Cartwright, *A Treatise of the Christian Religion or the whole bodie and substance of Divinitie* (London, 1616. Posthum.), 219-29 for an extended exposition of the function of the sacraments.

79. E.g., John Hooper, *The Later Writings of Bishop Hooper*, C. Nevinson, ed. (Cambridge: Parker Society, 1852), p. 43.
80. Martin Bucer, *Commonplaces of Martin Bucer*, D. Wright, trans. and ed. (Appleford, 1972), p. 39.
81. Nonetheless, not all Puritans held to the presence of discipline as a mark of the true church. Two very important Puritan leaders who did not were William Perkins and Thomas Cartwright. Both argued numerous times that Word and sacrament were the constituting marks and argued against assigning such importance to discipline, though, of course, they were given to pressing for holiness of life in the churches. Cf. William Perkins, *The Combat between Christ and the Devil*, second edition (London, 1606); A. F. Scott Pearson, *Thomas Cartwright and Elizabethan Puritanism 153-1603* (Cambridge: Cambridge University, 1925), pp. 308ff.
82. E.g., Whitgift, I.416; II.90; Hooker, EP V.vi-x.
83. E.g., Whitgift, I.184-185; II.227-228.
84. Instructive here is a then-contemporary analysis of Puritan ecclesiological development presented by Bishop Thomas Cooper, *Admonition to the People of England* (London, 1589), p. 160. The principal biblical warrants cited by the Puritans for their method were Deuteronomy 4:2 and 12:32. For a declaration of Puritan sentiment, see Thomas Cartwright in John Whitgift, I. 21-22.
85. The best edition is the Keble edition of Hooker's works (cf. *supra,* note 75), vol. III. 475-550.
86. Richard Hooker, "A Learned Discourse of Justification, Works, and How the Foundation of Faith Is Overthrown," sects. 4-6.
87. Hooker, "Learned Discourse," 7-19.
88. Cf. Hooker, "Learned Discourse," 18, 26, 33; also see EP V.vi.2.
89. Cf. Hooker's close reading of the decrees and canons of the Council of Trent in the notes of the *Learned Discourse* at sects. 5-6, 11.
90. Hooker, "Learned Discourse," 26 and 33.
91. Cf. C. J. Sisson, *The Judicious Marriage of Mr. Hooker and the Birth of the Laws of Ecclesiastical Polity* (Cambridge: Cambridge University, 1940) for a critical biog-

raphy and a study of the problems surrounding Hooker's EP. In short, the basic problems have been an Izaak Walton too gullible in his biographical judgment and a Bishop Gaudens too self-serving in his work with vol VII. Also cf. F. J. Shirley, *Richard Hooker and Contemporary Political Ideas* (London:SPCK, 1949), pp. 41-57.

92. Cf. EP I.xiv.1-5.
93. E.g., EP III.viii.12-13.
94. EP V.xxii.1
95. E.g., Thomas Cartwright in John Whitgift, II, 374-92.
96. EP V.xxii.1-20.
97. Thomas Cartwright, in John Whitgift, *Works* I.127-60, even insisted that the reading of homilies was not preaching. Also see II. 363-92.
98. EP V.xxii.1-20.
99. Cf. EP V.xxii.10, including Hooker's manuscript note.
100. EP II.1.2.
101. EP V.1.1 (ie., V.50.1).
102. EP V.1.3 (i.e., V.50.3).
103. Cf. EP V.lvii.1.
104. EP V.lvii.2. This much, any but the most radical Puritan would be willing to say.
105. EP V.lvii.4-5.
106. EP V.lvii.3.
107. Cf. Hooker, "Fragments of an Answer to the Letter of Certain English Protestants." John Keble, ed., I.xxviff. gives an account of the "Fragments." They are most readily available in the Everyman's Library edition of EP I-V (nos. 201 and 202; London; J. M. Dent and Sons; New York: E. P. Dutton, 1907), 202.490ff. Here Hooker works successively with free will, grace, the sacraments, and pre-destination. The order and connections demonstrate the point made here.
108. Cf. H. F. Woodhouse, *The Doctrine of the Church in Anglican Theology: 1547-1603* (London:SPCK, 1954). Woodhouse believes that Hooker's distinction between visible, mystical, and visible mystical is really only a distinction between visible and mystical (invisible) and that Hooker is simply confusing.
109. E.g., EP III.i.3 and 8; V.lvi.7 and 11.

110. EP V.1.1 (i.e., V.50.1).
111. EP V.xxiv.1.
112. EP IV.i.1-4.
113. EP V.lvii.1-6; Cf. esp. 4.
114. EP III.i.3 and 7.
115. EP V.xxiv.1.
116. EP III.i.2.
117. EP III.i.7.
118. EP III.i.8.
119. EP III.xi.14.
120. EP III.xi.11-12.
121. E.g., EP III.xi.16. Hooker does believe episcopacy to be nearer the ideal than any other polity. Also cf. John Whitgift, *Works* I.184-85; II.227-28.
122. Whitgift, *Works* I.6, 184-85.
123. Cf. Article XXXVII of the Thirty-nine Articles.
124. E.g., Thomas Cranmer, *The Remains of Thomas Cranmer*, H. Jenkyns, ed. 4 vol. (Oxford: Oxford University, 1833), I.117. Whitgift, *Works* II.263, says they are not equal, but the inequality is pragmatic, not theological.
125. At first glance, Puritan ecclesiology, in its biblicism, would appear to resemble Anabaptism. Closer examination, however, seems to show the Anabaptists far less bibliocentric than the Puritans. For the Anabaptists, the Bible is the means by which the life of the Kingdom is revealed; for the Puritans, it is the very constitution of the true church, the fellowship of the elect.
126. Richard Field, *Of the Church, Five Books by Richard Field, Doctor of Divinity* (London, 1606 [books 1-4], 1610 [book 5]). Modern edition: *Of the Church,* edited by Ecclesiastical History Society (Cambridge: Clarendon, 1852).
127. *Of the Church,* I.vii.
128. *Of the Church* I.x.
129. *Of the church* I.ix.
130. *Of the Church* II.ii.
131. *Of the Church* II.vi.
132. *Of the Church* V.xxvii.
133. *Of the Church* III.x1.

134. E.g., William Laud, *A Relation of the Conference between William Laud, Then Lord Bishop of St. David's, Now Lord Archbishop of Canterbury, and Mr. Fisher, the Jesuit* (London, 1639), preaf. The conference took place in 1622.

135. E.g., *Articuli Lambethani: vol. IV Lanceloti Andrewes Tou Panu* (1651) *(Judgment of the Lambeth Articles); Responsio ad Apologiam Cardinalis Bellarmini* (1610).

136. E.g., *A Just Vindication of the Church of England from the Unjust Aspersion of Criminal Schism* (1654); *Schism Guarded* (1658); *A Vindication from the Presbyterian Charge of Popery* (1672, posthumous).

137. E.g., *The Old Religion* (1628); *Episcopacy by Divine Right Asserted* (1639). Hall was a Puritan who advocated the episcopal form of government. His treatise on episcopacy underwent considerable tampering by William Laud but the decision to print it was Hall's.

138. E.g., *Schism and Schismatics* (1642).

139. E.g., *View of the Directory and Vindication of the Ancient Liturgy* (1645); *Of Fundamentals in a Notion Referring to Practice* (1654).

140. E.g., *A Plain Exposition of the Church Catechism* (1655); *An Apology for the Discipline of the Ancient Church* (1659).

141. E.g., *An Epilogue to the Tragedy of the Church of England* (1659).

142. E.g., *The Orthodox Faith and Way to the Church Explained and Justified: in Answer to a Popish Treatise* (1617).

143. E.g., *The Way to the True Church; Wherein the principal Motives persuading to Romanism and Questions touching the Nature and Authority of the Church and Scriptures are familiarly disputed and driven to their issues* (1610).

144. Laud, praef.

145. Laud, p. 245.

146. Laud, praef. Also see Hammond, *View . . . and Vindication . . .* , pref.

147. Laud.

148. Laud.

149. Laud.

150. Cf. pp. 39-49, for Laud's exposition of these sources.
151. John Overall, *The Convocation Book of 1606*, p. 147. This work is also known as *Bishop Overall's Convocation Book Concerning the Government of God's Catholic Church and the Kingdoms of the Whole World.*
152. Cf. his *Dissertationes quator quibus epsicopatus jura ex S. Scripturis et primaeva antiquitate adstruuntur* (1638).
153. Jeremy Taylor, *Episcopacy Asserted* (London, 1646), dedicatory epistle. (The edition perused for this essay was that of 1650, bound with *A Discourse of the Liberty of Prophesying*.)
154. Taylor para. 9 and 10.
155. Barclay's written works present several problems. The work usually referred to as *Truth Triumphant* is actually a collection, the first edition of which was published in London in 1692. The preface printed there was probably written by William Penn. A three-volume edition was published in London in 1718. The first edition is the one used for this essay. Its full title: *Truth Triumphant through the Spiritual Warfare, Christian Labours and Writings of that Able and Faithful Servant of Jesus Christ, Robert Barclay.* The *Apology for the True Christian Divinity* was written in Latin and published in the Netherlands. I have not seen this edition. I have perused the second Latin edition, published in 1729. The first English edition was published in the Netherlands in 1678. References in this essay are to the stereotype of this edition published in Philadelphia by the Friends' Bookroom, 1908. *Truth Triumphant through the Spiritual Warfare* will be designated by the abbreviation TT; *Apology* by *Apol.*
156. *Apol.* X.x.
157. Cf. TT, p. 697.
158. *Apol.* VIII passim. Also cf. TT, p. 230.
159. *Apol.* X.v.x.
160. Cf. *Apol.* X.x.
161. Cf. *Apol.* X.iii; also TT, pp. 203-207.
162. Cf. *Apol.* X.x.xxiv-xxvii, xxxiii.
163. E.g., TT, p. 185. Here, Barclay is defending the Quakers against the charge that they are fanatic individualists.

164. *Apol.* XI.vi-vii,ix.
165. George Fox, *The Journal of George Fox,* John L. Nickalls, ed. (Cambridge: Cambridge Universty, 1952), p. 668.
166. Cf. TT, p. 211.
167. *Apol.* VIII passim, but esp. i-ii.
168. Cf. *Apol.* XI.iii, vi, xvii.
169. *Apol.* XI.iii.
170. *Apol.* XI.xxi.
171. *Apol.* XI.xvii.
172. *Apol.* XI.x.
173. *Apol.* XI.xviii.
174. *Apol.* XI.vii.
175. E.g., *Apol.* XI.vi.
176. *Apol.* XI.ix. Silence was to become a more nearly normative characteristic of Quaker worship after Barclay's day.
177. *Apol.* XI.ix.
178. *Apol.* XI.xvii.
179. *Apol.* XII.vi.
180. Apol.
181. *Apol.* XIII.ii.
182. *Apol.* XIII.ii-iii.
183. *Apol.* XIII.xi.

Melvin E. Dieter (Ph.D., Temple University), vice-provost and professor of church history, Asbury Theological Seminary

The Concept of the Church in the Nineteenth-Century Holiness Revival

IT WAS INEVITABLE that the question of the nature of the Church and its mission should arise in the course of the holiness revival that began about 1840 and continued to grow within the American churches for half a century. Hundreds of small renewal groups sprang up within the churches to promote the preaching of Christian perfection and to call Christians to greater commitment. In essence and function they were counterparts of the Pietistic *ecclesiolae in ecclesia* that had expressed similar concerns for a more authentic representation of the Christian life within the Lutheran and Reformed churches in the post-Reformation era.[1] Because of their special concern for fellowship and their dedication to disciplined Christian living, the presence of these holiness fellowships within the American churches—especially those within the Methodist churches—created nagging tensions within the established structures. They were tensions that small groups commonly have produced within the larger bodies of less-involved Christians as the renewal groups seek to revive or reform the Church as a whole around their own concepts of what constitutes the true Christian life. Ultimately they challenged the adequacy of the concepts of the nature of the Church that prevailed in the established denominations.

These nineteenth-century revivalists, like the Pietists of the seventeenth century, strongly declared their loyalty to the churches of which they were members. For almost sixty years after the revival began, most holiness adherents proved the sincerity of their claim by continuing to propagate their concerns for renewal as members of the mainline denominations of the day. They could have identified readily with the father of German Pietism, Jacob Spener, when he contended that his followers were using all their energies "to improve the Church," not to divide it.[2] Critics of the movement, however, from the earliest days of the revival, saw nothing but schism ahead if the holiness associations were allowed to continue their activities from within their denominations. In the end, on the question of loyalty or schism, both the movement and its critics proved to be right. The main stream of the movement has always maintained that holiness adherents, for the most part, were forced out of rather than left the churches of which they were members. There were only minor disruptions of fellowship up to the end of the century. It was only then that the formative elements of the present holiness churches began to separate and organize new denominations out of the hundreds of loosely organized holiness associations and bands that had been spreading their message throughout American Methodism and other Protestant bodies.

The denominational pedigree of one or the other of almost every extent American church could be discerned in the make-up of one or more of these new holiness churches; they nevertheless displayed a remarkable unity of doctrine and purpose centered in their common commitment to the necessity for a personal experience of grace subsequent to that of justification and regeneration by which the believer's heart could be made free from the necessity (but not the possibility) of willful sin and be filled with the Holy Spirit. By 1900, most of the preaching of the movement associated this deeper Christian life crisis-experience with the baptism of the Holy Spirit and the Pentecostal experience of the early church. This renewed emphasis on the presence and power of the Holy Spirit in the churches was reinforced by the movement's teaching on the gifts of the Spirit, especially the gift of healing, and upon Spirit guidance in the lives of individual Christians and the Church.

When major sectors of the revival movement finally began to create their own denominational organizations, their understanding of the nature and mission of the Church in many ways differed little from what prevailed in the established denominations of the day. Their polity was in most instances clearly reminiscent of the Methodist or Baptist churches from whom they drew the largest number of their adherents. There are several dominant historical phenomena discernible in their development, however, that left indelible and unique imprints upon their ecclesiological understanding. Three of the most critical of these phenomena are (1) the small group, (2) the camp meeting, and (3) the concept of "the age of the Spirit."

The reflections on the revival's historical and theological developments that follow may help us to identify certain ecclesiological ingredients in the movement's self-understanding that tend to distinguish them as a distinct group within Protestantism. Each of these three rather comprehensive ingredients involve wide-ranging issues that move beyond our immediate interests; for our purposes we are concerned specifically with how each of these influenced the ecclesiology of the holiness movement and churches to which it gave birth or shape.

THE HISTORICAL CONTEXT

A brief historical introduction to the holiness revival is essential to understanding the discussion of these issues. Small "holiness" or "deeper life" renewal groups began to appear in the Protestant churches of America in the wake of the Second Great Awakening. The centers quickly coalesced into a perfectionist revivalist movement. The Wesleyan Methodist Connection and The Free Methodist church, upon their separation from Methodism in 1843 and 1860 respectively, both officially espoused the essentially Wesleyan doctrine of Christian perfection that lay at the heart of the movement's revivalistic thrust. In each instance their founders were dubious of the future of the doctrine in main-line Methodism. When the movement finaly took institutional form, the Church of the Nazarene, the Pilgrim Holiness church, the Church of God (Anderson, Indiana), the Salvation Army, and a host of smaller churches and agencies had joined with these two older Methodist bodies to form what are known today as the holiness churches. Today they constitute the seventh-largest family of Protestant churches around the world.[3]

Next to the sometimes irritating presence of these renewal groups within the established churches, the extended success of the holiness revival itself was the most significant factor in raising the church question within the holiness tradition. The evangelistic call of the revivalists to a personal commitment to the life of Christian holiness was directed to those who already professed Christian experience; but, in practice, the movement's evangelism often proved to be equally effective in bringing new converts into the faith. Many of these had had few religious attachments of any kind. How and by whom these new Christians should be nurtured and fellowshiped were difficult questions to answer. The obvious suggestion that they should become members of some existing local church in the established denominations frequently did not seem to be a viable one.

The problem was especially complicated for those holiness converts who were more familiar with non-Methodist rather than Methodist religious traditions and terminologies. There was little encouragement in the churches of the Reformed tradition for those who had responded to the strongly perfectionist teachings of the holiness evangelists, although that and almost every other Protestant tradition had been affected by the revival. Charles G. Finney and Asa Mahan of Oberlin fame both had influenced Congregationalism and Calvinistic evangelicalism in general by their vigorous espousal of perfectionism at Oberlin College. Absalom Earle and Edgar Levy had done the same in the Baptist churches; William Boardman and others represented adherents to the revival in the Presbyterian tradition. But these, along with the other non-Methodists who testified to a "second blessing" of some kind, represented only a healthy beachhead in their denominations. Reformed theology had had to go through a long series of transformations before the theology and methods of the revivalism of Finney had become acceptable to significant sections of the Calvinist churches. However, neither Finney nor other holiness evangelists were able to create a synthesis between Calvinism and the essentially Wesleyan message of entire sanctification as widely acceptable as that which they had created for their

"New Methods." Nevertheless, in spite of the fact that holiness revivalism smacked of both Methodism and perfectionism, "higher life" doctrines did take permanent hold upon the churches of the Calvinistic tradition; the Keswick movement eventually became the conservator and continuing perpetuator of the message in the Calvinistic churches.[4]

Throughout the history of the revival, however, Methodism provided the only readily available haven for the converts of the holiness movement. But there was no definite assurance that these new Christians would either desire or could find a sympathetic fellowship that would nurture their commitments even in the local Methodist churches. Many of the persons whom the holiness associations gathered up in their evangelistic efforts had already for one reason or another slipped through the nets of established Methodism. It was difficult for such persons to take up with a group with whom there was already some sense of alienation or disappointment. It was often difficult as well for Methodists "on the holiness line" to press their coverts enthusiastically into the local Methodist fellowships wherever the pastor and people might not be sympathetic to the spiritual concerns of the revival. If the ethos of the local Methodist church retained the fervor and the ambience of the revival and the camp meeting, the church question usually was muted among holiness movement adherents. In such instances, the holiness converts became a major feeder to the swelling stream of members for burgeoning Methodism. However, the tendency for the Methodist churches to become more and more representative of mainstream American culture made this ethos increasingly difficult to find. In the minds of those who had been initiated into the Christian faith by the generally more conservative holiness leaders, the church had begun to reinterpret or even abandon some of the traditional values which lay at the heart of the Wesleyan faith.[5]

The issues that B. T. Roberts and the Free Methodist movement raised in mid-nineteenth-century Methodism demonstrate the reality of these tensions. At their separation from the Methodist Episcopal church in 1860 the Free Methodist charged the Methodist Episcopal church with abandoning primitive Methodism; they claimed that they had forsaken the poor, the slave, Christian discipline, and the Wesleyan commitment to Christian holiness. There is other evidence from within that church that the issues beginning to be pressed by renewal groups were not merely the dissonant clamor of purported malcontents. Nathan Bangs, one of the early Methodism's most prominent leaders, expressed his own concern for the spiritual integrity of the church. He felt the thousands of new adherents who were continuing to flock into Methodist folds at mid-century should be disciplined through the class system that had served the church so well as "schools of holiness."[6] The decision of the Methodist Episcopal Church South, in 1866, not to require the classes for new members and the northern church's increasing failure to enforce the class system reinforced the fears of conservatives for the future of the movement. An understanding of these groups and their dynamics is essential to an understanding of how the church question was finally answered in the formation of the denominational organizations that developed out of these smaller fellowships. The conscious or unconscious preservation of the ethos and emphases of these small groups directly affected the worship, polity, and sense of mission of the new churches.

THE IMPORTANCE OF THE SMALL GROUP

This gradual abandonment of the discipline in spiritual-

ity and community fellowship that had been the genius of
Wesley's class meetings was of special concern to the
holiness revival's leaders, rooted as they were in the class
meeting tradition. Small group fellowship became a formative force in the movement's development. These early
holiness small groups were linked historically to the Wesleyan class-meeting structure. The "Tuesday Meeting for
the Promotion of Holiness," the early role setting meeting
of the revival, was begun by Sarah Lankford and her sister
Phoebe Palmer in 1835. It was the direct outgrowth of a
class meeting which they had moved from the Allen Street
Methodist Church to the parlor of their New York City
home.[7] In their purpose they reflected the purpose of Wesley's class meetings in which a group of earnest Christians
came together weekly for nurture, discipline, and witness.
The intense pursuit of holiness in which both women
engaged at this same time represented one of the primary
concerns John Wesley had had when he first structured the
class meeting system to encourage the spiritual growth of
the converts of his own revival. The birth of a renewed
concern for Christian holiness in the Tuesday meeting setting was, therefore, a natural one. Hundreds of similar
small group fellowships became the seed-bed of the
higher-life movement in America and around the world.
Had the Methodist Episcopal church pressured Sarah
Lankford and Phoebe Palmer to move the meetings of
their small-house church back into the more structured
atmosphere of their local church even as the Evangelical
Lutheran church had required Spener to do with his early
eccesiolae, the history of the revival might have been quite
different from what it was.[8]

What were some of the dynamics of this "church in the
house" that carried forward into the ongoing revival and
the church organizations?

First of all, these early small-group fellowships gave
focus to the mission of the movement. Mission is central

to ecclesiology. At the heart of the Methodist holiness meetings and the Finney-Mahan Oberlin holiness meetings that abetted them from within the American Calvinistic tradition there was the deep concern to bring the converts of the Second Great Awakening to Christian maturity and practical Christian living—to bring those already in the Church to wholehearted Christian faith and life. As the revival developed, its broader mainline-Methodist stream expressed its goals for Christian perfection in Wesleyan terms of entire sanctification—a second work of grace subsequent to regeneration that cleansed the heart from the remains of inbred sin and filled the Christian believer with the wholehearted love of God and neighbor. The holiness revival in the Calvinistic churches tended to define the second experience of grace as "the higher Christian life," "the victorious Christian life," or "the second rest"; but whatever terminology was used, present holiness through faith and the Spirit's cleansing and infilling was the goal. When the churches that were formed out of the movement took the name "Holiness" churches to themselves, they were identifying with this basic impulse of the movement; they were witnessing not to their own holiness in distinction from the other Christian churches, but rather they were indicating the central evangelistic concern that had brought them into being as a distinct group in nineteenth- and twentieth-century religion. They were urging the churches to take a new step of faith into a larger arena of spiritual power and effectiveness.

This highly focused concern of the movement, nurtured in small dedicated societies such as the Tuesday Meetings, contributed to the development of a sense of exclusiveness as church structures ultimately formed out the more informal associations of the revival. This tendency to sectarianism became most noticeable as the churches turned inward during their organizational stages. They became more culturally isolated from the mainline religious bodies from which many of their members had either come out or been forced out.[9]

Because of this dedication to evangelism and their special concern for "the higher Christian life," both the movement and the churches spawned by it were often accused, especially from within Methodism, of riding "a hobby."[10] Their critics claimed that they lacked a broad view of the Church and its mission. The subsequent history of the movement both proves and disproves the charge; some holiness adherents held to the central focus on the holiness experience so exclusively that the personal profession of the experience of entire sanctification became determinative not only for doctrine but for fellowship. The church, too, tended to maintain a small-group ethos conditioned by their adaptability to a more ready discipline of life and ministry. Separation and smallness justified in the name of purity and discipline became a part of the movement's institutional life. In its most radical and atypical expressions, this showed up in early fanaticisms in which spouses refused to associate with husbands or wives who were not professing the experience;[11] this in rare instances paralleled the use of the ban in the Anabaptist tradition. In spite of the movement's intense commitment to a second-crisis experience and a life of victory over willful sin as the norm for the Christian life set by the post-Pentecostal church. A personal profession of entire sanctification, however, became the norm for full membership in only one holiness church, the Holiness Church of California (founded in 1882?). It represented the most concrete expression of this focus in the formal ecclesiology of the movement. That standard for membership was dropped when the church merged with the Pilgrim Holiness church in 1946.[12]

But this extreme exclusiveness did not develop in the movement as a whole. Guarded by its own roots, though often vaguely perceived, in the Methodist-Anglican historical tradition, the holiness adherents regarded their promotion of entire sanctification not as an appeal to some sort of avant-guarde spiritual experience, but rather, as the contemporary expression of the concern for Christian perfection that has been a persistent element in the Christian tradition. With Wesley, their spiritual father, they believed it was to be found in the teachings of Christ and the doctrine and practice of earnest Christians from the primitive church on through all subsequent life of the Church; they regarded it as a natural development in the normal Christian's growth in Christ. The urgent call to discover the power for the holy life in a new infusion of the Holy Spirit, therefore was not the "hobby" of an aberrant group. It was, rather, a call to open up all the fullness of Christian life to the present experience of the individual and the Church by a wholehearted commitment in faith in the sanctifying grace of God already begun in every believer in regeneration.[13]

In their attempts to overcome the exclusivistic image that their commitment to the promotion of Christian holiness often presented within the communities where they ministered, most of the groups that had originally taken the term *holiness* into their official denominational name in their formative years eventually eliminated it.[14] One can conclude that their willingness to take such radical action and at the same time keep a strong commitment to the holiness movement, indicates that they may have had a more broadly oriented theological and missional self-understanding than their critics commonly allowed.

This desire to present to the society a more latitudinarian stance represents the fact that the holiness tradition in the churches, though highly focused upon its central concern, nevertheless placed itself in the much broader Christian tradition and wished to be regarded as such. Another active ingredient in this name-change development was also the attempt to dissociate their churches from the Pentecostal holiness tradition by removing the name *Pentecostal* from their institutional names after that movement began to flourish at the beginning of the twentieth century.[15] The sociological changes that gradually moved the holiness churches into middle-class status also helped to overcome the image of exclusiveness they tended to take on in their developmental stages.

A second aspect of the Tuesday Meeting that becomes significant for the historical interpretation of the movement and its self-understanding is the revivalists' use of the word *promotion* in designating the purpose of their meetings. The ecclesiology of the movement from the very beginning was shaped by an evangelistic urgency that marked the revival's sense of mission. There was the ever-present conviction that it was not enough for the church to confess its belief in the doctrine of Christian perfection; rather, both personal and corporate witness to the experience were necessary to the fullest enjoyment of the Christian life as well as to the success of the churches in responding to the new challenges to Christian faith that were rising in contemporary culture. The purifying and empowering of the church by a new baptism of "Holy Ghost fire" were seen as the only adequate answer to radical intellectual and social theories that were perceived as threats to the faith (e.g. evolution, higher criticism, a new secularism, and others).[16]

It would be difficult to overemphasize the telling effects that this sense of responsibility for getting the message before individual Christians and the churches had upon the ecclesiology of the movement. The urgency of evangelism has always dominated the theology of ministry of the churches of the holiness tradition. The mission shaped the ministry. The always-present goal of introducing persons to the biblical validity of the experience of entire sanctification and the possibilities of the higher life was a powerful force for activism. The emphasis on the Christian's responsibility in responding fully to the revealed will of God that became so critical to the revivalism of Finney was equally a part of the revivalism of the holiness tradition. The promise that the doctrine seemed to provide for healing the malaise of spirit in the churches, together with the heritage of spiritual synergism that they shared with Wesley, and the New Methods of American revivalism, all came together to create an evangelistic urgency that has left permanent marks on the movement. The rapidity with which the movement spawned evangelistic bands, holiness associations, camp meetings, conferences, periodicals, and publishing houses demonstrates the sense of mission that dominated both lay and ministerial adherents to the experience.[17]

A third characteristic of the small group ambience that has continued to cast its hues over all subsequent ecclesiological landscapes in the holiness tradition was its social function. The parlor meetings with their emphasis upon prayer, Bible study, and testimony served as powerful centers for reinforcement of doctrine and life. Sandra Sizer points out the importance of the function of this type of meeting to revivalistic movements in her study on the gospel music of the revivals. She concludes that the "social religious meeting" of this period marked the beginning of the attempt to build a new Christian community united by intense feeling.[18] The prayer meeting pattern of the Revival of 1857-58 tended to reinforce the central importance of the small group concept to revivalism itself. George Marsden's analysis of revivalism indicates that the use of such small support groups constituted the formative base not only for the holiness movement but for the fundamentalist, premillennial, and Pentecostal movements as well.[19]

Many of the elements that became part of the holiness movement's understanding of the nature of the people of

God, of what constituted true worship, and of how the Church could receive and respond to the leadership of the Holy Spirit were fashioned out of the dynamics of the small religious gatherings. The effectiveness of personal testimony for either exhortation or affirmation; the intimacy that allowed individuals to share personal doubts and spiritual aspirations; the brother-sister fellowship that brought ministers and laypersons, men and women, into a relationship that was predicated on mutual acceptance around common religious experience; the common search for the mind of the Spirit—all raised a pattern of expectation for a type of Christian community different from what they felt was prevailing in mainline American Christianity.

They were attempting to realize a new community or a renewed community patterned after the Pentecostal community of the primitive church. Henry Fish, who wrote one of the early manuals for Methodist class meetings, recognized that something different was being said about the nature of the Church in these small fellowships; in his mind what was being said resonated with the descriptions that the Scriptures gave of that early Christian community. "Something more than Church communion in the sacrament of the Lord's Supper was enjoyed by the primitive Christians," he said. Intimate personal interaction and the opportunity to "meet together for the purpose of conversing on experimental religion and the state of each other's souls" were essential elements of the Church; Christians and churches, he concluded, who do not incorporate this concept into their understanding of the Church "are not based on the model of the apostolic churches."[20] These concepts were important in the structuring of the holiness churches at the end of the nineteenth century. Charles Jones demonstrates how the kind of fellowship and community that holiness adherents had experienced in the Methodist and other revivalist churches of the pre-Civil War period became the basic motif of the churches they gathered together as they organized into denominations.[21]

Howard Snyder has also dealt extensively with how this type of fellowship influences the nature of the Church. He sees Wesley's use of classes and bands as the heart of his renewal of the church in his day. Here, he wove his view of holiness into his ecclesiology.[22] Colin Williams suggests that

> Wesley believed that the necessity for mutual encourage ment, mutual examination, and mutual service within the context of the means of grace, required more than the hearing of the Word, the participation in the sacraments, and the joining in the prayers of the "great congregation." He believed that the gathering together of believers into small voluntary societies for mutual discipline and Christian growth was essential to the Church's life.[23]

The Tuesday Meetings of the holiness revival participated in this sense of the Church; unfortunately, the integration of the quest for inner holiness and the life of discipleship that Wesley emphasized so vigorously was not maintained as well in the nineteenth-century revivalistic counterparts.

The Tuesday Meeting pattern of intimate Christian community and holiness promotion became an established and integral part of the ongoing development of the movement. After the Civil War, however, the movement adopted the camp meeting as its primary means of promotion, and the small-group dynamics that had shaped the early years of the revival were to be modified significantly.

The Influence of the Camp Meeting

Within a decade of the founding of the Tuesday Meetings, Phoebe Palmer was pressed into a more public ministry by the interest in the higher Christian life that she and her colleagues had created in the churches. She discovered that the Methodist camp meeting was a fruitful field of holiness promotion. She and her husband spent most of their summers holding special services, urging Methodist campers to experience entire sanctification. Contrary to the impression created by Charles Johnson's study of the frontier camp meeting, the camp meeting was far from a dying institution by the Civil War period.[24] It had continued to be a significant feature in Methodism from its origins on the Kentucky frontier at the beginning of the century until the significant revival of the institution as an instrument of holiness evangelism immediately after the Civil War period. Like the small renewal group, the camp meeting was also a social gathering unusually well-adapted to the evangelistic purposes of the holiness movement.

When the leadership of the movement was assumed by Methodist ministers after the Civil War they, too, quickly realized the potential of the camp meeting for wider promotion of the doctrine. John Inskip, Alfred Cookman, John Wood, and other leading Methodist pastors organized the National Camp Meeting Association for the Promotion of Holiness after their first highly successful camp meeting for the promotion of holiness held at Vineland, New Jersey, in July 1867.[25] The attendance at these "national camps" rivaled that of the fabled Cane Ridge, Kentucky, camp of 1801. The National Committee revived old Methodist camp centers, and new camps were begun; the Ocean Grove, New Jersey, camp meeting became one of the first and most influential of the latter.[26]

The continuation of the perfectionist ethos created within the parlor meetings of the early revival into the camp meeting milieu illustrates the accuracy of Daniel D. Williams's observation, "It was inevitable tha the pietists would discover in the camp meetings . . . that the . . . patterns of the conversion [in this instance, second blessing] experience could become the liturgy and sacrament of religious fellowship."[27] This uniquely American institution, both a part of the religious establishment and yet always a step removed from strict ecclesiastical control, has always provided "safe ground" for experimentation and creativity in religious development in America. The camp meeting had become so much a part of Methodist style and worship that it had established its legitimacy as part of the Church's institutional life. It was more church oriented than the small house meetings of the early movement, and yet it had no official definition within the discipline of the Church. It provided a context for the growth of the movement free from strict control by traditional denominational lines of authority and yet under degree of denominational sanction and favor.

These large open air meetings provided centers that, more than any other, became the molding force in creating holiness churches and other agencies out of the revival. In these "forest temples" the numerous, loosely organized holiness associations gradually combined into larger likeminded groupings that finally became the organized holiness churches of America. The worship patterns of those churches also were shaped in large measure in the camp meeting milieu and ambience. The camp meeting became the halfway house for the movement on its way to creating its own patterns of faith and order. These meetings in nature's great cathedral provided the room within the religious structures of the day for the holiness leaders and people to reflect the spiritual freedom in worship, testimony, and song that could not have come into reality within the strictures of the established structures of their local churches except for those churches in which the holiness message prevailed.

As the center of holiness revival promotion moved from the parlor meeting to the "feasts of tabernacles" that thousands attended year after year in the fields, forests, or on the beaches of America, the small-group dynamics of the Tuesday meetings were preserved to a remarkable degree in spite of the modifications in emphasis that the change in surroundings and style dictated. The sense of

fellowship that characterized the small group was continued in the larger mass meetings. The outdoor gatherings
retained the intimacy of family gatherings. One camp
meeting advocate noted that "without some such meeting,
the members of a large city church will . . . remain strangers to each other and though they might be seated side by
side in heaven, would need the angel Gabriel to give them
an introduction." At the camp meeting, on the other hand,
they became "one happy family."[28] They became
significant occasions for the establishment and renewal of
relationships among holiness adherents. There they
learned the doctrine and personal commitments to disciplined Christian living that were unappreciated in many of
the local churches from which the campers came. The
freedom, the openess, the fellowship, the unity and sense
of the divine of the camp meeting became a metaphor for
the fully sanctified life itself as Jones has demonstrated.[29]

But there were significant adaptations as well. The
preaching of the doctrine became more central than the
personal witness to it, although in their "ring meetings"
and other "testimony meetings" personal experiential witness continued.[30] Lay leadership tended to give way to
ministerial direction. The greater organization that the
large camp meetings required also tended to move the
movement toward regulation and institutionalization. The
evangelist who proclaimed the message to thousands in attendance had great influence and power. The need to ac-
credit holiness ministers as to their personal character and
doctrinal integrity and assign them to ministerial and administrative roles became more and more pressing. The
movement's strong commitment to "the leadership of the
Spirit" became more difficult to reconcile with the institutional demands of the expansion of the revival, although in
the camp meeting they were reconciled more readily,
perhaps, than in other worship structures of the time.[31]

The ten days usually spent together by the campers in

concentrated, yet relaxed spiritual development within a fellowship of commitment and purpose allowed them to experience some of the special dynamics of Christian community that Dietrich Bonhoeffer attributes to such a milieu in his *Life Together*. Life begun together beginning at the break of day; the joining together in morning prayers and Scripture; the intense worship in corporate singing, formal and free prayers; the common meals of the family; working together in the labor of setting, maintaining, and breaking up the encampment; evening prayers in every tent or cottage—all represented elements that Bohoeffer believed were essential to true Christian communion.[32] The opportunity for discussion of the Scriptures, doctrine, and Christian life between preachers and laity as they lived together in close proximity for an extended period of time belies the concern that camp meetings were merely times of high emotional excitement. The interaction of lay people and ministers was evident at every point. Holiness people came to expect that the worship of the church should be like that.

T. M. Eddy, a Methodist minister of the Civil War period, caught the ambience that shaped the expectations of camp meeting worship and of the churches that molded their own worship style in its image. He rejoiced that the time for the "feasts of tabernacles," as camp meetings were often called, had come, for, he said,

> There is something truly inspiring in the scenery—the snow-white tents, or rude, primitive structures—the hearty greetings, the sweet songs, the gathering thousands, the green wood arch, ringing with the song caroled by a thousand voices! Ay, we feel we worship God in the temple of his own building.[33]

The Rev. Alfred Cookman, one of Methodism's most respected pastors at mid-nineteenth century, and one of the founders of the National Camp Meeting Association, reported to his sister after the first "National Camp," that after the Vineland experience, every other religious meeting would seem "tame."[34]

It was a lofty standard. Hannah Whithall Smith, Quaker author of the classic *Christian's Secret of a Happy Life*, became an adherent and evangelist of the holiness movement. In her later years in England, she became somewhat disenchanted with some of the emotional extremes that she had experienced in the revival. Her involvement, however, had made her an avid observer of religious movements and phenomona. Toward the end of her life she confessed that her most moving spiritual experiences took place in the holiness camp meetings that she and her husband, Robert Pearsall Smith, attended during the post-Civil War revival.[35] It became very difficult for persons for whom the camp meeting setting was both the high point and norm for worship and fellowship to appreciate the week-to-week routines of the regular churches, especially as their services became more structured.

THE AGE OF THE SPIRIT

The highly focused purpose of the movement to bring men and women into the experience of the fullness and power of the Spirit which the small group and the camp meeting both created and fostered found one of its most distinct ecclesiological expressions in those sectors of the revival that understood the move of God in eschatological terms. It would have been most exceptional if the holiness movement, where the emphasis on the present activity and power of the Holy Spirit had been promoted as persistently as at any time in church history, should not have begun to think that the world had entered a new era of divine activity in the affairs of people and nations. The ideal of Pentecost and the certainty that the revival marked the beginning of a new "age of the Spirit" eventually became the dominant force in shaping their vision of the Church and its mission.

As early as 1857, a report on the Palmers' Tuesday Meetings picked up the Pentecostal and millennial theme. A participant saw in the meetings "the germs, the dawnings of millennial glory." They were "strikingly imitative of the pentecostal" and "similar to the upper room at Jerusalem, where the early disciples assembled with Mary, the mother of Jesus . . . till God gave them power from on high, the tongue of fire, . . ." "Is this the baptism now called for . . . ere the world blossom as the rose?" he asked in conclusion.[36] The pentecostal theme continued to swell after the Civil War. L.R. Dunn, a Methodist holiness evangelist, wrote in 1871 that "God is now wondrously moving among the nations . . .; a mighty upheaval is now going on; all men are looking on and wondering what will come out. O blessed, Holy Comforter, finish speedily Thy great work in the world."[37] Holiness revivalists believed that in the renewal of the Pentecostal experience and gifts, the Church and world were experiencing the final stage of history before the consummation of all things in Christ. William Arthur's *Tongue of Fire*, published during the same time, urged upon the churches the necessity for recovering the power of the Holy Spirit in their life and that of their members.[38] Terms such as "The Baptism of the Holy Spirit," "The Gift of the Ghost," and "The Promise of the Father" charged the religious atmosphere of American evangelicalism, Calvinistic and Wesleyan.

The Church of God (Anderson, Indiana) reformation movement, which was born out of the crest of the first wave of post-Civil War holiness evangelism in the late 1870s, provides an example of how this sense of the final "age of the Spirit" influenced the ecclesiology of a particular segment of the revival. One of the most significant characteristics of the Church of God was its understanding of itself in apocalytic categories. Daniel Warner, the foun-

der of the movement, saw the holiness revival of his time
as the instrument that God was using at the end of history
to bring the true church to the purity and the unity that
human organization and creeds had denied to it for so
long. It was the means of God's final reformation of the
Church, final not only because of the universal extent of
the revival, but also because of the ability of its purifying
message to destroy the last vestige of sin in the Church—
sectarianism. It was the "evening light" spoken of by the
prophet Zechariah, "the age of the Spirit," in which the
one invisible church, hidden among the many sects of the
time, would finally be revealed as the one true visible
"Church of God." The sanctifying message of the revival
would cleanse the true believers then in the churches from
the "mildew" of Babylon (sectarianism) and gather them
into one unified fellowship organized by the Spirit and not
by humans.[39]

The "sin consuming flames of the Sanctifier" and the
baptism of the Holy Ghost were the means by which God
would bring the new fellowship to reality and visibility.
The church of Pentecost was the model that could be
realized again as "the peculiar heritage of the present dispensation." The intense competetion and bitterness that
he felt were being demonstrated between the denominations of his time were an indication that those structures
were "wood, hay and stubble" which the "fire of holiness" would consume so that the true church as the temple of God could appear in "primitive glory." In the holiness revival, he declared that God was revealing the
"mystery" hidden in the "book . . . which no man in
heaven or earth could open." It was the "cleansing of the
sanctuary," the restoration of "the true worship of God as
in days of yore—as it existed in apostolic times."[40]

The degree and manner in which the final "age of the
Spirit" in time might participate in the timeless perfection
of the age to come varied considerably in different sectors

of the movement. However, Warner's understanding of a church under the leadership of the Holy Spirit was characteristic of the movement as a whole. The Church was the dwelling place of the Spirit; there was an emphasis upon Spirit baptism and upon the primacy of Spirit leadership and organization of the Church. He insisted that persons cannot ordain those who have been called by the Holy Spirit but rather, merely recognize the Spirit's sealing of the individual. More traditional, denominationally oriented groups such as the Church of the Nazarene or the Pilgrim Holiness church that came out of the revival a generation after Warner's failed to join him in his radical anti-sectarianism. Nevertheless, they exhibited the same "age of the Spirit" motifs that formed the heart of the Church of God reformation movement. God within them, individually and in their fellowship collectively, through the sanctifying Spirit molded their concepts of the nature of the fellowship, the purity of the Church, their concept of the ministry and the qualifications that it required, ministerial education, and the mission and place of the Church in the world and in history.[41]

Jurgen Moltmann's discussion of the relationship between trinitarian theology and the kingdom of God provides worthwhile theological and historical background for understanding the kind of interaction between eschatology and ecclesiology that was shaping the movement's concept of human history around an "age of the Spirit." A review of Moltmann's reflections may also help us to better understand the latent but dimly defined antagonisms that often seem to color discussions between Reformed and Wesleyan scholars on the nature of the Church. As interesting as Moltmann's main thesis concerning the relationship between a truly trinitarian theology and human freedom may be, that is not the point that touches our concerns most directly; his insights into the importance of the work of Joachim of Fiore and his concept of "the age of the Spirit" hold special relevance for our discussion.[42]

Moltmann notes the continuing importance of Joachim's understanding of history; it lies in his integration of Augustine's concept of history as consisting of seven ages corresponding to the pattern of the seven days of creation with the Cappadocians' trinitarian understanding of history as successive dispensations of the age of the Father, the age of the Son, and the age of the Holy Spirit. Joachim's eschatology combines the seventh or final period of history, the Sabbath rest period of Augustine, with the "Age of the Spirit" concept of the Cappadocians. Moltmann contends, contrary to the claims of Thomas Aquinas, that this succession of sovereignty in history, as conceived by Joachim, does not signify the dissolution of the Trinity in history. The full Trinity was active in each of the ages, although one was sovereign.[43] Joachim's idea of a last great revelation of the Spirit before the ushering in of the perfect kingdom of God is, of course, much older than his development of it; it is rooted in Joel's biblical promise of the coming of the Holy Spirit as well as in the Paraclete passages of the Gospel of John, and the whole of the Acts of the Apostles. Ever since the Montanists, prophetic reform movements in the Church have drawn upon this textual syndrome at some point or other.

Joachim's scheme is as follows:

> The mysteries of the Holy Scripture point us to three orders (states or conditions) of the world: to the first, in which we were under Law; to the second in which we were under grace; to the third which we imminently expect, and in which we shall be under a yet more abundant grace. . . . The first condition is therefore that of perception, the second, that of partially perfected wisdom, the third of fullness of knowledge. The first condition is the bondage of slaves, the second is the bondage of sons, the third is liberty.

> The first in fear, the second in faith, the third in love.
> The first in the condition of thralls, the second of freemen, the third of friends.

The first of boys, the second of men, the third of the aged.
The first stands in the light of the stars, the second in the
light of the dawn, the third in the brightness of day . . .
The first condition is related to the Father, the second to
the Son, the third to the Holy Spirit.[44]

The Kingdom of the Spirit is made up of people who have
been reborn by the Spirit. They become people of the
Spirit whose experience of the Spirit is immediate. The
Spirit guides, the Spirit teaches, the Spirit appoints,
everyone is taught by the Spirit.

Moltmann's comparison of the three-fold pattern of Lutheran and Reformed eschatology with the trinitarian pattern of Joachim helps us to appreciate the self-understanding of holiness leaders like Warner and others who
came to look upon the holiness revival in this manner.
Moltmann sees this pattern in the three-fold nature of
Christ's kingly office: the *regnum naturae*, the *regnum
gratiae*, and the *regnum gloriae*. There is a difference,
however, between these three and the trinitarian patterns
of Joachim. His three kingdoms or eras actually come before the final consummation of all things; in fact the kingdom of the Spirit is the final era of history and leads to the
fourth kingdom. This fourth kingdom is the kingdom of
glory, the consummation of history itself in the kingdom of
the triune God.[45]

It would be difficult for historians of the nineteenth-
century Wesleyan holiness movement or of the later Pentecostal movement to fail to discern the parallel development of thought in their understanding of their eschatology
and history with that of Joachim's. The tendency of these
movements to finally relate the movements of the Spirit in
which they felt they were participating with the consummation of history shaped every aspect of their thinking,
especially their concept of the Church and its mission. It is
not surprising, then, that John Fletcher, the intimate of
Wesley and the first systematic theologian of the Wesleyan

movement, should connect a trinitarian dispensationalism similar to that of the Cappadocians and Joachim to develop his hermeneutic of Wesley's doctrine of Christian perfection centered as it was on the Pentecost event and the age of the Spirit. Fletcher defines the "pentecostal church" as the "kingdom" of believers made perfect in love.[46] Nor is it surprising that John Fletcher's identification of the experience of entire sanctification as Wesley taught it with the "baptism of the Holy Ghost" should have become the dominant motif for understanding and proclaiming their doctrine at the time that the holiness churches were seeking to formulate an understanding of the nature and mission of the Church. The millennial ethos that was woven and interwoven in all aspects of American culture and politics in the nineteenth century merely encouraged this emphasis upon the "age of the Spirit" that was to usher it in.

Moltmann diagrams the difference between the Lutheran and Calvinistic understandings of history and Joachim's as follows:

Joachim:

The kingdom of the Father	the kingdom of the Son	the kingdom of the Spirit	the kingdom of glory

Orthodox Protestantism:

Regnum naturae	regnum gratiae		regnum gloriae[47]

If these three eras of Joachim are not taken as a merely modalistic pattern of history, but are seen, as Moltmann suggests, as a trinitarian interpretation by which the kingdom sovereignty of the Father, Son, and Holy Spirit respectively mean "continually present strata and transitions in the kingdom's history,"[48] then his understanding becomes useful for contemporary evangelical dialogue. It provides a means of getting at some of the subtle theological differences that have caused evangelicals of the Reformed tradition and evangelicals of the Wesleyan tradition to come so close to each other on ecclesiological and eschatological questions without being able to define exactly what the differences are which seem to preclude completely corresponding responses to such issues.

How each tradition might respond to the concept and nature of an "age of the Spirit" affords us a good example of the difficulties that often arise between them, and the light that an interpretation of Joachim such as Moltmann's may shed on the problem. If one follows the motif of the three periods of Christ's reign rooted in the Reformed tradition, there is actually little room for an understanding of such a dynamic operation of the Spirit in history. There is less likelihood that the very concept of an "age of the Spirit" can be developed as readily as it was either by Joachim or by the holiness and Pentecostal traditions. The theological framework simply is not there. There is no place for a trinitarian concept of such a period of Spirit sovereignty and activity that constitutes part of the history of the Kingdom within time.

Reformed theology has portrayed magnificently the liberating Christ and the grace of the redemption to life which he brought through his cross; the kingdom of the servant redeemer is the grand theme of the kingdom of grace. But the themes that arise out of Pentecostal and post-Pentecostal milieus or "the age of the Spirit" are not commonly a part of Lutheran or Reformed understanding of history and time. Luther himself may have realized this lack when he complained that there was too much of the preaching of the cross and not enough of the preaching of Pentecost in the messages of his preachers.[49] Lutheran and Reformed theology also follow a trinitarian pattern in that the kingdom of the Father opens up all of creation to the future; so, too, the kingdom of the Son opens up the future to men and women by freeing them to be servants of God and no longer slaves to themselves and the world.

The Son makes us free for freedom. *The activity of the Spirit, however, is either subsumed in the age of grace and of the Son or in the final Kingdom and consummation of all things in the age to come.*

What, then, is the nature of the Kingdom of the Spirit if it is in time and not in glory or subsumed in either or both the age of grace and of glory? Moltmann contends that

> the kingdom of the Spirit is experienced in the gift conferred on the people liberated by the Son—the gift of the Holy Spirit's energies. That is the reason why the kingdom of the Spirit is as closely linked with the kingdom of the Son, as the kingdom of the Son is with the kingdom of the Father. In the experience of the Spirit we lay hold of the freedom for which the Son has made us free. Through the mediation of Christ we experience a kingdom of God. The mystics were right to call this 'the birth of God in the soul.' Through faith and by listening to his conscience, a person becomes God's friend. In the powers of the Spirit, the energies of the new creation are experienced, too. In the Spirit that new community comes into being which is without privileges and subjection, the community of the free. In the Spirit the new creation in the kingdom and 'earnest' or pledge of glory, the kingdom of the Spirit is directed towards the kingdom of glory; it is not itself already that kingdom's fulfillment.[50]

The intonations and intimations of this summary would have set well within the milieu of the nineteenth-century holiness movement. They believed that by ignoring the implications of the Pentecost event and the signs of a new spiritual age, the churches had hindered the reformation of the Church and left its mission unfulfilled. They were convinced that the holiness revival was the first fruits of better things for the Church and the world. The songs and hymns of a spiritual movement often offer the deepest insight into its mood and theology. One of the many songs that caught up the movement's eschatological vision of the Church in the "new age" was Francis Bottome's Pentecostal hymn "The Comforter Has Come." It lifted all the notes of victory and triumphalism that marked the ethos of the revival:

O, spread the tidings round, wherever man is found,
Wherever human hearts and human woes abound;
Let every Christian tongue proclaim the joyful sound:
The Comforter has come!

The long, long night is past, the morning breaks at last;
And hushed the dreadful wail and fury of the blast,
As o'r the golden hills the day advances fast!
The Comforter has come!

Refrain:

The Comforter has come! The Comforter has come!
The Holy Ghost from heav'n, The Father's promise giv'n
O' spread the tidings round, wherever man is found,
The Comforter has come![51]

CONCLUSION

The sense of community and mission born out of their small group beginnings, the worship and order fashioned within the context of the freedom and expectancy of the camp meeting ethos, the understanding of their place and that of the church in history dominated by the vision of Pentecost repeated in the new and final "age of the Spirit" permanently stamped the ecclesiological identity of the holiness revival. The maturation and acculturation that the contemporary holiness churches have since experienced have weakened these earlier dynamics either by fixing them in the immobility of honored traditions or by de-mythologizing them into weaknesses. Although this aging process has had its effect in slowing down the movement, the momentum of its initial concept of its place and mission as part of the universal church continues to allow the holiness churches to demonstrate somewhat better than average growth. It seems that in the contemporary cultural milieu it is a little more difficult "to see" and "to do" with the same measure of certainty that the founding generations appeared to enjoy.

Notes

1. See Dale Brown, *Understanding Pietism* (Grand Rapids: Wm. B. Eerdmans Publishing Co., 1978).
2. Brown, p. 53.
3. See David B. Barrett, *et al.*, eds., *World Christian Encyclopedia* (Oxford University Press, 1982), p. 14. The editors unfortunately separated the Salvation Army out of the holiness statistics; together they number more than 7 million members.
4. For amplification of these summaries see Timothy L. Smith, *Revivalism and Social Reform: American Protestantism on the Eve of the Civil War* (Baltimore: Johns Hopkins University Press, 1980); the same, "Righteousness and Hope: Christian Holiness and the Millennial Vision in America, 1800 to 1900" in *American Quarterly* XXXI (Spring 1979), pp. 21-45; Melvin E. Dieter, *The Holiness Revival of the Nineteenth Century* (Methuchen, N.J.: The Scarecrow Press, 1980).
5. Dieter, pp. 144-46.
6. Bishop John P. Newman, "Introduction," in John A. Roche, *A Life of Mrs. Sarah A. Lankford Who for Sixty Years Was the Able Teacher of Entire Holiness* (New York: George Hughes and Co., 1898), p. 10.
7. R. Wheatley, *The Life and Letters of Mrs. Phoebe Palmer* (New York: W.C. Palmer, Jr., 1876), pp. 238-57.
8. Brown, *Pietism*, pp. 61-2.
9. Timothy Smith develops this theme in his *Called Unto Holiness: The Story of the Nazarenes, the Formative Years.* (Kansas City, Mo.: Nazarene Publishing House, 1962); see especially p. 322.

10. "Holiness a Hobby," *Beauty of Holiness* VIII (April 1857) pp. 103-4.

11. Dieter, *Holiness Revival*, p. 215.

12. Dieter, pp. 268-70.

13. The Pilgrim Holiness church, founded in 1897, did this when it united with the Wesleyan Methodist church to form the Wesleyan church in 1968. The latest change was the change of the name of the Holiness Christian church to the Evangelical Christian church.

15. The most significant of these was the change of name by the Pentecostal Church of the Nazarene to the Church of the Nazarene in 1919.

16. "Timely Words for All Churches," *Divine Life and Expositor of Scriptural Holiness*, IX (May 1886), p. 305.

17. See Charles Jones, *Perfectionist Persuasion: The Holiness Movement and American Methodism, 1867-1936* (Metuchen, N.J.: The Scarecrow Press, 1974), pp. 49-57.

18. As noted by George M. Marsden, *Fundamentalism and American Culture: The Shaping of Twentieth-Century Evangelicalism, 1870-1925* (Oxford: Oxford University Press, 1980), p. 45.

19. Marsden.

20. As quoted from Henry Fish, *Manual for Class Leaders* by Charles C. Keys, *The Class Leader's Manual. . . .* (New York: Lane and Scott, 1851), pp. 43-4.

21. Jones, *Perfectionist Persuasion*, pp. 107ff.

22. Howard Snyder, *The Radical Wesley* (Downers Grove, Ill.: Inter-Varsity Press, 1980), p. 119.

23. As quoted in Snyder, *Radical Wesley*, pp. 118-19.

24. Charles A. Johnson, *The Frontier Camp Meeting: Religious Harvest Time* (Dallas: Southern Methodist University, 1955).

25. William MacDonald and John E. Searles, *The Life of Rev. John Inskip, President of the National Association for the Promotion of Holiness* (Chicago: The Christian Witness Co., 1897), pp. 194-95.

26. Jones, *Perfectionist Persuasion*, pp. 25-34; Dieter, *Holiness Revival*, pp. 103-119.

27. "Tradition and Experience in American Theology," James

Ward Smith and A. Leland Jamison, eds., *Religion in American Life* (vol. 2), No. 5 of Princeton Studies in American Civilization (Princeton, N.J.: Princeton University Press, 1961), I, p. 454.

28. *Zions Herald* XXI (July 31, 1850), p. 1. Also see Smith, *Called Unto Holiness*, p. 66.

29. Jones, *Perfectionist Persuasion*, p. 110.

30. For the best description of the order and ethos of a holiness camp meeting, see Adam Wallace, ed., *A Modern Pentecost: Embracing a Record of the Sixteenth National Camp Meeting for the Promotion of Holiness Held at Landisville, Pa., July 23 to August 1, 1873* (Philadelphia: Methodist Home Journal Publishing House, 1873).

31. Wallace, p. 29.

32. Dietrich Bonhoeffer, *Life Together*, John W. Doberstein, trans. (New York: Harper and Bros., 1954). For a summary of the "Community at Worship," see Dallas M. Roark, *Dietrich Bonhoeffer*, in Bob E. Patterson, ed., *Makers of the Modern Mind* (Waco, Tex.: Word Books, 1972), pp. 64-67.

33. "Camp Meetings," *Beauty of Holiness*, VIII, p. 228.

34. Henry B. Ridgaway, *The Life of Rev. Alfred Cookman: With Some Account of His Father, The Rev. George Crimston Cookman*, Introduction by the Reverend R. S. Foster (New York: Harper and Bros., 1873), p. 327.

35. Melvin E. Dieter, "The Smiths: A Biographical Sketch with Selected Items from the Collection," *Asbury Seminarian*, XXXVIII (Spring 1983), p. 31.

36. "Meetings for Holiness-Sectarianism," *Beauty of Holiness*, VIII (December 1857), pp. 364-65.

37. L. R. Dunn, *The Mission of the Spirit, or The Office and Work of the Comforter in Human Redemption* (Carlto and Lanahan, 1871), p. 299.

38. William Arthur, *The Tongue of Fire: or The True Power of Christianity* (New York: Harper and Bros., 1856).

39. John W.V. Smith, *The Quest for Holiness and Unity: A Centennial History of the Church of God* (Anderson, Ind.: Warner Press, Inc., 1980), p. 96.

40. For an extended discussion see Dieter, *Holiness Revival*, pp. 249-54; see especially, p. 248, note 40; Smith, *Quest for Holiness and Unity*, pp. 94-100.

41. For discussions of the theology of the Church that illustrate the diversity of detail and yet unity of mood see John P. Brooks, *The Divine Church: A Treatise on the Origin, Constitution, Order and Ordinances of the Church* (Columbia, Mo.: Herald Publishing House, 1981); William B. Godbey, *Bible Theology* (Cincinnati, Ohio: God's Revivalist Office, 1911); and Seth Cook Rees, *The Ideal Pentecostal Church* (Cincinnati, Ohio: God's Revivalist Office, 1898).
42. Jurgen Moltmann, *The Trinity and the Kingdom, the Doctrine of God* (San Francisco: Harper and Row, Publishers, 1981), pp. 202-13.
43. Moltmann, p. 203.
44. *Concordia Novi Ac Veteris Testamenti, Venice 1519,* Lib. V, 84, 112, E. Benz, trans., *Eranos-Jahrbuch*, 1956, pp. 314ff., as quoted in Moltmann, *Trinity and Kingdom*, p. 204.
45. Moltmann, p. 207.
46. Laurence W. Wood, *Pentecostal Grace* (Wilmore, Ky.: Francis Asbury Publishing Co., Inc., 1980), p. 187. See same, pp. 177-229, for development of Fletcher's position.
47. Moltmann, p. 208.
48. Moltmann, p. 209; Wood, pp. 114, 115.
49. *Luther's Works*, vol. 41, *Church and Ministry*, III (Philadelphia: Fortress Press, 1966), p. 114.
50. Moltmann, p. 211.
51. Clarence B. Strouse, ed., *Hosannas to the King and Praise Service Hymns* (Philadelphia: Pepper Publishing Co., 1901), p. 126.

Clarence Bence (Ph.D., Emory University), assistant professor of
church history, Marion College

Salvation and the Church:
The Ecclesiology of
John Wesley

AFTER TWO HUNDRED YEARS, followers of John Wesley find many of his ideas quite suitable for discussion and application in the modern context. His doctrinal views on sin, human nature, and salvation are pertinent to current theological debate. His practical comments on such wide-ranging topics as pastoral care, religious experience, faith development, and discipleship training offer fresh insights to the field of applied theology. And many of his concerns for oppressed and underprivileged persons are echoed in calls for social justice from Christians today.

But how does one relate the ecclesiology of an eighteenth-century Anglican priest to modern understandings of the Church, shaped so significantly by the forces of American democratic and revivalistic ideals? Wesley would find few familiar elements from his tradition and personal practice in the organizational structure, programs, and worship forms of those denominations that most openly promote the doctrine of holiness he preached. Any attempt to superimpose the structures of either Wesley's Church of England or Methodist societies on our various contemporary expressions of church organization reveals the sharp incongruities that exist between his world and our own.

There have been various attempts to rediscover Wesley's ecclesiology and apply his principles and forms to modern concepts of the Church. However, given the complexity of the situation surrounding the origins of Methodism within, and later separate from, the Church of England, it becomes rather easy to find in the multifaceted Wesley warrant for any number of divergent perspectives on the Church and ministry. Those who see the life of the Church in the spiritual dynamic of small groups point to the class meeting and the loose organization of the Methodist societies for their model of the Church.[1] Others with more institutional and ecumenical concerns stress Wesley's life-long allegiance to the Church of England and view him as the champion of conciliation and reform from *within* the ecclesiastical strutures.[2] Some would point to Wesley's conservative policies regarding the administration of sacraments and use of liturgical forms in their criticism of the free style of worship in many American churches; in rebuttal others would point to Wesley's willingness to discard the practices of the established church for the flexibility of field preaching and extemporaneous prayers. It would appear that the eclectic nature of Wesley's thought and actions creates the same problem for ecclesiology that also plagues those who endeavor to find some hermeneutical key for his systematic theology.

It is not the purpose of this study to trace all the various elements and shifts in Wesley's understanding of the

Church throughout his lifetime. The evolution of Methodism from the Oxford Holy Club to its break with the Church of England has already been carefully researched by Albert Lawson and Frank Baker.[3] And although such investigations provide interesting insights for historians, the radical changes in both church and society during the past two centuries make any attempt to repristinate Wesley's structures a futile task.

The most striking and ever-relevant feature of Wesley's ecclesiology is its soteriological focus, an emphasis that shaped almost every aspect of his thought and actions. By examining the central place that salvation plays in Wesley's understanding of the nature, mission, structure, and final destiny of the Church, we can better apply his ecclesiology to the exigencies of the twentieth century.

Salvation and the Nature of the Church

Wesley's childhood years in the parsonage at Epworth provided the rudiments of his understanding of the Church. Both of his parents had left dissenting congregations to join the established church and they remained faithful communicants in the Church of England until their deaths. Apparently, something of the zealousness of these converts was imparted to their son, for he observes, "In my youth, I was not only a member of the Church of England, but a bigot to it, believing none but the members of it to be in a state of salvation."[4] This view, reflecting Augustine's assertion that "outside the church there is no salvation," closely associates membership in the kingdom of God with adherence to the rituals and rules of an institution rather than an inward experience of regeneration through faith.

This sacramental view of salvation persisted during Wesley's years at Oxford as he sought to attain holiness by rigorous devotion to various spiritual practices of the primitive church. Through ecclesiastical disciplines of fasting, frequent partaking of the Lord's Supper, and observing the Christian holy days, he hoped to gain assurance of a right standing before God. Even during his missionary trip to the American colonies, Wesley maintained a formal ecclesiology that did not suit the needs or tastes of his rough parishioners in Savannah. They failed to see the spiritual benefits of early-morning services and triune immersion of feeble infants. Reflecting on his rigid formalism in Georgia, Wesley later wrote, "Can anyone carry high church zeal higher than this? And how well have I been since beaten with my own staff."[5]

Pastoral failures in America pushed Wesley to the brink of spiritual despair. Contact with Moravian Christians, however, opened up new prospects for assurance of salvation, and upon his return to England those prospects became personally appropriated in his evangelical awakening. After Aldersgate, Wesley advocated a new means for attaining spirituality; in addition to creedal assent to the truths of Scripture, a Christian must possess "a sure confidence in Christ's pardoning mercy, wrought in us by the Holy Ghost."[6] No longer was salvation determined by one's relationship to the ecclesiastical institution. The priorities of life and ministry were now altered; soteriology took the central place in Wesley's understanding and all other doctrines, including ecclesiology, established their character and validity in relation to the saving work of Christ. Lawson notes,

> After his evangelical conversion, churchmanship seems to have taken a subordinate place in Wesley's thinking. It did not, as some have supposed, become unimportant. Rather, it must be flexible enough to be adapted to changing circumstances and never be in opposition to his evangelical endeavors.[7]

Wesley continued to hold to the Articles of the Church of England, and in particular to its definition of the church militant: "The visible church is a congregation of faithful men in which the pure Word of God is preached and the sacraments are duly administered."[8] However, the concept of "faithful men" was significantly redefined. No longer was this phrase understood in terms of sacramental rites or birthright privileges alone; rather the Church must be seen as the congregation of "men endued with *living* faith."[9] In his *Notes on the New Testament*, Wesley describes the Church and its distinguishing marks in these succinct words:

> . . . a company of men, called by the Gospel, grafted into Christ by baptism, animated by love, united in all kind of fellowship, and disciplined by the death of Ananias and Sapphira.[10]

The divine work of God in calling and converting, coupled with the visible expressions of love and personal discipline form the basis for the Christian community.

Late in his life, Wesley wrote the sermon "On the Church" in response to critics who saw him as antagonistic to institutional Christianity. His emphasis throughout the sermon is on the spiritual character of its constituents, not its organizational structure. His premise is, "The catholic or universal church is, all the persons in the universe whom God hath called out of the world, as to be 'one body,' united by 'one Spirit;' having 'one faith, one hope, one baptism; one God and Father of all.'" Wesley then proceeds to elaborate the evangelical aspect of each term, relating the Spirit to the work of regeneration, faith to personal trust in the gospel, and baptism to the inward assurance of the transforming work of grace in the believer. He concludes by identifying all those whose character conforms to these evangelical criteria as members of the true church.[11]

Creedal affirmations and conversion experiences were significant elements in Wesley's ecclesiology, but in themselves they did not suffice. Since salvation was "the whole work of God," embracing both his justifying and sanctifying work, true believers must manifest their salvation to the world through a daily ethic of faith and love. Wesley wanted Methodists who were visible saints, "living witnesses to every part of that Christianity which we preach, which is held out to the world."[12]

The pattern for this "proper Christian Church" was to be found in the primitive community established by the disciples of Jesus. Not only had Christ taught the truths of religion, but after Pentecost, he "effectually planted it on earth" in the living witnesses of first-century Christians.[13] But that primitive model of an evangelized and evangelizing congregation soon deteriorated in the Constantinian age, not so much through political dominance and corruption as through the accumulation of material wealth and the consequent loss of spiritual zeal among its members.

Wesley's vision was to restore the Church to that original purity and he countenanced no compromise with nominal Christianity in the fellowship, any more than he tolerated some darling lust or residue of carnality in the individual who was pressing on to perfect love. The Spirit's sanctifying work was crucial in the life of the Church as well as in the life of the believer. Wesley wrote,

> The Church is called *holy* because it is *holy*; because every member thereof is holy, though in different degrees, as He that called them is holy. How clear is this! If the Church, as to the very essence of it, is a body of believers, no man that is not a Christian believer can be a member of it. If the whole body be animated by one Spirit, and endued with one faith, and hope of their calling; then he who has not that Spirit, and faith, and hope, is no member of that body.[14]

However, this demand for genuine Christianity in the Church never degenerated into sectarian pride or exclusiveness. Wesley accepts any person with a "desire to flee the wrath to come" into the fellowship and when one's heart was right (i.e. one was pure in intention and open to the Spirit's direction) Wesley could disregard deviations in both doctrine and liturgical practice in order to further the task of evangelism around the world.

The saving work of Christ was the heart of Wesley's understanding of the Church. Faith in that redemptive work was the primary prerequisite for membership in the body of Christ; but the ongoing process of "faith working by love" resulted in a holy people who proclaimed to the world the reality of the transformation wrought by the Spirit.

SALVATION AND THE MISSION OF THE CHURCH

If a personal experience of saving grace is the essential prerequisite to incorporation in the body of Christ, it necessarily follows that the proclamation of the gospel of Christ is essential to Wesleyan ecclesiology. "Mission is the primary task of the church," declares Colin Williams.[15]

Although the Anglican priest in Wesley never died, it was soon overshadowed by his concern for evangelism. Second only to his concern for his own salvation was his desire to bring others into a right relationship with God. Wesley described his vocation in a letter to William Hervey: "I have only one thing to do, to save my own soul and them that hear me."[16] For more than fifty years he traveled across the British Isles "offering Christ" to any who would hear him. To his brother Charles, he wrote, "I think every day lost, which is not (mainly at least) employed in saving souls. *Sum totus illo*. [I am totally in this]."[17]

In time the established structures and practices of the Church became restrictive to Wesley's evangelistic endeavors. He was forced to affirm the priority of his soteriology over his ecclesiastical views. He asks,

> What is the end of all ecclesiastical order? Is it not to bring souls from the power of Satan to God, and to build them up in His fear and love. Order, then, is so far valuable as it answers these ends; and if it answers them not, it is worth nothing.[18]

The Church was the divinely appointed means of establishing the kingdom of righteousness, peace, and joy. As a God-ordained institution it merited respect and obedience; but only insofar as it remained the means and not an end in itself. Wesley affirmed his allegiance to the Church and the limitations of that allegiance when he wrote, "I would observe every punctilio of order, except where the salvation of souls is at stake. Then I prefer the end [salvation] to the means."[19]

What was vital to Wesley, he expected to be a priority of his followers. His instructions to his preachers were simple and direct: "You have nothing to do but save souls. Therefore spend and be spent in this work."[20] This evangelistic commission was extended to all who called themselves Methodists, not just to a clerical class. Outler observes, "He taught his Methodists to be martyrs and servants. . . . They learned it from him and so became evangelists themselves, not many of them as preachers, but all of them as witnesses whose lives backed up their professions."[21]

Evangelism included both a message proclaimed and a life-style manifested to others. Wesley never tolerated a truncated soteriology that divorced the crisis of conversion from the pursuit of personal or social holiness. Sin, in whatever form it manifested itself in individuals or social institutions, was to be opposed by the body of believers. Wesley wrote,

There is abundant cause for all the servants of God to join together against the works of the devil; with united hearts and counsels and endeavors to make a stand for God, and to repress, as much as in them lies, these "floods of ungodliness."[22]

The pervasive nature of sin called for an all-encompassing assault by the forces of righteousness joined together in Christ.

The inclusive nature of Wesley's soteriological mission is nowhere more apparent than in his oft-quoted description of the geographical boundaries of his ministry. What is significant in the context of this statement is the priority of mission over any institutional limitations. It is his vision of the task, not his analysis of the inefficiencies of Anglican polity that elicits the outburst:

God in Scripture commands me, according to my power to instruct the ignorant, reform the wicked, confirm the virtuous. Man forbids me do this in another's parish; that is, in effect to do it at all, seeing I have no parish of my own, nor probably ever shall. Whom then shall I hear, God or man? "If it be just to obey man rather than God, judge you. A dispensation of the gospel is committed to me, and woe is me if I preach not the gospel."

I look upon *all the world as my parish*; this far I mean, that in whatever part of it I am I judge it meet, right, and my bounden duty to declare unto all that are willing to hear the glad tidings of salvation. This is the work which I know God has called me to, and sure I am that His blessing attends it.[23]

SALVATION AND THE STRUCTURE OF THE CHURCH

Wesley's vision of his parish was global, but it was still an Anglican parish and Wesley persistently declared, "I live and die a member of the Church of England."[24] But why this loyalty to ecclesiastical structures? Would not the

same soteriological commitment that forced him to ignore
geographical boundaries also permit him to disregard institutional limitations as well?

Here lies the central issue in Wesleyan ecclesiology. It
is possible to read either of two very divergent views into
Wesley's understanding of the Church. The catholic view
emphasizes the historical institution, established through
apostolic succession and vitalized through sacramental activity. The other free church position stresses the Church
as a fellowship of believers validated by the apostolic experience and perpetuated by evangelistic zeal. Baker
notes, "The first sees the church in essence as an ancient
institution to be preserved, the second as a faithful few
with a mission to the world."[25]

The early Wesley was committed to the institutional
concept of the Church and endeavored to pursue holiness
through strict adherence to its rubrics and disciplines. In
the Georgia experience and in the months subsequent to
his return to England, he came to realize that the apostolic
constitutions were not sacrosanct and that Scripture and
tradition—even ancient tradition—did not always coincide.

The Aldersgate experience did not lead to a repudiation
of the institutional church, but forced Wesley to see the
primacy of the soteriological mandate. The result, according to Robert Paul, was an "evangelical pragmatism," a
functional understanding of ecclesiology "controlled by
the gospel message and justified by the mission of the
church."[26]

A test case for this new understanding came soon after
his evangelical experience when George Whitefield asked
Wesley to come to Bristol and assist him in open-air
preaching. Wesley expressed his misgivings in his journal:

> I could scarce reconcile myself at first to this strange way of
> preaching in the fields, of which he set me an example on
> Sunday; having been all my life (till very lately) so tenacious
> in every point relating to decency and order, that I should

have thought the saving of souls almost a sin if it had not been done in the church.[27]

But Wesley observed that souls were being saved without the confines of the church and he was compelled to accommodate his views accordingly and "submitted to be more vile, and proclaimed in the highways the glad tidings of salvation."[28]

This was only one of many modifications that Wesley accepted in his commitment to save the souls of those who heard him. Methodist societies, class meetings, bands, and various agencies for social reform were created, not as substitutes to the established structures of Anglicanism, but as supplemental means of enabling the church to fulfill its mission to bring full salvation to the world.

The validity of each of these new structures was confirmed by the sources of authority commonly associated with Wesley: Scripture, reason, tradition, and experience. In an explanation of the Methodist system to a clergyman in 1748, Wesley indicated the interplay of these elements in his functional ecclesiology:

> But I must premise, that as they had not the least expectation, at first of any thing like what has since followed, so they had no previous design or plan at all; but every thing arose just as the occasion offered. They saw or felt some impending or pressing evil, or some good end necessary to be pursued. And many times they fell unawares on the very thing which secured the good, or removed the evil. At other times, they consulted on the most probable means, following only common sense and Scripture: Though they generally found, in looking back, something in Christian antiquity likewise, very nearly parallel thereto.[29]

The origin of these structures was a perceived need, suggesting the priority of *praxis* in Wesley's understanding of the Church. From the perceived need, the early Methodists moved to experience, developing structures either by conscious design or fortuitous discovery. It is difficult to argue that Wesley had a self-conscious ecclesiological plan from his many references to the serendipitous nature of these new structures. Frank Baker concludes that "the original cause of most of his separatist actions was spiritual need rather than theological conviction."[30]

However, the pragmatic nature of this approach was always tempered by the appeal to reason (common sense) and Scripture, as well as the traditions of the Church. No program or institution could be justified unless it conformed to scriptural teaching. "In all cases, the Church is to be judged by Scripture, not the Scripture by the Church."[31] But in studying the biblical warrants for ecclesiological practice, Wesley soon discovered that the Scriptures were not as explicit in this area as he had once believed. "Scripture," he decided, "in most points, gives only general rules; and leaves the particular circumstances to be adjusted by the common sense of mankind."[32] This allowed Wesley considerable flexibility in forming his view of the Church.

Wesley's reading of Lord King's *An Enquiry into the Constitution, Discipline, Unity and Worship of the Primitive Church* forced him to conclude that even the hierarchical structure (deacon, priest, bishop) of the Church of England was not dictated by Scripture. Further study forced him to conclude "that neither Christ nor his apostles prescribed any particular form of church government, and that the plea for the divine right of the Episcopacy was never heard in the Primitive Church."[33]

Such conclusions did not lead Wesley to repudiate the church altogether; he did not consider its structure to be contradictory to Scripture or common sense. But no longer could he defend any given ecclesiology as the only proper means of achieving the divine purpose of the Church. He announced to his preachers, "we are not assured that God ordained that the same plan should obtain through all the ages."[34]

Freed from the strictures of his earlier ecclesiology, Wesley could be innovative in mobilizing his Methodists for evangelism while still maintaining a loyalty with the established church, convinced that "with all her blemishes, [it] is nearer the scriptural plan than any other in Europe."[35] To those who cried for separation, he preached against schism, declaring such an act at worst would be sinful and at best would not be expedient. He affirmed his loyalty to the institutional structures in the strongest terms:

> I dare not renounce communion with the Church of England. As a minister, I teach her doctrines, use her offices, I conform to her rubrics, I suffer reproach for my attachments to her. As a private member I hold her doctrines, I join her offices, in prayer, in hearing, and in communicating.[36]

Resisting pressures to form a new dissenting body of believers in England, Wesley died a faithful communicant in the Church of England.

Wesley's sympathies for the institution were countered, however, by a driving passion for renewal within the church and society. When the spread of scriptural holiness was thwarted by ecclesiastical structures or leaders, Wesley felt justified in deviating from accepted practice to form new means of maintaining the primacy of salvation in the church. In the Conference Minutes of 1747, he defined the limits of ecclesiastical authority—"We will obey the rules and governors of the church whenever we can consistently with our duty to God. Whenever we cannot, we will quietly obey God rather than man."[37]

For almost half a century Wesley was able to maintain a creative tension between obedience to his church and his inward sense of the will of God for the Methodist societies. Although his followers were not always met with approbation, he tenaciously held to the conviction that they could serve as much-needed "leaven for the whole Church."[38] There were signs, however, that the fragile alliance of Anglicanism and Methodism could not be indefinitely sustained. Rather than withdraw from his commitment to evangelism and spiritual nurture, Wesley pressed on with an ever-expanding movement, arguing, "We cannot with good conscience neglect the present opportunity of saving souls while we live, for fear of consequences which may possibly or probably happen after we are dead."[39]

Those consequences finally came, precipitated by the war for independence in the American colonies. As Anglican clergy returned to England, leaving the American congregations bereft of leadership, and as Methodism spread to the frontier where no Church of England even existed, Wesley became acutely aware of the need for ordained Methodist clergy to administer the sacraments, administrate the Methodist societies, and perpetuate the movement in America. Receiving no help or sympathy from the established church, he acted "not by choice, but necessity"[40] and ordained several lay-preachers for the ministry in America in 1784.

This action transformed Methodism from an ancillary movement within the Church of England to an autonomous ecclesiastical body, at least in the States. Subsequent ordinations freed Methodism from its parent body in Ireland, Scotland, and eventually England itself. But these denominational beginnings did not indicate a new ecclesiology in the "late Wesley"; rather they were the logical and inevitable outcome of Wesley's decision to place soteriological concerns above those of institutional commitments.

Wesley cannot be viewed as an iconoclast. His ecclesiology was basically conservative and the innovations he fostered came with a certain reluctance for fear he would be misunderstood as a schismatic. But his functional understanding of the church permitted him to accommodate the structures of worship and administration to the spiritual needs of the people he sought to serve. In doing so, he offers a valid model for creative approaches to evangelism and discipleship within the institutional structures of our churches today.

SALVATION AND THE DESTINY OF THE CHURCH

"Wesley's understanding of the church was that it is an *act*, a function, a mission in the world rather than a form and institution."[41] Albert Outler has described well the functional character of Wesley's ecclesiology in this comment. However, one should be careful not to reduce the church to utilitarian activity, a transitory agency for the evangelization of the world that can be discarded when its goals are accomplished. The Church is a substantial reality as well; for Wesley it is the body of Christ, the company of the redeemed and the visible manifestation of the kingdom of God. As purity of heart was glory begun for the individual, the Church was the foretaste of the eternal social order to come and as such it participated already in eschatological realities.

The moral and spiritual climate of eighteenth-century England would lend support to pessimistic views of history. Wesley's own study of church history had led him to conclude that since the Constantinian age "the church and state, the kingdoms of Christ and the world, were so strangely and unnaturally blended together,"[42] that prospects of a pure church of holy believers was rather doubtful, short of the return of Christ to establish his rule on earth.

But the Kingdom, obscured by the corruption of sin, was nevertheless a present reality. "Wheresoever the gospel of Christ is preached, this kingdom is nigh at hand," he wrote.[43] Those who repented and believed had the opportunity to enter that kingdom, the company of regenerated individuals who comprised the true body of Christ. That kingdom was a spiritual kingdom, and Wesley would never equate the institutional church with the kingdom of God. But neither could the kingdom be totally abstracted from the visible community, and placed in some future transcendent world.

> [The kingdom] is not barely a future happy state in heaven, but a state to be enjoyed on earth; the proper disposition for the glory of heaven, if not the possession of it. It properly signifies the gospel dispensation, in which subjects are to be gathered to God by his Son, and *a society to be formed*, which is to subsist *first on earth*, and afterwards with God in glory.[44]

The Church, especially as it was leavened by committed believers, was that visible society, God's eschatological colony in the world. Wesley believed in a coming kingdom of glory but he did not make a sharp differentiation between that coming reality and the present work of grace manifested in the visible institution. The eschatological future was merely "the continuation and perfection of the kingdom of God on earth" at the present time.[45]

In his commitment to *full* salvation, and all that entails for both individual and society, Wesley was an optimist. He dared to believe that the cure of the cross was equal to, even greater than, the curse of the fall.[46] Through grace, the time would come when Christianity would cover the earth. Indeed, God had raised up the Methodists to be the primary catalysts in this transformation of the world. He wrote,

> Against hope, believe in hope. It is your Father's good pleasure to renew the face of the earth. . . . And "all the kingdoms of earth shall become the kingdoms of God." Be thou a part of the firstfruits, if the harvest is not yet.[47]

The structures of both the Church of England and the Methodist Societies were eschatological structures, ordained by God for the establishment of the kingdom of righteousness in time and space. When asked why Methodism had arisen in England, Wesley indicated the breadth of his vision by replying, "To reform the nation, and in particular, the church; to spread scriptural holiness over the entire land."[48] The Church was not a stop-gap measure, a feeble holding action until Christ's victorious return. The destiny of the Church was one with the goal of history—a social order that glorified God in all its aspects.

In an address given to the Society for the Reformation of Manners, Wesley outlined the soteriological agenda he envisioned for the Church:

Men who did fear God and desire the happiness of their fellow-creatures, have, in every age, found it needful to join together, in order to oppose the works of darkness, to spread the knowledge of God their Savior, and to promote his kingdom upon earth. Indeed He himself has instructed them so to do. From the time that men were upon the earth, he hath taught them to join together in his sevice, and has united them in one body by one Spirit. And for this very end He has joined them together, "that He might destroy the works of the devil;" first in them that are already united, and by them in all that are about them.

This is the original design of the Church of Christ. It is a body of men compacted together, in order, first, to save each his own soul; and then to assist each other in working out their salvation; and, afterwards, as far as in them lies, to save all men from present and future misery, to overturn the kingdom of Satan, and set up the kingdom of Christ. And this ought to be the continued care and endeavor of every member of his Church; otherwise he is not worthy to be called a member thereof, as he is not a living member of Christ.[49]

Here is the proper context for speaking of Wesley's

concern for social holiness. It is more than individuals doing acts of charity for others; it is even more than the institutional church speaking to the social injustices of society in general. Social holiness is the penetration and permeation of the gospel into all aspects of the social order with the intent of changing that order into the kingdom of God. Wesleyan ecclesiology as an expression of his soteriology must be transformational in its deepest sense. The goal of the Church is to be the firstfruits of the coming kingdom, to be the first installment of God's reign on earth.

Thus Wesley combined the functional concept of the Church as *act*, with a substantial view of the Church as the new social order, breaking through from the eschatological future into the present age. His willingness to dispense with structures that were ineffective or inefficient was balanced by his reverence for the institution as the visible manifestation of the work of God in transforming the creation into its original design and purpose.

Having experienced the reality of saving grace, Wesley committed his life to sharing that good news with others, confident that God would honor his endeavors. Those who joined his societies were expected to have "no design but to promote the glory of God, and no desire but to save souls from death." Wesley and his Methodists sought to call the Church to her true mission and to shape that ministry by such programs as would be effective means to the end of saving souls. The various structures of early Methodism need not be seen as normative for contemporary ecclesiology, since Wesley himself rejected any single ecclesiastical form as being the exclusive biblical option.

The heart of Wesley's ecclesiology is his combination of loyal respect for the Church as God's visible witness to the reality of the present kingdom with his flexibility in finding new ways of accomplishing the mission of that church in restoring the fallen world to right standing with God. In a letter to his brother, Samuel, during the early years of his new movement, John Wesley spelled out the creative tension in his ecclesiology:

> You cannot confine the Most High within temples made with hands. I do not despise them any more than you do. But I rejoice to find that God is everywhere. I love the rites and ceremonies of the church. But I see, well pleased, that our great Lord can work without them. And howsoever and wheresoever a sinner is converted from the error of his way, nay, and by whomsoever, I thereat rejoice, yea, and will rejoice.[50]

"To save souls," and to see the church as the agent and goal of that great enterprise is Wesley's legacy to the present age.

Notes

1. Howard Snyder, *The Radical Wesley* (Downers Grove, Ill.: Inter-Varsity Press, 1980).
2. Frank Baker, *John Wesley and the Church of England* (New York: Abingdon Press, 1970); Albert Outler, *John Wesley* (New York: Oxford University Press, 1964).
3. Albert Lawson, *John Wesley and the Christian Ministry* (London: SPCK, 1963), and Baker, *John Wesley and the Church of England*. A Ph.D. dissertation by Luke Keefer, "John Wesley: Discipline of Early Christianity" (Temple University, 1982), deals extensively with Wesley's views of the Church.
4. John Wesley, *The Works of the Rev. John Wesley, M.A.*, Thomas Jackson, ed. (London: Wesleyan Conference Office, 1872), XIII, pp. 268ff. Hereafter referred to as *Works*.
5. *Works*, II, p. 150.
6. *Works*, V, p. 205.
7. Lawson, p. ix.
8. *Works*, VI, p. 396.
9. *Works*, VI, p. 396.

10. John Wesley, *Explanatory Notes on the New Testament* (Cincinatti: Hitchcock and Walden, n.d.), Acts 5:11, p. 287. Also Jude 19, p. 649.

11. *Works,* VI, pp. 392-400.

12. John Wesley, "Ought We to Separate from the Church of England?" cited in Baker, p. 337.

13. *Works,* VI, p. 256.

14. *Works,* p. 400.

15. Colin Williams, *John Wesley's Theology Today* (New York: Abingdon Press, 1960), p. 209.

16. John Wesley, *The Letters of the Rev. John Wesley, A.M.,* John Telford, ed. (London: Epworth Press, 1931), VII, p. 63. Hereafter referred to as *Letters.*

17. *Works,* XII, p. 139.

18. *Letters,* II, p. 76.

19. *Letters,* IV, p. 146.

20. John Telford, *The Life of John Wesley* (London: Kelley, 1910), p. 229.

21. Albert Outler, *Evangelism in the Wesleyan Spirit* (Nashville: Tidings, 1971), p. 103ff.

22. *Works,* VI, p. 150.

23. John Wesley, *The Journal of the Rev. John Wesley, M.A.,* Nehemiah Curnock, ed. (London: Epworth Press, 1938), II, p. 217ff.

24. *Works,* XIII, p 274.

25. Baker, p. 137.

26. Robert Paul, *The Church in Search of Itself* (Grand Rapids: Eerdmans Publishing Co., 1972), p. 123.

27. *Journal,* II, p. 167.

28. *Journal,* II, p. 172.

29. *Works,* VIII, p. 248. Keefer observes that Wesley was a conservative leader, departing from traditional patterns slowly and only when necessity or careful reflection indicated the need (p. 693).

30. Baker, p. 2.

31. *Works,* X, p. 142.

32. *Works,* VIII, p. 255.

33. *Works,* XIII, p. 211.

34. "Minutes of the Conference of 1747," cited in John Simon,

John Wesley and the Methodist Societies (London: Epworth Press, 1923), p. 261.

34. *Works,* XII, p. 211.
36. *Works,* VIII, p. 444.
37. Baker, p. 113.
38. *Works,* VIII, p. 201.
39. *Works,* VIII, p. 201.
40. *Minutes of the Methodist Conferences:* 1744-1824 (London: Thomas Cordeux, 1812), I, p. 191.
41. Albert Outler, "Do Methodists Have a Doctrine of the Church?" in *The Doctrine of the Church,* Dow Kirkpatrick, ed. (New York: Abingdon Press, 1964), p. 19.
42. *Works,* VII, p. 164.
43. *Works,* V, p. 181.
44. Wesley, *Notes* (Matthew 3:2, 4:1), p. 14 (italics mine).
45. *Works,* V, p. 334.
46. *Works,* VI, p. 223.
47. *Works,* V, p. 277.
48. "Minutes of the Conference of 1763," cited in Baker, p. 118.
49. Works, VI, pp. 149ff.
50. "Letter to Samuel Wesley" (October 27, 1739), *Proceedings of the Wesleyan Historical Society,* XXXIII, p. 101.

Daniel N. Berg (D. Phil., Glasgow University), associate professor of theology and ministry, Seattle Pacific University

The Marks of the Church In the Theology of John Wesley

FROM THE TIME of the Council of Constantinople (381 A.D.) the Church has declared itself to be "one, holy, catholic and apostolic." Until the time of the Reformation these four marks of the Church were the basic elements in the Church's self-identity. Occasionally the number of the marks (*proprietates, signa, criteria,* and *notae*) would change, always by increasing.[1]

This proliferation of the marks of the Church at the height of the Reformation reflected the intense interest among Roman Catholics and Protestants alike in identifying the "true" church. What had, to that time, been only pedagogic touchstones for explaining the nature of the Church were now becoming polemical trump cards to be played out in disputes with Protestants.

319

If Tridentine Catholicism sought to defend the Church by increasing the distinguishing marks of the Church, the defensiveness of Protestantism may be seen in its shifting the grounds altogether. Although Protestantism did not reject the four ancient marks of the Church (unity, sanctity, universality, and apostolicity), it did, with a consistency remarkable for an era of such conflict, set forth two other marks as the essential identifiers of the "true" church. These marks have to do with the preaching of the gospel and the administration of the sacraments.

Article VII of the Augsburg Confession says, "The Church is the congregation of saints [the assembly of all believers], in which the Gospel is rightly taught [*purely preached*] and the sacraments rightly administered [according to the Gospel]."[2] Calvin, in the *Institutes*, is obviously informed by the Augsburg Confession: "Wherever we see the Word of God purely preached and heard, and the sacraments administered according to Christ's institution, there, it is not to be doubted, a church of God exists."[3] Likewise, Article XVIII of the Scot's Confession:

> The notes therefore of the trew Kirk of God we beleeve, confesse, and avow to be, first, the trew preaching of the Worde of God, into the quhilk (which) God hes revealed himselfe unto us, as the writings of the Prophets and Apostles dois declair. Secundly, the right administration of the sacraments of *Christ Jesus,* quhilk man be annexed unto the word and promise of God, to seale and confirme the same in our hearts.[4]

The objective of this chapter is to examine John Wesley's theological consciousness of these two marks of the Church. That he knows about them is beyond dispute and the use to which Wesley puts these two marks both in doctrine and practice is consistent. He rejects them as the polemical marks they were intended to be. He accepts them and values them only as means of grace. Wesley is quite conscious of the importance of the gospel truly preached and the sacraments duly adminstered, but not as much as marks of the "true" church as divinely ordained means of grace.

One ramification of Wesley's use of the marks is also instructive. Wesley will allow no facile trade-off of word on the one hand and sacrament on the other. As means of grace rather than marks of the "true" church both are to be humbly received as God's provision and neither is to be granted supremacy over the other.

There is no reasonable question that Wesley was theologically conscious of the two Protestant marks of the Church. The disquiet occasioned within Anglicanism by Wesley's ordinations of preachers for America drove him to produce and later (1786) to publish in the *Arminian Magazine* a sermon titled "Of the Church." In it Wesley makes explicit reference to the nineteenth Article of Religion: "The visible Church of Christ is a congregation of faithful men, in which the pure word of God is preached, and the sacraments be duly administered."[5]

Wesley's dependence upon the article is also obvious in his own Article XIII "Of the Church" for Methodists.[6] One cannot, however, escape noticing that in both of these direct references to the Anglican Article of Religion on the Church Wesley ignores an entire sentence. The full article of the Church of England is virtually unchanged since 1563 and reads:

> The visible Church of Christ is a congregation of faithful men, in the which the pure word of God is preached, and the Sacraments be duly administered according to Christ's ordinance, in all those things that of necessity are requisite to the same.
>
> As the Church of Jerusalem, Alexandria, and Antioch, have erred; so also the Church of Rome hath erred; not only in their living and manner of Ceremonies, but also in matters of Faith.[7]

The excision of this final sentence in Wesley's sermon "Of the Church" and in his Article of Faith for Methodists "Of the Church" is not incidental. In the sermon the reasons for the deletion are virtually explicit.

Referring in the sermon to only the first sentence of the Anglican article, Wesley writes, "I will not undertake to defend the accuracy of this definition."[8] The chief point of his reluctance is the insistence of the Article upon the preaching of the word of God and the duly administered sacraments *as signs of the church*. In the first place these marks appeared to Wesley as addenda to the forthright description of the church provided by the text he had taken for his sermon, Ephesians 4:1-6. Of this text he says:

> Here, then, is a clear unexceptionable answer to that question, "What is the Church?" The catholic or universal Church is, all the persons in the universe whom God hath so called out of the world as to entitle them to the preceding character; as to be "one body," united by "one Spirit;" having "one faith, one hope, one baptism; one God and Father of all, who is above all, and through all, and in them all."[9]

For Wesley, the church on every level is best described by the unities expressed in the text. With regard to the Church of England as to the Church generally, Wesley says, "This and this alone is the Church of England, according to the doctrine of the Apostle."[10]

At the outset Wesley contends that "this account (Eph. 4:1-6) is exactly agreeable to the nineteenth Article of our Church, the Church of England."[11] In a parenthesis, however, he confesses that "the Article includes a little more than the Apostle has expressed."[12] Within a few paragraphs the "little more" is referred to as "much more" and the inclusion of the Protestant marks in the Article is referred to as a "remarkable addition."[13]

But it is not just the character of these marks as addenda to the scriptural description of the Church that troubles

Wesley. He evaluates them for their polemical intent and draws back from the impractical results of a polemical application. Here is the clearest reason for deleting the final sentence of the Anglican Article.[14]

> I dare not exclude from the Church catholic all those congregations in which any unscriptural doctrines, which cannot be affirmed to be the "pure word of God," are sometimes, yea, frequently preached; neither all those congregations in which the sacraments are not "duly administered." Certainly if these things are so, the Church of Rome is not so much as a part of the catholic church; seeing therein neither is "the pure word of God" preached, nor the sacraments "duly administered." Whoever they are that have "one Spirit, one hope, one Lord, one faith and one God and Father of all," I can easily bear with their holding wrong opinions, yea, and superstitious modes of worship: Nor would I, on these, accounts, scruple still to include them within the pale of the catholic Church; neither would I have any objection to receive them, if they desired it, as members of the Church of England.[15]

Wesley's caution with regard to the Protestant marks of the Church is unmistakable. He receives them reluctantly from the pertinent article of religion. He edits that article to delete the most exclusionary element in it. And finally he limits the authority of the article by reference to the Scripture. Wesley, as we will insist, is reluctant about neither word nor sacrament in themselves. What Wesley fears is that the marks of the Church will be applied polemically to the disruption of the Church's unity. Unity, for Wesley, is a more biblical mark of the Church than either word or sacrament. In fact, word and sacrament can be used only to described the Church for pedagogical and not for polemical reasons.

The ramification of Wesley's unwillingness to use the marks polemically is that they remain as they are fundamentally, means of grace. As such they can be distorted but they are not to be ignored. Their abuse is insufficient reason to set either aside. There is no more vivid account of this thrust in Wesley than in his conflict with the Fetter Lane Society where both sacamental observance and preaching (hearing the word) had been deserted for "quietism."

Much has been written already about Wesley's view of sacraments and preaching.[16] That he has left no fully developed, systematic sacramentology and that his remarks *passim* concerning the sacraments are largely reactions, sometimes polemical, to situation make him appear in various doctrinal configurations. However, the attempt to extract from him a high church sacramentology must founder on his opinion that the Eucharist is as much a convincing as a confirming ordinance. The table of the Lord is as open as Wesley's view of atonement. Likewise the attempt to identify Wesley with anabaptism must also fail. Wesley steadfastly adheres to a sacramental and normative view of the Church.[17] The suggestion that the unevenness of Wesley's sacramentology is to be explained in terms of his own theological process is likewise unsatisfactory. What remains after any examination of Wesley's sacramentology is not a system, but a conviction that the sacraments are not incidental to the life of the Church or the Christian.

A similar observation might be made concerning Wesley's understanding of the function of the hearing of the Word. He defends the apostolic authenticity of his preachers on the dual grounds that they are subordinates to the authority of the Church and that they, in fact, contribute to the Church.[19] These apologies are not systematic treatises upon the place of preaching in the life of the Church, but they assert strongly that preaching must be disciplined by reading and the church to be worthy, and that such preaching is a central means of grace.

What we have to examine, then, if we want to discover

Wesley's esteem for both word and sacrament are not systematic accounts of the place of each in Christian thought and practice (although there are examples of such, consider his treatise "On Baptism"). Instead we have occasional papers, responses, and reactions both within Methodism and without that triggered Wesley's ecclesiological instincts. What we have received from Wesley is the conviction that there is no facile trade off of Word on the one hand for sacrament on the other.

In Wesley's controversy with the "Quietists" at Fetter Lane, Wesley directed his efforts toward steering a course between those who abuse the means of grace (Roman Catholics) and those who despise the means of grace (the Quietists). The issues were set for him, as for church members in general, by a question about the extent to which the means of grace are either salvific or symbolic. In Roman Catholicism, sacraments were the means of God's saving grace. Baptism cleansed away the guilt of original sin and the Eucharist was celestial food or the medicine of immortality. Furthermore, the list of sacraments included five other rites that provided grace for the nurture and sustenance of the believer throughout life and at death. In Roman Catholic theology and practice, saving grace was mediated through the sacraments. The Word is incomplete apart form the sacraments.

As movements within Protestantism distanced themselves from their Roman Catholic roots the sacraments were accorded lesser importance. Lutherans especially, but also Calvinists, managed to maintain a prominent and active place for the sacraments in their doctrines of salvation. Other Protestant groups, however, although they did not forsake sacramental teaching and practice, accorded the sacraments a symbolical meaning only. Their commitment to the doctrine of salvation by faith alone seemed to project a negative sense of "work righteousness" upon sacramental observance. Baptism and the Lord's Supper assumed more incidental roles and the additional five sacraments of Roman Catholicism were rejected altogether. For such Protestants the faith by which we are saved is not mediated by sacramental observance. Salvation is symbolized by the sacrament. But the faith that saves comes by hearing and hearing by the Word of God (Rom. 10:17). The place of primacy and action in the salvation of the individual is filled completely by the proclamation of the Word of God. Sacraments are outward and visible symbols of an inward and spiritual act. Sacraments apart from the Word are incomplete.

The temptation that follows from these two positions is to conclude that since one or the other mark of the Church is accorded primacy as a means of saving grace, the remaining mark is incidental or purely formal. What we have received from Wesley is the conviction that neither mark is only incidental or formal. As means of grace both word and sacrament are essential to the Church.

In his sermon "The Means of Grace" Wesley includes both preaching and the Lord's Supper when he defines his own position as separate from both "those who *abused* the ordinance of God, . . . [and] those who despised them."[20] The first error, abusing the ordinances, is reflected in Wesley's succinct treatment of the relationship between the ordinances and God's grace.

> Settle this in your own heart, that the *opus operatum,* the mere work done, profiteth nothing; that there is no power to save, but in the Spirit of God, no *merit,* but in the blood of Christ; that, consequently, even what God ordains, conveys no grace to the soul, if you trust not in Him alone. On the other hand, he that does truly trust in Him, cannot fall short of the grace of God, even though he were cut off from every outward ordinance, though he were shut up in the centre of the earth.[21]

The abuse of the ordinances consisted in mistaking the *"Means* for the *end,"* the imagining that though religion did not principally consist in these outward means, yet there was something in them wherewith God was well-pleased; something that would still make them [the worshipers] acceptable in this sight, though they were not exact in the weightier matters of the law, in justice, mercy, and the love of God.[22]

The opposite error, *despising* the means of grace, was as roundly condemned by Wesley who had, in the summer of 1740, withdrawn from the Fetter Lane Society over the issue of "stillness." "Stillness" was the result of preaching the futility of good works, including among such works the ordinary means of grace. Those who would practice stillness were pressed, "not to run about to church and sacrament, and to keep their religion to themselves; to be still, not to talk about what they had experienced."[23] The appeal of the doctrine was strong. "Christ has fulfilled the law for *you*. You are no longer subject to ordinances. You are now to *be still,* and *wait* upon God."[24]

Wesley himself confessed the appeal of "stillness" in a *Journal* entry concerning a visit to Islington in 1742.

I found there several of my old acquaintances, who loved me once as the apple of their eye. By staying with them but a little, I was clearly convinced, that was I to stay but one week with them, (unless the providence of God Plainly called me so to do,) I should be as *still* as poor Mr. St_____. I felt their words, as it were, thrilling through my veins. So soft! so pleasing to nature! It seemed *our* religion was but a heavy, coarse thing; nothing so delicate, so refined as theirs. I wonder any person of taste (that has not faith) can stand before them.[25]

The influence of "stillness" was widespread. Charles Wesley mourned that nine out of ten of the brethren at Fetter Lane were "swallowed up in the dead sea of stillness."[26] When the showdown over the issues of stillness came on July 20, 1740, Methodism moved to its new headquarters in the Moorefields "Foundery." "Stillness," however appealing, would not preempt the hearing of the Word and the observance of the sacraments among the Methodists.

John Wesley was prepared to understand the value of "stillness" and the good intentions of the originators in England. They were the counters to those who abused the means of grace. Their intentions were (a) to affirm "that outward religion is worth nothing without the religion of the heart;" and (b) to avoid "that horrid profanation of the ordinances of God which had spread itself over the whole church, and well nigh driven true religion out of the world."[27]

Nevertheless, good intention and high motive are insufficient to justify the continuation of an unworthy practice. However necessary might be the corrective for the abuse of the means of grace, to despise the means of grace itself needed correcting. For Wesley, the (non) practice of stillness stood condemned.

> I rode for Epworth. Before we came thither, I made an end of Madam Guyon's "Short Method of Prayer," and "Les Torrents Spirituelles." Ah, my brethren! I can answer your riddle, now I have ploughed with your heifer. The very words I have so often heard some of you use, are not your own, no more than they are God's. They are only retailed from this poor Quietist; and that with the utmost faithfulness. O that ye knew how much God is wiser than man! Then would you drop Quietists and Mystics together, and at all hazards keep to the plain, practical, written word of God.[28]

But what of the phrase "means of grace"? This, the Quietist objected, is not the language of Scripture either. Wesley concedes the point but argues that

> if the sense of [the term] undeniably is found [in Scripture], to cavil at the term is a mere strife of words. But the sense of it is found undeniably in Scripture. For God hath in Scripture ordained prayer, reading or hearing, and the receiving of the

Lord's Supper, as the ordinary means of conveying his grace to man.[29]

What Wesley gives us, then, in his critique of those who abuse and those who despise the means of grace is a critique of error in both Catholic and Protestant assumptions gone astray. While the first group values only one of the marks of the Church, sacraments, the latter group values neither. Wesley can be seen as calling the Protestant church to her own identity when he asserts the value of both. But finally for Wesley, the means of grace are established on their own merit. They are not primarily marks of the Church. They are channels of God's redeeming grace. Where the Church is truly alive there will be neither abuse nor neglect of either the hearing of the Word or of the sacraments. Nor will one be displaced by the other as if there were a primacy of one over the other. Wesley called the Methodists to affirm in doctrine and practice both the hearing of the Word and the celebration of the sacraments. To do anything less is not so much to fall short of the status of the "true church" as it is to miss the gracious opportunities afforded to every church.

Notes

1. *The Church* (New York: Sheed and Ward, 1967), p. 266.
2. "The Augsburg Confession" in Philip Schaff, *The Creeds of Christendom with a History and Critical Notes,* 3 vols. (Grand Rapids: Baker Book House, 1966) vol. III, pp. 11-12. Brackets enclose additions made with the translation from the Latin text into German.
3. John Calvin, *Institutes of the Christian Religion,* vols. XX and XXI of The Library of Christian Classics, John Baillie, John T. McNeill, Henry P. VanDusen, eds. (Philadelphia: The Westminster Press, 1960) XXI, p. 1023.
4. The Scott's Confession adds a third mark perhaps derived

from the Belgic Confession, article XXIX: "Last, Ecclesiastical discipline uprightlie ministered, as Goddis Worde prescribes, whereby vice is repressed, and vertew nurished." This third "mark" does not appear in the Thirty-nine Articles of Religion of Anglicanism but it is included in the Homily for Whitsunday: "The true Church . . . hath always three notes or marks whereby it is known: pure and sound doctrine, the sacraments ministered according to Christ's holy institution, *and the right use of ecclesiastical discipline.*" In Henry Wheeler, *History and Exposition of the Twenty-five Articles of Religion of the Methodist Episcopal Church* (New York: The Methodist Book Concern, 1908), pp. 245-46.

5. John Wesley, "Of the Church," *The Works of John Wesley,* 14 vols. (Kansas City, Mo.: Nazarene Publishing House), vol. VI, p. 396. See also "An Earnest Appeal to Men of Reason and Religion," vol. VIII, pp. 30-31.

6. "The visible Church of Christ is a congregation of faithful men in which the pure Word of God is preached, and the Sacraments duly administered according to Christ's ordinance, in all those things that of necessity are requisite to the same." In Wheeler, *History and Exposition of the Twenty-five Articles,* p. 237.

7. E. J. Bicknell, *A Theological Introduction to the Thirty-Nine Articles of the Church of England* (London: Longmans, Green and Co., 1919) p. 291.

8. *Works,* vol. VI, p. 397.

9. *Works,* vol. VI, pp. 395-96.

10. *Works,* vol. VI, p. 397.

11. *Works,* vol. VI, p. 396.

12. *Works,* vol. VI.

13. *Works,* vol. VI, p. 397.

14. Bicknell interprets the intention of the final sentence in the article as "denying (Rome) infallibility. As she has erred in the past, so she may err again at the Council of Trent. The allusion is to such events as the acceptance by Pope Liberius of an Arian creed, the acquital of Pelagius by Pope Zozimus and the lapse of Pope Honorius into Monotheletism." This historical nicety is lost on Wesley,

who reads the article not in terms of its intentions but in the way it would be read by those who would most sense its exclusionary qualities.

15. Bicknell.
16. On Wesley's doctrine of the sacraments see, among others, Frank Baker, *Methodism and the Love-Feast* (London: Epworth Press, 1957); Bernard G. Holland, *Baptism in Early Methodism* (London: Epworth Press, 1970); John R. Parris, *John Wesley's Doctrine of the Sacraments* (London: Epworth Press, 1963); Maximim Piette, *John Wesley in the Evolution of Protestantism* (New York: Sheed and Ward, 1937); John E. Rattenbury, *The Eucharistic Hymns of John and Charles Wesley* (London: Epworth Press, 1949).
17. Howard Snyder, *The Radical Wesley and Patterns for Church Renewal* (Downers Grove, Ill.: Inter-Varsity Press, 1980), p. 115.
18. John R. Parris, *John Wesley's Doctrine of the Sacraments* (London: Epworth Press, 1963), p. 100.
19. *Works,* "A Farther Appeal to Men of Reason and Religion, VIII, 220ff.
20. *Works,* V, p. 186.
21. *Works,* V, p. 201.
22. *Works,* V.
23. "Journal" for May 25, 1742; *Works,* I, pp. 372ff.
24. "Journal" for November 3, 1745; *Works,* I, p. 327.
25. I, pp. 364ff.
26. *Journal of Charles Wesley,* entry for May 14, 1740.
27. Sermon "The Means of Grace," *Works,* V, p. 186.
28. "Journal" for June 5, 1742, *Works,* I, p. 376.
29. "Journal" for June 25, 1740, *Works,* I, p. 278.

David L. Cubie (Ph.D., Boston University), chairman of the division of religion and philosophy, Mount Vernon Nazarene College

Separation or Unity?
Sanctification and Love in
Wesley's Doctrine of the Church

IN 1744, Wesley invited three Anglican clergymen, closely associated with him in the Evangelical Revival, and some of his leading preachers to meet with him in conference. In consultation with these, Wesley sought to search things to the bottom,[1] that is, to find principles and guidelines for the expanding societies. To the question "What may we reasonably believe to be God's design in raising up the Preachers called Methodists?" they and he gave the answer "Not to form any new sect; but to reform the nation, particularly the Church; and to spread scriptural holiness over the land."[2]

The reformation of nation and Church and the spread of scriptural holiness over the land were seen by Wesley as one calling. If they were one calling, then how did he interrelate them? Much has been written examining Wesley's application of love and holiness to the social sphere. What needs to be explored is the influence of his doctrine of holiness on his and the Methodist societies' relationship to the Church of England and on his doctrine of the Church.

Some preliminary observations need to be made. First, for Wesley, holiness, described by its model, is Christlikeness: "Holiness is the mind that was in Christ,"[3] but described qualitatively, it is love: "Love is the sum of Christian sanctification."[4] Thus though holiness is stated as the governing principle of the revival, holiness itself is defined by love. Second, the revival brought Wesley and his Methodists into repeated conflict with churchmen. In the midst of this, while pressing toward reformation of the Church, he affirmed loyalty to it; yet he was accused of separation from it, both in practice and goal. While he denied the accusation, his societies developed a structure and ministry that were independent of the Church and which, following Wesley's death, completed that separation.

The contrasts of sanctification with love and of loyalty with separation suggest the question, How, despite Wesley's definition of holiness as love, were sanctification and love in tension? That is, did the terms *sanctification* and *holiness* tend to cluster the ideas of separation around them and did love and its associate terms tend to attract the concepts of union, fellowship, and redemption around them? The themes of separation and union have existed side by side, both within Methodism and in its various branches. Wesley, though seeking to keep his Methodists in the Church of England, was torn between separation and loyalty. As he wrote to Charles, "For these forty years I have been in doubt concerning that question, 'What obedience is due to "heathenish priests and mitered infidels"?'"[5] He was driven on the one hand toward unity and evangelism within the Church, and on the other he taught distance from the sinners in the Church, whose predominance he expressed by saying, "I find few exceptions."[6] In times of hostility he sought for the protection of his sons and daughters in the gospel from their persecutors in the church and explored the advisability of separation from the national church. Yet throughout his life, he looked for a dynamic *via media* in which separation and union could both operate in creative tension for the reformation of Church and nation and, in his later years, for the reformation of the world.

Wesley sought to fashion his Methodists into that redemptive *via media* of being in the Church for its transformation while maintaining some distance from the sinful elements within it. As the Father of "the people called Methodists," he sought to unite Christians of different backgrounds and opinions. With a sympathetic tolerance for this diversity, he served both as arbitrator and unifying symbol. As Dr. Whitehead, Wesley's friend and biographer, records:

> It was highly pleasing to see rigid Churchmen, and equally rigid Dissenters of all denominations, assembled together in a Methodist preaching-house; hearing the truths of the gospel preached, and each feeling the beneficial influence of them on their own hearts. This tended gradually to lessen their prejudices against each other; and however they might still differ, as to modes of worship, it brought them nearer together in Christian charity and brotherly love.[7]

Wesley's ability to unite persons of diverse views was cradled in his concepts of Church, sanctification, and love. Each of these was complex. This complexity also enabled him to affirm, and in some cases dictate, unity with the Church of England while lending a sympathetic ear to those advocating separation. Charles was John's conscience for unity. On the other side were Thomas Walsh and Charles Perronet,[8] who in mid-century asserted their

right to administer the sacraments, a tacit form of separation, and Thomas Coke, who was an open advocate of
separation in Wesley's closing years.

Wesley's ability to hold views of both union and separation was possible because for him the visible church
existed under two formulations—the Church composed of
believers and the Church composed of all those who profess faith; or, to restate the contrast, the Church as nurturing and the Church as sacramental community. The organizational Church contains those who profess to believe and
has doctrines, sacraments, and polity. Though Wesley at
times blurs the distinction between the two, it must be
kept in mind, if one is to understand his teaching, that the
believer should separate from the wicked yet also receive
the sacraments in the parish churches, though from unworthy ministers.[9] Wesley held that the unworthy priest or
Church cannot interrupt the sacramental grace that must
be received through these ordained channels. Though
Wesley taught and practiced frequent communion—partly
because refusal to take the sacraments was *de facto* separation from the Church—the seeds of both division and
nonsacramentalism were present. Preaching and the nurturing community take primacy over the sacraments as a
means toward salvation.[10] The primacy of preaching is
indicated by his description of the prophet (or preacher) as
one sent directly by God, while the priest is one whose
office and ministries, though ordained by God, are commissioned by men.[11]

Both the church of believers and the Church composed
of those who profess faith exist in both universal and particular forms. Thus the Church composed as a "congregation of believers"[12] (1) at its outermost circle includes all
those who fear God and work righteousness (Acts 10:35):
"[He] *is accepted of him*—Through Christ, though he
knows Him not. The assertion is express, and admits of no
exception. He is in the favour of God, whether enjoying

His written word and ordinances or not.''[13] (2) Next is the church universal defined as

> all the persons in the universe whom God hath so called out of the world as to entitle them to the preceding character ["the saints," "the holy persons"]; as to be "one body," united by one "Spirit;" having "one faith, one hope, one baptism; one God and Father of all.''[14]

(3) Then follows, in a more particular form, the true national church: "those members, of the Universal Church who are inhabitants of England. . . . This and this alone is the Church of England, according to . . . the Apostle.''[15] (4) At its most particular there is the nurturing fellowship, including the Methodists, regarding whom he can say,

> Their Teachers are the proper successors of those who have delivered down, through all generatins, the faith once delivered to the saints; and their members have true spiritual communion with the 'one holy' society of true believers: consequently, although they are not the whole 'people of God,' yet are they an undeniable part of his people.[16]

The unity, character, and orthodoxy of this Church of believers, whether in whole or in part, are kept inviolate because every member is holy:

> And this church is. . . . 'ever holy;' for no unholy man can possibly be a member of it. It is 'ever orthodox;' so is every holy man, in all things necessary to salvation: 'Secured against error,' in things essential, 'by the perpetual presence of Christ; and ever directed by the Spirit of truth,' in the truth that is after godliness.[17]

This holiness, though final, is actual because every member thereof is holy, though in different degrees. Willful transgression is ended and they are alive unto God.[18]

Similarly, the Church defined as "a congregation professing to believe, "Church" . . . taken, in a looser sense,[19] also exists from its most general and inclusive to its particular. The following is Wesley's description of it:

> The *vineyard of the Lord*, taking the word in its widest sense, may include the whole world. All the inhabitants of the earth may, in some sense, be called "the vineyard of the Lord". . . . But, in a narrower sense, the vineyard of the Lord may mean the Christian world; that is, all that name the name of Christ, and profess to obey his word. In a still narrower sense, it may be understood of what is termed the Reformed part of the Christian Church. In the narrowest of all, one may, by that phrase, "the vineyard of the Lord," mean, the body of people commonly called Methodists.[20]

Representative of the narrowest sense, the Church of England could have been named instead of the people called Methodists. As Wesley indicates in the following, even zealous members of the organized church may not be members of the true church:

> Can anything then be more absurd, than for men to cry out, *"The Church! The Church!"* and to pretend to be very zealous for it, and violent defenders of it, while they themselves have neither part nor lot therein, nor indeed know what the Church is?[21]

One value of this church is that it is a bridge between the true Church and the world. Even carnal zeal is used by God for his purpose:

> Imagining that they are members of it themselves, the men of the world frequently defend the Church: Otherwise the wolves that surround the little flock on every side would in a short time tear them in pieces.[22]

But beyond that, as Wesley adds, "we know not how soon God may call them too out of the kingdom of Satan into the kingdom of his dear Son."[23] Thus the Church is mixed with the world and is subject to decay. As such it can be considered as part of the nation and of the Christian world and, like Israel of the old covenant, an institution under

God's providential concern. The Methodists have this same institutional existence and the same potential for decay.

This Church, "by law established,"[24] can bear on the one hand his approving description of the Church of England: "(the best constituted national Church in the world),"[25] and on the other his negative evaluation of every union of church and state from "that evil hour, when Constantine the Great called himself a Christian"[26] when "the kingdoms of Christ and of the world, were so strangely and unnaturally blended together."[27] The post-Constantine Church, the Church of Christendom, and the Church of England are equally condemned:

> So totally void of true religion were the generality both of the laity and clergy, so immersed in ambition, envy, covetousness, luxury, and all other vices, that the Christians of Africa [while Cyprian was Bishop of Carthage] were then exactly the same as the Christians of England are now.[28]

The reality is "they will hardly ever be divided till Christ comes to reign upon earth."[29]

Despite the presence of the ungodly in the institutional Church and the indistinct line between it and the world, this Church has continuity. Before 1745, when he read Lord Peter King and Bishop Edward Stillingfleet,[30] Wesley identified continuity as through apostolic succession. After that he saw the institutional church as having ordinary authority through legal establishment, but gaining spiritual authority through the Church of believers, that is, through "a succession of Pastors and Teachers; men both divinely appointed, and divinely assisted; for they convert sinners to God."[31] True succession and authority come through the visible saints. Throughout his life, at least after 1745, his thought was that the Church of believers takes priority over the institutional church, but he was too aware of history to think that he could establish a pure institutional church. The institutional church, in all its organizational forms, including the Methodist societies, was subject to decay.[32] His original calling was to reform the church, that is, to insure the increase of the true Church within the institutional church. He describes all the attempts to reform by separation in the following from his poem "Primitive Christianity" [c. 1743]:

Ye different sects, who all declare
'Lo! here is Christ!' or 'Christ is there!'
Your stronger proofs divinely give,
And show me where the Christians live.

Your claim, alas! ye cannot prove;
Ye want the genuine mark of love:
Thou only, Lord, thine own canst show,
For sure thou hast a church below.[33]

The distinction between the Church composed of believers and that of those who profess to believe is sometimes blurred, especially when Wesley uses the definition of the Church given in the Thirty-Nine Articles, rather than a biblical definition. From it he gained his way of referring to the true church as "a congregation of believers"[34] or "a company of faithful (or believing) people: *coetus credentium*."[35] This, he says, is "a true logical definition, containing both the essence and the properties of a church."[36] Yet he also observed, "I will not undertake to defend the accuracy of this definition,"[37] his reason being that he must include an institution such as the Church of Rome in which "neither is 'the pure word of God' preached, nor the sacraments 'duly administered.'"[38] His possible reason is that the Church as constituted in history, including the Roman church, gains its validity from the true church within, rather than apostolic succession or any other external sign. He then continues, whoever they are that have "one Spirit, one hope, one Lord, one faith, one God and Father of all," I can easily bear with their holding wrong opinions, yea, and superstitious modes of worship: Nor would I, on these accounts, scruple still to include them within the pale of the catholic Church; neither would I have any objection to receive them, if they desired it, as members of the Church of England.[39]

Wesley's doctrine of sanctification is also complex, being protective, disciplinary, and redemptive in its concerns. Protection and discipline interrelate. In order to keep the righteous from contamination, the wicked are to be banished from the Methodist societies. He describes their contaminating influence upon others as follows:

It was dangerous to others; inasmuch as all sin is of an infectious nature. It brought such scandal on their brethren as exposed them to what was not properly the reproach of Christ. It laid a stumbling-block in the way of others, and caused the truth to be evil spoken of.[40]

The model church is that described in Acts which, among other characteristics, is "disciplined by the death of Ananias and Sapphira."[41] The Methodists were a disciplined fellowship. Thus those who persist in their sins were not allowed to remain in the societies.

Individual self-discipline also involved protection, principally by keeping a distance from the wicked. In 1784, he indicated that he had practiced this from his Oxford days: "When it pleased God to give *me* a settled resolution to be, not a *nominal*, but a *real* Christian, (being then about twenty-two years of age,). . . . I resolved to have no acquaintance by chance, but by choice; and to choose such only as I had reason to believe would help me on my way to heaven."[42] The separation theme of holiness is expressed by such phrases as "separating ourselves from unholy men," inviting "no unholy person to your house, unless on some very particular occasion" (such as business), and refusing "any invitation from an unholy person."[43] Charles Wesley also lived by this principle. In July 1754, while traveling with Charles Perronet, he was overtaken by James Wheatley, a former Methodist preacher, who had been dismissed because he had been accused by several women "for some horrible practices."[44] Charles Wesley records;

> Charles [Perronet] . . . forced him to stop, and speak to us. He asked how I did; to which I made no answer. Charles cried out, "Ride on, James, ride on; do not talk to us. I pray God, give you repentance." He asked me how my brother did; but still I said nothing.[45]

The concept of holiness as separation is found in John's sermons. In his sermon "Of the Church" (1786), he states:

> The Church is called *holy,* becuase it *is* holy, because every member thereof is holy, though in different degrees, as He that called them is holy. . . . It follows, that not only no common swearer, no Sabbath-breaker, no drunkard, no whoremonger, no thief, no liar, none that lives in any outward sin, but none that is under the power of anger or pride, no lover of the world, in a word, none that is dead to God, can be a member of his Church.[46]

More explicitly, in his sermon "In What Sense We Are to Leave the World" (1784), which is an exposition of Paul's words "come out from among them, and be ye separate, saith the Lord, and touch not the unclean thing" (2 Cor. 6:17), he wrote against "conversing with ungodly ["unholy"] men when there is no necessity."[47] His reason is that "As Christ can have *no concord* with *Belial*; so a believer in him can have no concord with an unbeliever. It is absurd to imagine that any true union or concord should be between two persons, while one of them remains in the darkness, and the other walks in the light."[48] Wesley limits the application to unholy individuals and denies that it means separation from the Church. To apply this scripture to the Church, Wesley says, is totally foreign to the design of the Apostle. . . . [To have] done so, . . . would have been a flat contradiction both to the example and precept of their Master. For although the Jewish Church was then full as *unclean,* as unholy, both inwardly and outwardly, as any Christian Church now upon earth, yet our Lord constantly attended the service of it.[49]

Though this principle affected the relationship of the righteous to the unrighteous within the National Church, he denied that his societies were a separation from the Church. He did this by making a distinction between the Church and the unholy in the Church. In this case, the Church with its ordinances, sacraments, and polity is identified with those who believe, while those who only profess to believe, especially those with open wickedness or who deny the doctrines of the Church of England, are described as "the worst Dissenters" or "gross Dissenters."[50] While teaching separation from the unholy in the Church, he did not advocate separation from the Church. Ideally, the Church was to be a disciplined fellowship, but realistically he observed that it had never been. Thus wickedness in the Church was not a reason for separation from it. As he accused the Anabaptists (Baptists), "There are unholy, outwardly unholy men, in *your* congregations also."[51] To be true to their principle, he reminded them that "if no man ought to be *admitted* . . . who has not actual faith and repentance, then neither ought any who has them not to *continue* in any congregation."[52]

Separation was especially wrong because it went against the reason for Methodism's existence, which, as noted, is "to reform the nation, particularly the Church."[53] He was persuaded that separation would end the revival. As he said:

It has chiefly been by this means that many revivals of religion have been of so short a continuance. . . . Hence the world received no more benefit from them; and by degrees their own love waxed cold, till either their memorial perished from the earth, or they remained a dry, cold sect.[54]

While Wesley sought to prevent separation, he was also persuaded that if the Methodists were driven out, God would sustain them.[55] Though he never says as much, he does allow for the providential expulsion of the righteous remnant from an apostate Church. By 1788, he was convinced that "the Clergy . . ., far from thanking them for continuing in the Church, use all the means in their power, fair and unfair, to drive them out of it."[56] For the Methodists to leave voluntarily would contradict their purpose of evangelism and reformation and, as we will note, their guiding principle of love.

Though Wesley maintained a position of both unity and separation, many of his followers were unable to do so. Wesley blamed this in part on the dissenting origins of many who "brought in more and more prejudice against the Church."[57] Yet others of Anglican origin, such as Thomas Coke, were leaders in separation. To Whitehead, who sided with Charles Wesley against separation, Coke was a seceder in principle:

> The Seceders laid the very foundation of their work, in judging and condemning others: we laid the foundation of our work, in judging and condemning ourselves. . . . Dr. Coke, in laying the foundation of his new church in America, . . . quitted those of the old Methodists.[58]

Coke had condemned the pre-Revolutionary Anglican church in America as "filled with the parasites and bottle companions of the rich and great" and as deniers of "such 'fundamental doctrines' as that of Justification by Faith."[59] Similarly, Francis Asbury saw the Anglican church as "man made [and] worldly."[60] Later, Coke was to renounce his statement and seek reconciliation, a possibility which was abhorrent to Asbury. Wesley took a middle position regarding his American Methodists. Without renouncing the Church of England, he encouraged the American Methodists in their providential freedom from the English bishops.[61] They were a new church in a new land.

The difference between Wesley and many of his followers may be that the latter failed to fully incorporate love
into holiness. Asbury, for example, when talking about holiness typically does not include the concept of love. Asbury
did extract from the works of Burroughs and Baxter
his *The Causes, Evils and Cures of Heart and Church Divisions*,[62] whose theme is the responsibility of love to
maintain unity, but this was prepared during the O'Kelly
separation from the Methodists. In his journal Asbury
states the polemical purpose of the book: "In this work I
promise myself good arguments against our separating
brethren."[63] With Wesley, the organizational theme of
love was always present.

This difference between Wesley and his followers can be
seen by comparing two descriptions of the bands and
societies, Wesley's and one by Charles Perronet, who with
Thomas Walsh had been an early proponent of the
preachers' right to administer the sacraments. Both
Charles and John Wesley saw this as resulting in separation, for if a full ministry were provided, the Methodists
would no longer need to attend the parish church. Attendance at "all the ordinances of the Church at all opportunities" was Wesley's consistent way of distinguishing
between remaining in or leaving the Anglican church.[64]

Charles Perronet, in his "Of the Right Method of Meeting Classes and Bands, in the Methodist-Societies,"
expresses primary concern for personal holiness. The perspective is self-examination. "The particular design of the
classes" is defined as follows:

> Whether they aim at being holy [and] devoted to God. . . .
> [Whether they] Oppose Self-love in all its hidden forms. . . .
> Whether they can cordially love those that despitefully use
> them! Justify the ways of God in thus dealing with them? And
> in all they suffer, seek the destruction of inward Idolatry, of
> Pride, Self-will, and Impatience? . . .
> To inquire concerning. . . . Consciousness of their own
> vileness and nothingness. . . .

> Whether they had a clear, full, abiding conviction, that
> without inward, compleat, universal holiness, no man shall
> see the Lord?[65]

To this, Wesley adds the postscript,

> I earnestly exhort all leaders of Classes and Bands, seri-
> ously to consider the preceding Observations, and to put them
> in execution with all the Understanding and Courage that God
> has given them.[66]

Wesley recognized Charles Perronet's ideas as useful, but
the preceding passage does not reflect Wesley's way of
thinking.

Wesley's own "A Plain Account of the People Called
Methodists" does contain such concerns as "a desire to
flee from the wrath to come,"[67] "to inquire how their
souls prosper,"[68] and to "confess our faults one to another,"[69] and the practice of expulsion because "sin is of
an infectious nature."[70] Another expressed concern for
personal holiness is that "a select company" was to provide fellowship with those "to whom," as he says, "I
might unbosom myself on all occasions."[71] Despite this,
his major concern is for others: for Methodists, for other
Christians, and for others in need. The class leader was
"to inquire how [the class members'] souls prosper."[72]
The result described was, "Many now happily experienced that Christian fellowship of which they had not so
much as an idea before. They began to 'bear one another's
burdens,' and naturally to 'care for each other.' As they
had daily a more intimate acquaintance with, so they had a
more endeared affection for, each other."[73] Among the
Bands a smaller company gathered "in order to 'confess
[their] faults one to another.'"[74] Wesley began the love
feasts "that we might together 'eat bread,' as the ancient
Christians did, 'with gladness and singleness of heart.'"[75]
These intimate friends were not only "delivered from the
temptations out of which, till then, they found no way to

escape," but they were also "strengthened in love, and more effectually provoked to abound in every good work."[76] To promote love for those Christians who were not Methodists, he "allotted one evening in every month to read, to all who were willing to hear" accounts of what God was doing in other churches and in other lands as a "method of preventing . . . a narrowness of spirit, a party zeal, a being straitened in our own bowels; that miserable bigotry which makes many so unready to believe that there is any work of God but among themselves."[77] Concrn for the needy is indicated by reference to Stewards, Visitors of the Sick, Physic for the Sick, a Poor House, a School for Children, and Loans to the Poor.[78]

That holiness as separation is not dominant in his thinking is evidenced by his application of the bride theme of the New Testament. In his *Notes on the New Testament*, when the sanctification of the Church as the bride could have been used as a call to holiness with the goal of preparation for heaven, Wesley refers to her mission and her being in the world: "The Spirit of adoption in the bride, in the heart of every true believer. *Say*—With earnest desire and expectation. *Come*" (Rev. 22:17). Similarly, the cleansing of the Church is "*That he might present it*— Even in this world. *To himself*—As His spouse" (Eph. 5:27). Wesley, by these, indicated that his primary concern was not with the holiness of a mystical and invisible body but with the mission and holiness of the visible church.

The organizational principle by which all of Wesley's doctrines are either molded or measured is love. The centrality of this theme is evidenced by his comment on the verse "God is love" (1 John 4:8):

> This little sentence brought St. John more sweetness, even in the time he was writing it, than the whole world can bring. God is often styled holy, righteous, wise; but not holiness, righteousness, or wisdom in the abstract, as He is said to be love: intimating that this is His darling, His reigning attribute,

the attribute that sheds an amiable glory on all His other per-
fections.[79]

Though God's wrath is affirmed as an essential part of the
doctrine of the atonement ("if . . . God never was offended, there was no need of . . . propitiation. And, if so,
Christ died in vain"[80]), he rejected the Calvinist's doctrine
of decrees because they "represent God as worse than the
devil; more false, more cruel, more unjust. . . . No scripture can mean that God is not love, or that his mercy is not
over all his works; that is, whatever it prove beside, no
scripture can prove predestination." It were "better . . . to
say it had no sense at all, than to say it had such a sense as
this."[81] Christian perfection is repeatedly defined as "the
pure love of God and man; the loving God with all our
heart and soul, and our neighbour as ourselves."[82] "The
highest of all Christian graces, is properly and directly the
love of our neighbour."[83] Similarly, about religion he can
state, " 'The heaven of heavens is love.' There is nothing
higher in religion; there is, in effect, nothing else."[84] And
as already noted, "Love" is "the sum of Christian sanctification."[85] One of his earliest descriptions of the Church
is that it is "the Catholic seminary of divine love."[86] It is
where the seed of love is sown and nurtured towards its
full ripeness.

To say that "love is the sum of Christian sanctification"
does not define the way that sanctification interrelates with
the doctrine of the Church. Wesley's doctrine of love is a
complex of ideas that serve as his rationale for both redemptive inclusion and protective exclusion by the
Church. Thus *agápe* concepts of love, whether genuinely
New Testament, or late twentieth-century interpretations
of it, cannot be presumed. Wesley's concept of love is nurtured by the *Caritas* tradition[87] with its intricate ethical
heritage, and by the concept of benevolence, a term used
by such diverse writers as William Law (1686-1761),

Joseph Butler (1692-1752), Jonathan Edwards, Sr. (1703-1758) and Jonathan Edwards, the younger (1745-1801) to express the universal command, "Thou shalt love thy neighbor as thyself." In Joseph Butler and William Law, the concept of benevolence became a modern expression of the *Nomos* motif. It was expressed as a "disinterested" (equal) application of law, with its rewards and punishments. Wesley, in contrast, emphasized equal application of love with its mercy and compassion, for *"God is not a respector of persons"* (Acts 10:34).[88] That which makes Wesley creatively different from both of these influences is that he consciously sought to correct all ideas by the New Testament. Notice his interpretation of love in First Corinthians as referring to the "love of God, and of all mankind for His sake" rather than love in the abstract.[89] The term *benevolence* was used by him to advocate sacrificial love for all humankind.

The terms for love that Wesley uses in his teaching regarding the Church are (1) *storgé*: love or loyalty to family and nation; (2) benevolence or beneficence: an equal compassion and care for all; (3) complacence, delight: love for the saints; (4) reciprocal love: the *Koinonia* fellowship love which is the opposite of schism; (5) catholic love: a comprehensive love that includes all the preceding, plus an ecumenical concern for the whole Church; (6) zeal: love aflame, but organized according to the degree of value in its object.[90] It is by the interplay of these concepts that Wesley explains and defends his relationship to the Church of England.

The love terms that Wesley uses to maintain union with the Church of England are *storgé* and *benevolence*. He also uses the concept of unity which, though not a term for love, is a primary characteristic of it. He defines *storgé* as "a kind of natural affection for our country."

We look upon *England* as that part of the world, and the

> *Church* as that part of England, to which all we who were
> born and have been brought up therein owe our first and chief
> regard. We feel in ourselves a strong . . . *storgé*, a kind of
> natural affection for our country, which we apprehend Chris-
> tianity was never designed either to root out or to impair.[91]

In this essay titled "Ought We to Separate from the
Church of England," written originally for the "crucial
Conference of 1755,"[92] he affirmed that the clergy who are
"friends to the truth, or neuters, or enemies to it" are still
"our brethren" and the Church is still "the mother of us
all."[93] They are "that part of our countrymen to whom we
have been joined from our youth up by ties of a religious
as well as a civil nature."[94] They furthermore have a place
in God's purpose:

> We look on the *clergy*, not only as a part of these our breth-
> ren, but as that part whom God by his adorable Providence
> has called to be watchmen over the rest, for whom therefore
> they are to give a strict account.[95]

He described his own churchmanship in this way: "I am
an High Churchman, the son of an High Churchman"[96];
though by 1775, when this letter was written to the Earl of
Dartmouth, his high churchmanship may have been more
political than ecclesiastical. This strong natural affection
had been developed in him from infancy. Gottlieb
Spangenburg observed in his diary (June 30 to October 18,
1736), after conversation with Wesley, "He has moreover
several quite special principles, which he still holds
strongly, since he drank them in with his mother's
milk."[97] The term *benevolence* is not used in the crucial
article on the Church and the clergy; yet the concepts of
the benevolence idea are expressed in his description of
the attitude which one ought to have toward "the clergy,
our brethren" who may be enemies to the truth:

> If these then neglect their important charge, if they do not
> watch over them with all their power, they will be of all men

most miserable, and so are entitled to our deepest compassion.[98]

Storgé could not function by itself but required benevolence if it was to function for unconverted clergy.

In his correspondence with Charles in 1785, one senses a change in his mood regarding the Church and the unconverted clergy.[99] After the ordination of Coke to superintend the Methodist in America, Charles admonished John to take no further steps toward separation, blaming John's actions on pressure from Coke and the preachers—"all seek their own, and prefer their own interest to your honor."[100] In a letter dated August 14, 1785, he also argued from the loyalty John owed to his family:.

> So much, I think, you owe to my father, to my brother, and to me, as to say till I am taken from the evil. I am on the brink of the grave, do not push me in. . . . Let us . . . leave behind us, the name and character of honest men.[101]

John responded by referring to Charles's poetic line, "heathenish priests, and mitred infidels,"[102] as "a sad truth. . . . and I find few exceptions to it."[103] Charles then reminded him that "That 'sad truth' is not a new truth. You saw it when you expressed in your *Reasons* [1755] such tenderness of love for the unconverted clergy."[104] Benevolence was still to be the attitude toward the unconverted clergy and thus a continuing influence toward unity.

Though he never advocated separation, John in his later years was more open to the possibility. After Charles's death in 1788, when Coke proposed "that the whole Methodist body should make a formal separation from the Church,"[105] John did not vehemently oppose the idea; instead he remarked:

> Dr. Coke puts me in mind of the German proverb, which I may apply to himself and to myself. 'He skips like a flea; I creep like a louse.' He would *tear* all from top to bottom. I will not *tear*, but *unstitch*.'[106]

Despite the possibility of separation, benevolence was always a force toward unity. Thus in 1755 he wrote:

> By such a separation we should only throw away the peculiar glorying which God has given us, that we do and will suffer all things for our brethren's sake, though the more we love them the less we be loved, but should act in direct contradiction to that very end for which we believe God hath raised us up. The chief design of his Providence in sending us out is undoubtedly to quicken our brethren, and the first message of all our preachers is to the lost sheep of the Church of England.[107]

The same conviction was expressed in 1779:

> If it be said, "He could have made them a separate people, like the Moravian Brethren;" I answer, This would have been a direct contradiction to his whole design in raising them up. . . . to leaven the whole nation.[108]

What is benevolence for Wesley? It is his "equitable rule" by which you "do good to all men; not only friends, but enemies; not only to the deserving, but likewise to the evil and unthankful?"[109] It is his contrast and antidote to the legalistic benevolence of equal justice, that is, of "condemning the guilty in a higher degree than he deserves," and is expressed by the "strongest and tenderest affection."[110] In language similar to that used about sinful clergy, he asked:

> Should we have no pity for those
>
> > Who sigh beneath guilt's horrid stain,
> > The worst confinement, and the heaviest chain?
>
> Should we shut up our compassion toward those who are of all men most miserable, because they are miserable by their own fault?[111]

In his "Sermon on the mount, III" (1739), benevolence characteristics are given as essential for "the peacemaker," who, like his Heavenly Father, is not a respecter of persons:

a peace-maker is one that, as he hath opportunity "doeth good unto all men;" one that, being filled with the love of God and of all mankind, cannot confine the expressions of it to his own family, or friends, or acquaintance, or party, or to those of his own opinions,—no, nor those who are partakers of like precious faith; but steps over all these narrow bounds, that he may do good to every man, that he may, some way or other, manifest his love to neighbours and strangers, friends and enemies. . . . He does good, not of one particular kind, but good in general, in every possible way; employing herein all his talents of every kind, all his powers and faculties of body and soul, all his fortune, his interest, his reputation.[112]

The role of peacemaker was one to which he aspired in all his relationships with officials of the Church. His stated principle is,

O beware, I will not say of *forming*, but of *countenancing* or *abetting* any *parties* in a Christian society! . . . Follow peace with all men, without which you cannot effectually follow holiness. . . .

Happy is he that attains the character of a peace-maker in the Church of God.[113]

The concept of benevolence toward sinners, which included working all things toward their salvation, was an important argument against separation.

Besides the terms *storgé* and benevolence, another influence toward remaining in the national church was Wesley's conviction that "it is the nature of love to unite us together."[114] The sermon "On Schism" (1786), in which he makes the previous statement, is in part a defense of the emerging separation of the Methodists from the national church,[115] but it also has the other thrust of seeking to keep the Methodists in the Church. That which argues against division is that a principle purpose of the Church is to develop love. Unity works love and love naturally seeks unity. Thus he wrote in his sermon "On Zeal"

(1781) "that his followers may the more effectually provoke one another to love, holy tempers, and good works,
our blessed Lord has united them together in one body,
the Church, dispersed all over the earth."[116] The Church
is "a body of men compacted together."[117] That love
works toward unity is evidenced by the Church at Pentecost. Wesley asks:

> "How came they to act thus, to have all things in common,
> seeing we do not read of any positive command to do this?" I
> answer, There needed no outward command: The command
> was written on their hearts. It naturally and necessarily re-
> sulted from the degree of love which they enjoyed.[118]

Love was to motivate the Methodists in their relationship
to the Church of England. We have seen this already in his
application of benevolence toward even the wicked and
unbelieving in the Church.

He was especially concerned for unity among the
evangelical clergy in the Church despite indifference and
open opposition to the idea by many of them. As he wrote
to George Downing, chaplain to the Earl of Dartmouth,
the friend of Lady Huntingdon, in 1761,

> For many years [twenty] I have been labouring after this—
> labouring to unite, not scatter, the messengers of God. Not
> that I want anything from them. . . . But I want all to be
> helpful to each other, and all the world to know we are so.
> Let them know who is on the Lord's side.[119]

His efforts increased during that decade, even seeking to
establish a basis of union. He records in his journal for
March 16, 1764:

> I met several serious Clergymen. I have long desired that
> there might be an open, avowed union between all who
> preach those fundamental truths, Original Sin, and Justifica-
> tion by Faith, producing inward and outward holiness.[120]

He was even willing to push aside differences over "absolute decrees on the one hand, and perfection on the other.''[121] What he wanted was an active expression of ''Catholic love.'' To this end he proposed that they

1. Remove hinderances out of the way? Not judge one another. . . .
2. Love as Brethren? Think well of and honour one another? . . .

      ''Speak respectfully, honourably, kindly of each other . . . .

      This is the union which I have long sought after.[122]

This union never materialized. Instead, division increased. Near the end of the century, when the numbers of Calvinistic clergy in the Church of England were increasing, those who spoke against Christian perfection were included with the Arians among those Anglican clergy that Methodists ought not to have to hear if they were persuaded that hearing them would be spiritually damaging.[123]

The love concept around which Wesley's separation ideas orbit was complacence, though unity concepts are also derived from it. It is this delight love which is most in tension with his concept of benevolence. In his sermons, ''On Friendship with the World'' (1786) and ''In What Sense We Are to Leave the World'' (1784), he distinguishes between benevolence to all and complacence or delight, which is reserved for the saints. In these sermons the language of love for the neighbor, or benevolence, is as forceful as ever. Notice in the following his description of God as ''the universal Friend,'' that is, that he is no respecter of persons:

> We may, we ought, to love them as ourselves; (for they also are included in the word *neighbour;*) to bear them real goodwill; to desire their happiness, as sincerely as we desire the happiness of our own souls; yea, we are in a sense to honour them, (seeing we are directed by the Apostle to ''honour all men,'') as the creatures of God; nay, as immortal spirits, who

are capable of knowing, of loving, and of enjoying him to all
eternity. . . . We are never willingly to grieve their spirits, or
give them any pain; but, on the contrary, to give them all the
pleasure we innocently can; seeing we are to "please all men
for their good." . . .

We ought to do them all the good that is in our power, all
they are willing to receive from us; following herein the
example of the universal Friend, our father which is in
heaven.[124]

Complacence qualifies this love by placing limitations on
the quality of love and on the time and circumstances in
which it is given. Complacence expresses delight in the
object, but unlike benevolence, it must not be given to the
world. To do so would be to have friendship with the
world (James 4:4). The Christian's affection must accord
with that of the psalmist when he said, "All my delight is
upon the saints that are in the earth, and upon such as
excell in virtue" (Ps. 163).[125] Regarding time and circumstances, he states, "We may, doubtless, converse with
them, First, on business. . . . Secondly, when courtesy requires it; only we must take great care not to carry it too
far: Thirdly, when we have a reasonable hope of doing
them good."[126] Self-protection and calculated distance are
also necessary because

We may easily hurt our own souls, by sliding into a close
attachment to any of them that know not God. This is the
friendship which is "enmity with God;" We cannot be too
jealous over ourselves, lest we fall into this deadly snare; lest
we contract, or ever we are aware, a love of *complacence* or
delight in them.[127]

We have seen this practiced by Charles Wesley in his
treatment of James Wheatley. John Wesley's view of holiness as separation has a close affinity to his complacence
concept of love. Thus to say that "love is the sum of
Christian sanctification,"[128] for Wesley, does not rule out
separation.

The danger is that through complacence, legalism and bigotry may enter into human relationship. Though Christian perfection may be defined in terms of love for God and neighbor, a diminishing of love, identified as a mistake, can occur in relationships without, in Wesley's evaluation, love being any less perfect. As he states in his sermon "On Perfection": "From a wrong apprehension, I may love and esteem you either more or less than I ought."[129] This limitation of love by one's evaluation of the other person tends toward bigotry or of loving only those of one's own group. In 1761 Wesley himself warned those professing perfect love regarding this danger. He admonished them: "I entreat you, beware of bigotry. Let not your love or beneficence be confined to Methodists, so called, only; much less to that very small part of them who seem to be renewed in love. . . . O make not this your Shibboleth!"[130] Complacence is in danger of limiting benevolence to those in the circle of delight and approval. Wesley's concept of benevolence was a counteraction against bigotry. Regarding love for "the enemies of God, the unthankful and unholy," he asks, "Could you 'wish yourself' temporarily 'accursed' for their sake?"[131]

Though not entirely free of legalistic love, Wesley did avoid bigotry, in part because he had a broad inclusive definition of the word *saint*. For him, *saint* was defined in ethical terms rather than religious. He states, describing his own delight, "Let my soul be with these Christians, wheresoever they are, and whatsoever opinion they are of. 'Whosoever *thus* doth the will of my Father which is in heaven, the same is my brother, and sister, and mother.' "[132] Though normally the object of delight was one who can answer yes to the question "Dost thou believe in the Lord Jesus Christ?" potentially any person who works righteousness, even though "Jew, Deist, or Turk" can be an object of delight. Regarding anyone who casts out devils, defined as turning "men from all manner of sin to holiness of heart and life," Wesley says:

Speak well of him . . . defend his character and his mission. Enlarge, as far as you can, his sphere of action; show him all kindness in word and deed; and cease not to cry to God in his behalf, that he may save both himself and them that hear him.[133]

Righteousness is central. As he states, "Religion is . . . the love of God and man, producing all holiness of conversation. . . . But how very slender a part of this are opinions, how right soever!"[134] This righteousness is not humanistic because

the work under consideration is of such a nature (namely, the conversion of men from all manner of sin, to holiness of heart and life) that if it be at any time wrought at all, it must be the work of God: seeing it is God alone, and not any child of man, who is able to "destroy the works of the devil."[135]

Because Wesley's doctrine of complacence was not narrow, it could also contribute to unity with the national church. Thus Robert Barclay, William Law, and others who, from Wesley's perspective, did not understand evangelical truth, are still within the Church. As he notes,

However confused their ideas may be, however improper their language, may there not be many of them whose heart is right toward God, and who effectually know "the Lord our righteousness?"
". . . Only let men be humbled as repenting criminals at Christ's feet, let them rely as devoted pensioners on his merits, and they are undoubtedly in the way to a blessed immortality."[136]

The generality of his followers did not retain these distinctions. Thus while Wesley was striving to keep them in the Church, his ideas regarding love contributed to separation. The ecclesiological implications of complacence are evident in the Methodists' relationship to the Anglican church. Though John Wesley had *storgé* love for the Church of England, a large portion of his followers did not. Many of them had only been nominal Anglicans. Others had been Dissenters.[137] This is evidenced by the following comment by one of Wesley's helpers, Henry Moore, on the sermon "The Ministerial Office": "His love to the Church, from which he never deviated unnecessarily, had, in this instance, led him a little too far."[138] Because complacence (or delight) and reciprocal love could only be given to those judged to be righteous, the unity requirement of love was countermanded. Thus love did not persuade them unequivocally to remain in the Church of England. In fact, Asbury and others rejected the Church of England as an apostate church. Despite Wesley's arguments to the contrary,[139] a doctrine which separates the righteous from the unrighteous in the Church inevitably moves toward a separation of the "true church" from that which is perceived to be less than true. Francis Asbury could desire union with the Presbyterians as a disciplined and evangelical Church,[140] but be "exceedingly averse,"[141] according to Coke, to any reunion with the Protestant Episcopal church. Asbury said of both the latter church and the Church of England: "If they have the doctrine, they do not preach it at all. They are settled, man made, worldly ministry under no discipline and always have been."[142] To him, they were, in a derogatory sense, "those people."[143] The settled, human-made, worldly ministry and episcopacy of Anglicanism was part of the "rubbish" not cleared out at the Reformation.[144] The Methodist Episcopal church was, in contrast, a restoration of the primitive order. " 'I am satisfied,' " he wrote in his "Valedictory Address to [Bishop] William McKendree," using the words of Thomas Haweis, " 'that the Methodist mode of episcopal government is more apostolic than the Church of England ever was, will, or can be, without a radical reformation from its essential form of locality, written sermons and prayers, State laws, and human policy.' "[145]

Complacence or delight, as we have seen, can serve not only as an affectional and rational motive for separation; it also serves to unite. Complacence or delight can be expressed, to use Johannine language, as love for the brethren. As such, it was the motivation both for union with evangelicals within and beyond the Church of England and for unity in the local fellowship. As ecumenical love, it was the major component in what Wesley calls catholic love. As love expressed in face-to-face fellowship, it was reciprocal love and the counterforce to schism. Wesley's ideal Anglican church was a disciplined, yet broadly evangelical church, a church composed of all those who are genuinely children of God. Realism, along with loyalty, kept him from leaving a church in which there were the wicked. Catholic love, on the other hand, motivated him toward fellowship both within and beyond the confines of that Church. In his sermon ''On the Death of Mr. Whitefield,'' he defined *catholic love* as

> that sincere and tender affection which is due to all those who, we have reason to believe, are children of God by faith;—in other words, all those, in every persuasion, who ''fear God and work righteousness.''[146]

It moved beyond complacence in two regards, not only that it is ecumenical, but also that it includes benevolence as a constant concern. Thus it is required that both the one who practices catholic love and the one who is to receive it are not only to delight in the saints but also have universal benevolence. The heart of this one ''is enlarged toward all mankind, . . . neighbors and strangers, friends and enemies.''[147] The potential recipient of catholic delight, among other things, is asked,

> 17. Is thy heart right toward thy neighbour? . . . Do you ''love your enemies''? Is your soul full of good-will, of tender affection, toward them? Do you love even the enemies of God, the unthankful and unholy? Do your bowels yearn over

them? Could you "wish yourself" temporally "accursed" for their sake? . . .

18. Do you show your love by your works? While you have time, as you have opportunity, do you in fact "do good to all men," neighbors or strangers, friends or enemies, good or bad?[148]

If the answer to these is affirmative, then he says: "If it be, give me thy hand."[149] Catholic love will bind them together despite differences "in opinions or modes of worship." For Wesley, though formal unity may be desirable, true ecumenism is a supportive love across organizational and confessional distinctions. As he asked:

> But although a difference in opinions or modes of worship may prevent an entire external union; yet need it prevent our union in affection? Though we cannot think alike, may we not love alike? May we not be of one heart, though we are not of one opinion? Without all doubt, we may.[150]

There is, though, a qualitative difference between catholic love and benevolence. As he wrote to those evangelicals with whom he desired unity:

> I mean, First, love me: And that not only as thou lovest all mankind; not only as thou lovest thine enemies, or the enemies of God, those that hate thee, that "despitefully use thee and persecute thee;" not only as a stranger, . . . no; "if thine heart be right, as mine with thy heart," then love me with a very tender affection, as a friend that is closer than a brother; as a brother in Christ, a fellow-citizen of the New Jerusalem, a fellow-soldier in the same warfare, under the same Captain of our salvation. Love me as a companion in the kingdom and patience of Jesus, and a joint-heir of his glory.[151]

Wesley's concern for unity was not surface. He exchanged "heart and hand" with the Congregationalist, Phillip Doddridge, who himself was censored for his friendship with Wesley, and who wrote to Wesley that both separatists and establishment clergy "are coming nearer to the harmony in which I hope we shall ever be one in Christ Jesus."[152] Wesley had particular difficulty in accepting Scottish Presbyterianism. Thus after Dr. John Gillies opened the pulpit of the University Church in Glasgow to him, when a downpour made field preaching impractical, Wesley recorded in his journal:

> Surely with God nothing is impossible! Who would have believed, five-and-twenty years ago, either that the Minister would have desired it, or that I should have consented to preach in a Scotch kirk?[153]

Two years later, when Dr. Gillies preached for Wesley in Newcastle, Wesley rejoiced, "Shall we not have more and more cause to say,—

> Names, and sects, and parties fall; /Thou, O Christ, art all in all?"[154]

Though Wesley sought to maintain unity both with the national church and his evangelical friends, his primary concern was for his Methodist societies, which he saw as the nurturing community of believers. Though avoiding the term *church* for them through most of his life, preferring "the people called Methodists," he in the 1780s was referring to them as "the Churches of God that are under my care."[155] The nurturing community was where the Church as a congregation of believers really functions. It was to this group, whether connectional or local, that Wesley applied the concepts of reciprocal love and schism.

For Wesley, the local Anglican church, to a large extent, was a sacramental and worshiping community, which did not function to create primary face-to-face social responsibility. As in Germany, where Pietism developed the *ecclesiolae in ecclesia,* religious societies developed in England independently of the structural church, though usually with the local rector as their spiritual guide.[156] In contrast to the dissenting chapels, the local church was not a nurturing fellowship. Wesley's societies, initially at least, were a continuation of the religious societies. His father before him had also organized societies as an auxiliary to his parish ministry in Epworth.

When Wesley, as early as 1748, was accused of schism, that is, of "destroying Christian fellowship" on the local level by gathering his converts into societies, he answered, "That which never existed, cannot be destroyed."[157] The kind of fellowship which generally did not exist in the local parish, but should, is expressed by his asking,

> Who watched over them in love? Who marked their growth in grace? Who advised and exhorted them from time to time? Who prayed with them and for them, as they had need? This, and this alone, is Christian fellowship. . . . Are not the bulk of the parishioners a mere rope of sand?[158]

As he observed in 1754 in his *Notes* on 1 Corinthians 11:18, "the indulging any temper contrary to this tender care of each other is the true scriptural schism." In his sermon "On Schism" (1786) his definition was very similar. Commenting on 1 Corinthians 12:25, he stated: "Schism here, means the want of this tender care for each other. It undoubtedly means an alienation of affection in any of them toward their brethren."[159] Reciprocal love is the same type of love as delight or catholic love, but it functions not so much as a desire of approval for the righteous as mutual care. In the community of believers, "delight" and "complacence" are part of the conceptual context by which Wesley challenges the Christians to love one another. Schism is the opposite of reciprocal love. Though schism may be defined as "A causeless separation from a body of living Christians"—for example, from the churches of Rome and England—this is only "in a remote sense" schism.[160] Wesley's preferred definition is that schism "is not a separation *from* . . . but a separation *in* a Church,"[161] meaning in the fellowship of believers. Separation "from a body of living Christians, with whom we were before united," he says, "is a grievous breach of the law of love. It is the nature of love to unite us together; and the greater the love, the stricter the union."[162]

Wesley's principal application of the Scriptures against schism was to division within his societies, even as Asbury applied the theme of love to American Methodism when he wrote his *Mind and Heart of Love* at the time of the O'Kelly division. Thus Wesley warns,

> If you would avoid schism, observe every rule of the Society, and of the Bands, for conscience' sake. Never omit meeting your Class or Band; never absent yourself from any public meeting. These are the very sinews of our Society; and whatever weakens, or tends to weaken, our regard for these, or our exactness in attending them, strikes at the very root of our community.[163]

For most of Wesley's followers, the community of believers began in the Methodist societies. Thus while Wesley could say in 1781, "For many years I have earnestly advised . . . all in connection with me, who have been brought up in the Established Church, to continue therein,"[164] his primary application of his opposition to division was within the nurturing community, that is, within the Methodist societies. As he advised,

> Beware of schism, of making a rent in the Church of Christ. That inward disunion, the members ceasing to have a reciprocal love 'one for another,' (1 Cor. xii:25,) is the very root of all contention, and every outward separation.[165]

The repeated theme, the central motif in all of this advice against schism is that it transgresses the law of love. Because the issue is "reciprocal love," the blame for separation is not always placed on the one who separates but on the failure to love, whether by the person who stays away or the person who gives offense. Thus he advised the

"Greatest Professors [of Christian Perfection] in the Methodist Societies" to

> beware of tempting others to separate from you. Give no offence which can possibly be avoided; see that your practice be in all things suitable to your profession, adorning the doctrine of God our Saviour. . . . Avoid all magnificent, pompous words; indeed, you need give it no general name; neither perfection, sanctification, the second blessing, nor the having attained. Rather speak of the particulars which God has wrought for you.[166]

Similarly, though not directed toward the problem of forcing others to separate, he "Caution[s] . . . the Greatest Professors" to

> beware of bigotry. Let not your love or beneficence be confined to Methodists, so called, only; much less to that very small part of them which seem to be renewed in love; or to those who believe yours and their report. O make not this your Shibboleth![167]

Any action or attitude that tends to make distinctions within the body of Christ, Wesley said, is contrary to love.

At first glance, a contradiction seems to exist between Wesley's continued claim to loyalty to the Church of England and the gradual separation, which he began to see as inevitable. As we have observed, love itself, as *storgé* and benevolence, was his rationale for unity, by which he sought to overcome the extensive opposition of the Anglican clergy and hierarchy. On the other hand, love as complacence tended both toward separation from the Church and as reciprocal love, to rebuke schism within the nurturing community. Within his complex concept of love, forces for both unity and separation were present. His underlying principle that love tends to unite, was always a restraining argument against any final separation.

Two further concepts also serve toward explaining how Wesley could hold these diverse ideas of the Church together. They are the doctrines of degrees and of eschatology. Perfect love, for Wesley, was not the perfection of love's increase, but rather the absence of its contrary, sin. Thus regarding love itself, he can say, "There is no *perfection of degrees*."[168] "Love is the sum of Christian sanctification; it is the one *kind* of holiness, which is found, in various *degrees*, in the believers who are distinguished by St. John into 'little children, young men, and fathers.' The difference between one and the other properly lies in the degree of love."[169] Even as 'saintliness exists in degrees, so also the principle of delight was applicable in degrees, according to the degree of good in the object. This was specifically applied to the Church in a doctrine of priorities. Choice is guided by a love which compares. The term with which he made this comparison was *zeal*. His sermon "On Zeal," which he identified as a treatise on "comparative divinity,"[170] describes zeal as "always exercised *en kalō,* in that which is good . . . [Thus] . . . it is always proportioned to that good, to the degree of goodness that is in its object."[171] Like complacence, and in harmony with the Augustinian ethical tradition, zeal measures love according to the value of its object. *Zeal* itself he defined as "fervent love." As he stated, "True Christian zeal is no other than the flame of love. This is the nature, the inmost essence, of it."[172] Zeal, like complacence, is not given unless the object is good. In fact, objects of zeal must have superlative value, because "fervor for *indifferent things* . . . [or] *opinions* is not Christian zeal."[173] They are to be worthy objects of "fervent love" and "the flame of love." The Church is a worthy object of zeal. Thus the Christian is "to be earnestly desirous of its welfare and increase."[174]

John Wesley placed these worthy objects of zeal in a hierarchy or ladder of value. It is in that comparative grouping that the Church is "the lowest step"[175] and a means to all the other worthy goals. As such, zeal for the

Church must be less than for the higher goals, because "true zeal . . . should . . . rise higher and higher according to the scale mentioned above."[176] In this scale, love itself is the *summum bonum,* not love in the abstract, but "the love of God and all mankind." Thus, "see that you be most zealous for *love.*"[177] The Church is the means, in ascending order, to "works of piety," those *"ordinances* which our blessed Lord hath appointed,"[178] and *"works of mercy,* whether to the souls or bodies of men."[179] Nearest to love as objects of zeal are "all holy tempers;—long suffering, gentleness, meekness, fidelity, temperance."[180]

Though not stated in an ascending order, the Church in particular has priority over the Church in general. As he stated, "Be zealous for *the Church;* more especially for that particular branch thereof wherein your lot is cast."[181] The face-to-face characteristic of this "particular branch" was expressed by the clause, "that his [the Lord's] followers may . . . provoke one another to love, holy tempers, and good works."[182] Though he did not say that the Church is no longer the Church when it is not a means, the conclusion could be and was drawn by his followers. On the contrary, Wesley's view already noted was that the Church, at least in its sacramental function, is still a means of grace even though the administrator of it is unworthy.

The organized church, for Wesley, was a means, not an end. Even private conscience takes priority. Thus he told a Moravian friend, "I dare call no man Rabbi. I cannot yield either implicit faith or obedience to any man or number of men under heaven."[183] This was particularly true in relationship to his call:

> To be more particular: I know God has committed to me a dispensation of the gospel; yea, and my own salvation depends upon preaching it: "Woe is me if I preach not the gospel." If then I could not remain in the Church without omitting this, without desisting from preaching the gospel, I should be under necessity of separating from it, or losing my own soul.[184]

This concept of priorities in which the Church and its authorities, though of great importance, were secondary to convictions was present from his Oxford days. Comparative divinity, this way of assessing degrees of value in the object, was also a means of assessing where obedience belonged, even though it went against authority in the family and in the Church. His very independent family sought to use the argument of authority to persuade him to take the Epworth living: his father, "the authority of a parent,[185] and his brother, Samuel, "*The order of the Church.*"[186] Even his independent mother argued that he ought not to " 'break his rank', for in so doing 'he breaks the eternal order of the universe and abuses his Christian liberty.' "[187] Wesley's priorities, then and throughout his life, were to give glory to God, save his own soul, and promote holiness in himself and others.[188] His father had written to him that "the glory of God and the different degrees of promoting it are to be our sole consideration and direction in the choice of any course in life." John wrote in response, "I entirely agree."[189] As he stated before the Society for the Reformation of Manners in 1763,

> the original design of the Church of Christ . . . is a body of men compacted together, in order, first, to save each his own soul; then to assist each other in working out their salvation; and, afterwards, as far as in them lies, to save all men from present and future misery, to overturn the kingdom of Satan, and set up the kingdom of Christ. And this ought to be the continued care and endeavour of every member of his Church; otherwise he is not worthy to be called a member thereof, as he is not a living member of Christ.[190]

This evaluation of responsibilities from degrees of value was utilized in his life as a reformer. In Georgia, his reformation was that of returning the Church toward the practices of the primitive church. Regarding these rules, he said, "I believe [*myself*] it a duty to observe, so far as I can [*without breaking communion with my own*

Church]."[191] Here the Church is described as taking priority, but one senses his willingness to go contrary to leadership or custom in the Church if conscience required it. Late in his life the Church had a lower priority. As early as 1744 even potential schism in the Church after his death had to give way to "the present opportunity of saving souls while we live."[192] In 1755, when there was much agitation for the separation of the Methodists from the Church of England, John wrote the following to his brother Charles:

> I have no fear about this matter. I only fear the preachers' or the people's leaving not the Church but the love of God and inward or outward holiness. To this I press them forward continually. I dare not in conscience spend my time and strength on externals. If (as my lady says) all outward establishments are Babel, so is this Establishment. Let it stand for me. I neither set it up nor pull it down. But let you and I build up the City of God.[193]

In the 1750s the possibility of separation was very real. Though he argued that Methodists were not separating, he was not, as we can see in the following, willing to sacrifice practices that had been redemptively useful to the Church:

> At present I apprehend those, and those only, to separate from the Church who either renounce her fundamental doctrines or refuse to join in her public worship. As yet we have done neither; nor have we taken one step farther than we were convinced was our bounden duty. It is from a full conviction of this that we have, (1) preached abroad, (2) prayed extempore, (3) formed Societies, and (4) permitted preachers who were not episcopally ordained. . . . If we cannot stop a separation without stopping lay preachers, the case is clear—we cannot stop it at all.[194]

These differences eventually included the ordination of preachers, which for Charles Wesley and Dr. Whitehead, despite John's disclaimer, was separation in and of itself.

Wesley the reformer did not trust the unreformed national church to care for the converts and continue the revival. In 1755, when Walker of Truro advocated restoring the Methodist societies (and lay preachers) into the parish system of the Church of England, Wesley objected because he questioned whether the parish minister "could or would give that flock all the advantages for holiness which they now enjoy."[195] This was in contrast to his reply in December 1734 when he declined his father's anxious request that he seek the Epworth charge. At that time he wrote, "And He that took care of the poor sheep before you was born will not forget them when you are dead."[196] Was he being self-centered in his reply to his father? His father thought so and wrote, "To this I answer—1. It is not dear self, but the glory of God."[197] Nevertheless, for the later John Wesley, who had become the father of the "people called Methodists," the salvation of souls was the only worthy end, while the Church, though a worthy object of zeal, was a means. As he stated, "I would observe every punctilio of order, except where the salvation of souls is at stake. There I prefer the end before the means."[198]

Separation also occurred among the Methodists contrary to Wesley's original design, which was that there be an inclusive fellowship of Moravian, Calvinistic, and Arminian evangelicals within the Anglican church. Wesley, though seriously considering separation in the conference of 1755, took steps to maintain identity with the Church of England. He had great difficulty in keeping the preachers, who were laymen, from serving the sacrament. Due to local circumstances, the preachers in Norwich had been serving the sacraments without vigorous objection by John Wesley. Finally at the conference of 1760 the practice was stopped. Howell Harris, Welsh layman, preserved a full account of the conference. Regarding the proceedings of August 29, he observed, "Mr. John and Charles Wesley spake their opinion strong of the unlawfulness of a layman administering the ordinances." Regarding the next day, he recorded:

> Charles and I were the rough workers, and John more meekly, . . . and said if he was not ordained he would look upon it as murder if he gave the ordinances. He struck dumb the reasoners by saying he would renounce them in a quarter of an hour, that they were the most foolish and ignorant in the whole Conference.[199]

Many had proposed that he ordain them, but he refused because it would have meant separation from the Church. Similarly, in 1758 he had advised his preachers "not to frequent any Dissenting meeting" lest the Methodists, by their example, begin to choose to attend those Sunday church services rather than those of the Church of England.[200] Refusing to receive the sacraments at an Anglican church would also have meant separation.

Wesley's "Sermons on Several Occasions," published in 1788, include a remarkable group of sermons which deal with humanity's fall and restoration. These are influenced in part by Milton's *Paradise Lost* and *Paradise Regained* and are a theodicy by which Wesley is seeking to "justify the ways of God with men."[201] For Wesley, the Fall was the "fortunate fall." Because of the Fall, persons can know God's redemptive love and that which results from it, our love to God and persons. Yet to Wesley, personal redemption was not adequate to explain the sin and misery in the world and the division within the Church. The final answer is in the eschatological age: "At that time will be accomplished all those glorious promises made to the Christian Church, which will not then be confined to this or that nation, but will include all the inhabitants of the earth."[202] This restoration is given by Wesley as

> the answer, yea, the only full and satisfactory answer that can be given, to the objection against the wisdom and goodness of

God, taken from the present state of the world. It will not
always be thus: These things are only permitted for a season
by the great Governor of the world, that he may draw immense, eternal good out of this temporary evil.[203]

That which kept Wesley from mentally calcifying the
present realities of separation between churches into permanent monuments was a teleological idea of love. Love is
eschatological in its nature. Through love, what ought to
be works creatively on what is. Zeal, as love, may claim
holy love for God and neighbor as a first priority, but it
never forgets the Church. Though the present reality may
be formal separation, the future is unity. Love works
toward the future and transforms the present to be in harmony with it.

Eschatological hope for the world was expressed early
in Wesley's ministry as well as toward the end. In his second discourse of the Sermon on the Mount, written in
1739, he encouraged true Christians who were being oppressed by persecuting Christians as follows:

> O God! how long? Shall thy promise fail? Fear it not, ye little
> flock! Against hope, believe in hope! . . . Surely . . . the in-
> habitants of the earth shall learn righteousness. . . . They
> shall all be without spot or blemish, loving one another, even
> as Christ hath loved us.—Be thou part of the first-fruits, if the
> harvest is not yet. Do thou love thy neighbour as thyself. The
> Lord God fill thy heart with such a love to every soul, that
> thou mayest be ready to lay down thy life for his sake! May
> thy soul continually overflow with love, swallowing up every
> unkind and unholy temper, till he calleth thee up into the re-
> gion of love, there to reign with him for ever and ever![204]

Similarly, he desired the end of division in the Church. In
1749, when he recommended "the true primitive Christianity" of catholic love, he asked, "O when shall it spread
over all the earth!"[205] In the same year, while describing
his monthly meeting for reading what God is doing

"among those of various opinions," to the end of "breaking down the partition" between churches, he asked, "O when shall it once be!"[206]

The means toward that goal may be Christ's return, a mighty endowment of his Spirit, the gradual reconciliation of Christians and their institutions, or a combination of all these. Thus God works through both continuity and discontinuity (e.g., the Second Coming) to bring to pass his future work through his Church. As Wesley stated in his sermon "The General Spread of the Gospel" (1783), which deals with transformation of the Church for mission,

> All unprejudiced persons may see with their eyes, that He is already renewing the face of the earth: And we have strong reason to hope that the work he hath begun, he will carry on unto the day of the Lord Jesus; that he will never intermit this blessed work of his Spirit, until he has fulfilled all his promises, until he hath put a period to sin, and misery, and infirmity, and death, and re-established universal holiness and happiness.[207]

The mission of the Church continues through eschatological fulfillment. In fact, as in Fletcher, a new Pentecost is to be the means by which God will renew, equip, and prepare his Church: "The grand 'Pentecost' shall 'fully come,'" and 'devout men in every nation under heaven,' however distant in place from each other, shall 'all be filled with the Holy Ghost.' "[208] Fletcher's similar vision and hope was,

> I still look for an outpouring of the Spirit, inwardly and outwardly. Should I die before that great day, I shall have the consolation of seeing it from afar. . . . I want to see a Pentecostal Christian Church; and, if it is not to be seen at this time upon earth, I am willing to go and see that glorious wonder in heaven.[209]

A degree of discontinuity is part of all eschatology. For example, in the sermon "Of Former Times" (1787), church and state, which Wesley describes as so strangely and unnaturally blended together, are seen as probably not being separated "till Christ comes to reign upon earth."[210] Wesley, by this time, had put aside the concept of the Church as existing in an unbroken line. Thus the continuity of the Church composed of those who believe is continued by and through the Church which is composed of those who only profess to believe and which lacks continuity. God is one who raises from the dead and creates *ex nihilo* even in relationship to his Church. Thus in 1784, he wrote,

> God has constantly, from time to time, raised up men, endued with the spirit which they [others] had lost: Yea, and generally this change has been made with considerable advantage: For the last were, not only (for the most part) more numerous than the first, but more watchful, profiting by their example; more spiritual, more heavenly-minded, more zealous, more alive to God, and more dead to all things here below.
>
> . . . In the room of those that have fallen from their steadfastness, . . . he is continually raising up out of the stones other children to Abraham. . . . He is raising up those of every age and degree. . . . And we have no reason to doubt, but he will continue so to do, till the great promise is fulfilled; till "the earth is filled with the knowledge of the glory of the Lord, as the waters cover the sea; till all Israel is saved, and the fulness of the Gentiles is come in."[211]

Wesley saw his ordinations, with all their implications for division, as steps toward God's future. His "Sermons on Several Occasions," which includes several sermons dealing with eschatological hope, was published at the same time as he began to ordain his preachers. In the rapid growth of the Methodist societies in England and America, he saw the first fruits of the eschatological renewal of the Church, including the Church of England. The Methodists' separation from the Church of England was not to be the end. Instead, reconciliation is God's end. The order in which this is to be accomplished is "from the least [his

Methodists] to the greatest." In fact, for Wesley the fullness of the eschaton will be such that "Before the end, [not only the poor but] even the rich shall enter into the kingdom of God."[212]

Wesley was not unrealistic about the present. For one thing, he saw no evidence that people would ever think alike; they never had in the past, not even among the apostles.[213] As he stated, "I can no more think, than I can see or hear, as I will."[214] In 1765, while in dialogue with his Calvinistic opponents, he asserted, "allow me liberty of conscience herein: . . . Allow me to use it [the phrase "imputed righteousness . . . and the like expressions"] just as often as I judge it preferable to any other expressions."[215] In terms of present necessity, Wesley states in the same sermon:

> It is not easy for the same persons, when they speak of the same thing at a considerable distance of time, to use exactly the same expressions, even though they retain the same sentiments: How then can we be rigorous in requiring others to use just the same expressions with us?[216]

Similarly, he observed regarding the possibility of administrative unity that

> whensoever our Lord is pleased to send many labourers into his harvest, they cannot all act in subordination to, or connexion with, each other. Nay, they cannot all have personal acquaintance with, nor be so much as known to, one another.[217]

This realism regarding human opinion and practice was present in the separation of Moravian and Lady Huntingdon's societies from Wesley and the separation of some of Wesley's own flock from him either over perfection or the right of the unordained to administer the sacraments or the control of the preaching houses by local trustees. Despite his attempt at maintaining a "religious society . . . which requires nothing of men in order to their admission into it, but a desire to save their souls,"[218] he still found it necessary to provide a Trust Deed which, among other things, required that "the persons preach no other doctrine than is contained in Mr. Wesley's 'Notes upon the New Testament,' and four volumes of 'Sermons.'"[219] Wesley originally had settled the preaching houses in the hands of local trustees, but some of these trustees, because of differing doctrinal views or the desire to have the sacraments or to retain a favorite preacher, chose to become independent of Wesley and the Methodist plan.

That which distressed Wesley the most was that physical separation could end the practice of love. He wrote in 1749, in his sermon "Catholic Spirit":

> Although a difference in opinions or modes of worship may prevent an entire external union; yet need it prevent our union in affection? Though we cannot think alike, may we not love alike? May we not be of one heart, though we are not of one opinion? Without all doubt, we may. Herein, all the children of God may unite, notwithstanding these smaller differences. These remaining as they are, they may forward one another in love and good works.[220]

Earlier that year (July 18, 1749), he wrote his "Letter to a Roman Catholic" in which he expressed the same sentiments:

> I hope to see you in heaven. And if I practice the religion above described, you dare not say I shall go to hell. You cannot think so. None can persuade you to it. Your own conscience tells you the contrary. Then, if we cannot as yet think alike in all things, at least we may love alike. Herein we cannot possibly do amiss. For of one point none can doubt a moment,—"God is love; and he that dwelleth in love, dwelleth in God, and God in him."[221]

As noted, Wesley's "Old Plan" was that the Methodists would not separate from the churches from which they originated, but would serve as a leaven within Church and nation. When disagreement occurred with the Moravians (and later with the Calvinists), Wesley's view was that it was not on "points of opinion, but of practice."[222]

Realism is also present in what he had to say about the Gospel promises. After the sermons that proclaim the restoration of all things in Wesley's "Sermons on Several Occasions" (1788),[223] he placed his candid sermon, "The Imperfection of Human Knowledge." Here he lists, one after the other, various ways in nature, in the Church, and in personal salvation in which God does not act as we would hope. Regarding Christianity itself, he asked:

> Who can explain why Christianity is not spread as far as sin? Why is not the medicine sent to every place where the disease is found? But, alas! it is not: "The sound of it is" not now "gone forth into all lands."[224]

Similarly, regarding those unreached by the gospel, he stated:

> Nothing is more sure than that "without holiness no man shall see the Lord." Why is it, then, that so vast a majority of mankind are, so far as we can judge, cut off from all means, all possibility of holiness, even from their mother's womb?[225]

Despite these realities, his conviction was that God would fulfill his promises in this life. Not only is the individual to be delivered from all sin, but creation itself is "to be set free from its bondage to decay and obtain the glorious liberty of the children of God" (Rom. 8:21).

Nevertheless, present reality must give way to vision. Even in one of his more skeptical statements, the possibility that the Church can be transformed is implied. The vision is there: Christ will come "to reign upon earth," and the union of "Church and State, . . . so strangely and unnaturally blended together [by Constantine], . . . will be divided."[226] At the same time that he was castigating the national church (1783-1789), he was affirming his eschatology of renewal: "all these transient evils will issue well.''[227] In his letter to ''Our Brethren in America,'' which accompanied his commission to Thomas Coke to ordain Francis Asbury first as deacon and elder and then to serve with Coke as general superintendent over the Methodists societies in America, he states: ''They are now at full liberty simply to follow the Scriptures and the Primitive Church. And we judge it best that they should stand fast in that liberty wherewith God has so strangely made them free.''[228]

Separation was never the last word. While Asbury could say that the Anglicans and Protestant Episcopalians were ''a settled, man made, worldly ministry under no discipline and always have been,''[229] and, by implication, always will be, Wesley could not. Though he could speak strongly about ''mitered infidels'' and wicket priests, he always kept in sight the promise of restoration. Thus, he wrote,

> Then shall ''the times of'' universal ''refreshment come from the presence of the Lord.'' The grand ''Pentecost'' shall ''fully come,'' and ''devout men in every nation under heaven,'' however distant in place from each other, shall ''all be filled with the Holy Ghost;'' and they will ''continue steadfast in the Apostles' doctrine, and in the fellowship, and in the breaking of bread, and in prayers;'' they will ''eat their meat,'' . . . ''with gladness and singleness of heart. . . .'' and they will be ''all of one heart and of one soul.'' The natural, necessary consequence of this will be the same as it was in the beginning of the Christian Church: ''None of them will say, that aught of the things which he possesses is his own; but they will have all things common.''[230]

It should be noted that Asbury had a similar vision for union with the Presbyterians, his colaborers in the great frontier revival. He expected union soon to occur, but when the Presbyterians began to withdraw into strict confessionalism, he wrote,

> Friendship and good fellowship seem to be done away be-

tween the Methodists and Presbyterians; few of the latter will attend our meetings now; well, let them feed their flocks apart; and let not Judah vex Ephraim, or Ephraim, Judah; and may it thus remain, until the two sticks become one in the Lord's hands.[231]

The future held the possibility of reunion.

For Wesley at least, whatever may have been Asbury's ecumenical vision, though division may be unavoidable at present, it was not the last word. The last word is reunion when "they will all be of one heart and soul." This vision included the mission of reaching all the world,[232] the means toward which will be the "holy lives of Christians" and the conversion of the Church. Then "Malabarian Heathen will have no more room to say, 'Christian man take my wife: Christian man much drunk: Christian man kill man! *Devil-Christian!* me no Christian.' "[233] Listen again to Wesley's account of his vision:

At that time will be accomplished all those glorious promises made to the Christian Church, which will not then be confined to this or that nation, but will include all the inhabitants of the earth. . . . [Thus] thou [the Church] shalt be encompassed on every side with salvation, and all that go through thy gates shall praise God. . . .

This I apprehend to be the answer, yea, the only full and satisfactory answer that can be given, to the objection against the wisdom and goodness of God, taken from the present state of the world. It will not always be thus: These things are only permitted for a season by the great Governor of the world, that he may draw immense, eternal good out of this temporary evil. This is the very key which the Apostle himself gives us in the words above recited: "God hath concluded them all in unbelief, that he might have mercy upon all." . . . [God] is already renewing the face of the earth: And we have strong reason to hope that the work he hath begun, he will carry on unto the day of the Lord Jesus; that he will never intermit this blessed work of his Spirit, until he has fulfilled all his promises, until he hath put a period to sin, and misery, and infirmity, and death, and re-established universal holiness and happiness.[234]

We need, even as did Wesley, some purposeful means for breaking down the partition-walls which either the craft of the devil or the folly of men has built up; and of encouraging every child of God to say, (O when shall it once be!) "Whosoever doeth the will of my Father which is in heaven, the same is my brother, and sister, and mother."[235]

Notes

1. John Wesley, "Minutes of Several Conversations . . . ; From the Year 1744, to the Year 1789," Q. p. 2; *The Works of the Rev. John Wesley* (London, 1872), VIII, p. 299. This edition is a reprint of the third edition, edited by Thomas Jackson, 1829-31; hereinafter referred to as *Works*.
2. Wesley, "Minutes of Several Conversations," Q. p. 3.
3. Sermon: "The General Spread of the Gospel" (1783 AM), Sec. 13; Works, VI, p. 281. The dates indicated for the sermons are those assigned by Timothy Smith: "Chronological List of John Wesley's Sermons and Doctrinal Essays," *Wesleyan Theological Journal,* 17 (Fall 1982). The dating of Wesley's sermons is not simple. As Wesley notes in his "Preface" to "Sermons on Several Occasions," published in 1788, all of which except six had been previously published in *The Arminian Magazine* between 1778 and 1788, "they were occasionally written, during a course of years, without any order or connexion at all." (*Works,* VI, p. 186). Some of Smith's dates are being questioned at present. The great value of his "Chronological List" is that he has compiled in one apparatus not only information derived from his own research in primary sources but also that of E. H. Sugdon, Nehemiah Curnock, Richard Green, and others. His work is very useful and should push the academic community toward a standard

apparatus. It serves the purpose of our present study and, as far as I am aware, does not distort the evidence. AM refers to the publication date in *The Arminian Magazine,* hereinafter referred to as AM.

4. Sermon: "On Patience" (1784 AM; 1761 Smith), Sec. 10; *Works,* VI, p. 488.

5. Letter to Charles Wesley (Aug. 19, 1785); *The Letters of the Rev. John Wesley,* John Telford, ed. (London: 1931), VII, p. 284; hereinafter referred to as *Letters.* He is quoting Charles's, "An Elegy on the Death of Robert Jones, Esq." [c. 1741-1746], *The Journal of the Rev. Charles Wesley, . . . To Which Are Appended Selections from His Correspondence and Poetry,* Thomas Jackson, ed. (London: 1849), II, p. 299; hereinafter referred to as C. Wesley, *Journal.*

6. Letter to Charles Wesley (Sept. 13, 1785); *Letters,* VII, p. 288.

7. John Whitehead, *The Life of the Rev. John Wesley, . . . to which is prefixed . . . the life of the Rev. Charles Wesley* (Boston: 1844), II, 306; hereinafter referred to as *Whitehead.* He is referring to what both he and the Wesleys called "the old economy," which excluded preaching during the hour of morning worship. Thus Methodists, whether Anglican or Dissenter, could attend their church service. In this plan, the preachers did not need to take on sacramental and parochial authority.

8. Charles Perronet, son of Vincent Perronet, Vicar of Shoreham, was, along with his brother Edward, one of Wesley's preachers. He, his brother, and Thomas Walsh were leaders among the preachers in 1755 who wished to administer the Lord's Supper for those "who felt unwilling or unable to go to their parish churches," "After three days' consideration, the Leeds conference decided 'that, whether it was *lawful* or not to separate, it was no ways *expedient*' " (Telford, notes regarding John's letter to Charles, June 20, 1755; *Letters,* III, p. 129). At this time Wesley wrote of him to Charles, "Here is Charles Perronet raving 'because his friends have given up all,' and Charles Wesley 'because they have given up *nothing*' " (Letter to

Charles Wesley, June 20, 1755; *Letters*, III, p. 130). Later, during his illness, he was invited by Wesley to make the Foundery his home. (See notes by Telford, *Letters*, VI, p. 133.) Later Wesley was to write of Perronet's saintliness. He saw him at Canterbury on December 14, 1775, and wrote, "What a mystery of Providence! Why is such a saint as this buried alive by continual sickness?" *(The Journal of the Rev. John Wesley*, Nehemiah Curnock, ed. (London: Epworth Press, 1909), VI, p. 89; hereinafter referred to as *Journal).*

9. Sermons: "In What Sense We Are to Leave the World" (1784 AM), Works, VI, pp. 464-75, and "On Attending the Church Service" (1788 AM), VII, pp. 174-85.
10. Sermon: "The Ministerial Office" (1790 AM), Sec. 17; *Works*, VII, pp. 273-81.
11. "The Ministerial Office," Sec. 17, pp. 273-81.
12. Sermon: "Of the Church" (1786 AM), Sec. 16; *Works*, VI, p. 396.
13. Wesley, *Explanatory Notes Upon the New Testament* (1754), (Naperville, Ill.; Reprint 1958); hereinafter referred to as *Notes.* Wesley's way of viewing the Church from its most inclusive form to its narrowest occurred throughout his life. Thus this very inclusive picture of the church of believers, written in 1754, can be compared with the most inclusive form of the church composed of those who profess to believe, written in 1789. Similarly, the description of the universal church, written in 1786, is similar to that given in his "Letter to a Roman Catholic" (July 18, 1749): "this catholic, this universal Church, extending to all nations and all ages, is holy in all its members, who have fellowship with God the Father, Son, and Holy Ghost" (Sec. 9; *Works*, X, p. 82).
14. Sermon: "Of the Church" (1786 AM), Sec. 14; *Works*, VI, pp. 395-96; see also Sec. 7; p. 394.
15. "Of the Church," Sec. 17; p. 397.
16. Letter, "To the Editor of the London Chronicle" (Feb. 19, 1761); *Works*, III, p. 42.
17. *Works*, III.
18. Sermon: "Of the Church" (1786 AM), Sec. 28; *Works*, VI, p. 400.

19. "Minutes of Some Late Conversations," Conversation I (1744); June 27, Q. 1; *Works,* VIII, p. 280.
20. Sermon: "On God's Vineyard" (1789 AM; 1779 Smith); *Works,* VII, p. 202.
21. Sermon: "Of the Church" (1786 AM), Sec. 29; *Works,* VI, p. 400.
22. *Works,* VI.
23. *Works,* VI.
24. Letter, "To the Printer of the Dublin Chronicle" (June 2, 1789), P.S.; *Works,* XIII, p. 271.
25. "Letter to Dr. Coke, Mr. Asbury, and Our Brethren in North America" (Sept. 10, 1784), Sec. 4; *Works,* XIII, p. 252.
26. Sermon: "The Ministerial Office" (1790 AM), Sec. 8; *Works,* VII, p. 276.
27. Sermon: "Of Former Times" (1787 AM), Sec. 16; *Works,* VII, p. 164.
28. Sermon: "The Mystery of Iniquity" (1783 AM), Sec. 25; *Works,* VI, p. 261.
29. Sermon: "Of Former Times," (1787 AM), Sec. 16; *Works,* VII, p. 164. Notice an earlier evaluation when some said "the church is only a creature of the state?" Wesley, in response, referred to King Edward the Sixth's action in sending priests to "search into the law of God and teach it to all the people," and then commented, "we allow it is, and praise God for it." Wesley, "Ought We to Separate from the Church of England" (1755), Sec. II.[44]; in Frank Baker, "Appendix," *John Wesley and the Church of England* (Nashville: Abingdon, 1970), pp. 330-31; hereinafter referred to as Baker *JWCE.*
30. Baker, *JWCE,* pp. 145-50.
31. Letter, "To the Editor of the *London Chronicle*" (Feb. 19, 1761); *Works,* III, p. 42.
32. Sermon: "On God's Vineyard" (1789 AM; 1779 Smith), Sec. V. 1-7; *Works,* VII, pp. 211-13.
33. Stanzas 9 and 10. Included in the second edition of "An Earnest Appeal to Men of Reason and Religion" (1743). *The Works of John Wesley,* XI, Gerald R. Cragg, ed. (Oxford: 1975), p. 91; hereinafter referred to as *Works,* Oxford.

See Cragg's discussion of the dating, p. 90, n.4, and "Appendix," p. 543.

34. Sermon: "Of the Church" (1786 AM, Sec. 16; *Works,* VI, pp. 392-401.

35. "An Earnest Appeal . . ." (1743), Sec. 76; *Works,* Oxford, XI, p. 77. Cragg notes that Wesley's memory was imprecise in this place. The original Latin was *coetus fidelium,* p. 77, n.1.

36. Letter to Charles Wesley (Aug. 19, 1785); *Works,* XIII, p. 254; see also *Letters,* VII, p. 284.

37. Sermon: "Of the Church" (1786 AM), Sec. 19; *Works,* VI, p. 397.

38. "Of the Church," Sec. 19, p. 397.

39. "Of the Church," Sec. 19, p. 397.

40. "A Plain Account of the People Called Methodists: In a Letter to the Reverend Mr. Perronet, Vicar of Shoreham" (1748), Sec. II.1; *Works,* VIII, p. 252.

41. *Notes* (1754), Acts 5:11.

42. Sermon: "In What Sense We Are to Leave the World" (1784 AM), Sec. 23; *Works,* VI, p. 473.

43. Secs. 20-21; p. 472.

44. C. Wesley (June 11, 1751); *Journal,* II, 82; see also J. Wesley (July 8, 1751); *Journal,* III, p. 531-32.

45. C. Wesley (July 20, 1754); *Journal,* II, p. 103.

46. Sermon: "Of the Church" (1786 AM), Sec. 28; *Works,* VI, p. 400.

47. Sermon: "In What Sense We Are to Leave the World" (1784 AM), Sec. 6; *Works,* VI, p. 466.

48. "In What Sense." Sec. 8; p. 467.

49. "In What Sense." Sec. 2; p. 464.

50. "Journal," (Feb. 6, 1740): *Works,* I, pp. 262-63. He used these terms to refute the accusations that he had turned "Dissenter from the Church of England."

51. "A Farther Appeal to Men of Reason and Religion, Part II" (1745), Sec. III.3; *Works,* Oxford, XI, pp. 252-53.

52. *Works,* Oxford, XI, p. 253.

53. "Minutes of Several Conversations" (1744-1789), Q. 3; *Works,* VIII, p. 299.

54. "Thoughts upon a Late Phenomenon" (1788), Sec. 4;

Works, XIII, p. 265. Wesley lists twelve reasons why separation "is by no means expedient." "Reasons against a Separation from the Church of England" (1758), Sec. 1; *Works,* XIII, pp. 225-27.

55. "A Farther Appeal . . . , Part I" (1745), Sec. VI.11; *Works,* Oxford, XI, p. 185. "We *will not* leave the ship: if you *cast us* out of it, then our Lord will take us up." See "Minutes of Several Conversations" (1744-1789), Q. 41; *Works,* VIII, p. 319.

56. "Thoughts upon a Late Phenomenon" (1788), Sec. 8; *Works,* XIII, p. 266.

57. Sermon: "On Attending the Church Service" (1788 AM), Sec. 4; *Works,* VII, p. 175.

58. Whitehead, II, p. 261. See Wesley, "Minutes of Several Conversations" (1744-1789), Q. 45; *Works,* VIII, p. 321.

59. John Vickers, *Thomas Coke: Apostle of Methodism* (Nashville: Abingdon, 1969), p. 104.

60. Frances Asbury, Letter, "To George Roberts " (Feb. 11, 1797); *The Journal and Letters of Francis Asbury,* III (Nashville: Abingdon, 1958), p. 160; hereinafter referred to as Asbury, *Journal and Letters.*

61. Letter, "To 'Our Brethren in America' " (Sept. 10, 1784), Sec. 6; *Letters,* VII, p. 239; see also *Works,* XIII, p. 252.

62. Francis Asbury, *The Causes, Evils, and Cures of Heart and Church Divisions, Extracted From the Works of Burroughs and Baxter,* Thomas Q. Summers, ed. (Nashville, 1855); Reprint, *Heart and Church* (Salem, Ohio, Schmul Publ. 1978).

63. Asbury (Nov. 11, 1780); *Journal and Letters,* I, p. 388.

64. Letter to Charles Wesley (Aug. 19, 1785); *Letters,* VII, p. 284.

65. *The Arminian Magazine,* 4 (1781), pp. 604-606. Charles Perronet died on August 12, 1776. Wesley evaluated him as follows: "Why is such a saint as this buried alive by continual sickness?" ("Journal," Dec. 14, 1775; *Works,* IV, p. 63.) Again, "I looked over the manuscripts of that great and good man, Charles Perronet. I did not think he had so deep communion with God. I know exceeding few that equal him; and had he had an University education, there

would have been few finer writers in England" ("Journal," Jan. 8, 1777, p. 91.)

66. *The Arminian Magazine,* 4 (1781), p. 606.
67. "A Plain Account of the People Called Methodists" (1748), Sec. 8; *Works,* VIII, p. 250. Telford observes that "Vincent Perronet . . . was for the thirty-nine years his [J. Wesley's] most intimate clerical friend and adviser. Charles Wesley called him the Archbishop of Methodism. . . . Two of his sons became Methodist preachers" (*Letters,* II, p. 292). Charles Perronet was one of these.
68. "A Plain Account of the People Called Methodists" (1748), Sec. II.5(1); *Works,* VIII, p. 253.
69. "A Plain Account," Sec. VI.3; p. 258.
70. "A Plain Account," Sec. II.1; p. 252.
71. "A Plain Account," Sec. VIII.2; p. 260.
72. "A Plain Account," Sec. II.5(1); p. 253.
73. "A Plain Account," Sec. II.7; p. 254.
74. "A Plain Account," Sec. VI.3; p. 258.
75. "A Plain Account," Sec. VI.5; pp. 258-59.
76. "A Plain Account," Sec. VI.6; p. 259.
77. "A Plain Account," Sec. V; p. 257.
78. "A Plain Account," Secs. IX-XV; pp. 261-68.
79. *Notes,* 1 John 4:8.
80. *Notes,* Rom. 3:25.
81. Sermon: "Free Grace" (1739), Sec. 26; *Works,* VII, p. 383.
82. "Thoughts on Christian Perfection" (1759); "A Plain Account of Christian Perfection" (1725-1777), Sec. 19; *Works,* XI, p. 397.
83. Sermon: "The Reward of the Righteous" (Preached before the Humane Society, 1777), Sec. I.6; *Works,* VII, p. 131.
84. "Farther Thoughts on Christian Perfection" (1761); "A Plain Account of Christian Perfection," Sec. 25, Q. 33; *Works,* XI, p. 430.
85. Sermon: "On Patience" (1784 AM; 1761 Smith), Sec. 10; *Works,* VI, p.488.
86. "A Collection of Forms of Prayer for Every Day in the Week" (1733, 9th ed., 1749), Sunday Evening; *Works,* XI, p. 208.
87. See Anders Nygren, *Agape and Eros* (Philadelphia:

Westminster Press 1953) and my Dissertation, "John Wesley's Concept of Perfect Love: A Motif Analysis" (Boston University, 1965).

88. *Notes,* Acts 10:34. Regarding disinterested love, see "A Letter to . . . the Lord Bishop of Gloucester" (Nov. 26, 1762), Sec. III.4-7; *Works,* Oxford, XI, pp. 528-29.

89. *Notes,* 1 Cor. 13:1. There is a special emphasis on love for neighbor. See his notes on verses 1, 4-7.

90. In relation to Nygren's motif analysis, "benevolence" is the term Wesley uses to express *Agape.* His other terms are influenced by the *Caritas* tradition. See my dissertation, "Wesley's Concept of Perfect Love: A Motif Analysis," 178-80.

91. "Ought We to Separate . . ." (1755), Sec. V; Baker, *JWCE,* "Appendix," p. 337. "Reasons against a Separation from the Church of England" (1758) is a later edition; see Sec. 3; *Works,* XIII, p. 228.

92. Baker, *JWCE,* p. 326.

93. "Ought We to Separate . . ." (1755), Sec. V.1, 4; Baker *JWCE,* pp. 338, 339.

94. "Ought We to Separate . . . ," Sec. V.1; p. 337.

95. "Ought We to Separate . . . ," p. 338.

96. Letter, "To the Earl of Dartmouth, Secretary of State for the Colonies" (June 14, 1775); *Letters,* VI, p. 156.

97. Quoted by Martin Schmidt, *John Wesley: A Theological Biography* (New York: Abingdon, 1962), I, p. 138.

98. "Ought We to Separate . . ." (1755), Sec., V; Baker, *JWCE* p. 338.

99. Letters to Charles Wesley (Aug. 19 and Sept. 13, 1785; see also letter from Charles to John, Sept. 19, 1785); *Letters,* VII, 284-85, 288-89, p. 289.

100. Letter, Charles Wesley to John Wesley (Aug. 14, 1785); Whitehead, II, p. 265.

101. *Ibid.*

102. Letter, John Wesley to Charles Wesley (Aug. 19, 1785); Whitehead, II, p. 266. Charle's poem "Elegy on the Death of Robert Jones, Esq." was written around 1745.

103. Letter to Charles Wesley (Sept. 13, 1785); *Letters,* VII, p. 288.

104. Letter, Charles Wesley to John Wesley (Sept. 19, 1785); *Letters,* VII, p. 289.

388   David L. Cubie

105. Baker, *JWCE*, p. 311.
106. As quoted by Baker, *JWCE*, p. 311; from the *Proceedings of the Wesley Historical Society*, XVIII, pp. 25-6; cf. *Wesleyan Methodist Magazine*, 1845, p. 113.
107. "Ought We to Separate . . ." (1755), Sec. III.12; Baker, *JWCE*, p. 336.
108. Sermon: "On God's Vineyard" (1789 AM; 1779 Smith), Sec. II.8; *Works*, VII, p. 208.
109. "An Earnest Appeal . . ." (1743), Secs. 21-22; *Works*, VIII, p. 9.
110. Sermon: "Sermon on the Mount, X" (1742), Sec. 10; *Works*, V, p. 397.
111. "An Earnest Appeal . . ." (1743), Sec. 22; *Works*, VIII, p. 9.
112. Sermon: "Sermon on the Mount, III" (1739), Sec. II.4; *Works*, V, p. 284.
113. Sermon: "On Schism" (1786 AM), Secs. 20-21; *Works*, VI, p. 410.
114. "On Schism," Sec. II; p. 406.
115. "On Schism," Sec. I.1; p. 402.
116. Sermon: "On Zeal" (1781 AM; 1758 Smith), Sec. II.5; *Works*, VII, p. 60.
117. Sermon: "Preached Before the Society for the Reformation of Manners" (1763), Sec. 2; *Works*, VI, p. 150.
118. Sermon: "The Mystery of Iniquity" (1783 AM), Sec. 10; *Works*, VI, p. 256.
119. Letter, "To George Downing" (April 6, 1761); *Letters*, IV. p. 146.
120. "Journal" (March 16, 1764); *Works*, III, p. 161.
121. "Journal," (April 19, 1764), *Works*, p. 170.
122. "Journal," (April 19); *Works*, pp. 170-71.
123. "Of Separation from the Church" (July 22, 1786); *Works*, XIII, p. 257.
124. Sermon: "On Friendship with the World" (1786 AM), Secs. 8, 9; *Works*, VI, p. 455.
125. Sermon: "Catholic Spirit" (1749), Sec. I.2; *Works*, V, p. 492.
126. Sermon: "On Friendship with the World" (1786 AM), Sec. 10; *Works*, VI, p. 456.

127. "On Friendship with the World," Sec. 11; p. 456.

128. Sermon: "On Patience" (1784 AM; 1761 Smith), Sec. 10; *Works*, VI, p. 488.

129. Sermon: "On Perfection" (1785 AM; 1761 Smith), Sec. I.3; *Works*, VI, p. 412.

130. "Farther Thoughts on Christian Perfection" (1761); "A Plain Account of Christian Perfection," Sec. 25, Q. 34; *Works*, XI, p. 431.

131. Sermon: "Catholic Spirit" (1749), Sec. I.17; *Works*, V, p. 498.

132. "A Farther Appeal . . . ., Part III" (1745), Sec. IV.10; *Works*, Oxford, XI, p. 321. This work plus the sermons "A Caution against Bigotry" (1749) and "Catholic Spirit" (1749) [*Works*, V, 479-92 and 492-504] and his letter to Rev. James Clarke (Sept. 18, 1756) [Letters, III, pp. 200-4] were written to defend Wesley's lay assistants' right to preach. His argument, as stated in his "Caution . . . ," is they "cast out devils," meaning, they convert sinners, thus proving that they were sent by God (Sec. III.3; *Works*, V, p. 487).

133. Sermon: "A Caution against Bigotry" (1749), Sec. IV.5; *Works*, V, p. 491.

134. Letter, "To the Reverend Mr. Clarke" (Sept. 10, 1756), Sec. 7; *Works*, XIII, p. 215.

135. "A Farther Appeal . . . , Part III" (1745), Sec. II.3; *Works*, Oxford, XI, p. 281.

136. Sermon: "The Lord Our Righteousness" (1758; Pub. 1766), Secs. 16-17; *Works*, V, p. 243.

137. Sermon: "On Attending the Church Service" (1788 AM), Sec. 4; *Works*, VII, p. 175.

138. Quoted by Jackson, ed., *Works*, VII, pp. 273-74, from Moore's *Life of Mr. Wesley*, II, p. 339.

139. Sermon: "On Attending the Church Service," (1788 AM), *Works*, VII, p. 174-85.

140. Asbury (Aug. 19, 1806); *Journal and Letters*, II, p. 515.

141. *Journal and Letters*, Thomas Coke, Letter, "To Bishop White" (April 4, 1791); III, p. 96.

142. *Journal and Letters*, Asbury, Letter, "To George Roberts" (Feb. 11, 1797); III, p. 160.

143. *Journal and Letters,* Asbury, Letter, "To George Roberts" (May 31, 1804); III, p. 293.

144. *Journal and Letters,* Asbury, "A Valedictory Address to William McKendree, Bishop of the Methodist Episcopal Church" (Aug. 5, 1813); III, p. 475.

145. *Journal and Letters,* p. 479. Thomas Haweis, as noted, "had charge of Lady Huntingdon's College," n.38.

146. Sermon: "On the Death of the Rev. Mr. George Whitefield" (1770), Sec. III.7; *Works,* VI, p. 180.

147. Sermon: "Catholic Spirit" (1749), Sec. III.4; *Works,* V, p. 503.

148. "Catholic Spirit," Sec. I.17-18; pp. 498-99.

149. "Catholic Spirit," Sec. II.1; p. 499.

150. "Catholic Spirit," Sec. 4; p. 493.

151. "Catholic Spirit," Sec. II.3; p. 500.

152. Letter to John Wesley, June 29, 1746 (July 2, 1746); *Journal,* III, p. 244.

153. "Journal" (April 20, 1753); *Works,* II, 286-87.

154. "Journal" (May 29, 1755); p. 330.

155. Letters, "To Jonathan Crowther" (May 10, 1789); *Letters,* VIII, p. 136; "To Richard Whatcoat" (Nov., 1790); *Letters,* VIII p. 249. See Baker, *JWCE,* pp. 284-85, for discussion.

156. J. Wickham Legg, *English Church Life from the Restoration to the Tractarian Movement* (London: 1913), pp. 291-92.

157. "A Plain Account of the People Called Methodists" (1748), Sec. I.11; *Works,* VIII, p. 251; see also *Letters,* II, p. 295.

158. *"A Plain Account,"* I, II; *Works,* p. 251.

159. Sermon: "On Schism" (1786 AM), Sec. I.7; *Works,* VI, p. 405.

160. "On Schism," Sec. I.10; p. 406.

161. "On Schism," Sec. I.1; p. 402.

162. "On Schism," Sec. I.11; p. 406.

163. "Cautions and Directions Given to the Greatest Professors in the Methodist Societies (1762): "A Plain Account of Christian Perfection," Sec. 25, Q. 37; *Works,* XI, pp. 433-34.

164. "Some Thoughts upon an Important Question" (Nov. 19, 1781), Sec. 1; *Works,* XIII, p. 244.

165. "Cautions and Directions . . ." (1762): "A Plain Account of Christian Perfection," Sec. 25, Q. 37; *Works,* XI, p. 433.
166. "Cautions and Directions . . .," p. 434.
167. "Cautions and Directions . . . ," Sec. 25, Q. 34, p. 431.
168. Sermon: "Christian Perfection" (1739), Sec. I.9; *Works,* VI, p. 5. See also "A Plain Account of Christian Perfection," Sec. 12(1); *Works,* XI, p. 374.
169. Sermon: "On Patience" (1784 AM; 1761 Smith), Sec. 10; *Works,* VI, p. 488.
170. Sermon: "On Zeal" (1781 AM; 1758 Smith), Sec. II.5; *Works,* VII, p. 60. (Regarding the dates, the relationship of Methodism to the Church was of central concern in both these decades.)
171. "On Zeal," Sec. II.6; p. 61.
172. "On Zeal," I.3; p. 59.
173. "On Zeal," Sec. III.5-6; p. 64.
174. "Minutes of Some Late Conversations," Conversation I (1744), June 27, Q. p. 3; *Works,* VIII, p. 280. See "On Zeal," Sec. II.7; *Works,* VII, p. 61.
175. "On Zeal" (1781 AM; 1758 Smith), Sec. III.9; *Works,* VII, p. 65.
176. "On Zeal," Sec. III.7; p. 64.
177. "On Zeal," Sec. III.11; p. 66; see also Sec. II.11; p. 62.
178. "On Zeal," Sec. III.12; p. 66.
179. "On Zeal," Sec. II.5; p. 60.
180. "On Zeal," II, 5, p. 60.
181. "On Zeal," Sec. III.9; p. 65.
182. "On Zeal," Sec. II.5; p. 60.
183. "Journal" (June 7, 1746); *Works,* II, p. 15.
184. Sermon: "On Schism" (1786 AM), Sec. I.17; *Works,* VI, pp. 408-09.
185. Letter, "To his Father" (Dec. 10, 1734), Sec. 1; *Letters,* I, p. 166. This is implied by Wesley's reply.
186. From a letter of Samuel Wesley, Jr., quoted by Baker, *JWCE,* p. 37, from Joseph Priestly, ed., *Original Letters by the Rev. John Wesley and his friends illustrative of his early history* (Birmingham: 1791), pp. 18, 43.
187. Baker, *JWCE,* p. 37; from a manuscript letter, Nov. 10, 1725, in the Methodist archives, London.
188. Letter, "To his Father" (Dec. 10, 1734) Sec. 2; *Letters,* I,

pp. 166-78. Notice his father's letter of Nov. 20, 1734, responding to similar arguments John had raised: "To this I answer—1. It is not dear self, but the glory of God, and the different degrees of promoting it, which should be our main consideration in the choice of any course of my life." Quoted by Richard M. Cameron in *The Rise of Methodism: A Source Book* (New York- Abingdon, 1954), p. 75.

189. Sec. 1; *Letters,* I, p. 167.
190. Sermon: "Reformation of Manners" (1763), Sec. 2; *Works,* VI, p. 150.
191. From a document in which Wesley outlines apostolic procedure (c. 1735-36). The bracketed material was struck out by Wesley. See Baker, *JWCE,* pp. 40-1 and 350, where he quotes the document and analyzes it.
192. "Minutes of Some Late Conversations," Conversation I (1744), June 27, Q. p. 10(4); *Works,* VIII, p. 281.
193. Letter, "To his Brother Charles" (June 28, 1755); *Letters,* III, p. 132. "My lady" is Lady Huntingdon. See Telford's footnote.
194. Letter, "To Samuel Walker" (Sept. 24, 1755), Sec. 4; *Letters,* III, p. 146; see also *Works,* XIII, pp. 195-96.
195. Letter, "To Samuel Walker" (Sept. 16, 1767), Sec. 2; *Letters,* III, p. 223; see also *Works,* XIII, p. 202.
196. Letter, "To his Father" (Dec. 10, 1734), Sec. 26; *Letters,* I, p. 178; see also "Journal" (March 28, 1739), Sec. 22; *Works,* I, p. 185.
197. Letter, "Samuel Wesley, Sr. to John" (Nov. 20, 1734); Cameron, *The Rise of Methodism,* p. 75.
198. Letter, "To George Downing" [Chaplain to the Earl of Dartmouth] (April 6, 1761); *Letters,* IV, p. 146.
199. As cited by Baker, *JWCE,* p. 178, from Tom Beynon, *Howell Harris, Reformer,* pp. 79-80, 82-83. For a discussion of this see Baker, *JWCE,* pp. 176-79. Charles Wesley had marshalled the opposition to lay administration of the sacraments, having summoned Howell Harris and Rev. William Grimshaw to his aid. Charles had written to Grimshaw on March 27, 1760, about John's attitude regarding Norwich: "Three of our steadiest preachers give the Sacrament at Norwich with no other ordination or authority

than their sixpenny licence. My brother approves of it. All the rest will most probably follow their example. . . .

"He persuades himself 'that none of the other preachers will do like those at Norwich. That they may all licence themselves, and give the Sacraments, yet continue true members of the Church of England' " [. . . copy by Charles Wesley in Methodist archives, London." Quoted from Baker, *JWCE,* 176 and 376, n. 75]. Charles marshalled the opposition to anything that looked like separation. In 1784 when Wesley ordained Whatcoat and Vasey and set aside Coke for the superintendency, he did so in Bristol, while Charles was in residence without letting him know. Charles did not hear of the ordinations until two months later. He then wrote the memorable lines,

> So easily are Bishops made
> By man's, or woman's whim?
> Wesley his hands on Coke hath laid,
> But who laid hands on him?

Baker, *JWCE,* p. 273.

200. "Reasons against a Separation" (1758), Sec. 3(2); *Works,* XIII, p. 229.
201. Sermons: "God's Approbation of His Works" (1782 AM), Sec. II.3; *Works,* VI, p. 214; "On the Fall of Man" (1782 AM), Sec. 2; *Works,* VI, p. 216; "God's Love to Fallen Man" (1782 AM), Sec. 4; *Works,* VI, p. 233. Milton's line reads, "To justify the ways of God to men."
202. Sermon: "The General Spread of the Gospel" (1783 AM), Sec. 26; *Works,* VI, p. 287.
203. "The General Spread of the Gospel," Sec. 27; p. 287.
204. Sermon: "Sermon on the Mount II" (1739), Sec. III.18; *Works,* V, p. 277.
205. "Letter to a Roman Catholic" (July 18, 1749), Sec. 15; *Works,* X, p. 85.
206. "A Plain Account of the People Called Methodists" (1748), Sec. V; *Works,* VIII, p. 257.
207. Sermon: "The General Spread of the Gospel" (1783 AM), Sec. 27; *Works,* VI, p. 288.
208. "The General Spread of the Gospel," Sec. 20; p. 284.
209. Luke Tyerman, *Wesley's Designated Successor: The Life,*

Letters and Literary Labours of the Rev. John William Fletcher (New York: 1883), pp. 359-60.

210. Sermon "Of Former Times" (1787 AM), Sec. 16; *Works*, VII, p. 164.
211. Sermon: "The Wisdom of God's Counsels" (1784 AM), Secs. 22-23; *Works*, VI, pp. 335-36.
212. Sermon: "The General Spread of the Gospel" (1783 AM), Sec. 19; *Works*, VI, p. 283.
213. Sermon: "A Caution against Bigotry" (1749), Sec. II(3); *Works*, V, pp. 484-85.
214. Sermon: "Catholic Spirit" (1749), Sec. II(1); *Works*, p. V, 499.
215. Sermon: "The Lord Our Righteousness" (1758; Pub. 1766), Sec. II(20); *Works*, V, p. 245.
216. "The Lord Our Righteousness," II(2); p. 238.
217. Sermon: "A Caution against Bigotry" (1749), Sec. II(1); *Works*, V, p. 484.
218. "Journal" (May 18, 1788); *Works*, IV, p. 419.
219. "Minutes of Several Conversations" (1744-89), Q. 61; *Works*, VIII, p. 331.
220. Sermon: "Catholic Spirit" (1749), Sec. 4; *Works*, V, p. 493.
221. Letter, "To a Roman Catholic" (July 18, 1749), Sec. 16; *Letters*, III, p. 13; see also *Works*, X, p. 85.
222. "Journal" (May 29, 1745); *Works*, I, p. 496.
223. *Works*, VI, pp. 231-35.
224. Sermon: "The Imperfection of Human Knowledge" (1784 AM), Sec. 11.8; *Works*, VI, p. 346.
225. "The Imperfection of Human Knowledge," Sec. III.1, p. 347.
226. Sermon: "Of Former Times" (1787 AM), Sec. 16; *Works*, VII, p. 164.
227. Sermon: "The General Spread of the Gospel" (1783 AM), Sec. 27; *Works*, VI, p. 288.
228. Letter, "To 'Our Brethren in American' " (Sept. 10, 1784), Sec. 6; *Letters*, VII, p. 239.
229. Asbury, Letter, "To George Roberts" (Feb. 11, 1797); *Journal and Letters*, III, p. 160.
230. Sermon: "The General Spread of the Gospel" (1783 AM), Sec. 20; *Works*, VI, p. 284.

231. Asbury, "Journal" (Aug. 19, 1806); *Journal and Letters,* II, p. 515.
232. Sermon: "The General Spread of the Gospel" (1783 AM), Secs. 23-24; *Works,* VI, 285-86.
233. "The General Spread of the Gospel," Sec. 22; p. 285.
234. "The General Spread of the Gospel," Secs. 26-27; pp. 287-88.
235. "A Plain Account of the People Called Methodists" (1748), Sec. V; *Works,* VIII, p. 257.

III. The Church and Ministry

Donald M. Joy (Ph.D., Indiana University), professor of human development and Christian education, Asbury Theological Seminary

The Contemporary Church as "Holy Community": Call to Corporate Character and Life

NORTH AMERICAN CHRISTIANITY at the end of the twentieth century is deeply marked by nuclear individualism. By this I mean to suggest that concepts such as "the priesthood of all believers" and "homogeneous character" have become slogans of groups that distort congregations into mere extensions of isolated and lonely people. So, "priesthood of all believers" is thought to mean "every tub sits on its own bottom" and prays and intercedes for the self; whereas Luther's genius intended that we should sense that we had a priest at each elbow: no person serves the self as priest, but serves the corporate brothers and sisters. And "homogeneous units" have come to describe and justify amassing a gigantic congregation in which church growth amounts to recruiting clones of the isolated and barricaded self: a congregation of mirror images of narcissistic Christians.

A simple test of a congregation's inclination toward privatism emerges: (1) It appeals to a sense of anonymity—lost in a crowd of look-alike homogeneous people. (2) It sustains large numbers of these clones with minimal significant contact with other persons beneath surface and normally superficial exchanges at church meetings. (3) Individuals may move, drop out, or be victims of a tragedy without their loss being detected by others or being reported by them.

To the extent that this observation of the encroachment of "nuclear individualism" rings true to our real Christian world experience, to that extent it stands under the judgment of God, of Scripture, and particularly of an Anglo-Catholic-Wesleyan view of the nature of the Church. In this chapter, therefore, I wish to put forward foundations for a systemic (as opposed to systematic) theology of grace/faith and the Church. Then, I will trace a biblical vision for the value of persons, followed by an examination of how respect and authority are distributed in Jesus' kind of church. Finally, I will offer a synthesis and an exposition of John Wesley's concept of our "going on from grace to grace" and relate our life-long pilgrimage to that grace and to Jesus' holy community, the Church.

A Call For A Truly Wesleyan Theology

When Albert Outler quipped, in what appeared to be a mere aside, "How do you explain the fact that it seems never to have crossed John Wesley's mind to construct and publish a systematic theology, large or small, and that every attempt to transform Wesley's ways of teaching doctrine into some system of doctrine has lost something vital in the process?'' Royal Auditorium became very quiet.[1] Outler was in the midst of painting a portrait of Wesley as constantly taking Scripture to experience and of bringing experience back to Scripture, and working all of them through reason and tradition. For this reason, it became clear in piecing together Wesley's life records that he was unable to lock himself away from the realities of a thousand or more members of the class meetings to write a merely cognitive, logical, abstract theology. Though Outler did not reflect on it, it may have been the hymns of Charles Wesley that constantly transformed John Wesley's more cognitive preaching into the distinctly affective domain. The theology that we sing more likely makes its way immediately into our life-styles than the theology that we hold in logical syllogisms or in "systematic confessional theology,'' which stresses memorized word formulations.

I hold, therefore, that a wholistic theology is more nearly within reach of those of us within the Anglo-Catholic-Wesleyan perspective than any other. It is my hypothesis that John and Charles Wesley, perhaps unwittingly, formed the most viable wholistic theology since the close of the New Testament. I will further take the position that "systematic theology" is as old as the Fall, and that its central tendency is "scholastic,'' "anti-experiential,'' and is uniquely rooted in those left-hemisphere-dominated cultures that have been spawned and have dominated the world to the west of Babel. It is unlikely, therefore, that our perspective will survive to leaven a technological Cain-based world unless we take pains to differentiate our perspective from those that have given us the various distortions that characterize virtually all well-known theologies today.

Outler's concern that most United Methodist theologians were not trained in Wesleyan theology and hence United Methodist seminaries are not teaching Wesleyan theology is not particularly an indictment of one denomination. It is instead a state-of-the-art observation. To the extent that we put ourselves in the "systematic theology" trajectory, we will merely codify Wesley's teaching. Its brittle dogmas will then be of little more use to us or to our world than if we had bought into the schemas of the more contemporary systematic theologians. In an important sense Wesley's way is not that of a verbal "confessional" theology but of a dynamic wholistic "way of grace."

What we need is a different way of doing theology. I am appealing here for a wholistic theology, a theology that is "systemic." By systemic I mean a theology that fully synchronizes all reality and shows up everywhere from the root system to the finally ripened fruit—just as a systemic gardener avoids systematic spraying of vegetables and fruit in favor of a way of gardening that engenders health and resistance to disease, even predators, by getting the proper nutrients and inhibitors into the *system* of every living plant.

Jacques Ellul makes the point that Cain is the first to substitute "human achievement" for the Creation. He suggests that it was the curse on Cain that engendered fear and that Cain's urge to build the "city" was a means of contriving "security" and safety from the curse.[2] But in Cain we also see the contrast to Abel, who "by faith . . . offered God a better sacrifice than Cain did. By faith he was commended as a righteous man, when God spoke well of his offerings. And by faith he still speaks, even though he is dead."[3] Thus Abel is allied with God, "the judge of all men, to the spirits of righteous men made perfect, to Jesus the mediator of a new covenant, and to the sprinkled blood that speaks a better word than the blood of Abel."[4]

The impulse of Cain is to "do it my way," to marshall all human ingenuity to exalt the self, leading ultimately to the city, of which the tower of Babel is but one tower—all poised to defy the Creation and to exalt human mastery.

And it is at Babel that God came down to confuse the language. Evolutionist Carl Sagan projects backward through imagination to see us having redundant hemispheres of a left-handed right-hemisphere sort.[5] John Oswalt, left-handed Old Testament linguist, notes that clay tablets disclose the timetable when Akkadian ceased to be written with the left hand and the language became "right handed." The widely diverse cultures of East and West are now seen by some linguists and neurosurgeons as possible differentiations rooted in pictographic languages housed in the right hemisphere (East) and linear/abstract languages housed in the left (West).[6]

Behind Babel and Cain, however, examine the primal thumbprints of the Serpent: "Did God really say, 'You must not eat from any tree in the garden'?"[7] Seduction was couched in an appeal to "systematize" the God-human relationship. This strategy of dividing "relationship" from "cognition" by exalting cognition leads to the original sin. It is original sin because it incites the humans to pride and rebellious behavior, which fractures the God relationship. But it is also original sin because it established a fault line between "affect" and "cognition." This split between cognition and affect predicted the cognitive power plays by which relationships continue to be devalued and destroyed. Yet to be truly human is to be in full synchrony with cognition and affect fully integrated and fully functioning. It is to be in the line of Adam, Abel, Seth, Jesus, the Apostles, Bernard of Clairvaux, Count Zinzendorf, and the Wesleys. To exalt cognition at the expense of affect and relationships is to be in line of descent from Cain, Nimrod, the Gnostics, Augustine, Descartes, Calvin, and Darwin.[8] Paul Bassett ably traces the line of descent of the vision of Christian holiness in this present life from the Wesleys back to the New Testament, documenting its near eclipse following the Augustinian bypass, which relegated that holiness to the future life alone.[9]

Ironically, the detour to the left brain—the cognitive power play that devalues affect—left the laity without literacy, without cognitive balance, and the "dark ages" of magic, fear, and childlike license and games in the name of Christianity formed the alternative bypass to the right. Today's charismatic movement, located largely in the affect—the feelings—is a reminder of the tragic deformity when the affective right hemisphere is deprived of the balance of reason and the cognitive in theology.

Both detours emphasize the urgency of each generation to forge ahead to hold left and right in dynamic and synchronic union. Who are the prophets and saints of ages past whose life and vision encompassed the whole of our humanity? Who, to make a simple test, are those enshrined in ministries of mercy, wholeness, and healing? Are there homes for orphans or are there hospitals named for Augustine, Cain, Knox, Darwin, or Paine? Or are they named for St. Francis, St. Bernard, and Wesley? How do you account for that?

My appeal, then, is for a radicalization of theology that is truly Wesleyan. This will mean that systematic theology that exalts reason and epistemology in any kind of elitist cognitive or confessional sense will not suffice, even if it should be constructed out of Wesley categories. It means that the harvest of Augustinian theology, in any of its several contemporary versions, will be doomed to that appropriate to the inheritance of the Gnostics. Delbert Rose calls for a "theology of Chrisitan experience."[10] Albert Outler describes John Wesley as a "folk theologian."[11] Neither captures the expansive and encompassing balance necessary when truly cognitive and truly affective dimensions are kept in dynamic synchrony in our theology.

A BIBLICAL VISION OF PERSONS AND COMMUNITY

How are persons valued in your church? Are Christmas "food baskets" taken only to those who reciprocate properly with church attendance? Barbara Robinson describes *The Best Christmas Pageant Ever* in which her mother refused to beg the regular middle class children to try out for the parts. So instead she found herself with almost a full cast of poverty-stricken Herdmans for Mary, Joseph, the Wise Men, and the Angel of the Lord parts. The book unfolds the horrors of the rehearsals, during which Herdman violence, cigar smoking, and uncivil language offends almost everybody. But "Mother" sticks to her guns and keeps the Herdman children in the lead roles. At the actual presentation it pays off. As the angel choir hums, the door opens for Mary and Joseph to enter: "Ralph and Imogene were there all right, only for once they didn't come through the door pushing each other out of the way." The author tells how they "just stood there for a minute as if they weren't sure they were in the right place." There they stood, looking "like the people you see on the six o'clock news—refugees, sent to wait in some strange ugly place, with all their boxes and sacks around them."

Ultimately, the effectiveness of the church or any of its congregations may be tested by the question, Is a person safe there? Of Dwight L. Moody's Chicago Sunday school, it was known on the street that "they love a feller there."

I want to put forward here the thesis that (a) the value placed on persons, whether high or low, and (b) the distribution of authority, whether to the many or the few, provide us with a measure of the extent to which the Church will be effective in its mission to be "the body of Christ."

Value of persons. There is no more profound test regarding the value placed on persons than to ask the justice questions. Are rewards matched to the performance? Or are they calculated to punish and to make an example of the offender? Would all persons offending in the same way receive the same reward? Or would a weaker, younger, or more naive person receive an adjusted reward? In Figure 1, I have summarized what I call "objective engrossment."[12] I use that title to denote the justice concerns of a righteous God. In the same way, humans look after concerns of justice among humans.

The center "circle" of Figure 1 denotes that egocentric arena in which all justice issues look after the concerns of the self. It might be labeled "fairness" since the cry "no fair" is the earliest appeal for justice. So when church officials look after "the concern of the church" and choose to use punitive or expiative punishments against persons, it is clear that the church is egocentric and that it is protecting itself.

The middle ring of Figure 1 denotes a healthier stance toward justice issues among persons. Here everyone is safe from punitive or expiatory punishment; only the pure quality of justice rules here. All are treated equally; there is an even match between crime and punishment denoted by "reciprocity," and natural consequences or imposition of published penalties are found to be binding on the whole community. The highest form of justice, however, might be labeled forgiveness and it appears in the outer circle. "Equity" denotes a specialized form of justice in which the ability of the offender to perform is taken into account: age, knowledge, competency to stand trial. "Commutation" is the highest form of punishment, in which the governor, the president, or the Savior takes to himself the full consequences of another's crimes; it is always costly—at the next election, or on the cross—and it tends to offend the masses, who view it as capricious, malicious, or stupid.

What does it mean, then, to "be my brother's/sister's keeper"? How does our justice perspective get translated into our educational ministries, our evangelization processes, and our administrative policies? What is the witness

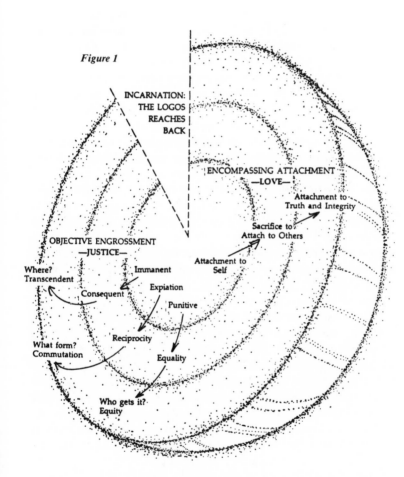

Figure 1

INCARNATION:
THE LOGOS
REACHES
BACK

ENCOMPASSING ATTACHMENT
—LOVE—

Attachment to
Truth and Integrity

Sacrifice to
Attach to Others

OBJECTIVE ENGROSSMENT
—JUSTICE—

Attachment to
Self

Where?
Transcendent

Immanent

Consequent

Expiation

Punitive

What form?
Commutation

Reciprocity

Equality

Who gets it?
Equity

of our congregational ground rules, our budgets, our unwritten traditions?

If justice is the inner face that reveals our true perspective on the value of persons, then "encompassing attachment" (Figure 1) is the outer face. "Attachment to the self" is the egocentric target of affection and tends to retain the congregation as a private club, expending its entire energy and resources on itself and is doomed to stagnation and eventual death. "Attachment to others" denotes the healthy concern for the outer world and the ability to absorb them into the common life of the congregation. At the outer ring, "attachment to truth and integrity" restores an even healthier balance between attention to others as well as to the self. We love the neighbor as we love the self; hence attention includes both inner and outer dimensions of our ministry.

These issues of justice and love may be tested in any of a thousand biopsies available to us in the church: What evidences indicate our commitment to the elderly and to the very young (special equipment, location of meeting places for them)? Are women as well as men serving in significant leadership roles? In our evangelization and educational outreach ministries, are we canvassing the whole populations around us, or are we selectively avoiding the wealthy? the poor? What proportions of our energy and resources are spent on maintenance of our own program? What proportion on the work of God beyond our community? What feelings are evoked in persons among us who experience unemployment, illegitimate pregnancy, divorce, or other tragedies or sensations of failure? If we "love a feller there," our congregations will tend to be a haven for those who have experienced serious failure or loss. But if we have our very own special scarlet letter for them, they will read that in our body language and will keep their distance. Is your church a "safe" place?

Distribution of authority. Perhaps the ultimate test for

the question about the actual "value of persons" within any structure is to ask how authority or power is distributed? Are all persons created equal, or are some more equal than others? Is every member a participant, or are some only observers?

The tradition of "observer only" is very strong in the church. People even choose a congregation on the basis of not being noticed, of anonymous spectatoring. My pastor once shocked me back to the radical nature of the Church when he intoned this call to worship:

If this were a performance,
I would be the actor.
God would be the prompter,
And you would be the audience.
But since this is not a performance.
But, instead, a service for the worship of God,
Then, YOU are the actors.
I am the prompter;
And God is the audience.[13]

In a connectional denomination, ministers are either local popes or they are under the general mandate to facilitate the work of God in territories to which they are sent. When a local church delegation demanded an appointment with the area bishop, he gave them one. They arrived with their young pastor in tow. And they protested the reappointment of their pastor of two years to a distant but larger parish. "We always have to take new young pastors," the committee objected, "and just when our church begins to come to life with them, you move them on." The young pastor had joined in the objections. At last the bishop turned to him, "Pastor," he said, "I am going to leave the decision about your appointment up to you. But before you decide, I must tell you that a committee made up of members of your annual conference made the appointment that would have moved you. They are not only the people who ordained you, but they are the ones who must look after the larger concerns of the work of our church in three states. But you may stay at Pleasant Valley if you feel you must.'' The young pastor responded quietly, ''When you put it that way, I cannot make my own appointment.''

In Figure 2, I have condensed the Lindgren and Shawchuck grid, which shows five management approaches that can be found in various congregations.[14] As a quick-test for your own preferred appetite for a particular style, simply read across at the lines marked ''Leader's Functions and Style'' and ''View of Persons.''

In Figure 3, I have composed a diagram that explores implications when the value of persons comes into interface with the distribution of authority. If a congregation has been functioning in a merely passive/spectator role as would be characteristic of the Traditional/Authoritarian quadrant, it is likely that the path to the Participative/ Facilitative quadrant lies either through Human Relations (in which the organization and structures are collapsed, perhaps even much of the program) or through Charismatic/Classical/Paternalism (in which the authoritarian dictator role is transformed into a benevolent monarch or the Big Daddy).

The summons of the New Testament calls us to the highest view of persons and to the widest distribution of responsibility. Jesus becomes the servant to collapse any idea of a ''chain of command.''[15] Then he brings the disciples up face to face to abolish the idea that they are his servants; they are not ''servants, but friends.''[16] And St. Paul affirms that Jesus ''gave some to be apostles, some to be prophets, some to be evangelists, and some to be pastors and teachers, to prepare God's people for works of service, so that the body of Christ may be built up.''[17]

LIFELONG PILGRIMAGE:
ADVENTURES FROM GRACE TO GRACE

Figure 2

	TRADITIONAL	CHARISMATIC	CLASSICAL	SYSTEMS	HUMAN RELATIONS
ORGANIZATIONAL THEORIES	○	△	△	Input → Transformation → Output	(circle with dots)
DESCRIPTIVE ORGANIZATIONAL AND THEOLOGICAL TERMS	Organizational: Patrimonial Theological: "The People of God"	Organizational: intuitive Theological: "The New Creation"	Organizational: Bureaucratic Theological: "God's Building"	Organizational: Organic Theological: "The Body of Christ"	Organizational: Group or democratic Theological: "The Fellowship of Faith"
CONCEPT OF ORGANIZATION	Maintaining a tradition	Pursuing an intuition	Running a machine	Adapting a system	Leading Groups
DECISION-MAKING PROCESS	Made and announced by the elders. Unhurried pace	Spontaneous, unpredictable proclamation by leader.	Issuance of orders from the top; conscious, rationalized, calculated.	Continuous adaptation with purpose kept relevant to environment.	Group decision through informal, intimate, and fluid relationships.
LEADER'S FUNCTIONS AND STYLE	To maintain the tradition and preserve the status quo. PATERNAL PRIESTLY	To lead and motivate through personal appeal. PROPHETIC INSPIRATIONAL	To direct by handing down decisions. AGGRESSIVE DIRECTIVE	To clarify goals, interpret environment, and monitor change. PROFESSIONAL ACTIVATOR	To create an atmosphere conducive to expression and participation. SENSITIVE NON-DIRECTIVE
VIEW OF "PERSONS"	Persons are secure in the status quo; little initiative is expected.	Persons are active and capable, but need constant direction and intervention.	Persons need controls and prefer direction.	Not all have same skills & knowledge. Can be motivated through goal clarification enablement and effectiveness.	Persons learn to seek and accept responsibility when properly motivated.
COMMUNICATION PATTERN	Leader transmits heritage, expecting unexplicit consent	Leader announces the content of intuition; he and his followers are bound to obey.	Leader issues detailed directives; most communication is downward from the top.	In all directions, through open channels and "linking" persons.	Leader encourages individual participation and contribution; the group shares.
GOALS	Generally assumed and seldom articulated.	Highly explicit, reflecting the philosophy and aims of the leader.	Objective and quantitative; arrived at by hierarchy and handed down.	Definitive and unifying, with consideration for environment.	Subjective rather than objective; purposes of the group emerge from discussion.

Figure 3
Some Leadership Styles

My friend Albert F. Harper, longtime anchorman for the curriculum ministries of the Church of the Nazarene, tells how an earnest evangelist in his experience was bringing the invitation to its conclusion. He told of a man in middle years who had never come to Jesus, though he would attend church courteously with his devout wife. The man, so the story went, told his wife on a Saturday night as they drove home from a revival service, "I see now that I have been wrong all these years, and tomorrow morning, I am going to go to the altar and be saved."

To make his point of the urgency of deciding now, the evangelist made the story wail: "But he never lived to be saved. In the night he died of a heart attack and went into eternity without God."

My friend Albert, with a gleam of truly Wesleyan insight, loves to say, "I nudged my wife and whispered, 'I don't think the evangelist knows where the man really went.'"

Left-brained, systematic understandings are preoccupied with words and formulations. Right-brained feeling approaches go for the ecstasy or the fear for the proof of reality. A synchronic and wholistic approach—what I have urged that we call "systemic" theology—holds that heart and mind, life and doctrine combine to form a dynamic and harmonious duet.

Albert Harper's evangelist held tenaciously to Wesley's doctrine of justification by faith alone, no doubt, but he had not examined Wesley's understanding of preventing/prevenient grace nor of converting grace. Preventing grace refers to God's grace, which reaches out to humans before they are aware of their need of God. Preventing grace reaches out to cover the young, the abused, the defective, and the naive. Its purpose is to lead and to draw those persons to the moment or the condition when they may freely reach out to Jesus, throwing themselves by converting grace into justifying grace where sanctifying grace is

begun. Like prevenient or preventing grace, so also converting grace originates in God.[18] All grace is God's grace,
and it is, by definition, nothing produced in humans. We
like to speak of our "having faith" in Jesus. But even the
ability to have faith originates in grace.

In Figure 4, I have tried to diagram the unfolding grace
of God as we experience it. First born in innocence grace,
we quickly are moving toward the awakening of personal
responsibility and the loss of innocence. Beneath this
plunging loss lies the preventing net of prevenient grace,
by which God is eager to turn our minds back toward love
and truth and integrity. Once triggered, awakened toward
God and enabled to "have faith," converting grace leads
quickly to justification grace, which triggers sanctification
and the pilgrimage toward entire sanctification grace.
Notice that this journey of grace always rides on God's
"imparted righteousness." But across a life-time, this real
righteousness God imparts to us is insufficient to meet
God's full standard of righteousness; hence God's imputed
righteousness fills the gap, making our garments white as
snow.

Notice that life-long repentance is designated by the letter r in the diagram. Throughout infancy and childhood the
almost-daily alignment of spirit and behavior requires honest exchanges and reconciliations between child and parent or other significant persons in the child's environment.
Christian parents often extend the child's repentance to
repair breaches in the relationships with Jesus or God.
Children are susceptible during the years of innocence to
"invitations" to repentance. In the Wesleyan perspective
of prevenient/preventing grace, we rejoice because maintenance repentance is a way of life for people in the Wesleyan spirit.

Notice the Repentance markers which coincide with
justification grace and entire sanctification grace. These
denote epochal and transformational events, of which

Toward Christian Holiness: John Wesley's Faith Pilgrimage

JOHN WESLEY'S "WAY OF SALVATION"

INNOCENCE GRACE

GLORIFICATION GRACE

". . . we go on from grace to grace"

ENTIRE SANCTIFICATION GRACE

SANCTIFICATION GRACE

Repentance

sanctification . . .

IMPARTED RIGHTEOUSNESS

JUSTIFICATION GRACE

Repentance

IMPUTED RIGHTEOUSNESS

"r" is "maintenance repentance"

Death

"through faith: the only condition of justification and sanctification."

PREVENTING GRACE

Birth   age 10   20 ± 5

Conscience *(Piaget)*	objective responsibility-external	subjective responsibility/"intentionality"	
Perspective *(Piaget)*	egocentric	heteronomous and increasingly "perspectivistic"	
Justice *(Piaget-Joy)*	immanent justice, expiatory and punitive	consequent justice, reciprocal and equalitarian	transcendent justice, commutative and equitable
Love *(Gilligan)*	love for life and survival	love as self-sacrifice to and for other persons	love as avoiding hurting self or others: nonviolence
The HOLY	experienced in terms of narcissism, magic, power such that the Holy is manipulated for personal gain	. . . in terms of external authority evoking obedience/trust for leap of faith, trusting in Christ alone for justification	. . . in terms of internal transformation/liberation of "good," "walking in the light as God is in the light . . . fellowship."

Figure 4

there are only two: repentance to trust entirely in the justifying grace of Jesus, and surrendering repentance to open
entirely the inner arenas of life to the flooding of sanctifying grace through and through.

I have been so bold as to suggest the age at which de-
clining innocence places the child in crucial need of converting, then justifying grace. But I have suggested a range
of age fifteen to twenty-five as the span during which converting grace is likely to deliver the young adult to justifying grace. There is a high jeopardy phase, then, between
abut age ten and age twenty-five when the chief protective
grace is the net of God's preventing/prevenient grace.

Any life that follows the grace-flow is a life oriented
toward honesty and integrity. It is a life-long orientation
toward confession and repentance. By repentance I do not
refer to feelings of shame or inadequacy, humiliation, or
inferiority. I regard this confession or repentance as the
healthy acceptance of responsibility, of accountability to
other persons, of embracing community, and of taking
personal steps to maintain relationships based on honesty
and integrity. Hence evangelism always is a call to
repent—to ''come home'' to honesty and integrity in all
relationships. Repentance presupposes living close to both
the Other and to others. Parenting that favors grace, then,
is parenting that fosters confession, honesty, and responsibility. Pastoral care that favors grace is always leading
persons toward new arenas of honesty and integrity in relationships.

Any life that goes against grace will move on deception
and deceit and will dip into the net of preventing/ prevenient grace. In this grace, pain and failure and the sting of
the consequences of selfish choosing often evoke awareness of guilt, the need for repentance, even the nostalgia of
days when life was easy in innocence grace—a yearning to
come home, to convert, confess, and repent. Wesley sees
all of these sensitivities as effects of God's preventing/
prevenient grace.

The net of preventing grace may be punctured, however, as narcissism, pride, and rebellion rip through the protective undergirding grace of God. In our care of persons, therefore, we will serve best as evangelists when we create environments in which honesty prevails, in which narcissism—the tendency to fall in love with oneself and to build the whole world around the self—is inhibited through service to others and deliberately formulating affirmation for others. Inappropriate self-love, pride, and rebellion are best cured within the holy community where transparency, honesty, and affirmation make self-centeredness conspicuous and unnecessary.

For those who puncture and fall through the net of preventing grace, there lie the descending levels of non-grace. *Hedonism* is the first non-grace level in the descent and it consists of having one's own way, of being one's own authority, of writing one's own ticket. A minor tragedy among life's consequences here may turn the person back in search of grace. The second tier downward consists of *rebellion*—the deliberate thrust to organize all of life around the self instead of God, around the human's "city" instead of around God's creation. Finally, *treason* denotes the ultimate blasphemy against the Holy One. Life is organized around one's own "good" and the Holy has become "evil." Thus God has no existence, no channel by which to be the ultimate resource for life or meaning, and there is no longer an option of repenting, since there is no home to return to. But God's seeking grace is always "tracing" persons even in a lost trajectory, yearning to draw them back to the net of prevenient grace and to the life of eternal righteousness.

Substantial territories remain to be examined as we consider how the person moves from grace to grace. I want now to hypothesize that (a) it is by grace/faith alone, with all resources derived as a gift from God, and (b) that the unfolding structures of perception and organization within the person order the sequence of possibilities and place some limits upon the timetable by which the pilgrimage marker points may be passed. I suggest further that (c) there are dynamic responses to grace which tend to predict future responses or to foreclose future grace options, and finally that (d) the grace pilgrimage includes two major transformational events, epochal and nonduplicative, by faith alone.

In the previous discussion of preventing and converting grace, I have put forward a summary of Wesley's observations. In the summaries on conscience, perspective, justice, love, and The Holy, in Figure 4, I have indicated likely parallels between the pilgrimage of grace and the unfolding structures and organization of perception. Jesus seemed often to rest comfortably knowing that those who had ears to hear and eyes to see would take proper steps in response to his summons. The major transition noted in the 20 ± 5 phase of life matches major physiological changes: the onset of pubescence with its agenda for both sexual pleasure and sexual responsibility and the completion of the meylinization of the correlation fibers of the central cortex[19] which makes rapid reflective/evaluative thinking possible, turns the mind inward to ask ultimate questions about personal worth and destiny, and sets the stage for intense self-awareness.

Unfolding structures. Elsewhere, I have drawn parallels and developed a significant critical evaluation in comparisons of Wesley's three "states" of man and Lawrence Kohlberg's three "levels" of cognitive structural development.[20] Here I wish only to summarize firm conclusions from those explorations and evaluations. The following set of statements represents the enormous distillation of some twenty years of primary research and theological reflection:

1. Piaget, Kohlberg, and Gilligan find an intrinsic deposit universally in humans which develops across time and

through experience into an increasingly complex moral system. While individual decisions and choices may differ, values are universally the same; value choices are limited by the options of which the person is aware. Theologically, this structuralist finding confirms the intrinsic "image of God" and identifies it explicitly with justice/ righteousness (studies primarily with males)[21] and with attachment/love (studies primarily with females).[22]

2. Biological ripening is prerequisite to advancing into higher and more complex moral reasoning, but it by no means guarantees that any advancement will occur. Theologically, this finding confirms that there is likely an earliest age or at least a prerequisite biological condition that will precede certain kinds of moral sensitivity ("subjective responsibility" for example), hence our teaching, our ministry, and especially our evangelism must attend to this prerequisite ripening. At the same time, we may *not* assume that biological maturity automatically advances any person along an axis of moral, ethical, or spiritual maturity.

3. Experience, not biological ripening, is the motor of advancing moral reasoning. Piaget goes so far as to identify "cooperation" as the particular form of experience most helpful to childhood maturing in moral reasoning. Kohlberg has noted the importance of "responsibility" as prerequisite to Level III moral reasoning. This includes a responsibility for (a) making final moral choices and interpreting them to all persons affected by the choice, (b) the care of other persons whose welfare is finally in the "keeper's" hands, and (c) enduring pain, grief, and stress; the "trough" is often the immediate matrix for major breakthroughs in moral reasoning. To this Kohlberg adds (d) the ability to see things from the other's point of view and to feel the consequences from that perspective, and (e) habitual reflective tendencies; the person continually reviews moral behavior and moral choices and evaluates the

self and the consequences of those choices.[23] Theologically, the parallels between Kohlberg's and Piaget's findings and the characteristics of the Christian pilgrimage are obvious. (1) Salvation is always in "community," never in isolation. (2) Obedience to Jesus takes us into life's responsibilities and its stresses to refine us and produce the fine gold of faithfulness (*vis-a-vis* the popularized "success syndrome" heresy now abroad in the land). And (3) doubt, even battles of despairing, often become the instruments of victory and new resolution of faith at a more complex and enduring level.

4. Construction of each new perspective is "reconstruction" of previous constructs! Hence, progression in structural development is consistently through the same observable "stages" and none of them may be skipped. What is more, the earliest constructs will still be identifiable after many transformations in highly complex and mature structures. Piaget called this phenomenon "hierarchical integration and transformation." Theologically, the salvation pilgrimage is "one step at a time." Each phase of God's grace released in our experience must be respected and completed in order to form the foundation for healthy construction at a later, more mature, more complex phase. The "law is a schoolmaster to bring us to Christ." We now see through a "glass darkly." We now understand as a child, think as a child, reason as a child, but we long for the day when we may put these behind and see perfectly and know as we are known.

It becomes crucial that we avoid projecting adult religious experiences onto children, yet in our eagerness to be faithful to the young we tend to impose *our present life agendas upon everyone*. We run the enormous risk of proselytizing—of making them twice as susceptible to hell as ourselves—by transmitting as verbalisms the bright and shining reality we won by the long and pain-filled ascent through experience and by grace. Ministry, and especially ministry with children and youth and the naive, is obligated to so evangelize and educate that every person is granted the luxury of personal entry in the pilgrimage at "square one." Mentors must be comfortable granting freedom and responsibility such that each learner may navigate the entire course and embrace each grace with the zest and eagerness of a thirsty sailor as he sights land. Entire sanctification must follow justification by faith, but the sequence is prerequisite in developmental and experiential ways, not in any mathematical sense. The sequence of two major epochal events is made necessary by the nature of pilgrimage, not by any arbitrary whim of God or any coercive statement in Scripture. So also, justifying grace cannot be built out of innocence grace without passing through the high-risk zone of dealing with narcissism, pride, and the temptation to arrogance and rebellion. Any bridge that denies the person those risks will deliver a deformed faith: a naive childhood faith that can survive only if it is isolated from all of life's other experiences and is thus deformed or irrelevant in a tragic sense if it survives to adulthood.

Keep in mind that "maintenance repentance" must characterize the child's life experience, the adolescent's, and ours: Wesleyan salvation is thus conceptualized as a life-long orientation toward repentance. Honesty and responsibility are necessary to maintain innocence before justification, and repentance characterizes the life of holiness as we take responsibility for acting with integrity in all relationships for all of our lives.

Dynamic responses. I wish now to bring alongside the structural evidences above quite another set of theoretical support from research in human development done by such persons as Erik Erikson, Abraham Maslow, Daniel Levinson, and James Fowler. Their perceptual roots lie in Sigmund Freud and hence are sometimes called "dynamic" theories. They are characterized by (a) tending to fix "responsibility" for events outside of the person, hence deterministic in the sense that blame rests on parents, environment, or other significant persons; (b) seeing "conflict" as the necessary life-long struggle, hence some of the systems pose "versus" or adversary positions at war within the self; and (c) pessimism, hence there is a strong attention to shame, guilt, sin, with sometimes a groveling in past events, blaming others, which of course leads to more resentment, more shame, guilt, and sin. Most significantly, the dynamic theories deny any positive instinctual or intrinsic deposit in the human. Fowler's "faith development"[24] is an "empty model" suited as well for tracing religious commitment of Black Panthers as for Wesleyans. Unlike structural findings that hold that justice and love are the core of morality, dynamic theories begin with spiritual chaos at best. Nonetheless, Erikson and Maslow especially throw light on both Wesleyan theology and structuralist findings.

Erikson is best known for his ladder of "eight stages of man," and best of all for his "identity crisis," fifth of the eight.[25] He regards movement through the life crises or stages as motivated by "epigenetic" seeding of future crises by the solutions of a particular one. As with structural stages of Piaget and Kohlberg, development is across each stage in a fixed sequence and none is skipped. See Figure 5 for an arrangement of Erikson's life crises, each represented as adversary polarities tending to pull the persons toward either a positive or a negative resolution of that crisis, and thus to influence epigenetically the tilt of the scale for the next.

Abraham Maslow offers a ladder of "basic human needs" which he sees as emerging in a "prepotency" manner. Hence, physiological needs, safety needs, belongingness and love needs, esteem needs, and self-actualization needs comprise this core; on this theory no need emerges unless the previous need(s) is met. To these,

The Beatitudes of Jesus in Structural-Developmental Perspective.

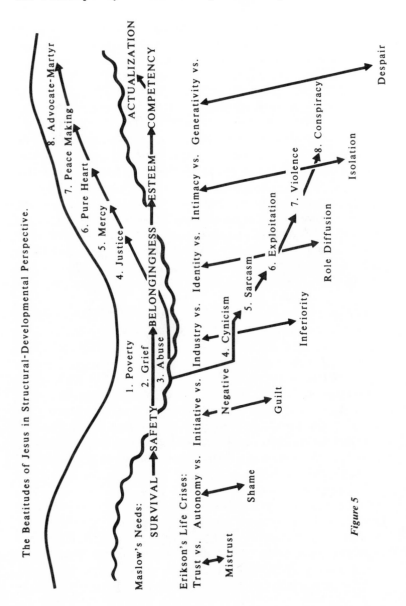

Figure 5

Maslow offers two which span the others: the need to know and to understand, and aesthetic needs.[26] These basic needs could easily be spread across the developmental grid in Figure 5 for purposes of comparison and illumination. In a similar way the "seasons of a man's life" from Levinson[27] and James Fowler's "stages of faith"[28] lend themselves to comparative study along the axis of John Wesley's perspective of our going on from "grace to grace." I wish to turn, however, to Erikson as both an example of how developmental theories may inform our theology of grace and how one developmental theory may serve to illuminate another.

Eight dynamic crises. Erik Erikson holds that each of his "stages" consists of a tension between two polarities and that a person resolves each life stage in a predominantly but not exclusively positive or negative way. To the extent that Erikson rings true with our experience, he may point to the importance of seeing each of life's marker points as a new "Eden," a new choosing and targeting for positive resolution and pursuit of holiness.

The first four life crises tend to occur during the prepubescent phase of life. *Trust versus Mistrust* is typically resolved positively or negatively by age two or soon after. *Autonomy versus Shame* is often given its tilt by toilet training, Erikson notes, since this task, once mastered, establishes the young person as able to take care of the self, whereas extended and harrassed toilet training tends to shatter the sense of self-worth and plunge the child into an orientation of shame.

Theologically, it is important to note that "shame" orientation early in life may delay movement into honest guilt. Shame is characterized by feelings of inferiority, weakness, the inability to take care of the self, and feelings of humiliation. Narcissism as an unsocialized love of the self is also a dimension of shame.

Initiative versus Guilt is the life task of the early elementary school years. It is the first clearly "social" task, and initiatives are being taken in the corporate setting, with a feeling of "doing well" or of "having failed" to do as well as one ought to do. If "shame" dominated in the previous resolution, then the guilt will be diffused here and amounts to a pseudo guilt, often leading to social withdrawal. Theologically the foundation of a "sense of social responsibility" may well lie in the resolution of this life crisis: initiative is characterized not only by taking responsibility to be a participating member of one's group, but also by owning one's failure and by arranging to make appropriate restitution. Guilt, on the other hand, is the lingering, correct assessment that one has failed and that one must act to make things right, honest, and restored. Guilt will linger, even lifelong, unless initiative is grasped and executed.

Industry versus Inferiority characterizes the middle elementary, prepubescent person. The extensions from the previous crises are evident. *Identity versus Role Diffusion* is the adolescent polarity. The identity task revolves around three questions: What is my vocation? Where did I come from? Where am I going? (Jesus, according to John's record in John 13:3, "knew" these things, and so he could wash the disciples' feet without concern that his "work" determined his worth.) Role diffusion, on the other hand, experiments with various "vocations" (student, drunkard, playboy, preacher) in a quick succession if a stable and abiding sense of identity does not emerge from the previous "industry" base. Justification by faith requires the possession of the self in identity in order to present the self to God.

Intimacy versus Isolation is the late adolescent/young adult task. Identity is sometimes established by early pursuit of an exclusive romantic relationship. To the extent that sexual intimacy becomes a means of "proving one's adulthood," or the occasion for "getting out of the house" and establishing adult status, it becomes confused and blurred back into the identity crisis. If so, it may be only one of the many "roles" being tried in experimentation. If not, it may set up the basis for early marriage and escape from the turbulence of the extended adolescence which characterizes North American culture at this time. The power of intimacy accounts for the mushrooming numbers of single adults in our culture who choose to live together in a modern equivalence to the ancient "common law" marriage. On the other hand, isolation is the actual estate of those who go through the motions of intimacy without accepting full responsibility for sharing the life of the other person. So, "sex without responsibility" in the teens and twenties is the marker for isolation, and predicts the negative resolutions that follow.

Generativity versus Stagnation establishes the polarities between which the thirties and forties will pass: either highly productive years or years of boredom and stagnation, feeling that life is passing them by without their achieving significant life visions. *Ego Integrity versus Despair* is the final polarity that Erikson chronicles. It is life's inventory marker and it calls for review and evaluation: either one is basically glad to have lived and loved and worked, or one moves toward despair and depression and gloom.

Erikson may have outlined the territory across which effective ministries of nurture and evangelization might usefully move. Note these generalizations:

1. All resolution toward the positive pole might be said to be "graced" by God's creation.

2. All negative resolution tends to be moving toward "non-grace" and hence describes the condition or outlook of persons who are the concern of the community of faith as it searches out the lost and the hopeless.

3. Christian mission, therefore, is always prepared to reach out to those caught by the negative pole, and to

move them to the positive resolution of that exact life crisis; the mission proceeds then to give them lifelong support through ministry relationships and programs to support their positive resolutions at all future crises.

Does Jesus Show Us How to Minister?

In this chapter, I have urged a "systemic" or wholistic pursuit of theology, in order to keep faith with the Scripture-experience-based theology of Jesus and John Wesley. I have offered an elegant perspective by which we view persons and have suggested alternative ways of dealing with issues of power and authority. Finally, I have examined John Wesley's "way of salvation" and have offered a way of enriching its understanding by focusing light from theories of human development on his grace markers along salvation's way.

There remains, I think, a further shaft of light in Jesus' teaching in the Beatitudes. My thesis is that ultimately the major life transitions are not completed at the marker points unless the person comes to a point of risk, of desperation, or of some other "leap" event at which possession of the new perspective requires the collapse of the present perspective. James Loder, in describing such a *Transforming Moment*,[29] notes that at the purely human level, when (a) *the lived world* is encountered by (b) *the self*, ordinary growth occurs. Before long, however, we tend to encounter conflict, pain, or ambiguity, which he calls (c) *the void*. Without supernatural intervention, the void turns inevitably to despair or cynicism. To those who live only in a two-dimensional reality (without grace), life may seem unfair, but they grind along. But God may break through with a fourth dimension, (d) *the Holy*. The Holy penetrates and transforms the void, turning pain and catastrophe into solution. Loder explicates the Emmaus Road event to illustrate how with a "double negation" the Emmaus couple receive the broken body from the risen Lord and he disappears from their sight, denoting the transformation of blinding grief into the blinding light of grace-bestowed reconstruction and discovery.

God's salvation scheme appears to be a grace-lubricated conveyor belt by which we are enabled to move from one transformation to another. In early or otherwise innocent experience, the grace is "prevenient." In later or otherwise self-reflective choosing experience, the grace is available and responsive. Note that the Beatitudes, like the epigenetic stages of Erikson's "life crises," or the "seasons" of Levinson, or the "hierarchy of human needs" of Maslow, unfold in a telescoping "prepotency" and come within reach only when the previous one is controlled. And like Piaget's structural stages, they are hierarchically integrated—all previous masteries remain accessible and undergird the highest functioning stage. (See Figure 5.)

Poverty, grief, and abuse may be literal and inescapable. Sometimes they are inward attitudes of negative self-worth. When they have been transformd by God's grace they may finally be inner marks of a transparent spirit; the grace-transformed person has allowed the void to be transformed by the Holy. (See Figure 5.)

I was present when the Christ's Community pastor preached from the Beatitudes. Of these first three, he said, "It isn't surprising that you rarely see these people in church. They are too preoccupied with their own emergencies: their poverty, their grief, and their own humiliation. But God has extended to them 'carte blanche' the Kingdom, his comfort, and a guarantee of inheriting the Creation." He went on to note that the remaining five beatitudes have implied or explicit contingencies. Each demands action: the pursuit of righteousness, the practice of mercy on other persons, the quest for a pure heart, the rigorous and dangerous work of arbitrating for peace, and the absolute risk of being defender and apostle of the true holiness. Eventually—given life's common doses of catastrophe and the uncommon transformations of God's grace—any of us may be expected to traverse the path from poverty to advocacy.

A negative trajectory is all that remains to those who grovel in the void and establish no transforming contact with the Holy. In an egocentric arena where it is "everybody for themselves," the path through the void tends to traverse through poverty, grief, humiliation, despair, cynicism, sarcasm, violence, arrogance, exploitation, conspiracy, and eventually to treason and to terror. The Incarnation and the Atonement were God's interventions aimed specifically at transforming the destructive effects of the void into the crowning redeemed sheaves of the holy.

OUR MINISTRY:
THE TRANSFORMATION OF THE VOID

A veteran pastor told me his miracle formula for church growth. "I search the admissions roster at the hospital every day. I look for people in trouble who have no pastor. I have literally filled every church I have served by ministering to people in pain. I have led whole families to Jesus in the months after officiating at the funeral of a member of the family." But such ministry will seem repugnant to pastors who have never suffered or who have glossed over and anesthetized the pain of their own lives.

It is not surprising to note that Jesus incarnated not only our humanity, but also this trajectory that begins with the descent into the void. He "became poor" and entered into our suffering and death, suffering humiliation and shame for us—all well-known theological facts. What is less easy to comprehend is that Jesus saw his ministry as the proclamation of liberating, perhaps even "prevenient," grace:

The Spirit of the Lord is on me,
    because he has anointed me
    to preach good news to the poor.
He has sent me to proclaim freedom
    for the prisoners and recovery of
    sight for the blind, to release
    the oppressed, to proclaim the year
    of the Lord's favor.[30]

In our well-appointed churches, the "gospel" we offer
to the broken, the ethnic minority, the fatherless, the
abandoned, and the widow is more often characterized by
our pursuit of righteousness and justice than by our willingness to become the advocate and defender of the
abused and the humiliated. Imagine what evangelism might
look like if we were, to begin where Jesus began. What,
then, might we discover to be the first doctrine of Christian holiness? Does "doing justice," "loving mercy," and
"walking humbly with God" consist of rescue, forgiveness, and radical advocacy of the poor, the bereaved, and
the humiliated? Jesus seems to have made such a summons explicit for those on whom he breathed that new-
creation breath—the Holy Spirit:

> "Peace be with you! As the Father has sent me, I am sending
> you." And with that he breathed on them and said, "Receive
> the Holy Spirit. If you forgive anyone his sins they are for-
> given; if you do not forgive them, they are not forgiven."[31]

We tend to be more skilled at refusing to forgive the
poor, the mourning, and the humiliated. One pastor recently brought a seventeen-year-old young woman to the
platform in a Sunday evening service and announced her
illegitimate pregnancy and demanded that she apologize to
the congregation. Matthew's picture of Jesus makes such
public humiliation seem distinctly pagan. He cites Isaiah's
picture of the redeeming servant of God:

> Here is my servant whom I have chosen,

the one I love, in whom I delight;
I will put my Spirit on him,
   and he will proclaim justice to the nations,
He will not quarrel or cry out;
   no one will hear his voice in the streets.
A bruised reed he will not break,
   and a smouldering wick he will not snuff out,
till he leads justice to victory.
   In his name the nations will put their hope.[32]

So, what might a congregation be doing if it were, indeed, Christ's redeeming community, the arena of grace in which the void is transformed by the holy?

It is clear that Christ's fully enabled Body will nourish not only the transformations of deep void, but also will sustain all of the members through all of life's variations and minor tragedies. The full-spectrum needs of people at various stages or seasons of their faith journey will be abundantly met by the many-splendored grace refracted through diverse persons whose gifts and grace-transformed experiences meet other pilgrims at junction points on their journeys.

I was deeply moved by Charles Hampden-Turner's observation that the late Dr. Martin Luther King "did not withdraw to the contemplation of Good within an academy of rich young men as the social system collapsed." Instead, King worked personally through to the top of the hierarchy of moral perspectives, deliberately to descend to its lowest point and to facilitate renewal, repair, and transformation at every level. He publicly claimed the rights of his people to safety (1) and to simple human pleasures (2). He inflamed a sense of offended justice by setting up brilliant televised moral pageants in which "black people were conventionally good and peaceful and white racists were stereotypically brutal" (3). He motivated civil rights legislation (4), and forged a social movement (5), all the while inspired by a personal vision of dignity and worth for his people (6).[33]

Surely we can catch the view of a holy community in
which a fuller spectrum of splendor reenacts the transforming words and works of Jesus of Nazareth as he is
incarnate in his body in the present world.

Notes

1. Albert C. Outler, "Repentance and Justification," Wilmore:
   The Asbury Seminary Tape Library, No. 82BB3, July 13,
   1982.
2. Jacques Ellul, *The Meaning of the City* (Grand Rapids:
   William B. Eerdmans, 1970), pp. 1-9.
3. Hebrews 11:4, NIV.
4. Hebrews 12:23-24, NIV.
5. Carl Sagan, *The Dragons of Eden: Speculations on the
   Evolution of Human Intelligence* (New York: Random
   House, 1977), pp. 173-74.
6. Atuhiro Sibatani, "The Japanese Brain: The Difference Between East and West May Be the Difference Between Left
   and Right," *Science/80* (December 1980), pp. 22 ff.
7. Genesis 3:1, NIV.
8. Charles Hampden-Turner, *Maps of the Mind* (London:
   Mitchell Beazley Publishers Limited, 1981), pp. 30-37.
9. Paul Bassett, "The Practice of Holiness in the Great Tradition," Holiness Emphasis Conference Lectures, Asbury
   Theological Seminary, October 6-7, 1982.
10. Delbert R. Rose, *A Theology of Christian Experience* (Min-
    neapolis: Bethany Fellowship Inc., 1965).
11. See also Albert C. Outler, *John Wesley* (New York: Oxford
    University Press, 1964).
12. See the work of Carol Gilligan, such as her book *In a Differ-
    ent Voice: Psychological Theory and Women's Development*
    (Cambridge: Harvard University Press, 1982).
13. Pastor Gary Walsh, Wilmore, Kentucky, Free Methodist
    Church, Based on concepts in Soren Kierkegaard's "Purity
    of Heart Is to Will One Thing."
14. Condensed and adapted from Alvin J. Lindgren and Norman

Shawchuck, *Management for Your Church: A Systems Approach* (Nashville: Abingdon, 1977), pp. 26-27.
15. John 13:1-17.
16. John 15:14-15, NIV.
17. Ephesians 4:11-12, NIV.
18. Steve Harper, *I Offered Christ: John Wesley's Message for Today* (Grand Rapids: Zondervan), 1982. See chapters 3 and 4, "Power to Begin" (Prevenient Grace), and "The Turning Point" (Converting Grace).
19. See, for example, Barry Tarshish, *An Introduction to Physiological Psychology* (New York: Random House, 1980), pp. 62-63. On the "correlation fibers of the central cortex," see the discussion in Clara Schuster and Shirley Ashburn, *The Process of Human Development: A Holistic Approach* (Boston: Little, Brown, and Company, 1980), pp. 138-39, for example.
20. Donald Joy, "Human Development and Christian Holiness," in *The Asbury Seminarian* (April 1976), pp. 5-27. See also, with major revision, the basic material with additional Wesley analysis in "John Wesley's Faith Pilgrimage," chapter 11 in my *Moral Development Foundations: Alternatives to Agnosticism* (Nashville: Abingdon, 1983).
21. Lawrence Kohlberg, *The Philosophy of Moral Development*, vol. 1 (San Francisco: Harper and Row, 1981).
22. See Carol Gillgan, *In a Different Voice*.
23. See John S. Stewart, *Toward a Theory for Values Development Education*, especially the section "Criteria for Principled Morality" (East Lansing: Michigan State University doctoral dissertation, 1974), pp. 400-39.
24. James W. Fowler, *Stages of Faith* (San Francisco: Harper and Row, 1981).
25. Erik H. Erikson, *Childhood and Society*, see especially chapter 7, "Eight Ages of Man" (New York: W. W. Norton, 1950).
26. A. H. Maslow, *Motivation and Personality* (New York: Harper and Row, 1954), pp. 80-106.
27. Daniel J. Levinson, *et al, The Seasons of a Man's Life* (New York: Ballantine Books, 1978).
28. James W. Fowler, *Stages of Faith*.

29. James Loder, *The Transforming Moment* (San Francisco: Harper and Row, 1981).
30. Luke 4:18-19, NIV.
31. John 20:21-22, NIV.
32. Matthew 12:18-21, NIV.
33. Charpes Hampden-Turner, *Maps of the Mind*, p. 139.

James Garlow (Ph.D., Drew University), pastor of Metroplex Chapel, Dallas/Ft. Worth, Texas

The Layperson
as Minister:
A Call for a New
Theology of the Laity

I HEAR the sounds of a revolution! I cannot see it yet. It's too far away. But I hear the sounds of it coming—a revolution that will liberate laity to a new self-perception. Laity will see themselves as ministers in the biblical definition of that word. Pastors likewise will be liberated to a new self-perception. Rather than viewing themselves as *the* ministers, they will view themselves as *trainers* of a vast army of ministers—lay ministers.

The "revolution" to liberate laity to ministry is not new. In fact it is very old. The Scriptures are clear that all God's people—the *laos*—share in a common priesthood. Throughout Christian history attempts have been made to

433

enable laity for roles of service. Some of these "lay ministry movements" were successful. Others were clearly reactionary and short-lived.

Some of the persons who emphasized the ministry of ordinary Christians through Christian history are well known: St. Francis, Peter Waldo, Martin Luther, John R. Mott. Others are not as well known: St. Dominic, Alexander Campbell. Yet none of these deployed laypersons more effectively than John Wesley.

John Wesley regarded laity with a seriousness that many of his theological offspring have overlooked. Admittedly, Wesley arrived at this understanding of the role of the laity by default rather than by design. Accounts of Wesley's "discovery" of laity are obscure and sometimes conflicting. The discovery may have occurred in 1739 or 1740 when the Wesleyan revival was in its infancy. In the absence of a scheduled preacher in London, Thomas Maxfield, a presiding layperson, took it upon himself to preach. This action by a bricklayer brought a storming Wesley quickly home from Bristol. Susanna, Wesley's mother, in her typical straightforward fashion, confronted John before he had opportunity to discipline Maxfield. She said, "John, take care what you do with respect to the young man, for he is as surely called of God to preach as you are."[1] Maxfield continued preaching.[2] Others followed. During Wesley's half century of ministry he trained 653 lay preachers. He also oversaw the selection and equipping of another group labeled "local preachers" in addition to a vast army of exhorters, class leaders, trustees, stewards, and "visitors of the sick."

In summary, the Evangelical Awakening in England of the 1740s would not have been so widespread had it not been for John Wesley's extensive utilization of laypersons. His claim to uniqueness does not lie in the fact that he utilized the laity, but rather the extent to which he deployed laity and the manner in which they were used.

Stephen Neill has correctly noted that the deployment of the class leaders was "a calling of the layman into responsible activity in the Church on a scale that had hardly even been before."[3] Franz Hildebrant suggested that "the scale on which [Wesley] recruited these forces in the service of Methodism was something of a revolution in church history."[4] The followers of Wesley, according to one writer "would claim that the priesthood of all believers in its fullness is part and parcel of the *raison d'etre* of the Church. No church among the larger denominations has given its laity more opportunity for service. Original Methodism understood the docrine and practices. Methodism would not have lived without it."[5]

What was vital to original Methodism is equally vital to all who consider themselves the sons and daughters of Wesley. It is imperative that laity in the twentieth century be taken with the seriousness manifested in the eighteenth century. Children of Methodism who chose to be faithful to their heritage will not limit ministry to clergy. Ministry is shared. It belongs to *all* God's people. The challenge of contemporary Wesleyanism is to liberate laity to ministry as creatively and effectively as the Awakening of the 1700s in England.

Wesley's most definitive explanations on the role of laity is found in his writing on the lay preachers. His deployment of lay preachers produced more criticism of Wesley than any other innovation of the revival. His defenses of lay preaching form the backdrop for a "Wesleyan vision" of lay ministry.

Much of the genius of Wesley's deployment of laypersons is reflected in his definition of the laity. The fact that they were not clergy did not prevent them from active ministry. Consistent with Wesley ecclesiology, the laity, as part of the Church, are activated into service. They are not perceived in purely passive roles capable of merely receiving ministerial actions from the clergy. The lay preachers were truly ministers in a sense that was not less important than, though different from, the clergy. Shipley noted that the proclamation of the gospel in the form of the "call to preach"

> is a unilaterally received vocation *in the context of the church*. The call from the Holy Spirit lays hold upon ordained and lay members of the church, including surprisingly enough, lay-women. "The call to preach" is, in no sense, definitely related to the doctrine of the orders of the ministry.[6]

Wesley appealed to several theological traditions, among them Presbyterian, Roman Catholic, and his own Church of England, as evidence that laypersons could legitimately minister.[7] John's grandfather by the same name likewise contended that the work of ministry was in no way dependent upon the office of the clergy.[8] Lawson was accurate in stating that "as far as Wesley is concerned, the main consideration is the preaching of the Gospel to the salvation of men's souls. Their ecclesiastical status is a minor matter by comparison."[9] The clerical hierarchy of the Church do not somehow possess more of the Spirit. The Spirit is common to all—laypersons or cleric.[10] The one-person rule over each church that developed after Constantine[11] did not justify the deprivation of the rest of the church of valid ministry.

Wesley's high view of the laity included clearly defined roles. Wesley did not permit laypersons to administer the sacraments.[12] Laypersons could, however, engage in mutual ministry. Laypersons could care for one another, bear one another's burdens, watch over one another, exhort one another, provoke one another to love and good works and confess faults to one another.[13] Boraine noted that Wesley "believed that the gathering together of believers in fellowship for mutual examination, encouragement, and service was indispensable for the life of the Church."[14] According to Wesley, the absence of this type of lay ministry among Whitefield's followers was most unfortunate. He wrote, "They were formed into no societies: They had no Christian connexion with each other's souls."[15] Perhaps one of Wesley's strongest statements of his high regard for lay ministry is found in "A Farther Appeal to Men and Religion":

> Why, must not every man, whether Clergyman or layman, be in some respects like the Apostles, or go to hell? Can any man be saved if he be not holy, like the Apostles; a follower of them, as they were of Christ? And ought not every Preacher of the gospel to be in a peculiar manner like the Apostles, both in holy tempers, in examplariness of life, and in his indefatigable labours for the good of souls? Woe unto every ambassador of Christ, who is not like the Apostles in this! In holiness, in making full proof of his ministry, in spending and being spent for Christ! And the same God who was always ready to help their infirmities, is ready to help ours also. He who made them "workmen that needed not to be ashamed," will teach us also "rightly to divide the word of truth." In this respect likewise, in respect of his "having help from God," for the work whereunto he is called, every Preacher of the gospel is like the Apostles.[16]

Wesley's firm conviction of the appropriateness of lay ministry permitted him to write so emphatically:

> Give me one hundred preachers who fear nothing but sin and desire nothing but God, and I care not a straw whether they be clergymen or laymen, such alone will shake the gates of hell and set up the kingdom of heaven upon earth.[17]

Wesley understood the laity in this activated sense. He viewed them as ministers even though he never allowed even the lay preachers to be called by the term. To Wesley, ministry was not dependent upon ordination. Ministry was expected of all followers of Christ—laity or clergy.

One of the major problems facing contemporary Christianity is the problem of a "deactivated" laity. How does one transfer Wesley's "activated" understanding of laity into the contemporary church. What ingredients of Wesley's understanding of the laity can be translated across two centuries of today's church?

It has been said that 95 percent of God's people are unemployed in meaningful kingdom service. Ministry for the most part has been that activity performed by ordained ministers. A minister, in the minds of many, is a person who is ordained, seminary or Bible-college trained, and who is responsible for public preaching. These definitions of *minister* and *ministry* are unscriptural. Furthermore, they do injustice to a Wesleyan understanding. The early Methodist societies were centers of lay vitality. Certain "lay ministry principles" were at work that produced an invigorated laity. Admittedly these principles are often subtly rather than overtly expressed by Wesley. Not everyone reading Wesley will use identical terms to describe his lay ministry principles. Nevertheless, the following four principles are present in Wesley, even if they are at times in somewhat primitive and undeveloped form. Wesley viewed laity as (1) A Called People, (2) A Gifted People, (3) A Trained People, and (4) A Sent People. Although these four concepts were used to apply to that band of Wesley's followers known as lay preachers, we shall use them here to apply to lay persons in general. These principles are as vital today as they were in the 1700s. The concepts are sufficiently universal to describe *all* God's people.

LAITY IN WESLEY'S DAY: A CALLED PEOPLE

Like St. Francis, St. Dominic, and St. Ignatius of Loyola, Wesley believed that the Church required called and dedicated laity to reinvigorate the Church in its apathy.[18] Wesley expected his lay preachers to have a call. The call to which Wesley referred was not so much an initial call to salvation as it was a call to active ministry. In addition to being converted, a potential lay preacher should be able to articulate his inward call from God. Wesley was criticized for the fact that his lay preachers lacked the outward call from the bishop. He did not oppose such a call, since he had one himself, but he refused to allow the absence of an outward call to invalidate the ministry that resulted from an inward call.

As with Israel in the Old Testament and the followers of Christ in the New, the call was not based upon privilege but upon servanthood. No lay preacher could ever gloat over having received such a call. Indeed, the lay preacher's attitude should be one of humility. The call of God to proclaim the gospel entailed much sacrifice and possibly persecution. Above all, it involved submission. As Charles Wesley's hymn noted,

> To serve the present age,
> My *calling* to fulfill;
> O may it all my pow'rs engage
> To do my Master's will![19]

John Wesley was certain not only of the call of God but of God's provision to follow the call. On this note Wesley once remarked,

> You trust in God; and you aim at pleasing Him only. And if He should call you even into the midst of a burning fiery furnace; "though thou walkest through the fire, thou shalt not be burned, neither shall the flames kindle upon thee."[20]

Today's Laity: A Called People

Wesley's emphasis upon a called people in his theology of the laity can inform contemporary thought on the topic. One work on the laity, appropriately titled *Buried Alive*, suggested that few things have deprived the laity of ministry more than the clerical concept of the call to be a pastor. Sometimes it is even referred to as the highest calling or the holy calling. The implications of this concept are both obvious and misleading. Laypersons must assume that they have no call, or if they do, it is a lower callng.[21] A biblical understanding of *laos* does not permit such distinctions. All individuals "to whom the Gospel has spoken meaningfully must take seriously the call which comes to them and become responsible participants in the covenant community."[22] Ayres, in his aphoristic style, made it unmistakably clear when he wrote,

> You are called. All Christians share the same calling. . . . "Call," "called," and "calling" denote God's call to repentance and faith, and to a life of service in the church. . . . The purpose of God, the task of the church, and the whole message of the Bible can be described in terms of calling and the appropriate response. Ministry . . . begins with calling and is a response to it.[23]

Ministry is not optional for the one who has responded in faith. Every believer is called to active, responsible membership in the community of faith. It is inappropriate for Christian ministry to be described as volunteer ministry. Followers of Christ are not volunteers, giving of their extra time. They are under orders, responding to a call to ministry.

Writing on the "common" call, Francis Ayres notes again that

> the basic, primary Biblical use of the term "calling" is an urgent invitation to enter into a life of service to God, a life of forgiveness, meaning, purpose, and freedom. It is issued to all men without distinctions of any kind. A clergyman, no matter how high his office, has received the call in exactly the same way as everyone else and for exactly the same purpose—to serve God in all areas of his life. . . . There is no instance in the Bible where a man is "called to be a clergyman or a statesman or a worker. . . ." Nevertheless the word "calling"

can be used in respect to the work of a clergyman—as long as one recognizes that it can be used in exactly the same sense for a salesman, a lawyer, a teacher, or an actor. . . . Secular occupations are to be regarded not as ends in themselves but as means to the service of God.[24]

Wesley's understanding of the call stems from his strong belief that each person could know with certainty that he or she was commissioned for a divinely appointed mission. The one receiving the call was undaunted by the doubts of others.

Laypersons in the twentieth century will *not* be "liberated" to this call to ministry until the word *minister* is used properly. So long as one person in each congregation is referred to as "*the* minister," other persons (specifically, lay persons) within that congregation will assume that they are *not* ministers. Thus they perceive of themselves as essentially passive. "Ministry," they will assume, should be done only by "*the* minister." If we view laity in a manner consistent with our biblical and historical foundations, we will learn that a congregation does not have one minister and two hundred parishioners; rather, it has one pastoral minister and two hundred ministering laypersons.

There is another equally important consideration. If we take seriously the notion that all God's people are called to ministry, we will view pastors differently. They are not to do the work of ministry alone. Rather, they are to prepare, or equip, others (laity) for ministry. A pastor is not *the* minister, but a *trainer* of ministers—lay ministers. Admittedly, no pastor has all the gifts needed to equip an entire congregation for ministry. Yet, as leader of the congregation, he or she is responsible to see that the equipping process is in motion, that laypersons are genuinely being outfitted for kingdom service.

This has profound implications for our Bible colleges and seminaries. The goal of such institutions, if we take lay ministry seriously, is not only to produce professional clergy but to prepare persons who can equip and mobilize persons for ministry. The organizationally and administratively gifted Wesley gathered around him a small group of Anglican priests who oversaw the vast army of enabled laypersons. Wesley was unsuccessful in attracting more than forty sympathetic Anglican clergy. Yet from this small group, thousands of laypersons understood the joy of active ministry.

LAITY IN WESLEY'S DAY: A GIFTED PEOPLE

John Wesley regarded the lay preachers as persons who had been gifted by God. So basic was this to his understanding of lay ministry that he made it one of the criteria upon which he selected laypersons. After conversion and a "call," Wesley looked for gifts. The minutes of the 1746 conference demonstrate Wesley's concern for discovering the gifts of his lay preachers.[25] Wesley likewise examined his exhorters to determine if their gifts corresponded with the work assigned them.[26]

With the awareness of the layperson's gifts came an accompanying sense of personal commitment and responsibility. The lay preacher, like the biblical steward, was admonished not to bury his talent. He was to be faithful with the gift or gifts that God had granted him for ministry.

Wesley's stress on gifts was not new. It was Pauline, appearing both in Romans and 1 Corinthians. Writing about Methodist local preachers one hundred years after Wesley's death, W. B. Pope noted that the Methodist church came near the model of the New Testament because it utilized the gifts efficiently.[27] In a limited way, Wesley followed this biblical model in that ministry was based upon one's gifts, rather than upon "institutional expectations" or "needs." One ministered to the extent and in the domain that he was gifted. Wesley's perception of gifts, though admittedly embryonic, has important implications for the relationship between clergy and laity. In his work previously quoted, Pope claims that this understanding of gifts provided the

> secret of the reconciliation between separated office and common priesthood; between the ordained ministry and all others. There is a class to whom, for the sake of order, the teaching and rule of the community is specially committed: that class is specially endowed; but it does not absorb all the gifts. The very gifts that are the necessary endowments of the pastoral office, government and teaching may be largely bestowed on the governed and taught. Then these must be used in teaching and catechising children, in cottage and street and village preaching, in administering affairs, in guiding souls, and in a thousand ways.[28]

Not all persons possessed the gifts associated with preaching. In a preliminary way, Wesley knew that. He recognized the variety of gifts with which God equips his people. One example of a unique gift was that required for prison ministry. One person who in his opinion possessed the gift for such ministry was Silas Told. Wesley wrote that no other man in the last hundred years had been so successful in working with prisoners.[29] John Wesley was well within the tradition of his grandfather by the same name when he recognized that God's gifting process was not the same for all persons. Some persons, according to the elder John Wesley, do not have gifts in preaching.[30] The younger Wesley, by the very act of selecting lay preachers from among the thousands of persons in the societies, recognized the diversity of gifts that characterized even the followers of Christ. All were called to minister. Yet their ministry took varying forms due to the differences in gifts.[31] Furthermore, Wesley taught the laity that they should not despise one another's gifts.[32] This diversity was a part of God's plan so that all needs could be ministered to.

One must be careful not to overstate Wesley's teaching on gifts. He was primarily concerned that the lay preachers possess certain gifts—understandably those gifts that would make them effective itinerants. He was not nearly so concerned with the wider range of gifts that might be present in a congregation. Yet Wesley's perception of the gifts, though embryonic in its development, was an important principle that merits our attention. He understood that ministry was not based upon ordination, but rather upon the gifts that God gave, thus enabling persons to respond to his call to ministry.

TODAY'S LAITY: A GIFTED PEOPLE

The stress on the study of spiritual gifts is receiving a much more extensive and intensive treatment in present-day studies on lay ministry than it did in Wesley's day. In the twelfth chapter of the first letter to the Christians at Corinth, Paul stressed the gifts that have been given to each person. In Paul's writings as well as in 1 Peter 4:10, one notes that the mere possession of a gift was regarded as implying a debt to other persons, which should be discharged by some form of ministry. There are different gifts for different persons, but the purpose for the gifts remains the same—ministry. The Spirit, who according to Paul is the giver of the gifts, bestows these gifts not to form a spiritual elite or an aristocracy, but rather for servanthood. In Romans 12, Paul listed the gifts beginning first with the gifts and then moving on to the persons exercising the gifts. In 1 Corinthians 12, he reversed the process, beginning with the persons and then the gifts. C. K. Barrett suggested that "the form as well as the content of the two lists indicates the very close connection between gift and function."[33] The gifting process is not an end in itself. It is the means to an end, the end being ministry or service.

If one believes that laity are truly gifted for ministry, then laity will not be recruited to fill vacant positions of service. They will not be coerced into ministries. Pastors who take seriously the notion that laypersons are truly gifted for ministry will (1) assist laypersons in discovering their unique abilities or gifts, and (2) assist laypersons in finding the ministries (or spheres of service) in which their gifts can be used best. Pastors are often tempted to recruit laypersons to fill positions that happen to be vacant. This is tragic in that it focuses concern on the lesser issue—the ministry position that needs to be filled, rather than the greater issue: the individual who has gifts to share. Lay ministry, when taken seriously, begins with the *person*, rather than the *position*. This means that the first question to be asked is not, Who will fill this position? but rather, What are the gifts of this individual? How can these gifts be most effectively used in kingdom service?'' If this understanding of giftedness were to be taken seriously in local church life, many laity would be set free from positions of service for which they have no abilities. They would be "liberated" to a new sense of ministry—one based upon their unique abilities. The results would be overwhelming. Service for Christ would be much more fulfilling to vast numbers of laity. They would respond more enthusiastically to ministries if they were assured that their "enabler," or pastor, was concerned primarily with maximizing their giftedness.

I once heard a pastor preach a sermon on lay ministry. He based it on a passage from Nehemiah. It was an excellent sermon. Unfortunately, he concluded the sermon by announcing to the congregation that there were two open Sunday school teaching positions and three open positions in the choir. He stated that some laypersons should immediately volunteer to fill those positions. What an unfortunate misunderstanding of what lay ministry really is. This method was unnecessarily guilt-producing.

How much better it would have been for the pastor to
ask those who had gifts compatible with the open positions
(assuming the congregation had received thorough instruction on how to discover one's gift) to give careful
consideration to the ministries of music and teaching. He
could have met with persons with appropriate gifts (individually or in a small group), explained the need, and then
asked them to consider the positions for a week or so. This
would have given each one an opportunity to counsel with
others and be sensitive to the Spirit's call upon his or her
life. If the layperson felt he or she was *not* to accept the
position after this time of consideration, the pastor should
recognize that the Spirit may be directing the layperson
into another area of ministry.

Note that it is not the pastor's responsibility to *call*
laypersons to service—it is God's. The pastor augments
this operation by assisting laypersons in understanding
their gifts and the spheres (ministries) in which those gifts
can be used most effectively. This approach takes the
pressure off the pastor in filling the position. It takes the
pressure off the layperson to volunteer for positions that
he or she does not feel called to fill. (Remember, if a
layperson does volunteer under pressure, the pastor will
probably be looking for someone to fill that same position
very soon!)

Laity in Wesley's Day: A Trained People

Initially Wesley was hesitant to grant to laity the responsibility of ministry. This was particularly true of his
lay preachers. But once the decision was made to employ
them, he proceeded to devise the best possible training
program.[34] He did not encourage them to exercise their
proper priesthood without first providing the training to
make such a priesthood a possibility.[35] Referring to young

believers, Wesley wrote that preaching that awakens persons without "training them up in the ways of God, is only begetting children for the murderer."[36] If Wesley regarded training as important for all Christians, one can appropriately anticipate the extent to which he insisted upon it for the lay preachers. Hildebrandt noted that Wesley's training of lay preachers was far superior to lay training as it is known today. Wesley "presupposed a training and quality of lay leadership which to our generation has become almost legendary."[37] Wesley's insistence upon quality training is reflected in his disinclination to develop the office of "local preacher."

How was it possible for one person to have been responsible for the training of 653 lay preachers, 57 percent of whom continued preaching under Wesley's guidance until their deaths? One method of analyzing Wesley's success is to note those pitfalls that he avoided. The *Proceedings of the Ecumenical Consultation* which was held in Gazzade, Italy, in 1956 noted several factors that had caused modern lay training to be largely unsuccessful. The following items were noted: training has not been integrated with daily life; too much instruction and not sufficient training through action; instruction from the top rather than beginning with the experience of the people involved; impersonalization; and limiting most Christian education to children.[38]

Wesley cannot be faulted with any of the above. His training was of such intensity that it pervaded one's total being. It was "integrated with daily life." One could not be a Methodist without understanding the way in which it altered one's function within society. On the second critique it must be acknowledged that Wesley's instruction did come from the top but was always the results of the "felt needs" of the "grassroots." Wesley's training was formed out of the experiences of those over whom he served as pastor. The training techniques used by Wesley were grounded not on some preconceived guidelines but rather emerged out of the crucible of the Wesleyan revival itself. Following the critiques of the Ecumenical Consultation further, one would note that Wesley's training was not impersonal, but was highly personalized. He examined potential lay preachers carefully. The lines of accountability were structured in such a way as to permit Wesley either to have personal awareness of an individual's progress or at least have access to that information through his helpers. The stress upon the small group as a training ground prevented any possibility of impersonalization. On the final critique, it is simply noted that Wesley concentrated his prime focus on adult training. Furthermore, he conceived of the Christian life in such a manner that one should never cease growing in the pilgrimage toward spiritual maturity regardless of age.

Wesley utilized several different methods in the training of the lay preachers. One was the annual conference, "one of those strokes of practical genius that marked off Wesleyan Methodism from the other vectors of the Evangelical Revival."[39] Although the conferences involved much discussion of theological issues, they also served as effective training centers for the practical concerns of lay ministry.[40] A second training tool was the rules. Wesley had a knack for writing rules for other persons. The famous *Rules for a Helper* were drawn up at the Leeds Conference in 1753 and included everything from punctuality to relationships with members of the opposite sex.[41] This list of rules was only one of many that Wesley produced to assist the laity in their personal lives and ministries.

Closely related to this method of training is the third one. This consisted of a proper combination of demonstration, delegation, and supervision. Wesley's own ministry served as a model for the lay preachers. In a sermon titled "The Ministerial Office," he noted the importance of being an example in ministry, *demonstrating* how to serve others.[42] Francis Asbury, a lay preacher whom Wesley trained and sent to America, clearly stated this principle when referring to the lay preachers subsequently trained by Asbury for the New World. When many of them wanted to settle down in the eastern cities, he responded, "I will show them the way," and embarked on a two-thousand-mile preaching tour through the wilderness.[43] The words "I will show them the way" embodied one of Wesley's methods of training. He frequently had lay preachers as traveling companions who watched and learned from him. "Demonstration" was not isolated from delegation and supervision. Outler notes that

> it was part of [Wesley's] genius to divine and delegate pastoral responsibility throughout a widening network ["connexion"] of local groups and leaders under his overall diligent supervision. Thus he was able to multiply and disperse his pastoral influence in quite extraordinary ways.[44]

A fourth method of training is more difficult to label and explain. Borrowing a term, I chose to label it simply the force of the revival itself. Warner wrote that "the process by which leaders were made was important. They were not created by arbitrary authority so much as designated by the self-expressed forces of the revival."[45] Laypersons were given leadership responsibilities by their fellow Methodists by a form of natural selection. The local leaders "grew up through the enlarging units of the societies until, at length, by the logic of events, they became general leaders."[46] Of some sixty-three Methodist leaders, at least fifty-two were elevated to leadership, stage by stage, in a gradual ascension. In spite of Wesley's alleged autocracy, the leadership of the Methodists was not imposed from above. Instead the movement produced its leaders.[47] Part of the organizational genius of Wesley was his ability to recognize the gift of leadership within his helpers, and to fine tune those gifts for expanded service.

The secret of this leadership training process is found in Wesley's vision that "ordinary people could do for themselves and others—and in so doing, make a significant contribution."[48] Wesley structured the Methodist segment of the Evangelical Revival in a way that, consciously or unconsciously, allowed persons to excel in leading others. Lay preachers, class leaders, exhorters, stewards, trustees, and visitors of the sick were not only set to work, but were given meaningful responsibilities.[49] This sense of mutual service alleviated whatever feelings of inferiority the common person might feel. Regardless of social qualifications, persons were given responsibilities for the welfare of their peers. In fact, Methodists were encouraged not to act as "gentlemen," but rather to be the servants of all.[50]

The fifth training tool was that of the small group or cell concept that characterized Methodism. Fitchett has noted two theories that have implications for training laity. One is the "tram-car theory," which places an arbitrary group of people side by side who happen to be going the same direction for a short period of time. During their brief journey they remain essentially strangers to each other. The second is the "family theory," which states that a church should consist of a circle of persons who are conscious of a close kinship one with the other.[51] As societies within Anglicanism, Methodism functioned by the latter theory, linking persons together who represented much diversity of background, education, and wealth.[52] Since the congregation and even the society were too large for nurture, Wesley developed the structures that allowed for face-to-face sharing of the Christian life. Christian fellowship was an ingredient of such importance that he expected it to be enjoyed by all members.[53] Admittedly this was not unique to Methodism. Other religious groups used the principle of small groups. Wesley's uniqueness is defined in the *extent* to which he capitalized on this innovation for purposes of pastoral oversight.[54] In addition to encouraging fellowship, the small groups served as excellent training ground for the laity who would continue the important ministries assigned to them.[55] This "cellular" unit of Methodism, providing the channels whereby laypersons could become equipped for ministry, was probably Methodism's greatest strength. So successful was Methodism at using the small group as an arena for training that other religious movements, "the trade unions, the Chartists, the Labour Movement, and to some extent the Communist Party, have paid it the compliment of imitating it."[56] In addition to knowing that they could not watch over one another unless they were closely united,[57] Wesley realized that the laity could not be trained without the same intimate unity. The class meeting and bands did much more than edify believers. They provided avenues for developing shared leadership.[58] These small cell units "produced an active and articulate laity such as no other denomination has produced, not only within the Connexion but in secular society."[59] Wesley knew that people could learn much more from one hour of discourse than from ten year's public preaching.[60] The encounters provided in the small groups were instruments to "tool" the laity for ministry.

Any theology that takes the ministry of the laity seriously must give adequate attention to training. Ministry is not automatic. It may not always require strict regimentation, but it does need structures for training and expression. Wesley lived out a theology of the laity by his insistence upon small group fellowships: In them, laypersons were trained for ministry by the sheer existence of arenas in which they could begin to exercise their gifts.

TODAY'S LAITY: A TRAINED PEOPLE

Lay ministry, taken seriously, states that laity are *called* to ministry and *gifted* for ministry. The use of the gifts can be improved by fine tuning. This fine tuning is referred to as being *trained* for ministry. The gifts that God gives are tools for ministry. Training improves the effectiveness of these tools.

It is strange indeed that lay training is not more common in Christianity. Much of what has been labeled lay training occurs by default rather than by design. Perhaps the greatest hindrance to lay training is a faulty ecclesiology that views the church building as a center for nurture rather than as a center for equipping and enabling. The church building is often viewed as a mess hall where people show up for chow rather than an armory in which they are outfitted for spiritual warfare. Contemporary church life rewards laity for merely attending church services. It frequently fails to sound a call to arms. Contemporary church phraseology lends itself to deactivating laity. Church auditoriums are described by how many they can seat (a passive term) rather than by how many they can equip (an active term) for service.

What might happen if lay ministry were taken seriously? Activities in the church building would be evaluated for their equipping potential. The church facilities would be described as a place where persons are outfitted for service, not *seated*! The minister would refer to himself or herself as the enabler, or person responsible for the enabling process. We would have nothing short of a revolution—a revolution that would be welcomed by every underchallenged layperson and every overworked pastor.

Some pastors are noticeably threatened at the thought of laity being trained for ministry. There is no reason for any pastor to be threatened by the current lay ministry emphasis. Present-day thinking on a theology of the laity does not advocate a "laitization of the clergy" or a "clericalization of the laity." Both extremes are a distortion of the biblical models to which a theology of the laity appeals.[61]

Clergy, functioning as enablers, have an important role in lay ministry. However, "the purpose of having an ordained ministry is not to establish any monopoly of ministering, but to ensure that the ministry shall be carried on."[62] The task of the ordained, then, is to teach and equip the *un*ordained for ministry.[63] Thus it becomes apparent that a high doctrine of the laity strengthens, rather than diminishes, a high doctrine of the ordained ministry or clergy.[64] Howard Grimes says it well:

> From this higher estimate of the meaning of the laity may be drawn what seems to me to be a false conclusion: namely, that ordination is of no significance, that a layman is called to do everything that a clergyman does, including even the celebration of the sacraments. . . . A more adequate generalization seems to me to draw upon the tradition within the Church which emphasizes order with a differentiation of *function* of members. All are called by God to service; the nature of that service varies, and it includes the particular work of the ordained ministry.[65]

Thus one notes that the clergy is essential in understanding the function of the people of God. Almost all churches and denominations recognize the need for a representative ministry. Often this recognition is most obvious for pragmatic reasons, for every social system must have certain structures in order to survive.[66] However, this seemingly pragmatic necessity is quite capable of being theologically justified.[67] This theological justification is rooted in the function of the enablers: to train all God's people for ministry. The two are inseparable. Thus

> the training of the laity cannot be divorced from the work of the clergy. The training of the clergy cannot ignore the work of the laity. The theological education of the ministry can no longer be regarded as a purely professional matter. It is crucial to the ministry of the laity.[68]

Ephesians 4:11-12 is one of the clearest biblical passages

relating to this theme. Citing this passage, Braun noted that the enablers are given to the Church to equip God's people for work in his service. Weber observed that the comma that in some translations appeared after the word *saints* (v. 12) is "a fatal comma," since it gave the appearance that the equipping of the saints and the work of ministry were separate functions of the clergy. In actuality the function of the clergy is to equip the believers for their ministries.[69] For this reason persons such as Rupert Davies have stated that "the old phrase 'ministry of word and sacraments' doesn't quite fill the bill."[70] This phrase neglects the theme of the pastor as the trainer of the total church. Far from being unneeded by the Church, a theology of the laity regards the pastor as one "chosen by God . . . prepared, trained and put where he is in order to ensure that the other members realize the significance of their ministry in the world."[71]

The pastor, as enabler, is not separate from the rest of the *laos* by status but rather by function. John Zizioulas clearly stated the issue at stake when he raised the question "whether ordination gives a certain objective grace ontologically possessed by the ordained person or is simply a commission to function in a certain way on behalf of Christ or the Church."[72] Though Zizioulas contended that neither "ontology" nor "function" are adequate descriptions, many persons, including myself, feel that the debate is an important one for a theology of the laity. The discussion as to whether ordination is functional or substantial "lies at the root of all discussions about laity."[73] To perceive the clergy as ontologically separate is to regard the laity as "second class citizens."[74] This kind of perception results in what one writer referred to as "clergy-laity game playing."[75] Gordon Rupp staged the question in humorous fashion by stating "that nobody can tell whether a difference between a difference of degrees and difference of kind is itself a difference of degree or of kind."[76]

A theology of the laity, if biblically grounded, asserts that the functions of laity and clergy can be considered equal without belittling either. The priesthood of the whole church and that of the ordained clergy are not different in kind. The activity of the clergy does not have separate status though it is clearly functionally different from that of the layperson.[77] Outler noted this functional difference in the following:

> The general priesthood of all believers and the ordination of the laity do not obviate the fact that there is also a particular ministry—what I prefer to call "the representative ministry"—in the church. All organisms above the level of the amoeba differentiate their various organs and functions and exhibit a functional hierarchy. All laymen are ministers; all ministers are laymen. However, all laymen do not have the same office; and the effectiveness of the Churches' ministry in and for the world depends as decisively on the differentiations of various offices as on the generality of ordination and *vice versa*.[78]

This understanding of the clergy-laity relationship means that a partnership in ministry exists, not a twofold division of labor. The dependence of the laity upon the clergy for training and equipping challenges those who would distort a theology of the laity into an attempt to usurp the function of the clergy. In contrast there is a "mutuality of ministry" that characterizes a biblical understanding of the priesthood of all believers, for there are enablers who equip the believers for their priesthood.[79]

It is important to note that laypersons are not trained for ministry as a "side job," something they will do if their other commitments permit them time. Being a member of the *laos* is far too central to one's being to be considered in that light.[80] Even the word *training* might suggest that ministry is something extraneous to the *laos*, something to be added. It is not. Others prefer the term *laity formation* over the word *training* or *equipping* simply because these terms suggest condescending notions that are incongruent with the understanding of *laos*. Still others dislike any reference to lay education for the same reason, fearing that it smacks of the old hierarchical divisions between clergy and laity.[81] These terminological fears are unfounded, for as Kist has pointed out, "modern lay training . . . does not consist of a one-track communication of thoughts between the leader and his audience." It is far more interactional than that.[82] At the core of "lay training" are the presuppositions that the people of God exist for service for which they need training, and second, that those who train them are their servants, not masters over them. Thus is it not in violation of a biblical perception of *laos* to speak of the need for "lay training."

Come has warned his readers that, while the theological understanding of lay training may be well in mind, the sociological findings demonstrate an absence of understanding of the Church's mission. A biblical understanding of the laity states that all God's people are to be trained, not for themselves, but for one another and for the world. However, in contrast to this

> sociologists are insisting that the majority of church members are interested only in what the Church can do in ministering to their personal needs—what [Come calls] the "caretaker" role of the Church. And those pastors who are anxious to train the laity for mission in the world, and who organize such training programmes, soon find they have two congregations—the minority who respond, and the majority who strongly resist such a "new" interpretation of the reason for the Church's existence.[83]

Part of the task of lay training is enlightening the total *laos* to its need for training. Lay training and equipping are not done purely for pragmatic reasons. It is rooted in the very purpose of God for his own creation.[84] The Church does not exist for itself but for the world. It is on a mission in the world.

Laypersons are equipped and strengthened for this mission most obviously in the liturgical, worship, and devotional aspects of the Church. Furthermore they are equipped by becoming involved in specific and concrete projects of mission, not simply by just "being" the Church.[85] Thus the "formation" of "training" of the *laos* takes more than one form. The local congregation is only one of several important spheres of training. Most recently, lay training centers with a stress on Church-world dialogue have become tools of learning. Retreat committees, Bible studies, and specialized study groups[86] are only a few of the environs in which the laity are being equipped.[87] By far one of the most effective settings is the "small group" or cell concept. It is here that the Church can truly become the body of Christ, exercising its gifts in an effective manner.[88]

Churches that regard lay ministry as important are discovering ways to "turn their churches into seminaries."[89] Some examples are Hollywood Presbyterian (Hollywood, California)—"Laos Academy"; The Crystal Cathedral (Garden Grove, California)—"Lay Ministers Training Center"; First United Methodist Church (Wichita, Kansas)—"University of the Spirit"; First Southern Baptist (Del City, Oklahoma)—LAMP (Lay Adult Ministry Preparation); First Nazarene Church (Bethany, Oklahoma)—LITE (Lay Institute to Equip).

LAITY IN WESLEY'S DAY: A SENT PEOPLE

Robert Barclay, writing in 1876, quoted the following statement by a Dr. Waddington:

In 1681, certain members of the laity of the Church of England published the following circular;—We find that divers and several of those people called Quakers are also very good Christians, and preach true doctrine according to Holy Scrip-

ture; and we therefore declare that it is our opinion that such
a voluntary ministry, to preach on free cost as aforesaid, is of
excellent use and exceeding necessary to be allowed in the
Church of England, not only in preaching to poor people in
tabernacles, who cannot pay anything sufficiently to maintain
a ministry, nor yet get pews in their parish churches, but also
it makes the learned clergy to be the more sober and studious
in their places, and therefore we can think of no other but that
such *voluntary ministers* are *sent of God*; for we remember
the Apostles were working men, of several trades as these
are, yet we do not believe God sent these to hinder the clergy
of maintenance, but only to season them as salt seasons meat.
In great parishes there is need to be at least two congregations: the parish church for the orthodox minister and the
rich, and a tabernacle for the lay prophets and the poor.[90]

With only the slightest modifications,[91] the previous quotation well reflected the views of Wesley. Of most
significance is the phrase "sent of God." Wesley viewed
his lay ministers in such a manner. As stated in the previous quote, Wesley's lay preachers were not sent to "hinder the clergy" but to "provoke" them, that is, encourage
them to better ministry. The lay preachers did not require
the hands of a bishop in order to know they were sent.
Their training, sincerity, and sobriety, along with other
qualifications, assured them of their "sentness."[92]

All believers should perceive their ministries in the light
of the ministry of Christ. As Christ is sent into the world,
ordained of God to fulfill a special *mission* for humankind,
so also the Christian is commissioned to fullfill the mission
with which he or she is entrusted.[93] This is demonstrated
in the fact that Christ sent out his followers to make
known his message. These evangelists whom Christ sent
out to proclaim the gospel to all the world were not ordained, yet they were still sent. Wesley viewed his lay
preachers as being in the lineage of these "sent"
evangelists.[94] Hildebrandt noted that one cannot understand such Methodist institutions as the lay preachers un-

less one comprehends that Wesley's mobilization of these laypersons is the result of an "extraordinary sense of urgency."[95] The urgency spoken about here was framed by a theology of universal salvation available to all who hear and respond to the beckoning call of God. This message of salvation was to be taken to all who would hear. On such a mission were Wesley's lay preachers sent. They were not sent into the Church. They were the Church sent into the world. And into the world they went.

Even the hymns that the laypersons sang spoke of the mission to the world. Charles Wesley's songs reflected a militaristic bent, portraying the early Methodists as the army of God being sent on a mission into the world. They sang:

> Soldiers of Christ, arise
> And put your armour on,
> From strength to strength go on.
> Wrestle, and fight, and pray,
> Tread all the powers of darkness down,
> And win the well-fought day;
> Still let the Spirit cry
> In all His soldiers, "Come,"
> Till Christ the Lord descends from high
> And takes the conquerors home.[96]

The hymns frequently reflected the victorious nature of their mission:

> This God hath bid us do,
> And man forbids in vain;
> . . .
> Resolved our Lord to obey
> In spite of man's command.[97]

Early Methodist laity, in responding to the call to be sent on a mission, were true followers of Wesley, for it is in just such light that Wesley viewed himself.[98]

In addition to the various pastoral functions, this mis-

sion included the command to preach. Wesley's theology
of the laity viewed the lay preachers as being not only
sent, but being sent with *authority*. They had the authority
to proclaim God's love. On January 14, 1747, Joseph
Crownley knelt down before Wesley in his room in the
Horsefair in Bristol. Wesley, first placing a New Testament in his hand, said to him, "Take thou authority to
preach the gospel." This was not an ordination, but was
rather a recognition.[99] Adam Clarke was admitted in a
similar fashion in 1782, yet he did not consider himself ordained.[100] Wesley was convinced that the lay preachers
were well within the range of biblical and ecclesiastical
precedence to claim to have authority to preach. Wesley
viewed his granting of such authority as "analogous to
Christ's commissioning of the disciples, who were not of
the priestly class and not of the pharasaical order of the
day."[101]

This conviction of Wesley's is an important aspect of his
theology of the laity. It accounts for such statements as
the one previously quoted in which Wesley called for one
hundred preachers, caring not if they are clergy or laypersons.[102] Preaching, that first principle of Methodism, was
in the "will of God" and was not dependent in any way
upon ordination.[103] To stop preaching would be a tragic
neglect of persons needing Christ.[104] It should be noted
that Wesley did not limit the task of proclaiming God's
love to that portion of the laity known as lay preachers.
Furthermore, it should be noted that preaching was not
necessarily something done with pulpit, stained glass,
pews, and organ. "Preaching" was simply making known
the gospel of Christ to those who needed to know. This
task belonged to the whole church and emerged from the
nature of the Christian gospel itself.[105]

TODAY'S LAITY: A SENT PEOPLE

Like the laity of Wesley's day, the *laos* are not only trained; they are sent. Kraemer suggested that a theology of the laity must begin with the fact that "God is concerned about the world."[106] One writer, noting this fact, stated that every Christian needs two conversions: a conversion from the world to Christ, and a conversion to serve Christ in the world.[107] In John 17:18, Christ stated that he had sent the apostles into the world just as he had been sent into the world. What was true of the apostles was likewise true of the whole church. They were sent on an apostolic mission.[108] Clifford Wright diagrammed this in the following manner: first the Christians are called into the Church from the world—gathered,

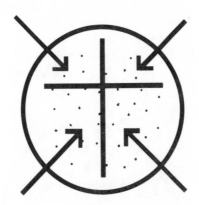

then the Christians are sent into the world—scattered to do the work of evangelism, bringing others into the life of the Church, and finally

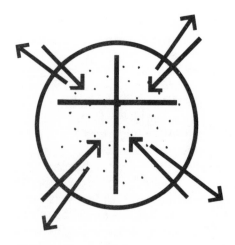

Christians are sent out, scattered to transform society. Christ sends out people not merely to extract others from the swamp (evangelism) but to clean up the swamp. The ministry of the *laos* is ultimately in the world.[109]

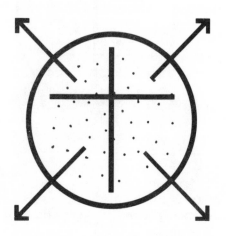

The Christian layperson is strategically placed in the world with an accessibility to it that is denied most clergy. It is in the arena of the world that the people of God can live out their calling. One author equated this task to an army that is equipped and disciplined and now awaits its assignment. The people of God exist to be sent on a mission.[110] In this "apostolic mission to the world,"[111] the goal is not merely to bring the world into the Church, but to be the Church, the *laos*, in the world.[112]

Many laity are unaware they are "sent" into ministry, in part because there is no "sending service" to validate their ministry. In contrast the ministry of clergy is validated by a "sending service." This is referred to as ordination. The ordination service is important because pastoral ministry is important. Since lay ministry is important it deserves the same kind of special event—a sending service. It is not necessary that the service be elaborate or that it be called ordination. It might be referred to as a commissioning service. The name is less important than the purpose: to assist laypersons in understanding who they are before God—his people sent into a world in his name. A sending service is one way of reminding laypersons of their ambassadorial status. It is a way of saying to them that their ministry is important. Having a sending service only for pastoral ministers, while omitting one for ministering laypersons, is to say that lay ministry is unimportant.

A sending service for laypersons may focus on their churchly ministries and be held for various groups such as Sunday school teachers. Or a sending service may validate their vocational call to ministry and thus recognize them by trades or professions. Or it might acknowledge their "calledness" in family commitments by recognizing their status within family units—fathers or mothers, for example. Although there are many creative ways of validating lay ministry through a commissioning service, the objective remains the same: to remind laity of who they are, by whom they are called, and for whom they are sent.

An equally important reason for having a commissioning service is that it underscores not only to whom one is sent but *by whom* one is sent. All of us, as we begin our ministries, are sent *by the church*, the visual representatives of Christ himself. So true is this that the visual representatives are actually called by the astounding title "the body of Christ." In other words, ministry is not solo flight. There is no lone ranger mentality in lay ministry, or any ministry. We as ministers (lay or clergy) are extensions of Christ, of his body. Ultimately, what makes ministry important is not whether it is lay or clergy. Ultimately, it is *his* ministry, the ministry of Christ. This perception of ministry makes our culturally imposed lay/clergy distinctions seem so unimportant! Ministry is done in his name, as a direct result of our joint life together in the Church. Thus a sending service is much more than a remainder of the world—*to* which we are sent. It is a remainder of the nature of the Church—*from* which we are sent. It is a reminder of our oneness in Christ. It is an affirmation of our interdependence upon one another. This is why it is so important for laity to understand not merely their "calledness," their "giftedness," their "trainedness," but also their "sentness." It is a necessary ingredient to a biblical understanding of the nature and mission of the Church.

The challenge to contemporary Christianity is to renew our commitment to the ministry of all Christians with the freshness, vigor, and creativity demonstrated by John Wesley two centuries before us. This renewal will occur to the extent that Wesley's vision for his lay assistants (generally known as lay preachers) becomes the conceptual foundation for our understanding of laity in general in the twentieth century.

Wesley's lay assistants were *called*. This was not a formal external call, but a yielding to the inward voice of the

Spirit. They were a Spirit-led people. They were expected to develop a sensitivity to spiritual concerns. Common villagers perceived themselves to be responders to the beckoning of their Creator.

Second, they were *gifted*. They were blessed people. In responding to the call of God upon their lives, they became recipients of God's gifts—gifts that prepared them for ministry. Wesley looked for certain gifts when selecting lay leaders. Possession of such gifts was not an excuse for self-exaltation, but was rather a reason for praising the Giver of these gifts.

Third, the lay preachers were *trained*. The training process involved diligence in both study and ministry activities. Whether reading on horseback to keep up with Wesley's rigorous assignments or inquiring about the spiritual conditions of the attenders of a class meeting, one's "tools" for ministry were forever being sharpened. They were a teachable people, always learning in the process of being more effectively trained and equipped for ministry.

Fourth, Wesley's lay helpers were a *sent* people. They were on a mission. There was a sense of urgency in their activities. One involved in such an important mission knew the value of each moment. One must so conduct one's life so as to be faithful to this mission.

A Wesleyan view of laity is one in which laity are seen with such seriousness. Contemporary Wesleyans and Christianity in general have much to learn from Wesley in many areas, but his theology of the place of laypersons in the Church is as profound and as practical as any. I hear the sounds of a revolution. I cannot see it yet. It's too far away. But I hear the sounds of it coming—a revolution that will liberate laity to new self-perception: called, gifted, trained, and sent. Pastors likewise will be liberated to a new self-perception in which they will understand their partnership in ministry with laity. Listen with me, and I think you will hear the sounds of the revolution, too.

Notes

1. William R. Cannon, "Accomplishments to Wesley's Death," *Methodism*, W. K. Anderson, ed. (New York: The Methodist Publishing House, 1947).
2. Accounts of the "first" lay preacher vary. Some suggest that the first lay preacher was Thomas Westell. Two other persons may have actually been first: Joseph Humphreys or John Cennick.
3. Stephen Charles Neill, "Britain," *The Layman in Christian History*, Stephen Neill and Hans-Reudi Weber, eds. (Philadelphia: The Westminster Press, 1963), p. 207.
4. Franz Hildebrandt, *Christianity According to the Wesleys* (London: Epworth Press, 1956), p. 48.
5. Douglas Blatherwick, *A Layman Speaker Again* (London: Epworth Press, 1964), p. 19.
6. David C. Shipley, "The Ministry in Methodism in the Eighteenth Century," *The Ministry in the Methodist Heritage*, Gerald O. McCulloh, ed. (Nashville: Board of Education, the Methodist Church, 1960), pp. 19-20.
7. John Wesley, *The Works of John Wesley*, Vol. VII, 1872, reprint ed. (Grand Rapids: Zondervan Publishing House, 1958), p. 76.
8. John Wesley, *The Journal of John Wesley*, Vol. V, Nehemiah Curnock, ed. (New York: Eaton and Mains, n.d.), p. 121.
9. Albert B. Lawson, *John Wesley and the Christian Ministry* (London: SPCK, 1963), p. 102.
10. *Works*, VIII, p. 467.
11. *Works*, VII, p. 276.
12. John Wesley, *Explanatory Notes Upon the Old Testament*, Vol. I, p. 821; *Letters*, VII, p. 372.
13. *Works*, VIII, p. 254; *Works*, VII, p. 412; *Works*, VIII, p. 224; *Letters*, II, p. 94; *Works*, VIII, p. 258; *Works*, VII, p. 278.
14. Alexander L. Boraine, "The Nature of Evangelism in the Theology and Practice of John Wesley" (Dissertation, Drew University, 1969), p. 248.
15. *Works*, VII, p. 411.

16. *Works*, VIII, p. 220.
17. *Letters*, VI, p. 272.
18. Shipley, "Methodism in the Eighteenth Century," p. 30.
19. *Wesley Hymn Book* (London: A Weckes & Co., reprint, 1958), no. 51. Italics are the author's.
20. John Wesley, *Standard Sermons of John Wesley*, Vol. II (London: Epworth Press, 1921), p. 504.
21. Paul G. Johnson, *Buried Alive* (Richmond, Va. John Knox Press, 1968), p. 34.
22. Howard Grimes, *The Church Redemptive* (Nashville: Abingdon Press, 1958), p. 59.
23. Francis O. Ayres, *The Ministry of the Laity* (The Westminster Press, 1962), p. 34.
24. Ayres, pp. 37-38.
25. Samuel E. Carruth, "John Wesley's Concept of the Church" (Th.D. dissertation, The Iliff School of Theology, Department of New Testament and Christian History, 1952), p. 124.
26. *Journal*, III, p. 307.
27. W. B. Pope, *The Methodist Local Preacher* (Lodon: Wesleyan Conference Office, 1879), p. 11.
28. Pope.
29. *Journal*, VI, p. 221.
30. *Journal*, V, p. 121.
31. Charles Atmore, *The Methodist Memorial* (London: Hamilton, Adams & Co., 1871), p. 282.
32. *Works*, VIII, p. 324.
33. C. K. Barrett, "The Ministry in the New Testament," *The Doctrine of the Church*, Dow Kirkpatrick, ed. (New York: Abingdon Press, 1964), p. 46.
34. Boraine, "The Nature of Evangelism," p. 261.
35. David Lyman Taylor, "Lay Leadership in Methodist Worship" (STM dissertation, Seabury-Western Theological Seminary, 1960), p. 20.
36. *Journal*, V, p. 26.
37. Hildebrandt, *Christianity According to the Wesleys*, p. 49.
38. *Laity Formation Proceedings of the Ecumenical Consultations, Gazzada, Italy, September 7-10, 1956* (Rome: World Council of Churches. Department of the Laity and the

Permanent Committee for International Congresses of the Lay Apostolate, 1966), p. 76.

39. Albert Outler, ed., *John Wesley* (New York: Oxford University Press, 1964), p. 135.

40. Boraine, "The Nature of Evangelism," p. 236.

41. Garth Lean, *John Wesley, Anglican* (London: Blanford Press, 1964), p. 59.

42. *Works*, VII, p. 270.

43. Frederick A. Norwood, "The Shaping of Methodist Ministry," *Religion in Life*, vol. 45, no. 3 (Autumn 1974), p. 350.

44. Albert C. Outler, "Pastoral Care in the Wesleyan Spirit," *Perkins Journal*, 25 (1) (Fall 1971), p. 5.

45. Wellman J. Warner, *The Wesleyan Movement in the Industrial Revolution* (Lodon: Longmans, Green and Co., 1930), p. 257.

46. Warner, p. 257.

47. Warner, p. 258.

48. Outler, "Pastoral Care," p. 7.

49. J. Ernest Rattenbury, *Wesley's Legacy to the World* (London: Epworth Press, 1928), p. 40.

50. Warner, *The Industrial Revolution*, p. 266.

51. W. H. Fitchett, *Wesley and His Century* (New York: Eaton & Mains, 1906), pp. 219-20.

52. Fitchett, p. 224.

53. Robert E. Chiles, "Values of the Class Meeting for Redemptive Life Today," in *Spiritual Renewal for Methodism*, Samuel Emerick, ed. (Nashville: Methodist Evangelistic Materials, 1958), p. 56; Herbert J. Cook, "Confirmation and the Lay Membership of the Church," *The Doctrine of the Church*, Dow Kirkpatrick, ed. (New York: Abingdon Press, 1964), pp. 118-19.

54. L. Rosser, *Class Meetings* (Richmond, Virginia: L. Rosser, 1855), p. 47.

55. Boraine, "The Nature of Evangelism," p. 249.

56. Rupert E. Davies, *Methodism* (London: Epworth Press, 1963), p. 54.

57. Hildebrandt, *Christianity According to the Wesleys*, p. 47.

58. Chiles, "Values of the Class Meeting," p. 64.

59. Eric W. Baker, *Fathers and Brethren* (London: The Epworth Press, 1959), p. 11.

60. Franklin Hamlin Littell, *The German Phoenix* (Garden City, N.J.: Doubleday & Co., 1960), pp. 145-46.
61. Haus Herman Walz, "The Lay Specialist or the Rediscovery of the Church," *The Student World*, vol. 43, no. 2 (Second Quarter, 1950), p. 133.
62. Philip S. Watson, "Ordination and the Ministry in the Church," *The Doctrine of the Church*, Dow Kirkpatrick, ed. (New York: Abingdon Press, 1964), p. 133.
63. Paul Crow, Jr., ed., *Consultation on Church Union, Digest of the Proceedings*, vol. IX (St. Louis: 1970), p. 13. As a further example, note the following: "The Christian community needs the special ministry which serves to coordinate and unite the different gifts in the community and to strengthen and enable the ministry of the whole people of God. . . . The minister, who participates, as every Christian does, in the priesthood of Christ, and of all the people of God, fulfills his particular priestly service in strengthening, building up and expressing the royal priesthood of the faithful"; *One Baptism, One Eucharist and a Mutually Recognized Ministry*, Faith and Order Paper No. 73, World Council of Churches (Geneva, Switzerland: 1975), pp. 33, 35.
64. Alden Kelly, *The People of God* (Greenwich, Conn.: The Seabury Press, 1962), pp. 33, 78; Blatherwick, *A Layman Speaks Again*, pp. 31, 34.
65. Howard Grimes, "The Vocation of the Laity," *Perkins School of Theology Journal*, vol. 13, no. 1 (Fall 1959), p. 17.
66. Note Emile Pin, "Some Sociological Thoughts on Ordination and the Authentication of the Ministry," *Study Encounter*, vol. 6, no. 4 (1970), p. 183.
67. Ronald Osborn, "The Ordination of the Presbyter," *Study Encounter*, vol. 6, no. 4 (1970), p. 194.
68. Mark Gibbs and T. Ralph Morton, *God's Frozen People* (Philadelphia: The Westminster Press, 1964), p. 159.
69. Neil Braun, *Laity Mobilized* (Grand Rapids: Eerdmans, 1971), pp. 107, 109; Hans-Ruedi Weber, *Salty Christians* (New York: The Seabury Press, 1963), pp. 31-32.
70. Rupert E. Davies, "An Ordination Charge," *Worship and*

Preaching, vol. 1, no. 5 (1970), p. 33.

71. Andre deRobert, "The Role of the Laity in the Life and Ministry of the Church," *Reprints from Laity No. 2-6* (Geneva: World Council of Churches, Department of Laity, 1962), p. 8.

72. John Zizioulas, "Ordination and Communion," *Study Encounter*, vol. 6, no. 4 (1970), p. 189.

73. *Laity Formation Proceedings*, p. 14.

74. Gibbs and Morton, *God's Frozen People*, p. 12. However, note Theodore O. Wedel, *Minister of Christ* (New York: Seabury Press, 1964), p. 25 for a defense of the term *priest* to be applied to clergy.

75. Taylor McConnell, *The Pastor as Educator* (Nashville: Board of Education of the United Methodist Church, 1972), p. 55.

76. Gordon Rupp, "The Pastoral Office in the Methodist Tradition," *Church Quarterly*, vol. 2, no. 2 (October 1969), p. 118.

77. Ayres, *The Ministry of the Laity*, p. 38; R. C. Moberly, *Ministerial Priesthood* (London: SPCK, 1969), p. xii; Odd Hagen, "The Ministry of the Church," *The Duke Divinity School Bulletin*, vol. 26, no. 2 (May 1961), p. 61.

78. Albert C. Outler, "The Pastoral Office," *Perkins School of Theology Journal*, vol. 16, no. 1 (Fall 1962), p. 5.

79. W. R. Pape and V. T. Kurien, "Helping Future Ministers to Train the Laity," *Laity*, no. 25 (July 1968), p. 35; William Robinson, *An Essay on a Lay Ministry* (London: J. Mason, 1832), p. 4; *Consultation on Church Union, Digest of the Proceedings*, vol. IV (Lexington, Ky.: 1965), p. 133; Blatherwick, *A Layman Speaks Again*, p. 33.

80. *Laity Formation Proceedings*, p. 23.

81. *Laity Formation Proceedings*, pp. 16-17; Gibbs and Morton, *God's Frozen People*, p. 119.

82. A. W. Kist, "Dynamics of Adult Education," *Laity*, no. 13 (July 1967), p. 23.

83. Arnold B. Come, "Lay Training in the U.S.A.," *Laity*, no. 19 (July 1965), p. 15.

84. *Laity Formation Proceedings*, p. 34.

85. Come, "Lay Training in the U.S.A.," p. 16.

86. See Gordon Bruns, *Laymen on the Frontiers* (Australia: Methodist Federal Board of Education, 1963), as a sample.

87. Note *Laity Formation Proceedings*, pp. 57ff.
88. Robert A. Raines, *New Life in the Church* (New York: Harper & Brothers, 1961), p. 103; Littell, *The German Phoenix*, pp. 144ff.; *Laity Formation Proceedings*, p. 39.
89. This phrase is borrowed from James Newby, who has authored a brochure titled "How to Turn Your Church into a Seminary," available from Yokefellow Institute, Earlham College, Richmond, Indiana.
90. J. C. M. Miller, "The Roots and Development of John Wesley's Organization," (Ph.D. thesis, University of Edinburgh, 1951), pp. 124-25, noting Robert Barclay (the younger), *The Inner Life of the Religious Societies of the Commonwealth* (London: 1876), p. 531, citing Dr. Waddington, *Congregational History*, first edition, n.d., p. 615.
91. Wesley, for example, did not advocate separate congregations. He did defend, however, having a second locale for preaching—the open field.
92. George H. Harwood, *The History of Wesleyan Methodism* (London: Whittaker, 1854), p. 67.
93. Cyril Eastwood, *The Priesthood of All Believers: An Examination of the Doctrine from the Reformation to the Present Day* (London: Epworth Press, 1960), p. 204.
94. John Whitehead, *The Life of the Rev. John Wesley, M.A.*, vol. II (Dublin: John Jones, 1805, 1806), pp. 498-99.
95. Hildebrandt, *Christianity According to the Wesleys*, p. 50.
96. J. Ernest Rattenbury, *The Evangelical Doctrines of Charles Wesley's Hymns* (London: Epworth Press, 1941), p. 325.
97. Rattenbury, *Evangelical Doctrines*, p. 322.
98. Lawson, *Wesleyan Local Preachers*, p. 262.
99. W. A. Goss, "Early Methodism in Bristol with Special Reference to John Wesley's Visits to the City," *W.H.S. Proc.* 19 (1934-5), p. 82. Note Wesley's Sermon, "The Ministerial Office."
100. A. Raymond George, "Ordination in Methodism," *London Quarterly & Holborn Review*, vol. 176 (1951), p. 157.
101. E. Herbert Nygren, "John Wesley's Changing Concept of the Ministry," *Religion in Life* 31 (1962), p. 272.
102. *Letters*, VI, p. 272.

103. *Works*, VII, p. 277; *Works*, XII, p. 90; *Letters*, III, p. 200.
104. *Works*, II (Oxford Edition), pp. 177-79; *Letters*, IV, p. 147; *Works*, VII, pp. 422-23.
105. Ronald G. Williams, "John Wesley's Doctrine of the Church" (Th.D. dissertation, Boston University School of Theology, 1964), p. 284.
106. Hendrik Kraemer, *A Theology of the Laity* (Philadelphia: The Westminster Press, 1958), p. 127.
107. Weber, *Salty Christians*, p. 49.
108. Ayres, *The Ministry of the Laity*, p. 50.
109. Clifford J. Wright, *Laymen Are Ministers* (Melbourne: Methodist Federal Board of Education, Methodist Church of Australia, 1961), pp. 12-13.
110. *All God's People* (Evanston, Ill.: General Board of the Laity, 1968), p. 43; Robert A. Raines, *Reshaping the Christian Life* (New York: Harper & Row, 1964), p. 52.
111. Hans-Ruedi Weber, *The Militant Ministry* (Philadelphia: Fortress Press, 1963), p. 33.
112. Raines, *Reshaping the Christian Life*, p. 34.

Everett E. Richey (Th.D., Iliff School of Theology), research librarian and professor of educational ministries, Azusa Pacific University

The Church:
Its Mission and Message

TWO IMPORTANT ISSUES have stood out in the history of the Church, namely, the questions of the nature of its message and the how of its mission. Without proper understanding and integration of these two, the Church ceases to be effective in its ministry.

To work toward a balance of these two components is to establish a check-and-balance system in which sane action is correlated with historical and eternal truth and in which the demands of the content and emphases of theoretical truth are tempered by ethical and moral action. There can be no sound proclamation of the message without the involvement of mission. Likewise, the execution of mission involves propagating and strengthening the components and tenets of the historic message of the faith.

GOD: OUR BEGINNING POINT

Evangelical Christians assume the revelation of God. This means that there are given elements—factors that have been made known and forever remain the same to humanity. By revelation, it is assumed, God has disclosed himself. This is personal and other than propositional. It may be categorized as "a divine visit, in which in his Son incarnate, God breaks in upon man's experience and makes himself known not merely by teaching something, but by doing something for man's salvation."[1]

God may be depicted as an actor playing out his role on the human scene.[2] In this context, "God is what God does."[3] He acted in creation and continues to act in bringing about growth, redemption, and the final consummation of humanity. In history, especially in the biblical record, we perceive God at work "both to will and to work for good pleasure" (Phil. 2:13). He is not one who forever ceased from activity on any given day but one who acts in the arena of the natural, the social, the environmental, the emotional, the moral, and what is referred to as the historical social-cultural scene where changes and adaptation are constantly taking place.

The concept of God is affected by one's assumptions and world-view. If God is one who is active in this world, then he cannot be a being separated from, above and beyond the world. In essence, he actively seeks to bring all aspects and dimensions of human essence and experiential life into an integrated unity, a wholeness that becomes qualitatively spiritual. R. C. Miller states:

> When we begin to understand how God works as a process of integration, as a principle which supplies structure to the natural, social, historical moral and spiritual orders, and as that power which sustains and transforms human beings in their spiritual quest for full lives, we have the basic data which provide the clues for our understanding of God's nature.[5]

God is everywhere! This is the message of the ages. Judaic and Christian proclamation declare that God is intimately involved in people's lives, seeking progressively to reveal himself and to affect their behavior redemptively. Any assumption that removes God from the human scene limits what God can do. To picture God as a being intimately linked with the world process, the change and growth in human nature, enhances learning. To separate the creature from the Creator, even in the act of rebellion by the created, is to limit the nature of what was created as well as the role of the Creator. "God is what God does." He is involved in human life. The learning process, the aspects and roles of ministry, the interpretation of the message, in each and every generation, must be couched in assumptions that make for integration of life and spiritual maturity. The end result must be one that is in keeping with the nature of humanity, which forever carries the imprint of *spirit* as a result of the creative work of God.

The Church, the object of our concern here, exists because of God. He designed it and brought it into existence. Christ said, "I will build my church and the powers of death shall not prevail against it" (Matt. 16:18). As members of the Church, we share a common ministry, a fellowship of learners and doers wherein we experience one another as creatures of God and the power and influence of God operative in and through the created order of the universe. To eliminate the natural or to minimize its significance is to shortchange the role of God in human lives. The arena of God's activity is his created order. All dimensions of human nature must be considered in the construction and interpretation of philosophy of ministry. The context in which persons live and the nature of their being are paramount to an enunciation of theory, philosophy, and content of the theological message.

THE PRIMACY OF MISSION

When one holds the previously described perspective, the fact that God is more and other than any given interpretation of his being, any theological dogma, it is essential to enunciate clearly the role of Christian mission and to understand its connection with the message of the gospel.

Mission arises out of people's understanding of God and their responses to his imperatives to them and the Church. In the beginning of biblical revelation we have God in the garden giving humanity dominion over what was created. Humanity is to "fill the earth and subdue it" (Gen. 1:28). Consideration of this primal mission, or cultural mandate, is necessary for any understanding of the role and function of the Church in society. The imperative, the commission, that came to Adam was one of responsible action, a demand that he relate to and manage his environment. He was to be an administrator, not to be separate from it or form a monastic cell, but rather to penetrate his world and bring nature into subjection.

It is in this context that we assert the primacy of mission over message while not nullifying the power or impact of message. In the Bible we note that "God so loved the world that he gave his only Son, that whosoever believes in him should not perish but have eternal life" (John 3:16). While believers are urged not to conform to the world (Rom. 12:2), it is clear that God sent his Son to redeem the world, that the Incarnation is central to the life and work of the Church, and that it typifies the attitude of God toward the world.

Consequently, the Church is to take its cue in its ministry and message from the central act of God in his relationship to and love of the world. The Incarnation is far more than symbol or dogma. It depicts "an immensity of love and service beyond the wildest dreams of man."[6] As Robert Paul continues, the New Testament writers

proclaim a divine love and compassion that elects the human race into fellowship with itself and into service for the rest of creation, and are saying that this fellowship and service are really not two different things but two parts of a single whole because they arise within the very nature of God himself. The 'glory' and the 'lordship' about which the gospel speaks are never symbols of status to be flaunted and exploited before others, but they are manifested as they were in Jesus through obedience to the Father's will so that this creation may become what it was intended to be.[7]

The Church's mission is to proclaim God's love. This love must not be lost sight of in the systemization of dogma or the adoption of practical programs. Theology is essentially a human enterprise. While it is a needful one, it has no priority rights over relationship with or value derived from one's experience with God.

Mission may best be described as the work of God in and upon people that motivates them to action on his behalf and the welfare of people. It is more and other than any methodology. While methods are essential, mission in and of itself is the active pulse-beat of a God-inspired motivation expressed in a Spirit-endued believer or community destined to affect the world for God; or one may say, it is the power of the Holy Spirit producing individual and communal activities. From the dawn of human history and through biblical, historical and modern periods, God has acted in and upon the conscience, spirit, and life of individuals. The result has been growth, a change for the better, and spiritual maturity both in individuals and community life.

Mission is closely related to and yet may be declared more and other than *praxis*, a term used to describe the methodology of integrating the components of a Christian learning experience. Some elements that are entailed in *praxis* are listed by Thomas H. Groome: (1) present action, (2) critical reflection, (3) Dialogue, (4) the Story, and (5) the Vision that arises from the Story.[10] In each of these the controlling perspective is shared experience, dialogue, and confrontation with Story and Vision that calls for response and responsibility. Strong emphasis, therefore, is placed on teachers and learners and their roles in furthering the cause of Christ and reaching *telos* faithfulness to the Christian message. While much may be said for methodology and the integration of all components of a learning experience, mission involves more than human responsibility. There is a God who continually acts to communicate to humanity. That communication may come via history, tradition, community, or perhaps direct personal revelation. God is not limited to any one theoretical formulation of a human-ward approach to learning.

Theological understanding and practical application, however, are essential tasks coupled with religious experience and Christian character. The sought-after integrity of the Church's life and work involves the task of integrating mission and message. To separate the two from each other or to overemphasize one to the detriment of the other is to lose balance and perspective. To confound mission and message with method and theology is to lower the perspective of spiritual vision to the mundane science of human enterprise. The revelation of God to persons produces the sense of supremacy of mission and endues persons with a message. The Church must grapple with these essential core concepts—of mission and message—and the subordinate roles of theology and methodology if it is to prosper and achieve its task in the world.

The Authenticity of Message

The revelation of God in Christ, his birth, his ministry, his crucifixion, his resurrection, and his life-giving quality could never have been perceived and understood by reason alone. It is revelation, specific in type, directed to the inner life of persons, to an inner self that perceives in

manners transcendent to the rational mind and far more
personal. Paul, in writing to the Corinthian church, stated,
"What no eye has seen, nor ear heard, nor the heart of
man conceived, what God has prepared for those who love
him, God has revealed to us through the Spirit. For the
Spirit searches everything, even the depths of God" (1
Cor. 2:9-10). The authenticity of the message stems from
the character of the revealer, God. Its credibility rests with
God. To affirm it, on our part, is to perceive and receive it,
to act upon it, to absorb it into one's character and life. In
and of itself, the revelation of God—the message—need
not be defended. It is its own defense. Apologetics, the
science of the defense of the faith, has its place but can
never do the work that revelation does in the soul of persons. Worship is the response of persons to God, but the
science of worship is only an explanation of what occurs,
not the act of worship. Service to one's fellow persons is
admirable. The "how-to" books of evangelism and education are needful, but the sciences of evangelism and education are neither evangelism nor education but only explanations of the art. The work of the Holy Spirit, the revealing of God to the souls of persons is an experience that
carries the authenticity of God's message far deeper than
reason or intellect attempts or designs.

Harry Emerson Fosdick has affirmed,

> One of the profoundest motives that can grip man's heart is
> the conviction that he is a fellow-worker with the Divine. To
> feel that there is a great cause, on behalf of which God himself
> is concerned, and, the furtherance of which we can be God's
> instruments and confederates, is the most exhilirating outlook
> of life conceivable.[9]

The historic Christian faith asserts that God's message to
humanity came *via* revelation. While revelation is the act
of God in communication, theology is humanity's interpretation of that message and its relationship to God. To confuse these two concepts or to make them identical robs

revelation of its power and theology of its usefulness. To perceive revelatory experiences and to interpret them is most productive and worthwhile, or, as Fosdick says, "exhilarating."

Theology is a human enterprise, the science that interprets God's communiqué to persons. Message is God's communiqué to humanity. It is primary; theology is secondary. The first projects the authenticity of God; the second, the authenticity, creativity, and fallibility of humanity.

Human experience accrues a mixture of values through experience and relationship with God and persons. Some of these values are primary; others are secondary. Theology attempts to interpret our experiences, systematize our thought, construct concepts and paradigms, and focus our minds on *truth*. Above and beyond this "truth" stands an eternal God who constantly reveals himself to persons through word and deed. The Bible stands as a record of that revelation. In and beyond that Bible, God's message is authentic; his Word is everlasting.

THE DANGERS OF PAROCHIALISM

The Church is not immune from the tendency to parochialize its message and/or its mission. Given a people, a structure, a culture and duration of time, more often than not parochialism emerges in one form or another with varying degrees of intensity. Form, in both message and mission, supplants function and purpose, and when this happens we have institutionalized Christianity in a given culture. This institutionalization, being a precise cultural expression of the faith, separates itself to degrees with other cultural expressions of the faith, thus becoming parochialized.

The ability of a community of believers to move beyond

its parochialized nature depends upon openness to its mission and the historic message of the faith. The degree to which newness emerges in a group, to which hope and anticipation are experienced depends upon a group's ability to move beyond its cultural mode and incorporate new expressions of the faith and perform its mission in new and dynamic patterns compatible with itself and the world around it.

No group of believers is immune from tendencies of parochialism. Cardinal Suenens, writing on the necessity of *pentecost* and the power of the Holy Spirit in the Church, states that there are two major classes of devotees to the faith: the "traditionalists" and the "progressives." The traditionalists are those who place primary emphasis on the Church, its hierarchial or governmental stance, its liturgical or worship patterns, its theological expressions of the faith or its canonical laws. In each case there is some aspect of form that often emerges where legalism demands conformity and the spirit of the Law is lost through emphasis on the letter of the Law (2 Cor. 3:6). The progressives, on the other hand, have little regard for the "established church" and seek to discover the communal expression of the faith through the relational dimension. The Church, to them, becomes a gathering of people involved in a "search."[10]

Evangelicals, with many others, have overemphasized (1) the supernatural, (2) institutionalized truth in creedal statements, (3) codified morality, (4) overregulated ministries. While it is necessary to work on the issues raised in the preceding discussion, at the same time it is supremely important how they are matured and expressed in the life and work of the Church. Aberrations of a component hinder; normal expressions help. Ideals that are worthy may become abnormalities that detract. We must detect the differences between the normal and those things that are malfunctions in the life and ministry of the Church.

The supporting historical arguments, used by denominations, scholars, and leaders to substantiate the existence of the Church and lend credibility to its structure and work, have, according to Robert S. Paul, also lacked credibility and are questioned. These, he points out, are apostolic succession, biblical restorationism, and spiritual pragmatism.[11] Apostolic succession fails to guarantee the fruits of the Spirit, which are the distinctive marks of the Church of Jesus Christ.[12] Biblical restorationism blatantly denies the unity of the Church when it calls for a litrugy and a polity, based on wrong assumptions of the Bible, in exact models as existed in the New Testament, not allowing for the expression of Christian unity and love. Spiritual pragmatism, on the other hand, emphasizes the practical at the expense of the gospel and sound theory. These and other aberrations cause polarization and bring about a parochialism that is unhealthy. In each case the gospel and its power are voided by undue emphasis on secondary matters.

Evangelicals, with their emphasis upon the supernatural grace of God, have not escaped the forces of social formation and the tendencies to parochialize that characterize all social organisms. The biblical motif of organism, so descriptive of Paul's doctrine of the Church (1 Cor. 12), leads to institutionalism unless counteracted with growth in the community of the Church. The resulting effects are rigidity, hierarchial structures, positional authority, crystallization of message, and the establishment of boundaries that limit fellowship, work, and ministry in the Church.

To *bond* mission and message requires that the biblical motif of *covenant* be emphasized along with the *organism* motif. While *organism* tends to an organizational heirarchy, *covenant* expresses a relationship between God and persons. The two motifs balance each other. Both are components of the biblical message affecting the life, structure, and ministry of the Church. If properly integrated, the Church does not legalize its message, codify its behavioral patterns, or rank organizational structure above life and work. As R. C. Miller states, "Theology in the background: grace and faith in the foreground."[13]

Paul, in writing to the Corinthians, says that God "has made us competent to be ministers of a new covenant, not in a written code but in the Spirit; for the written code kills, but the Spirit gives life" (2 Cor. 3:6). A code is a sign of parochialism; standards are goals projected with expectancy for response and behavior. Codes are enforced by legalism; standards are projected with courtesy and love.

PHILOSOPHY OF MINISTRY

The authenticity and vitality of the Church lie in its life-giving quality. To appeal to anything other than the authority of God is to place too little emphasis on the role God plays in one's growth and undue emphasis on secondary matters. To argue that one's creed, denomination, theology, or organizational system is biblically based and hence spiritually superior to all others is to fail the ethic of Christlikeness. The ministry of the Church is to be carried out in the reality of the revelation of God in Christ. This reality is experiential in the best sense of the term, calling for bonds of love and unity in the Church. It takes due cognizance of biblical theology, methodological factors, human nature, and goal orientation.

God is the beginning point.

To argue this is, for the Christian, to recognize the centrality of the Incarnation and its relationship to ministry, theology, and ecclesiology.

All this is from God, who through Christ reconciled us to himself and gave us the ministry of reconciliation; that is, in

Christ God was reconciling the world to himself, not counting their trespasses against them, and entrusting to us the message of reconciliation (2 Cor. 5:18).

In verse 20, Paul continues, "So we are ambassadors for Christ, God making his appeal through us." The ministry of reconciliation originates in God. This indicates no separation of the secular and the sacred. Neither does it indicate, for Paul or anyone else, special prerogatives because of one's position as an ambassador for Christ. Nor is the Incarnation to be considered a one-time historical event, but the continuing presence of God in the Christian community, wherein exists the presence and power of the Holy Spirit and of Christ to transform character and establish the Kingdom.

It is with this essential theology of the Incarnation that we should begin any consideration of the philosophy of the Church's ministry. Unless primary consideration is given to the role of God in human life and redemption, emphases placed on organization, structure, goals, and priorities become void of significance. For instance, emphasis placed on whether we are democratic, papal, presbyterial, or episcopal can lead us to a form of godliness that lacks the power of mission. Mission must always outdistance message; purpose and goal pull people beyond mere intellectual analysis to the level of experiential trust, to a hope in Christ that motivates them to action. This is where mission sanctifies the content of message and where both mission and message become one in purpose and goal.

A clear example of this is found in the life of Christ. Having chosen twelve disciples, he schooled them in the crucible of life's experience. Many of their prime lessons grew out of experiential involvements. Whether it was an involvement on mission or within the community of Christ, the Twelve were always caught in the grip of fulfilling life's goals and the consequent maturity that came as a result of confrontation with the demands of gospel and mission upon their lives. Jesus never established a plan of institutional governance for the Church. His emphasis in ministry was ethical and ideal, leaving secondary matters to be worked out in the cultural circumstances of oncoming generations. One author writes,

> It was Jesus' habit in teaching simply to hold up before men great ethical and spiritual principles which, having heard, they were to then apply to themselves. . . . It was the testimony of Jesus' early hearers that he "taught not as the scribes," and time and again throughout his ministry we find him setting himself in open and vigorous opposition to the legalistic ways of the Pharisees, who by their petty prescriptions for the regulation of human conduct were binding upon men "burdens grievous to be borne."[14]

The impact of this is that Jesus' ministry was first and foremost one of meeting people head-on with the demands for personal commitment to ideals of purity, righteousness, and honesty. When those ideals are accepted, individuals become one with God and are thereby able to enter into service to others free of the bondage of human molds and organizational patterns.

This is not to say that patterns of organization for the Church and its work need not be established. The point is that Jesus left such structural matters to each generation. To have freedom in this area is the right of every generation and of those who choose to work together in a community of believers and combine their efforts in ministry. The following are general principles operative in this area that give direction to the Church's ministry.

The Church's primay goals are experiential life's values.

Christ's church was established to meet the needs of people. "The sabbath was made for man, not man for the sabbath" (Mark 2:27). At no place does institutional stance, human authority, the rights of positional leaders, or the force of philosophical or theological systems have jurisdictional authority over the needs of humanity. These things exist to serve persons.

Insight arises through experience. Moses and the burning bush, Daniel in the lion's den, Peter walking on the water, Mary at the tomb—these and others all point to the fact that learning takes place in the crucible of experience. Experience first, concept second is the general rule. Through suffering, torment, trial, and confrontation one comes to know the value of victory, growth, and persistence, as well as the ascertainment of spiritual grace and maturity.

To be profitable, experience must have qualitative integrity. It is sought after directly by persons, contaminated by others, and fashioned in humanity's own image. Nevertheless, wholesome and qualitative experience is food for the soul, a stimulus to the emotions and liberation to the mind. It can provide a stimulus for action, challenge to fellowship, and a drive to motivation. In and of itself it becomes the medium through which the incarnation of Christ in the life-blood of the Church becomes reality. Without it, the message of the Church is lifeless.

The relationships of believers are built, not given.

Christ said, "I will build my church, and the powers of death shall not prevail against it" (Matt. 16:18). The community of faith is one built from the raw material of human individuality. Christ took twelve men, educated them, and trained them to become apostles. The gifts and talents of those men became channeled in avenues of service that enlisted other people into a community of concerned individuals.

This community has been viewed from many perspectives. Culturally speaking, it is a subculture in a community, national, or world culture. Psychologically speaking, it is a society of people who are conditioned to a mental perspective that incorporates Christian concerns. Sociologically speaking, it is one of many groups who commit themselves to objectives that assist individuals in personal and communal needs. Historically, it is an organization that stems from the ministry of Christ and continues to exist and minister to human needs.

Relationships are built. They do not exist by nature or come about by any other means than through human response and choice. Spiritually, the Church consists of humans who are affected culturally, psychologically, sociologically, and historically, and yet who are openly permeated by the divine and the eternal. The relationships of believers are built, not given.

Institutions are established as channels of service.

Institutions are channels of service. They exist to assist individuals to help other individuals. In institutional life and work, organizational channels direct the flow of help to those in need. The Church, as compared to the institution, is the body of believers—in Paul's terminology, the body of Christ. It is an organism in which each organ serves the total body. Institutional life, on the other hand, is a format of offices, boards, committees, and commissions with structured and delegated job descriptions. One cannot be identical with the other, but both are needed for the furtherance of cooperative work in the Church.

The Church itself is a servant community.

While institutions are established to provide channels for service, the Church by nature is a servant community. As members of that community, we seek to bring ourselves and others into conformity to the ideals and standards of the Christian life.

And his gifts were that some should be apostles, some prophets, some evangelists, some pastors and teachers, to equip the saints for the work of ministry, for building up the body of Christ, until we all attain to the unity of the faith and of the knowledge of the Son of God, to mature manhood, to the measure of the stature of the fullness of Christ (Eph. 4:11-13).

Through the Incarnation and the continuing presence of Christ in the Church, God calls the Church to become God's divine agency in the world for the redemption of humankind and the establishment of his kingdom in the lives and hearts of people. As such the Church is a servant community to bring the institutional life and organizational work subject to the mission of the Church and the message of the gospel. Herein, a tension often emerges between the Church as kingdom and as institution or organization. Such tension has been known to usurp the energies of the Church, rob the cause of mission, and crystallize the message.

The Church, as divine agency, is called upon to exert its influence and power to mold human behavior into a body of believers. In Jeremiah, the potter threw away a vessel that was not fit. In Jesus' ministry he stated that old wineskins could not hold new wine.

Theology guides the Church.

The practical value of a doctrine, creed, or theology lies in its positive effects upon lives. The purpose and function of theology is to provide guidance for individuals and groups seeking fulfillment in spiritual maturity.

Theology is *the science of God.* As such it depicts God at work in the world, seeking to redeem, purify, and perfect his people, the Church.

If the Church has the biblical revelation of God at its center, its essential task cannot be other than to proclaim this God in word, deed, and presence. It is not a structureless society of spiritual individualists, for the form it adopts is integral to its proclamation and should point to the nature of this God both in its institutions and in the way they operate: what the Church *is* is just as much a part of its total witness as what it proclaims from the pulpit or manifests in social service.[15]

Every generation sees the Church both in historical and current perspectives. Historically, the biblical portrayal of the Church is central, at least during the first century. Currently, the pattern rises out of the prevailing culture and the locale in which it is found. In either case, the Church is not a group of unidentified individuals, and is not *structureless*. In Biblical terminology, it is one body (Eph. 4:4), a peculiar people (1 Pet. 2:9), the true vine (John 15:5), the household of God (Eph. 2:19), lively stones (1 Pet. 2:5), and a spiritual house (1 Pet. 2:5). In each case there is structure, order, and unity in the functioning of the Church as a living organism. It identifies its members, engages in mission, adopts patterns of operation, delegates responsibilities, builds programs, evaluates progress, and works to achieve its objectives.

As a structured society, it integrates the interpretation of its nature and the organism itself with its practical work. To overemphasize one of these without regard to the other is to rob the Church of both message and mission. Doctrine overemphasized becomes lifeless, making the gospel of no effect. The "practical" overemphasized leaves the Church anemic, without the essence and power of the Word. Ministry includes both doctrine and practice; the Word lends itself to both concept and practice.

What the Church is (mission) is just as much a part of its witness as what it proclaims (message). These words point to the significance of being. The Church in its ministry recognizes the reality of valid experience as indicative of the work of God in and among God's people. As Paul expressed it, "For it is the God who said, 'Let light shine out of darkness,' who has shone in our hearts to give the light

of the knowledge of the glory of God in the face of Christ"
(2 Cor. 4:6). He continues in verse 7, "But we have this
treasure in earthen vessels, to show that the transcendent
power belongs to God and not to us."

This leads to the recognition of two facts; namely, the
experiential involvement and the theological interpreta-
tion(s) of Christian experience. It is safe to say that God
outdistances and outranks our interpretation of reality; but
that interpretation as such points to reality. The greatest
idolatry in the world is the attempt to capture God in one's
thought forms. Yet, thought and concepts are necessary as
ideas and symbols to express our belief and concept of
God. Theology, in this sense, becomes a guide for individuals and the Church.

Theology grow out of experience. Old and New Testament records and beliefs grew out of God's revelation to
persons and out of their experience as terrestrial beings
who contemplated God. To make theology the queen of
the sciences and to resist any reinterpretation of the data
of God-person relationship is to stifle faith, hinder growth,
and make the Church a depository of dogma rather than a
ministering organism communicating the gospel by word
and deed. Theology may be defined as "the-truth-about-
God-in-relation-to-man."[16] It guides the Church in understanding God, itself, and ministry.

Education enriches the Church.

Evangelism and education as facets of the Church's
ministry are essentially complimentary. In essence they
are so related that they should never be thought of as distinct or unrelated functions. There is education for evangelism and evangelism that necessitates education for the
sake of nurture and Christian maturity. Each of these may
be defined as facets or dimensions of the one task of the
Church, which is to communicate the gospel in such a

manner as to involve individuals in decision making that leads to Christian integrity and maturity.

John R. W. Stott states that "evangelism may and must be defined only in terms of *the message.*"[17] It is not, he states, to be defined in terms of recipients, results, or methods. Any one of these adulterates the biblical message if emphasis is placed on them rather than the Good News. Recipients do not have to receive it; results do not have to occur; methods are not primary. Evangelism is first and foremost the proclamation of the gospel, for it is the power of God unto salvation.

Education, on the other hand, is closely related. The Great Commission emphasizes that we are to teach disciples of all nations to observe all things that Jesus commanded. The biblical concept of *didaskontes,* here translated "teaching," carries with it an ethical requirement to produce understanding, to bring about achievement of insight. Yet, it is more. It is life itself, maturity, integrity. To teach is to educate, to make whole, to produce motivation, decision, and results. It is not for intellectual aggrandisement alone, but for total personality and spiritual development.

The biblical concept of dialogue adds example and understanding to the role of education in the mission of the Church. From the prophets to Christ to Paul and the apostles, God speaks to human beings. Always and ever the point of the conversation is for persons to hear and to act responsibly with God's instruction. The freedom of persons is not removed. Persons are partners, co-workers with God (2 Cor. 6:10). One shares responsibility in communication and results.

Dialogue, thus, is a conversation in which all parties, whether God or persons, take seriously individuals and subjects under consideration. Decisions made in this framework lead to growth and maturity. Education, thereby, involves dialogue. The process and example of

God as communicator to persons establishes guidelines for human communication and dialogue. It adds to the significance of education as a most important factor in fostering spiritual maturity and enrichment in the life of the community of the Church.

The purpose of education is to buildup the Church in love. In this context Paul states that the gifts are to lead persons to "the stature of the fullness of Christ" (Eph. 4:13). Every gift produces enrichment of the total body. Each gift, unique in itself, supplies spiritual nourishment, enriching some segment of the Church's life and fellowship. Whether it is evangelizing, teaching, helping, administering, witnessing, or whatever the deed may be, the whole organism is profited when such deeds are done in his name and for his sake.

The Church transcends culture.

The assertion here is that there are distinctive features in the organism of the Church that are not determined by the culture in which it operates. Culture is temporal and pluralistic; the Church is spiritual and eternal is dimension and hence not bound by the deterministic forces of this world's societies.

It is true that the church exists in culture(s), that it affects and is affected by culture, and that it creates its own culture. Yet, at the same time the Church is the church triumphant and not just the church terrestrial. The eternal, spiritual, and qualitative aspects of the Church are built and exist due to the operative forces of divine grace. The Church is and becomes an agency that transcends culture while at the same time it is operative within and upon culture.

Evangelicals must not be bound by a dualism that sets church against culture or identifies one with the other. The Church is a divine agency, a colony of heaven operative within the arena of the world but with hoped-for results in individual and social transformation. There can be no dualism that identifies the world with the devil and the Church with God. The creative force of God is operative and central where Christ's lordship is dominant. The psalmist declares, "The earth is the Lord's and the fullness thereof, the world and those who dwell therein" (24:1).

Evangelicals have been adamant at times in asserting the sinfulness of humanity and, at the same time, the responsibility of humanity. While grace is the force of God at work in the life of persons, responsibility for human sinfulness rests with humankind. Persons thus become co-creators with God, working cooperatively within culture for a life that reaches above culture. We seek to make our culture the best possible culture, an expression of the divine within culture.

The world therefore is the arena for the leavening influences of divine grace. The responsibility of Christianizing a community rests with the people of God, with people attuned to the spiritual arena, to a world beyond or what one may call a larger world—a frame of reference inclusive of life that is and is to be.

Religion is operative upon culture and culture upon religion. As evangelicals, we maintain that the influences of the gospel transform culture, making it amenable to the ministry and work of Christ. Culture never becomes the church, for by divine prerogatives the church that Christ built stands supremely, consisting only of those who have exercised faith in Christ's redeeming grace. By and of itself its nature is established for eternity, for "the powers of death will not prevail against it" (Matt. 16:18).

Within the world, the Church is the "salt of the earth" (Matt. 5-13), "a city set on a hill" (Matt. 5:14), a leaven in a lump. Whatever our weaknesses and our shortcomings, the Church remains the body of Christ, existing within culture, yet transcendent to culture, a preserving creative force at work for the good of humankind, destined to remain eternal in the heavens.

The tension that exists between the eternal and spiritual dimension of the Church and its cultural context and abode calls for a ministry involved in struggle, a theology of struggle, in growth and conquest. It is only through struggle and conquest, which forever confront the Church and its ministry, that the people of God become strong in their faith and their works.

Ministry is multifaceted.

The earthly and the spiritual, the individual and the social are revealing of the many facets facing the ministry of the Church. While the tasks are great and the methods varied in the Church's ministry, the message remains forever stamped on its heart. To be human was not too low a position for the Son of God to assume. The Incarnation remains forever the norm and example of what ministry is all about. And, just as the Incarnation is there, so the cross depicts the extent to which ministry goes to procure its goal and achieve results.

These twin factors—the Incarnation and the cross—are in essence the "content" of the Church's ministry expressed by whatever methodologies it chooses to use in reaching the hearts and minds of persons. Whether it be education, evangelism, counseling, preaching, missionary endeavor, youth work, children's ministries, or any other, the message of the gospel is Christ incarnated in the lives of people, expressing himself in and through them for their betterment and his glory.

In an age of humanism, with secularism rampant, everyone needs to be made aware again of a divine Christ who mediates grace to the heart of the individual. While there are programs that build societies that flourish and civilizations that endure for a time, Christ establishes a kingdom that lasts forever. The tensions between secularism and Christianity, humanism and God, are surmounted in an evangelical ministry in which God and person work together. God is not set against this world, but is involved in it. He designed it and continues to work within it. The creative forces God has structured in the universe may be relied upon to assist the ministry of salvation and personal and social enrichment.

The Christian educator, in harmony with sound principles of learning, leans heavily upon learning theory but is impelled by the nature of his or her mission to move beyond secular and human insight and correlate the message, the historic revelation of God, into mission. The manner in which this is done is conditioned by the determinants of the context in which the educator works.

The necessity of coming to grips with the incarnation of Christ and its continuing effects in the life of the church raises questions of great proportions. How are doctrine and revelation correlated with learning theory? How do we integrate content and process? What role does context play in formulating one's faith? Is reinterpretation of the message necessary in every generation. Does reinterpretation of the message sacrifice content? How does one first learn the message? What does it mean that the message was "once delivered unto the saints"? These and other questions formulate a core of concern as the Church faces its mission. There are no simple answers. The work of the ministry is multifaceted.

Message and mission are complimentary.

The problem of integrating message and mission is not new. In Matthew 22:1-14, Jesus tells of a man who appeared at a feast without a wedding garment. This man represented the Jewish-Christian community whose historic concern was for morals and conduct based on law. In

Luke 14:16-24, where the parable was originally recorded, a second invitation was issued—an attempt to get the response of outsiders. In the parables there are two emphases—the proper behavior of one who knows what to do and believe and the concern in reaching the outsider. This chapter has been concerned in how these two emphases—the Christian message (moral and theological) and mission (outreach and evangelism)—are properly balanced and integrated into a unity in the life and work of the Church.

For centuries the Church has been taught to believe. This often results in no more than mental assent to dogma. Herein one can accept without analysis, giving mental assent without confirmation or knowledge of the bases of action. This is nothing other than the pharisaism that Jesus objected to when he declared, "If a blind man leads a blind man, both will fall into a pit" (Matt. 5:14).

The necessity is to know where we're going, what we're doing, and upon what our action is based. More is expected than the transference of beliefs from one generation or person to another. Evangelicalism at its best calls for the development of personal and individual growth. This necessitates a theology of education where the foundational factors for learning are utilized in mission as well as theological tenets. To fail to do so is to jeopardize personal and spiritual growth. Learning occurs only when it becomes individualized and adapted to personal and social growth.

Psychologists have provided insight into ways in which growth and learning occur. To lift these insights to the spiritual dimension and integrate them into a philosophy of ministry is a must for evangelicals.

Christian education cannot use the raw findings from other fields. It asks educational questions of the other fields and receives answers in noneducational terms. Theory of Christian education builds on the evidences from various sources, but it exercises the right of prior jurisdiction for the reorganization of the material.[18]

It is safe to say that we learn our biblical convictions as we learn anything else. There is no separate and distinct approach in learning for a Christian. All learning occurs on a personal level where one exists.

It is true, however, that where Christianity is concerned the dimensions and context of learning are enlarged to take into consideration the whole field of spiritual experiences and the total message of the gospel. This makes for a philosophy of ministry that is all-inclusive and a range of thought that outdistances any psychological theory of learning.

Theology, thus, contributes to learning and learning theorists contribute to the teaching of theology. To assert the supremacy of one over the other is to nullify the possibilities of learning. One moves from the content of the gospel to confrontation wherein people respond in faith or from personal need to fulfillment through meditation of the grace of God. The latter is discovery before any thorough analysis of the Bible or the message of the gospel. In such cases it may be declared that the grace of God is operative before any significant formulation of dogmatic truths. One then may move either from theological concerns to learning and mission or from learning to theological concerns and mission; there is no set pattern to which all learning conforms.

The gospel and mission are the two *content* areas for learning. An individual is called into confrontation with God. This is fundamental to evangelicalism. The Word of God, the message, confronts the learner. The learner responds. The degree of response is conditioned by one's openness to intellectual and spiritual understanding. Insight and perspective build only through comprehension. Learning is more than rational. It is spiritual and personal. This involves the total personality—mind, body, and soul. Anything else is short of the goal.

Message and mission must forever remain complimentary, being servants one to another. Theology, distinguished from message, is systemized, conceptual patterns of truth. Revelation grants to Christian tradition given elements that remain forever true in any and all circumstances. The body of knowledge gained over the years is accumulated and shared through truth statements. Systematized and organized, it becomes known as theology. To distinguish between theology and message, the essential meaning of revelation, is a must for the Church in every generation. How this is done is essential. It was Jesus who declared, "If any man's will is to do his will, he shall know whether the teaching is from God or whether I am speaking on my own authority" (John 7:17). In this, Jesus declares that the basis of knowledge is experiential learning. And, evangelicals agree.

Notes

1. John Lawson, *An Evangelical Faith for Today* (Nashville: Abingdon Press, 1972), p. 26.
2. Randolph Crump Miller, *Biblical Theology and Christian Education* (New York: Charles Scribner's Sons, 1956), pp. 16ff.
3. Randolph Crump Miller, *This We Can Believe* (New York: Hawthorn Books, Inc., 1976), p. 52.
4. Miller, p. 52.
5. Miller, p. 52.
6. Robert S. Paul, *The Church in Search of Itself* (Grand Rapids: William B. Eerdmans Publishing Company, 1972), p. 309.
7. Paul, p. 309.
8. Thomas H. Groome, *Christian Religious Education* (San Francisco: Harper & Row, Publishers, 1980), p. 184ff.
9. Charles F. Kemp, *Thinking and Acting Biblically,* (Nashville: Abingdon, 1976), p. 110.
10. León Joseph Cardinal Suenens, *A New Pentecost* (New York: The Seabury Press, 1975), p. 3.

11. Robert S. Paul, pp. 275-76.
12. Paul, p. 276.
13. Randolph Crump Miller, *Christian Nurture and the Church* (New York: Charles Scribner's Sons, 1961), p. 33.
14. *Divorce and Remarriage: A Report to the Church* (Atlanta, Ga.: Division of Christian Relations, Board of Church Extension, Presbyterian Church in the United States, n.d.), pp. 17-18.
15. Roberts S. Paul, p. 24.
16. Randolph Crump Miller, *Education in Christian Living* (Englewood Cliffs, N.J.: Prentice-Hall, Inc., 1956), p. 60.
17. John R. W. Stott, *Christian Mission in the Modern World* (Downers Grove, Ill.): Inter-Varsity Press, 1975), p. 40.
18. Robert R. Boelhke, *Theories of Learning in Christian Education* (Philadelphia: The Westminster Press, 1962), p. 18.